UNLOCKING JAPAN'S DISTRIBUTION SYSTEM IN THE '90s

The complete exporter's guide

JAMES KEENAN

Canada	Groupe
Communication	Communication
Group	Canada
Publishing	Édition

Canadian Cataloguing in Publication Data

Keenan, James

Unlocking Japan's Distribution System in the '90s

Includes bibliographical references
ISBN 0-660-15389-0
Cat. no. K49-3/1994E

1. Japan — Commerce — Handbooks, manuals, etc.
2. Japan — Economic conditions — Handbooks, manuals, etc.
3. Japan — Social conditions — Handbooks, manuals, etc.
4. Canada — Commerce — Handbooks, manuals, etc.
I. Asia Pacific Foundation of Canada
II. Title
III. Title: Unlocking Japan's Distribution System in the '90s

HC462.95K43 1994 380.1'7952 C94-980305-7

Editor: **Shirley Zussman**

Cover design and charts: **Hélène St-Denis**
Comrem Inc.
(514) 670-0972

Available in Canada through

your local bookseller

or by mail from

Canada Communication Group — Publishing

Ottawa, Canada K1A 0S9

Catalogue No. K49-3/1994E
ISBN 0-660-15389-0

The Asia Pacific Foundation of Canada
wishes to thank our
project participants

Dentsu Burson-Marsteller

HAYASHIDA, KASHIWAGI & TAZAWA

Hongkong Bank of Canada

STIKEMAN, ELLIOTT
Canada's Global Law Firm

Table of Contents

Japan's Distribution Scene

PREPARING THE GROUNDWORK

DISTRIBUTOR AGREEMENTS

Managing Your Distribution Relationships

Planning and Reference

ANNEXES

General Introduction

Unlocking Japan's Distribution System in the '90s is a business guide designed for exporters of consumer products or capital goods who wish to know how best to select and manage intermediaries – dealers, distributors, agents and middlemen of all kinds – to maximize their chances of success in the Japanese market. My belief is that intermediaries play such an important role in the Asia Pacific region that exporters must devote as much time and energy learning how to sell to them as they do trying to understand end-users.

For the sake of simplicity, the word "he" is used throughout the book to refer to both genders. I hope my female readers will not interpret this as an indication that Japanese business life is closed to foreign businesswomen.

Using this Guide

Unlocking Japan's Distribution System in the '90s is written in such a way that it can be read from beginning to end or referred to quickly for facts on topics of special interest. If in doubt about where to look for specific information, consult the Table of Contents or the Index.

Its Limitations

Guidebook information is inevitably prone to become outdated. The material contained in this primer was assembled up to September 1, 1994, and unless otherwise indicated, is based on information available at that time. While the greatest care has been taken in the preparation of this book, the Asia Pacific Foundation of Canada, Canada Communication Group, Showa Ota & Co., Hongkong Bank of Canada, Dentsu Burson-Marsteller, Stikeman Elliott, and Hayashida, Kashiwagi & Tazawa (hereafter referred to as "the participants") cannot accept any liability for any consequences arising from the use of the information contained herein.

Where an opinion is expressed, it is that of the author and does not necessarily coincide with the views of the participants.

We welcome corrections and suggestions from our readers. Please write to:

Unlocking Japan's Distribution System in the '90s
Asia Pacific Foundation of Canada
8160 Sartre St.
Brossard, Qc
Canada J4X 1P2
Tel: (514) 923-9397
Fax: (514) 466-1156

ACKNOWLEDGMENTS

So little practical advice has been written about Japanese distribution that a research project on this subject is doomed to failure unless one is introduced to the right people – suppliers, distributors and consultants – all willing to take time off from their busy schedules to share their experiences. My first thanks go to the Tokyo office of the Asia Pacific Foundation of Canada for their guidance and support: James Yellowlees (Director), Yasuko Watanabe (my interpreter and assistant), Harumi Morisaki (who scheduled many of my meetings) and Megumi Tanabe. My thanks also to the many people who helped steer me in the right direction: Michael Adams (Ernst & Young), Peter G. Campbell (EAITC), Terry R. Greenberg (Canadian Consulate General-Osaka), Yuji Ioka (JETRO), Tsuneo Kato (JETRO-Montreal), Gary Nachshen (Stikeman Elliott), Ron Richardson (Asia Pacific Foundation of Canada) and Arnie Rusinek (Proact International).

To the many people who agreed to be interviewed, I extend my heartfelt thanks. Their willingness to share their time and expertise with me made my research work a pleasure and a privilege. In particular, I wish to acknowledge the support of a core group of interviewees and/or co-authors whose insights were instrumental in guiding my work: Mark Bain (Dentsu Burson-Marsteller), Larry D. Blagg (Market Makers Inc.), David E. Bond (Hongkong Bank of Canada), Ronald M. Finne (RBC Inc.), Shigeru Fujita (Showa Ota & Co.), Isao Kaneko (Canadian Embassy), Toshihiko Kashiwagi (Hayashida, Kashiwagi & Tazawa), Jerome Partos (Nichifutsu Boeki K.K.), John M. Powles (Council of Forest Industries-Canada), Brian G. Smallshaw (Develcon Electronics Ltd.) and Wayne Steinhauer (Austad's USA).

I am similarly grateful to Thomas Ainlay Jr. (McCann-Erickson Hakuhodo Inc.), Hidetoshi Akiyama (7-Eleven Japan Co. Ltd.), Mike Allen (Barclays de Zoete Wedd), William Attridge (High Technology Management), Robert J. Ballon (Sophia University), Harrison G. Bates (W.I. Carr-Tokyo), John A. Beale (Dentsu Burson-Marsteller), Robert Berry (ACCJ), Michel P. Boudriau (Government of Quebec), Michelle Brazeau (Directory of Canadian Business in Japan), Paul C. Brodek (Trek Japan Corporation), Paul-Henri Bunet (Canadian Embassy), Paul Brunette (Quebec Ministry of International Affairs), Anita Chandan (JETRO-Montreal), Ginette Charbonneau (APFC-Montreal), Jean-Pierre Coljon (Quebec Ministry of International Affairs), John Cotton (Government of Alberta), Ezio A. DiEmanuele (Canadian Embassy), Louise Do Rosario (Far Eastern Economic Review), François Donadieu (Clestra Hauserman K.K.), Manon Dumoulin (Government of British Columbia), Christopher L. Evans (CCCJ), Robert A. Food (Government of British Columbia), Hiro Fukuoka (Japan Council of Shopping Centers), Eve J. Gordon (American Standard Inc.), Suzanne Guy (Government of Quebec), Masuo Hachiya (Government of British Columbia), Hiroshi Homma (Japan Department Store Association), Yoshio Horiuchi (Canadian Consulate General-Osaka), Takenori Ishikawa (International Business Counselors Co. Ltd.), Kevin B. Iwanaga (Dun

& Bradstreet-Japan), Ken Kameyama (Dentsply Japan K.K.), Nobuo Kanemaru (JETRO), Robert Keating (Government of Quebec), Y. Chrys Kikuchi (Government of Quebec), Thomas F. Killilea (Anacomp Japan Ltd.), Hiroshi Kohda (MIPRO), Hiroaki Kosugi (Showa Ota & Co.), Norio Kudo (Government of Alberta), Fumiaki Kuraishi (JETRO), Tetsuya Kuroiwa (Japan Council of Shopping Centers), Regent Lapointe (Quebec Ministry of International Affairs), Mike Leslie (Canadian Beef Export Federation), Itsuaki Mabuchi (Japan Retailers Association), Heather Mackay (Seiyu Ltd.), Shojiro Makino (Grace Japan K.K.), Russell T. Mark (Canadian Embassy), Hiroshi Matsunaga (Canadian Embassy), Ray McCague (Ontario House), Amy McCarthy (Dentsu Burson-Marsteller), Paula McEachern (Nova Inc.), Tim McGauley (Go International Ltd.), Harold McNairnay (Canadian Embassy), Keizo Miyata (Japan Retailers Association), F. Alan Moore (Dentsu Wunderman Direct Inc.), Mashiko Morikawa (Uni-Supply Co. Ltd.), Carl Morris (McCain Foods Japan Ltd.), Kyle E. Murphy (KMG Japan Inc.), Shinichi Nagashima (Distribution Economic Institute of Japan), Yumiko Nagoshi (Osaka Chamber of Commerce & Industry), Renhard Neumann (European Business Community Investment Committee), Seiichi Okubo (Government of Alberta), Haruyasu Orihashi (Japan Franchise Association), Shichiro Otake (Ontario House), Susumu Saito (Osaka Chamber of Commerce & Industry), Duane Sandberg (Seiyu Ltd.), Minoru Sano (Nitto Shoji Ltd.), Kunio Sanuki (Japan Leasing Association), Hiroyuki Sato (Government of British Columbia), Yoichi Satoh (Nissho Iwai Corp.), Robin V. Sears (Ontario House), Takashi Seo (Pfizer Pharmaceuticals Inc.), Tadamichi Shiramatsu (MIPRO), Lennie Soo (Asian Sources Trade Media Group), John P. Stern (American Electronics Association-Tokyo), Eiji Suganuma (Asian Sources Media Group), Jun Sugii (Dun & Bradstreet-Japan), Seth R. Sulkin (Japan Development Institute), Akihide Takahashi (Dun & Bradstreet-Japan), Nobuhiro Takahashi (Japan Leasing Association), Yasushi Takaku (Takashimaya Co. Ltd.), Akihiro Tamai (Sumitomo Canada Ltd.), Sandy Taubenkimel (Howard Roberts Associates-Osaka), Victoria Taylor (EBC), Hiroshi Tokunaga (Dodwell Marketing Consultants), Dan M. Tyson (Varian), Kazuhiro Watanabe (Nissho Iwai Corp.), Yasujiro Yabe (Canadian Embassy), Yon Yamaguchi (McCain Foods Japan Ltd.), Tatsuo Yamamoto (Nova Inc.), Junichi Yasuda (A.T. Kearney), and Wataru Yoshida (JETRO).

Once again, I wish to thank Kerry Bingham of the New Brunswick government's Trade and Investment Division whose many comments on the first draft of this book did much to improve the final product. And finally, I owe a debt of gratitude to Shirley Zussman, my editor, for her patient efforts under highly pressured circumstances.

GLOSSARY

ACCJ	American Chamber of Commerce in Japan.
AEA	American Electronics Association.
Agent	A person or firm which has been granted the right to bind a supplier contractually in certain carefully defined sales transactions. See the section Defining Relationships for more details.
Allowance	An amount or percentage given to a distributor or retailer in order to reduce a payment because of stock shrinkage, damage, breakage, spoilage, impurities, etc.
Amae	Indulgent dependency.
Amakudari	Post-retirement employment of bureaucrats in big business.
APFC	Asia Pacific Foundation of Canada.
Bento	Box lunches.
BOJ	Bank of Japan.
Bucho	Department or general manager.
Catalog price	See list price.
CCCJ	Canadian Chamber of Commerce in Japan.
Channel leaders	For our purposes, Japanese trade intermediaries – importers, wholesalers or retailers – willing and able to offset the power of local producers with imported products.
Chiho ginko	Regional bank.
Choai wholesaler	An exclusive wholesaler who acts as a buying agent for a large retail group or as selling agent for a manufacturer. As buying agent, he receives a margin whether or not he physically handles a product.

CIF	Cost, insurance, and freight. "CIF Osaka" means that the seller's price includes all charges and risks up to the point where the ship carrying the goods arrives in Osaka. From that point, the buyer must bear all charges and risks, including unloading costs, lighterage and wharfage, and risks, unless the sales contract specifies otherwise. With Japanese distributors, sales quotations are usually given either CIF or CIF port of shipment, plus actual charges for freight and insurance.
Compatible products	Products which do not compete with each other and yet are intended for the same type of customer, e.g., car engines and spark plugs.
Consignment	The act of entrusting goods to a dealer for sale, but retaining ownership of them until sold. The dealer pays only if and when the goods are sold.
Creative	Direct marketing term. Preprinting aspects of catalog presentation: design, layout, copy writing and photography. It is used as a noun in the catalog business.
D/A	Document against acceptance.
DBM	Dentsu Burson-Marsteller.
DC	Documentary letter of credit.
Depato	Department store.
Diet	The Japanese parliament.
Discount	An amount deducted from a payment that is due because the buyer is paying cash (cash discount), making early payment (trade discount), buying in quantity (quantity or volume discount), or granting some other advantage to the seller.
Distributor	An independent company which takes ownership of its suppliers' merchandise, maintains an inventory, and deploys its own sales, marketing and after-sales service staff in passing the goods down the distribution chain. See the section Defining Relationships.
DM	Direct marketing.
D/P	Document against payment.

Dumping — The sale of a product in a foreign market at less than "fair market value." Fair value is usually the price at which the same product is sold in the exporting country or to third countries. Under U.S. law, however, dumping can also be established if the export price falls below estimated costs of production. The legal remedy for dumping is a special duty or "margin" equal to the difference between fair value and the actual sales price.

EBC — The European Business Community in Japan.

EEC — European Economic Community.

Endaka — Strong yen.

EOS — Electronic ordering system.

FDI — Foreign direct investment.

FOB — Free on board. Transportation term meaning that the invoice price includes delivery at the seller's expense and risk up to a specified point (often a port) and no further. Title normally passes from seller to buyer at the FOB point by way of a bill of lading.

Fulfillment — Direct marketing term. Responding to customer orders. Processing and filling orders.

FY — Fiscal year or from April 1 to March 31 in Japan. For example, FY91 refers to the period between April 1, 1991 and March 31, 1992.

Gaiatsu — Foreign pressure.

Gambare — Perseverance.

GATT — General Agreement on Tariffs and Trade.

GDP — Gross domestic product. The total value of a country's annual output of goods and services.

GNP — Gross national product. GDP plus income derived from property held abroad as well as the economic activity of residents abroad, minus the corresponding income of non-residents in the country.

Grey market — See parallel trade.

Gross (profit) margin	1. An amount. The dollar difference between sales and the cost of goods sold during a stated period of time. Also called gross profit. 2. A percentage. Gross profit as a percentage of sales. Also referred to as gross margin percentage.
Homon hambai	In-person sales.
Honne	Real intentions or motives. The opposite of *tatemae*.
HS	Harmonized Commodity Description and Coding System, or more simply Harmonized System. Japan's official trade statistics are classified according to the HS product coding system.
HSBC	The Hongkong and Shanghai Banking Corporation Inc.
Intra-industry trade	International selling and purchasing within a single industry. For example, Italy and Germany both manufacture cars, yet actively sell automobiles and auto parts to each other.
IPR	Intellectual property rights.
JADMA	Japan Direct Marketing Association.
JAS	Japanese Agricultural Standards.
JDB	Japan Development Bank.
JDMA	Japan Direct Mail Association.
JETRO	Japan External Trade Organization.
JICPA	Japan Institute of Certified Public Accountants.
JIS	Japan Industrial Standards.
JIT	Just-in-time.
JNTO	Japan National Tourist Organization.
JPO	Japan Patent Office.
JSA	Japanese Standards Association.
JSP	Japan Socialist Party.
JTB	Japan Travel Bureau.
JV	Joint venture.
Kacho	Section chief or assistant general manager.
Kaizen	Continuous improvement.

Karaoke	"Empty orchestra." A sound and video system providing an instrumental background for amateur singers.
Keidanren	Japan Federation of Economic Organizations.
Keiretsu	Industrial groups whose members cooperate with each other for strategic purposes. There are two major types of *keiretsu* in Japan: horizontal and vertical. See the section The Birth of a Growth Machine: 1945-1970.
Kohai	Junior, the opposite of *sempai.*
L/C	Letter of credit.
LDP	Liberal Democratic Party.
List price	The published or marked price, what the end-user is asked to pay. Also called retail price, catalog price, or suggested selling price.
Listing fee	A one-shot payment Japanese supermarkets sometimes ask of suppliers before giving them access to shelf space. Also called slotting fee.
LSRSL	Large-Scale Retail Store Law.
MAFF	Ministry of Agriculture, Forestry and Fisheries.
Manufacturer's representative	A person or firm which arranges or facilitates sales for its suppliers without having the right to bind them contractually. Manufacturer's representatives are paid on a commission basis and do not normally take ownership of the goods they sell. For more details, see the section Defining Relationships.
Markdown	A dollar or percentage reduction in retail price, usually because an item cannot be sold at the list or suggested price. Customer refusal to buy the item may be due to damage, soiling, style changes, an excessively high list price, etc. Percentage markdowns can sometimes be ambiguous. If the price is reduced from \$100 to \$75, for example, the markdown may be expressed as a percentage either of the former price (\$35/\$100, i.e., 25%) or of the reduced price (\$25/\$75, i.e., 33%).

Markup	The dollar or percentage increase between the buying price and the selling price. In dollar terms, it is identical to the gross profit. In percentage terms, however, it can be computed either as a percentage of the retail selling price, (the conventional way of doing it) or as a percentage on cost. A hat bought for $10 and resold for $15 can be said to have a 33% markup on price ($15 - $10=$5/$15=33%) or a 50% markup on cost ($5/$10=50%).
Meishi	A business card.
MFN	Most favored nation. According to GATT's "trade without discrimination" principle (also known as the "most favored nation clause"), all parties that are signatories to GATT are bound to grant each other treatment as favorable as they grant to any other nation in the application of import and export tariffs.
MHW	Ministry of Health and Welfare.
MIPRO	Manufactured Imports Promotion Organization.
MITI	Ministry of International Trade and Industry.
MLM	Multilevel marketing (also called network marketing). A form of direct marketing whereby a parent company distributes its products or services though a network of independent businesspeople who both sell directly and sponsor other people interested in selling.
MOF	Ministry of Finance.
MOSS	Market-Oriented Sector-Selective talks.
MOT	Ministry of Transport.
MPT	Ministry of Post & Telecommunications.
Nemawashi	The informal consultation preceding group decisions (see *ringi* system).
Net price	1. The price actually paid. List price minus all discounts, deductions and allowances.

Net price (cont.)	2. A price on which no discount will be allowed. Net distributor price is the supplier's minimum price for a given territory and should never be published in price list form because net prices are highly confidential and vary with different distributors. The only price lists given out by experienced exporters are retail price lists.
Net (profit) margin	1. An amount. The dollar difference between sales and the cost of goods sold during a stated period of time after expenses and taxes have been deducted. Also called net profit. 2. A percentage. Net profit as a percentage of sales.
NICs	Newly industrialized countries. Sometimes called NIEs (newly industrialized economies). Refers primarily to the four "Little Dragons": Hong Kong, Singapore, South Korea, and Taiwan.
NIEs	See NICs.
Nokyo	Agricultural cooperatives. Headed at the national level by the National Federation of Agricultural Cooperative Associations.
OL	"Office lady." Refers to any female white-collar support-staff worker.
Oligopoly	A market structure where the bulk of supply in a given industry is in the hands of a relatively few large firms selling to many small buyers.
Parallel trade	The international commerce in goods by traders who function outside of the official distribution networks established by the original manufacturers. Parallel trade is entirely legal. The goods thus traded are referred to as parallel imports (PI) or parallel exports.
PI	Parallel imports. See parallel trade.
POS	Point of sale.

Push/pull	Marketing strategies that focus the exporter's pricing, advertising, promotion and personal selling programs on the re-sellers (push) or on end-users (pull).
Rebate	Any refund made to the buyer after he has made full payment. Discounts, on the other hand, are made in advance of payment.
Retail price	See list price.
Ringi system	Group decision-making.
ROI	Return on investment.
RPM	Resale price maintenance.
Samurai	Warrior.
Salaryman	White collar worker.
SCAP	Supreme Command of the Allied Powers.
Seikyo	Consumer cooperatives. Their umbrella organization is the Japanese Consumers' Cooperative Union.
SEL	Securities and Exchange Law.
Sempai	Senior. The opposite of *kohai*.
Senmon shosha	Specialized trading company.
SII	Structural Impediment Initiative. Bilateral negotiations initiated in September 1989 between the Japanese and U.S. governments. Its purpose from the U.S. perspective was to pressure Japan into changing six non-tariff barriers blocking U.S. market entry: domestic pricing, the distribution system, Japan's high savings rate, the power of the *keiretsu*, discriminatory land use regulations, and certain exclusionary business practices (see The Odd Couple).
Slotting fee	See listing fee.
Sogo shosha	General trading company.
Soto	Outside. Outsiders (*soto* people) are not treated with the same consideration as people belonging to one's group. The opposite of *uchi*.
SPC	Statistical process control.

Suggested selling price	See list price.
Tarento	Celebrity talent.
Tatami	Tightly woven straw mats used to cover floors.
Tatemae	Pretense or official explanation. The opposite of *honne*.
Tegata	Promissory note.
TIC	Tourist information center.
Tonya	Wholesaler.
Toshi ginko	City bank.
Tsushin hambai	Media-contact sales.
Uchi	Inside. The group to which one belongs. The opposite of *soto*.
VA	Value analysis.
VAN	Value-added information network.
VAT	Value-added tax.
VE	Value engineering.
VER	Voluntary export restraint.
Wa	Harmony, peace, team spirit.
Yakuza	Gangster, Japanese mafia.
Zaibatsu	Pre-war, family-owned industrial conglomerates (see The Colonial Path: 1867-1945). The *zaibatsu* were dismantled at the end of World War II by the U.S. military occupation authorities.
Zaitech	Financial technology.

A CLASH OF CAPITALISMS

THE COLONIAL PATH: 1867-1945

Japan's astonishing industrial development after Commodore Perry's arrival in 1853 was achieved in an atmosphere of crisis. The overwhelming priority for her leaders was to escape the colonization process then swallowing up the rest of Asia. That required a large navy, a powerful industrial base, and a secure supply of raw materials from her Asian neighbors. It was Japan's push to become the dominant naval power in the northwestern Pacific that eventually brought her into conflict with America's strategic interests.

MEIJI RESTORATION: 1867-1912

Future shock

After centuries of Japan's self-imposed isolation, Commodore Perry's arrival in 1853 with a squadron of warships caused havoc in Tokyo. According to one source: "The whole city was in an uproar. In all directions were seen mothers flying with children in their arms, and men with mothers on their backs. The tramp of war-horses, the clatter of armed warriors, the noise of carts, the parade of firemen, the incessant tolling of bells, the shrieks of women, the cries of children, filled the streets of a city of more than a million souls."

America's motives were clear: she wanted to establish commercial relations and send missionaries, in that order of importance. The immediate consequence of this intrusion, however, was the rapid collapse of the Tokugawa Shogun and his replacement by a collective leadership working under the symbolic authority of a fifteen-year-old emperor. The society they inherited, backward though it was technologically, was not without certain advantages that served it well in the early years of its industrial development.

- Ethnically and linguistically the Japanese were highly homogeneous. Social consensus was thus easier to achieve.
- The military background of Japan's ruling elite made it quick to adopt Western technology in order to maintain its independence from foreign control.
- Compared to other pre-industrial Asian societies, Japan was highly urbanized. Tokyo alone with its population of over one million was perhaps the world's largest city in the 18th century, while Kyoto and Osaka had gone beyond the half-million mark. These cities were kept supplied from the countryside by means of a highly developed transport, wholesale and retail network.
- The population was well-educated. Nearly 60% of men and 15% of women could read, write and do simple arithmetic.

JAPANESE HISTORY AT A GLANCE

Foreign influences: c. 200-800

Written accounts of Japan first surface in Chinese records at a time when Japan's tribal society was being overrun by mounted invaders from the Korean Peninsula. By 500 AD an imperial line claiming descendance from the Sun Goddess (Amaterasu) had come into existence. (The present emperor Akihito is number 25.) It was this court society which spearheaded for centuries the widespread adoption of Chinese administrative and cultural ideas: Confucianism, Buddhism, an ideographic script and artistic standards for literature and the visual arts.

Heian period: c. 800-1200

Despite its great admiration for China, then the world's most advanced political and economic system, Japan's geographic isolation and linguistic uniqueness (Japanese is as different from Chinese as it is from English) helped its people retain a sense of their own identity. Politically, Japanese emperors became symbols of state authority whose time-consuming religious and ceremonial duties left them no time for affairs of state. True power could very easily drift into the hands of provincial lords unless a strong man, working in the shadow of the throne, asserted his authority. Artistically, the Kyoto-based imperial court was perhaps the most aesthetically refined in Japan's history. The world's first great novel, The Tale of Genji, *was written by a Heian court woman.*

Kamakura and Muromachi periods: c. 1200-1600

For 400 years, Japan alternated between military governments and periods of incessant warfare. In Kyoto, the imperial family remained as weak as ever even if its support conferred legitimacy to a succession of unstable regimes. Unless a strong man was in power (i.e., became Shogun), military might was the preserve of local warlords and their vigilante bands of warriors called samurai. *The prime duty of a samurai was to serve his feudal lord faithfully. Over the centuries, the samurai adopted a code of conduct (called Bushido, the "way of the warrior") which stressed total self-control, endurance, and the importance of an unblemished reputation, even at the price of death. Culturally, this period was dominated by the simpler aesthetic values of Japan's military elite. Expanded trade with China brought on more cultural imports such as Zen Buddhism which deeply colored the development of new aesthetic pursuits: the Noh theater, flower arranging, gardening, ink painting and the tea ceremony.*

Tokugawa period: c. 1600-1867

Japan was unified again as a succession of three brilliant leaders gradually subjugated less powerful feudal lords. The last of these leaders, Tokugawa Ieyasu, set up his headquarters in a small fishing village called Edo (now Tokyo). To maintain internal security, Ieyasu set up a highly centralized feudal system which weakened the power of the provincial lords. Social harmony was further buttressed by enforcing rigid behavior codes within a hierarchy of mutually exclusive social castes. At the apex of society were the samurai whose martial skills had become useless in a society at peace. Second were the peasants because the samurai's wealth was based on land. At the bottom were the despised merchants whose money-lending skills progressively impoverished the samurai class. It was the merchant class which put its stamp on Tokugawa art. Its Kabuki and puppet theaters, its novels and woodblock prints all reflect the urban-centered concerns of a growing commercial elite.

Externally, Japan could no longer count on the sea to protect itself from foreign incursions. European merchants and missionaries were already active in Kyoto by the mid-16th century. Indeed, European muskets played an important role in Ieyasu's eventual victory. To protect themselves against the disruptive influence of foreigners, therefore, Tokugawa authorities all but stamped out Christianity in the early 17th century. All foreigners were thrown out and their books banned. The only exception was the port of Nagasaki where specially licensed Dutch and Chinese merchants were allowed to conduct foreign trade.

This isolationist policy lasted for over 200 years until the United States dispatched Commodore Perry and his "black ships" in 1853 with instructions to force Japan to open its ports to foreign trade. The Tokugawa, weakened by internal revolts, collapsed in 1866.

Top-down revolution

The Meiji Restoration was one of the most innovative and achievement-filled periods in Japan's history. Within 45 years, a backward feudal country transformed itself into a modern industrial power with an overseas empire.

This remarkable transformation was not engineered by a single great leader. Rather, it was a small group of young, reform-minded samurai that used the symbolically charged figure of the emperor to unite the nation around their ideas. A national government was created from almost nothing, based on the fiction that the emperor had been restored to power by a group of reformers who were merely executing his will.

A series of changes followed in quick succession: local lords lost their titles, a new financial system was created, a postal system was organized, compulsory primary education was introduced and a nation-wide system of schools and universities established. The goal throughout was not only to unify the country administratively, but also, for the first time in Japanese history, to enlist the active participation of common people in national affairs. This was a complete reversal of the feudal order whereby rulers and commoners ignored each other except when taxes were due.

The visible hand

The merchant class was one group the Meiji reformers were particularly eager to attract. Their reticence to take risks, however, forced the government to invest in railway and steamship lines, mining pits and cotton spinning factories. Eventually, the government succeeded in selling some of these enterprises to powerful merchant families such as the Mitsui and Mitsubishi. And, even then, it was often found necessary to guarantee their profits by granting them exclusive mining rights and other privileges.

These family businesses, called *zaibatsu,* quickly diversified into a wide variety of industries – shipping, banking, foreign trade, textiles, real estate and shipbuilding being the most popular choices – to minimize risks and make the best use of scarce capital. Their management style was extremely autocratic even when day-to-day decision-making drifted within a generation or two from powerful founder-owners to salaried managers.

Military adventures

Such massive social changes created new winners and losers, and thus aroused opposition, at times violent. Disgruntled samurai, now stripped of privileges and disdainful of common employment, were a special source of concern. A massive rebellion flared up in 1877 over reduced samurai stipends, but by then the government's military reforms had taken hold. The revolt was crushed thanks to an army of conscripted commoners indoctrinated with a new sense of national identity based on absolute loyalty to the emperor.

Japan acquired Korea and Taiwan in a war with China in 1895 in part to keep its samurai employed and also to acquire new markets and sources of raw materials in the colonial style of their European role models. An armament drive followed, and ten years later, the Japanese decisively defeated the Russian Baltic fleet near Port Arthur. The link between a quick adaptation of Western industrialism and national power implied in Meiji Japan's national slogan, *fukoku-kyohei* (rich country, strong army), could not have been clearer.

Transition problems

By 1910, the small circle of reformist samurai that had led Japan since 1867 was rapidly dying off. The result was a power vacuum at the top because the reformers' 1890 constitution created a host of me-too parliamentary institutions designed more to impress Western powers with Japan's modernity than to function as effective state organs. The elected lower house, for example, had no power of its own; all appointments and policies were determined by the original reformers and then presented to the emperor for ratification.

Had Japan evolved a parliamentary democracy as the constitution implied, the death of the Meiji reformers would have permitted an easy transition. What happened instead was a struggle by various groups – court officials, big business (*zaibatsu*), political factions, bureaucrats and the army – to use an essentially passive emperor to control those institutions of Japanese society of most concern to them. To make matters worse, Emperor Meiji died in 1912 and his son, Taisho, was mentally handicapped.

DRIFT AND CATASTROPHE: 1912-1945

Wartime prosperity

World War I created enormous opportunities for Japanese industrial expansion because it cut Europeans off from their export markets in Asia. Demand over the period 1914-20 had the same dramatic consequences on the size and structure of Japanese industry as the Korean War did in 1950-54. Heavy industry in particular seized upon this opportunity for expansion. Production of iron and steel, ships and cement tripled.

This evolution towards heavy industry – a few large factories controlled by *zaibatsu* and other big enterprises – was strongly encouraged by a growing corps of economic bureaucrats through favorable regulations, tax breaks and subsidies even though more conventional calculations of "greatest comparative advantage" or "return on capital invested" should have led them to support light industry, then Japan's biggest employer and foreign exchange earner by far. Nevertheless, some heavy industries such as shipbuilding had obvious military spin-offs. They also brought with them high productivity growth and advanced Western technologies. Unfortunately, heavy industries also devoured ever greater quantities of raw materials until Japan, a net exporter in that area until 1890, had to depend on its colonies to keep its plants running. It is indeed ironic that a self-contained economy in 1860 should become a dependent one 40 years later, all in the name of achieving political autonomy.

Bad news

Excessive government subsidies and the *zaibatsu* tendency to match each other's investment projects led to over-capacity and a sharp recession in the 1920s when European exporters re-entered Asian markets after the war. A rash of bankruptcies ensued, leaving the four largest remaining *zaibatsu* – Mitsui, Mitsubishi, Sumitomo and Yasuda – with enormous influence over the domestic economy.

Compared to the rapid economic expansion and general optimism of the war years, the decade following 1922 was one of acute disappointment. Japan suffered its slowest growth of any decade between 1880 and 1940. Foremost among its problems was the Great Earthquake of 1923, which leveled much of Tokyo and Yokohama, and a string of harvest failures causing famine in the countryside. When the World Depression of the 1930s hit the country, the latent tensions between Japan's fractious power elites were bound to surface.

Officers amuck

Overall, the period between 1912-1932 saw a progressive deterioration in relations between the powerful institutional groups created by the Meiji Restoration. The political parties sought by every means possible to make the Cabinet (the emperor's close advisors) accountable to them (i.e., the Diet). Big business wanted more responsive bureaucrats and politicians. Court officials sought to gain control by influencing the emperor directly. Above all, the military, who interpreted Japan's growing reliance on foreign markets and raw materials as a *colonial* problem, wanted a more aggressive posture abroad and the weapons to achieve it. There was a drift towards lawlessness, anarchy and violence, which the political system was unable to control.

Power flowed outward. The politicians lost control over the generals as did the general staff over the junior officers. Control moved into the hands of the colonels in the field where access to colonial resources permitted some degree of independence. Anyone who resisted military expansion, politician or army commander, risked assassination.

Japan's expansion into Manchuria (China's three northeastern provinces) and thence to South China by an army essentially on its own led to a series of clashes with the political parties and to growing opposition abroad, particularly from the U.S. Many prominent ministers who opposed the army were assassinated, and by 1937, the year when the Japanese army stationed in northern China launched its southern campaign, the military had taken over the government. With the nation now at war, opposition became unpatriotic and subject to police repression.

The new bureaucracy

Government-business relations evolved quickly after the 1860s, from close personal relations within a small circle of Meiji reformers and merchant families to more bureaucratic interactions between much larger groups of technocrats and salaried *zaibatsu* managers in the 1920s. However, the belief that government had a crucial role to play in the process of rapid industrialization never faded. If anything, it only grew stronger as Japan's wartime economy gave her civil servants much greater scope to test their organizational skills. Many of their programs resurfaced again in altered form during the difficult early postwar years.

Figure 1-1

Japan prior to Pearl Harbor, December 1941

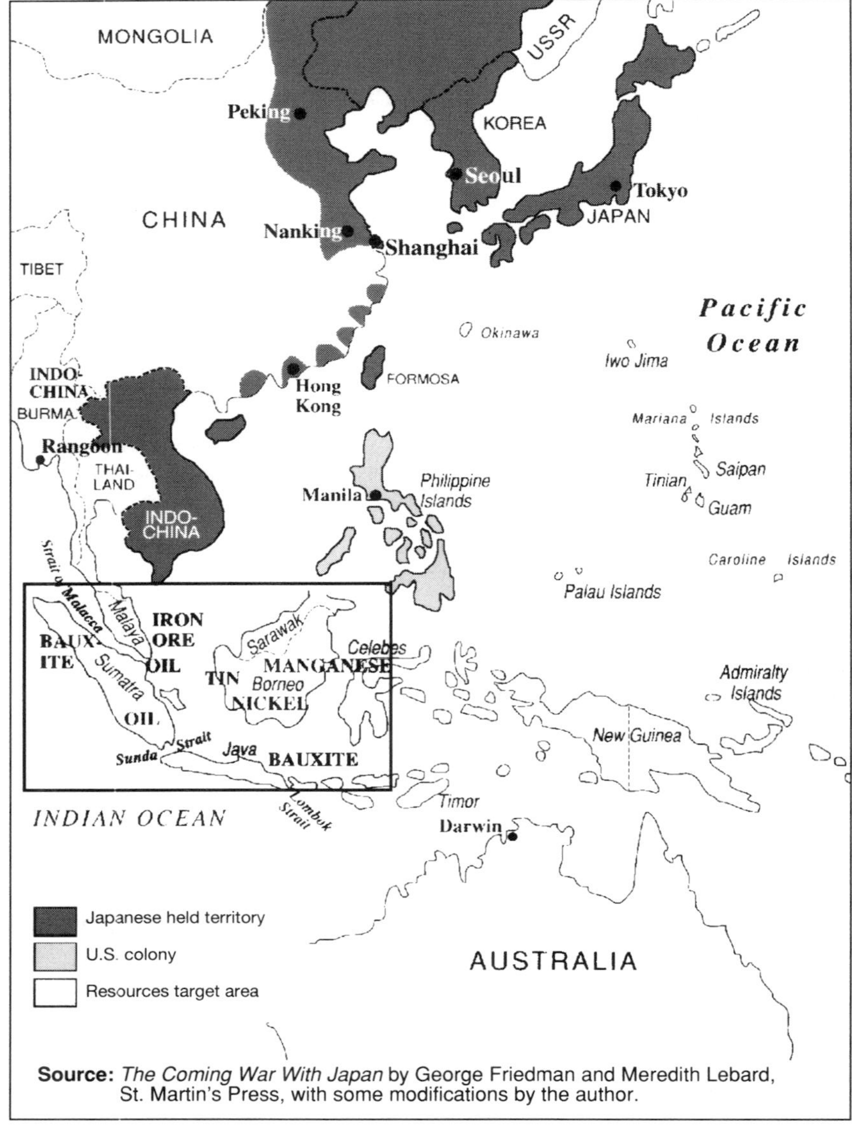

Source: *The Coming War With Japan* by George Friedman and Meredith Lebard, St. Martin's Press, with some modifications by the author.

- **Cartels** Government-sponsored mergers and cartels were organized to promote economies of scale. During the no-growth '30s, this entailed Soviet-style production quotas for each industry. Competition was replaced by cooperative public-private planning.
- **Trade block** Northern China, now a war zone, became the staging ground for a highly regimented resource extraction and transportation system feeding into Japan's industrial machine.
- **Rationing** With so many resources directed towards the war effort and labor shortages due to national conscription, industrial production began to fall after 1940. Japan's bureaucracy became very adept at devising "priority allocations systems" to keep a resource-starved domestic economy producing enough for survival.

Checkmated

In territorial terms, the Japanese army was at first very successful in China. City after city fell in its wake. But the Chinese army merely retreated into the interior, drawing the Japanese further and further away from their main supply lines. With an oil embargo by the U.S. in effect, Japan's war in China soon proved too costly. Japan either had to accept the unthinkable and withdraw from China or she had to expand into Southeast Asia to capture needed oil resources and raw materials. In her way stood the Philippines, then a colony of the U.S. protected by a naval fleet based in Pearl Harbor, Hawaii.

THE BIRTH OF A GROWTH MACHINE: 1945-1970

Although the Occupation eventually brought Japan into the Western Alliance, U.S.-style private enterprise proved unexportable. Japan's own brand of communitarian capitalism was primarily a response to her crisis-ridden postwar circumstances: uneven growth, massive urbanization, and an economy starved of fuel and raw materials for lack of foreign exchange. Market forces alone could not be relied upon, and so the bureaucracy sponsored the creation of export-driven oligopolies in target industries to take maximum advantage of her special relationship with America.

THE OCCUPATION: 1945-1952

Turning point

The American occupation marked the end of one chapter in Japan's isolationist relationship with the rest of the world. Ever since Commodore Perry's arrival in 1853, the overwhelming priority for Japan's leaders was to escape the colonization process swallowing up the rest of Asia. Fear and envy of the West and contempt for her "less advanced" Asian neighbors lay behind almost everything Japan had achieved and suffered through in the hundred years preceding her defeat.

Now, for the first time, she was occupied by foreigners who walked the streets giving orders and handing out rations. The first impression for most civilians was simple relief that they had escaped annihilation. With their leadership discredited, no one quite knew how to react.

Scavenging years

Getting along with GIs was far from the major concern of the moment, however. Over 8 million people were homeless; nearly one-third of Japan's cities had simply ceased to exist in any organized sense.

In theory, the government's rationing system continued in force. In practice, however, most food could only be obtained through the black market. City dwellers packed the trains daily to go barter family heirlooms for food in the countryside. There were days when fear of starvation could have pushed society into revolutionary chaos; the supply of rice reaching Tokyo from farming regions was only half the amount needed for a subsistence diet. Wartime rations had also been severe at times, but at least everyone had been equally poor. Now neighbor turned against neighbor, small thefts led to gang killings, and a criminal underworld of huge proportions was now in full operation. The crime rate was aggravated by the return of over

6 million soldiers and settlers from the colonies. Thirteen million Japanese were jobless and looking for work.

This desperate situation lasted until 1950, five years after the war had ended. American help never took the form of aid such as the Europeans were receiving under the Marshall Plan. Instead, a draconian stabilization plan (called the Dodge Plan) pushed the economy into a deep recession in 1949. Labor unrest only seemed to worsen as workers, encouraged by their leftist leaders, exploited their new-found right to strike. The rise of communist union leaders was particularly worrisome for the Japanese government because many of them played on growing popular hostility toward the occupation authorities, thus undermining by association the legitimacy of the Japanese politicians serving these authorities. Fortunately for the Japanese government, the Cold War changed all of this.

SCAP

Although General MacArthur is often credited for single-handedly managing the Occupation, many of the most fateful decisions were taken by Washington before he set foot on Japan. Germany would be led by a large military government. Japan, on the other hand, was to be governed by a much smaller "Supreme Command of the Allied Powers" (SCAP). This left the civilian bureaucracy largely intact and MacArthur would have to govern through it. In theory, this allowed the Japanese plenty of leeway to democratize themselves.

SCAP, however, was only a force of 200,000 supervising a nation of 70 million. And while it succeeded in instituting fundamental reforms, Japan's bureaucrats quickly became adept at diluting its efforts. It never was a simple process whereby the Japanese meekly accepted all that was thrust upon them. Still, the changes were fundamental:

- The **emperor** lost his divine status, but remained as symbolic head of state.
- **Land reform** freed peasants from serfdom and gave them land.
- Tens of thousands of wartime politicians, businessmen, bureaucrats and media personalities, deemed "militarists" by SCAP, were **purged**.
- SCAP legalized the right to assemble and form **labor unions**.
- The ***zaibatsu***, widely perceived in Washington as the main economic support of Japanese militarism and "feudalism," were dissolved and replaced by an economic system that favored smaller enterprises.
- **School** textbooks and courses were cleansed of emperor worship. Local school boards were given more independence from the Education Ministry.
- **Women** were granted equal rights under the Constitution.

By early 1948, much of SCAP's reformist energy had fizzled out. With the communists winning in China, a de-stabilized Japan could jeopardize Washington's interests in the area. These fears only grew stronger when North Korean soldiers invaded South Korea in June 1950. Reform took second place after economic reconstruction.

Red scare

The SCAP reforms which had the most immediate consequences were those related to unionism. Many of the labor leaders released from war-time prisons were hard-core communists willing to apply industrial muscle to political ends.

At first, workers met with little opposition. Managers, demoralized by Japan's defeat and fearful that their companies would be dissolved like the *zaibatsu* if unions were opposed, accepted whatever labor wanted. Inflation and rationing difficulties only worsened the labor climate. The turning point came in 1946-47 when government cutbacks and an election led to widespread strikes. Tens of thousands of workers rioted in the streets of Tokyo calling for the overthrow of the government.

As a result, SCAP sanctioned a revision of the labor laws which curtailed the right to strike and allowed managers to abrogate and re-negotiate hundreds of collective agreements concluded in 1945-46. The most crushing blow of all was the red purges of 1950, a series of events which weakened Japan's labor movement forever after. At a time of escalating East-West tensions, MacArthur ordered the dismissal of 24 top communist party leaders from public life. The Japanese government followed suit, purging alleged communists from the news media and universities. The campaign spread to the private sector and by the end of the year over 12,000 workers and officials had lost their jobs. There is no doubt that both the government and private industry used the red purge to kick out trouble-makers who were not communists, many of whom had been encouraged to agitate by SCAP a few years earlier.

Independence has a price

General MacArthur had once vowed that Japan would become "the Switzerland of the Pacific" and that suited most Japanese. They were a crushed but proud people who wanted most to be left alone.

By 1950, however, Washington had developed very different plans for Japan. The Occupation would end, in a manner of speaking, and Japan could formally re-enter the society of nations. However, it would have to do so as a loyal member of the Western Alliance with these five conditions:

- To minimize Soviet influence, Japan could only sign a treaty with the U.S. and its anti-communist allies.
- To contain China and the Soviet Union, the U.S. wanted the right to set up air, naval and ground bases in Japan.

- Japan would have to re-arm to some extent and ignore the renunciation of war clause in its American-made constitution.
- Japan would be a member of the Western Alliance. Swiss-style neutrality was out of the question.
- Japan would have to respect the U.S. embargo on contacts with Communist China and recognize Taiwan as the sole legitimate representative of the Chinese people.

These conditions met with widespread opposition from the Japanese public. They wanted an end to the Occupation and feared that such an exclusive alliance, far from protecting Japan, could drag it into a disastrous war between the U.S. and the Soviet Union . Nevertheless, Prime Minister Yoshida believed Japan's future lay with the West and that this was the best deal he could get at the time. The peace treaty was signed in San Francisco on September 1951 with the United States and 47 other nations.

The "San Francisco System," as the treaty came to be called, had momentous consequences for Japan. By accepting these limitations on her sovereignty, she benefited enormously from another part of the package: her close economic relationship with the United States. At the same time, however, it had a perverse effect on Japan's ability to interact with the rest of the world at any level other than economic. Shielded by U.S. protection and forbearance, Japan saw no need to develop a foreign policy except in the limited sense of encouraging exports. Her relationships with other countries were those of a trading company, not a nation state.

THE GROWTH MACHINE: 1950-1970

Imperfect hindsight

The Korean War in 1950 jumped-started an economy starved of fuel and raw materials for lack of foreign exchange. Within six weeks of the war's outbreak, the U.S. military had placed $40 million in procurement orders with Japanese firms, an amount that grew to a total of $4 billion by 1954. Japan was the base from which the U.S. fought the war and the destination of choice for troops seeking rest and relaxation.

The next two decades were years of stupendous growth. Japan's real GNP grew at 9% a year during the '50s and 10% a year during the '60s. By 1970, her output was over six times what it had been in 1950. By contrast, U.S. GNP increased only 3-4% a year during the same period. At that rate, Japan's economy was doubling every 7 to 8 years compared to 20 years for the U.S.

Nevertheless, the postwar order established by Japan's elite – bureaucratic, politicians and business leaders – reflected deep uncertainty, not confidence. The exceptional growth of these years was punctuated by sudden slowdowns and there was always the fear that the country would fall back into the social convolutions of the 1945-50 period. The short slump following the end of the Korean War was followed by a series of "booms" – the Jimmu boom (1956-57), the Iwato boom (1958-61) and the Izanami boom (1966-70) – closely tied to U.S. business cycles (see Fig. 1-2). The pattern was always the same. First exports would rise followed by a surge in capital investment and raw materials imports to feed increased production capacity. Very quickly thereafter imports would overtake the increase in export earnings; Japan's current account balance would slide into deficity; and foreign currency reserves would diminish until a foreign currency crisis forced the authorities to put a brake on expansion.

Along with this highly unstable growth dependent on foreign markets came a massive population shift. Within 20 years, a Japanese workforce which had been almost 50% agricultural in 1950 became 90% urban. Along the pacific coast of Japan, extending all the way from Tokyo to Osaka, a huge urban belt of 50 million people – roughly half of Japan's population – emerged plagued by transportation, housing, pollution and welfare problems.

Growth and social stability in such a heavily populated, export-dependent island-nation could not be left to chance or to uncertain market forces: elite consensus had to be achieved. And in the '50s and '60s, the key elite was the bureaucracy.

Figure 1-2

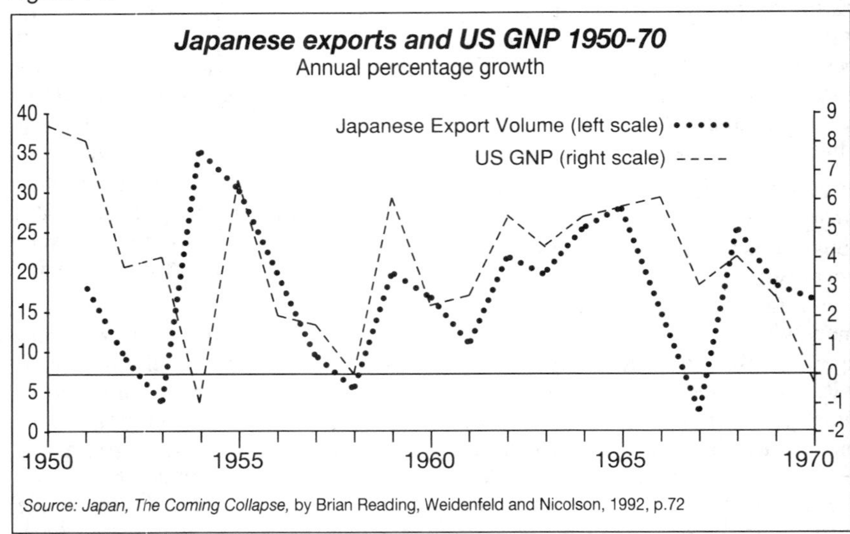

Mighty MITI

One group which escaped almost unscathed from SCAP's many reforms was Japan's economic bureaucrats. During the war years, they had kept an army spread across Asia supplied with equipment while maintaining production at home. The experience had made them a close-knit group with one outstanding skill: the capacity for large-scale planning.

By 1950, most of them were clustered in a new ministry, the Ministry of International Trade and Industry (MITI) and they lost no time in resuscitating the policy tools which had proven so effective in wartime. Their goals were simple:

- Establish sectoral priorities. Focus the country's limited resources on high-growth capital- and technology-intensive industries which seem to offer the steepest gains in labor productivity at the moment (coal and steel production in the '50s, automobiles in the '60s).
- Protect "infant industries" from foreign competition through capital controls and trade restrictions.
- Encourage industries to structure themselves to achieve the large economies of scale necessary to compete vigorously in export markets.
- Foster continuous process technology improvements in key industries by facilitating the massive importation of foreign know-how and the establishment of effective subcontracting networks.

In practice, this meant that MITI sponsored the creation of oligopolies in targeted industries to guarantee profits and prevent ruinous competition. However, this support came at a price: industrial beneficiaries had to compete internationally or see their privileges withdrawn. In time, as industries grew stronger and had less need of government financing, direct controls were eased and replaced by suggestions and exhortations, MITI's famous "administrative guidance."

Specific policy mixes for each industry were the product of a consultative process, not imposed from above. To improve communication between government and industry, MITI encouraged the creation of thousands of sector-specific trade associations. In addition to their monitoring function, trade associations were active in determining industry standards and controlling the entry of new competitors in their sectors.

Although MITI was the source of much industrial targeting, especially targeting destined for export-oriented sectors of the economy, it was not the only or even the most influential ministry guiding the business community. Other bureaucratic targeters included the Bank of Japan (BOJ), the Ministry of Finance (MOF), the Ministry of Post and Telecommunications (MPT), the Ministry of Transport (MOT), the Ministry of Health and Welfare (MHW), the Ministry of Agriculture, Forestry and Fisheries (MAFF), and so on. Most of these ministries worked with highly protected, domestically-oriented industries where government support became highly politicized (see The Dual Face of Globalization: 1970-1995).

Son of *zaibatsu*

One major roadblock facing ministerial targeters wishing to foster economies of scale was SCAP's Anti-Monopoly Law prohibiting collusive activities such as cartels, price-fixing and market-sharing agreements. Japanese bureaucrats never shared SCAP's aversion to big business. As far as they were concerned, only big companies could both serve Japan's development priorities and compete abroad. The Anti-Monopoly Law was therefore drastically weakened in 1953. The *zaibatsu* in their old form – family-controlled conglomerates – had ceased to exist, but they were promptly replaced by new business groups called *keiretsu* led by professional managers, not family dynasties.

Keiretsu come in two forms: horizontal (or "inter-market") and vertical (or "enterprise"). **Horizontal *keiretsu*** consist of fifty or more highly diversified companies revolving around a leading manufacturer, a top bank and a general trading company (*sogo shosha*). The biggest horizontal *keiretsu* – e.g., Mitsui, Sumitomo, Mitsubishi, Dai-Ichi Kangyo Bank (DKB), Industrial Bank of Japan (IBJ) – are now among the largest business entities in the world and possess tremendous economic power (see Fig. 1-3). The whole is held together by certain business practices:

- **Cross-shareholding** is extensively used and reflects the relative power of member companies. Equal firms exchange shares of equal value. Core units such as banks or trading companies, on the other hand, might own a larger share of smaller members.
- Members **exchange personnel** such as directors, auditors and managers.
- Years of doing business together and **preferential buying policies** lead members to think twice before purchasing outside their group.
- Members **borrow** from the same core bank and core trading company. Large members also help smaller ones financially.
- Members share **consultation bodies** such as presidential councils.
- Members develop a **common ethos**. Their personnel sport the same badges and share in the prestige which comes from group membership. This is very important in a society where employees are primarily "company men," not free agents with skills to sell.

Figure 1-3

The Mitsubishi Group
(a horizontal *keiretsu*)

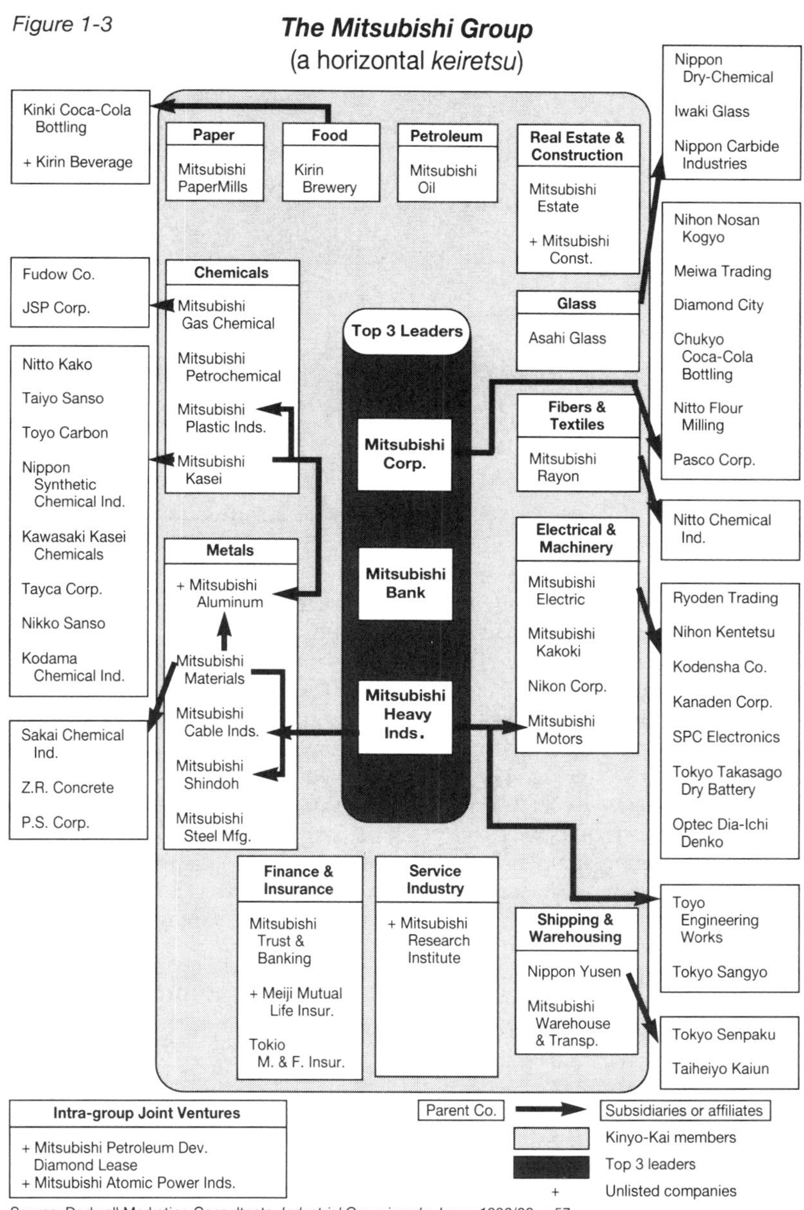

Source: Dodwell Marketing Consultants, *Industrial Groupings In Japan 1992/93*, p.57

Figure 1-4

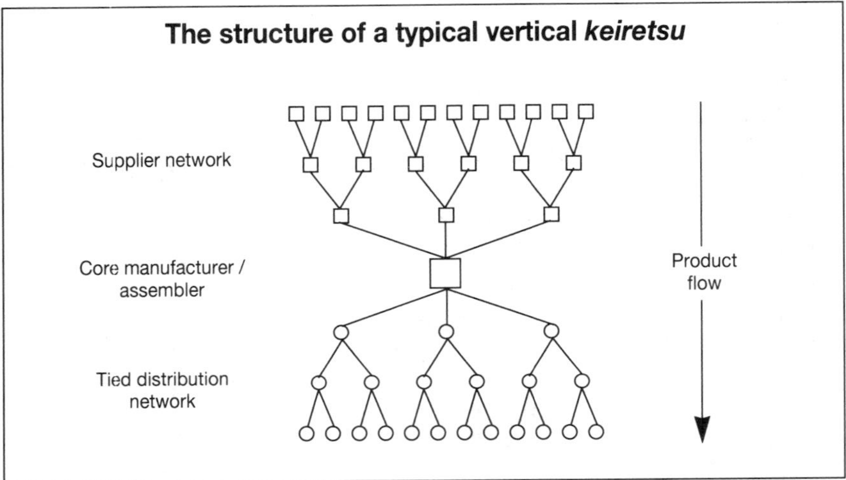

Vertical *keiretsu* revolve around powerful manufacturers and include a tiered family of suppliers at the input end (see Industrial Purchasing), and a captive distribution network (see Japanese Distribution Management – the outside view) to take care of sales and customer servicing (see Fig. 1-4). The core manufacturer's ownership interest in his member companies can go from 100%, making them mere subsidiaries, to a few percent, a token of good will. In any case, vertical *keiretsu* are much more narrowly focused than horizontal *keiretsu.* They predominate in industries such as automobiles, electronics, shipbuilding, and household appliances. Well known examples are Sony, Hitachi, Toyota, Nissan, and Nippon Steel.

The main purpose of these large groups was market stabilization, a crucial competitive asset for highly leveraged companies aiming for high growth in Japan's boom and bust economy of those years. Heavy industrialization required huge pools of capital and yet Japan's capital market was primitive and in disarray after the war. Major companies therefore became heavily reliant on debt, particularly bank debt. This required stable, long-term bank connections to work and *keiretsu* memberships offered this advantage among others.

A company culture

Another market the *keiretsu* were instrumental in stabilizing was the labor market. Japan's prewar and early postwar labor scene was marked by frequent strikes, harsh repression and high turnover rates. This old confrontational approach no longer suited rapidly growing companies in need of trained workers willing and capable of absorbing all the new Western technology being imported.

Organized labor, weakened by red purges and breakaway unions, abandoned its opposition to new technology in exchange for certain concessions which formed the basis of Japan's large company employment system. First, permanent employees were guaranteed work for life even if their jobs changed due to new technology. Secondly, wages were tied to productivity through bonus systems so that workers as a group could share in the benefits of improved production methods. Wage differences among workers were determined not by merit, but by a graduated seniority pay system (the "escalator") guaranteeing annual raises and pre-scheduled promotions to permanent employees remaining with the company. Lastly, a system of continuous consultation between committees of workers and management was established to discuss issues affecting labor relations.

This compromise had momentous consequences for Japanese society because it transformed large companies into self-contained communities capable of doing for their employees what the Imperial Army had done for poor farm boys adrift in the 1930s. Between 1955 and 1965 millions of young men left farms to look for jobs in the city. Most of them were country bumpkins fresh out of school with no experience of life in vast anonymous cities. The company fed them, provided housing and recreation, introduced them to friends with similar backgrounds, and even helped them find wives. What companies offered, in other words, was a vast social support system that replaced their employees' lost village network of family and friends. It had the desired effect: job hopping between large companies became rare; the "company man" was born.

This, however, only covered one-third of the total labor force. In Japan's small and medium enterprises, where most people worked, layoffs remained common in hard times and turnover high in good ones. Jobs and pay depended primarily on supply and demand. There was a corresponding gap between large and small firms in the degree of employee loyalty.

Market-share driven

High debt-to-equity financing and lifetime employment introduced high fixed costs, forcing large Japanese companies to seek ever-expanding market shares. And the fastest way to improve market share is to invest in new plant facilities, reduce per-unit costs and use low prices as the principal competitive weapon. This emphasis on market share was a rational choice in Japan's high growth economy even if it eventually collided head on with Anglo-American capitalism when Japanese products overran the U.S. market in the '70s and '80s.

Imagine organizing a company and electing at the outset to establish the following policies and procedures: the company will be leveraged to the hilt. It will have perhaps two or three times as much debt in its capital structure than is typical for other companies in its industry. It will be dependent on a single bank or a small group of banks for virtually all of that debt, most of which will be short term and secured against just about every asset the company owns.

The company will rely on a relatively small handful of suppliers and subcontractors in its trading relationships. Its dealings with them will be fairly informal. It will negotiate hard but will minimize reliance on painstakingly detailed written contracts. Once an understanding is reached, the trading partners will be trusted to uphold the spirit of the agreement, informally modifying the terms of trade as needed to adjust to changed circumstances.

The managers who will run this firm are to be hired right out of college (just a few good ones, however), trained at the company's expense, and effectively promised jobs for life. There will be little or no performance-based compensations, and promotion will be based primarily on seniority. Similarly, factory workers will be hired for life, with pay tied primarily to seniority. Decision-making will be a highly decentralized, bottom-up process.

The goals of the company will be growth and longevity, with profitability a distant third priority. In fact, independent shareholders will rank fairly low on the list of constituencies whose interest management is to represent. There would be no outside directors. The board of directors will be composed entirely of senior managers who will probably hold no equity in the company. Dividends will be small. Cash not needed for re-investment will be saved for a "rainy day" in bank deposits, government securities, or equities of other companies.

Today, few people would feel sanguine about such a company's prospects for lasting success. In fact, unless you were wealthy enough to provide most, if not all, of the equity capital yourself, it would seem challenging enough to get such an enterprise off the ground, let alone sustain its viability. Yet many of these policies are stylized versions of characteristics that have been common among many of Japan's largest modern corporations.

Source: W. Carl Kester, *Japanese Takeovers: The Global Contest for Corporate Control*, Boston, Harvard Business School Press, 1991, p. 21-22.

Under Anglo-American capitalism, companies operate for the benefit of shareholders whose dividends derive from company profits. Poor quarterly returns mean low dividends, depressed share prices and greater exposure to takeovers. Short-term profits must therefore be maintained at all costs. Large Japanese companies face a different challenge. As closed communities embedded in *keiretsu* networks, they operate primarily for the benefit of their managers, employees, suppliers and customers. Shareholders are less important because equity financing plays a smaller role, and in any case, most shares are held by friendly same-*keiretsu* companies willing to accept low ROI.

Anglo-American short-term profit and Japanese market share orientations foster very different perspectives on what constitutes "fair" competition. Anglo-American capitalism has a win-win ethos. Since short-term profits must be preserved, costs are passed on to the consumer even if it means slower growth and less market share. It is better to make high profits on low sales, than low profits on large sales. In good times, one company's price hike will probably lead to similar moves from the competition and everyone is happy making money. The opposite happens, of course, in bad times, but the fact remains that price competition is more the exception than the rule.

Market share is a much harsher task master. In Japan, price cutting is the rule except within stable oligopolies because you must undercut your competitors to increase market share. The ethos is no longer win-win but win-lose, for market share cannot exceed 100% and one company's gain must be another's loss. Declining market share in Japan is a very serious matter: it means lower sales, higher unit costs, weaker product development capacity and a salary cut for every employee starting with the president. Since mass lay-offs are not possible, the only way out is to borrow more money from the banks and recoup market share by increasing capacity or by developing new products, even at a loss.

What this implies, in the context of Japan's high growth economy of the '50s and '60s, is that bigness in all its manifestations was beautiful. Large enterprises could expand capacity despite short-term losses. They could also fix retail prices by the process of establishing their own outlets and refusing to sell to other shops. What distinguished winners from losers in the long run was not quality or productivity *per se* – all Japanese companies were striving for that – it was access to capital and a captive distribution network. The big boys with the deepest pockets and the best market access almost always maintained their share of the domestic market against smaller upstarts no matter how innovative their products or efficient their factories.

GNPism

Ruthless though they were in the competitive field, large Japanese companies became the focus of the nationalistic aspirations of the man in the street in the '50s and '60s. After one disastrous war and years of turbulence during the Occupation, ordinary

Japanese willingly accepted their managers' patriotic appeals for restraint, hard work, economic growth and above all social stability. Again and again, they were reminded that "Japan is a small island country with few resources. We must export to survive. Our country lives on trade." As such, Japan's company men became her foot soldiers, and her export industries, vehicles of national salvation.

GNPism, or the individual's sincere belief that the company's needs took precedence over family, friends and even personal health, achieved wide currency in large part because of the social equality of those years. The drastic income disparities of prewar Japan – her rural landlords and rich industrial families – had mostly been swept away by occupation reforms and postwar labor radicalism. Now the salary gap within each company between the lowliest employee and the president was very small. This change fostered a widespread assumption that all would benefit more or less equally from Japan's growth.

Japan's educational system was another powerful institution promoting both GNPism and social equality. From kindergarten through college, students were subjected to grueling discipline applied equally to everyone according to detailed instructions from the Ministry of Education. By stressing rote learning and frequent testing, the system provided employers with a steady supply of literate workers respectful of authority. The streaming of the best students into a hierarchy of colleges and universities also simplified the work of corporate recruiters looking for management material.

The result of GNPism was a high degree of consensus permeating Japanese society from the '50s till the end of the '70s. In the privacy of their homes, people grumbled about their wretched housing, high prices, polluted environment and poor transportation, but this discontent very rarely translated into organized opposition. At the end of the day, most Japanese accepted the established view of their corporate and government leaders: that Japan's prosperity could disappear overnight if social stability was not maintained.

THE DUAL FACE OF GLOBALIZATION: 1970-1995

The remarkable social and political consensus underlying Japan's postwar production-first economy was made possible by the system's "other face": the inefficient and largely tax-exempt service and agriculture sectors. These functioned as a de facto social security net subsidized by Japan's export champions and her consumers. This system is now under greater pressure than ever because of trade friction abroad and popular disaffection at home.

THE POLITICS OF PROTECTION

Foreign threats again

The '70s and '80s brought so many shocks to the international trading system that the preceding 20 years acquired an aura of peace and harmony in comparison. The traumas began with the collapse of the fixed exchange rate system and the forced revaluation of the dollar against the yen by President Nixon. Then came OPEC's first oil shock (1973-74), followed in quick succession by a world recession (1974-75), a second oil shock (1979-80), another recession (1980-81), a doubling of the yen's value (1985), five years of asset-price inflation (1985-90) and a recession (1990-95). These years were also marked by escalating trade friction with the United States.

For Japan's exporters, these changes seemed nothing short of catastrophic. Their early successes had been built on cheap oil, an undervalued yen and easy access to the U.S. market. The only way out was to raise productivity: bonuses were reduced, suppliers were squeezed, polluting and labor-intensive production was shifted to the NICs, and a lot of machinery was introduced to conserve energy and cut labor costs. GNP growth declined from its 9% average in 1960-74 to 4-5% thereafter.

From the government's perspective, lower growth was bringing into question the average man's belief in the corporate agenda (GNPism). New programs had to be created in response to old problems neglected in the past (e.g., environmental pollution, healthcare) and new demands by politically powerful groups such as farmers and small business. The most active power elite in this respect was not big business or the bureaucracy but politicians, or more specifically, the Liberal Democratic Party (LDP). But first, some background on special-interest politics Japanese style.

Re-distributive justice

One of the key goals of MacArthur's Occupation reforms was the creation of a participatory democracy strong enough to withstand manipulation by powerful minorities. Everything was done to broaden representation: 35,000 pre-war politicians were purged, women were enfranchised, and the principle of free speech was enshrined in the constitution. This fostered an active multi-party system, evenly split between right and left. By 1955, the conservative parties had united to form the LDP. The left was represented by the Japan Socialist Party (JSP) and the Japan Communist Party. Gradually, however, political life became curiously disconnected from the concerns of the urban majority. The rituals of democracy – elections, costly campaigns, and mass voting – remained intact, but politics became a spectator sport of no concern to anyone except professional politicians and special interest groups.

Much of this political apathy came from rural over-representation in the Diet. For 38 years (1955-93) the LDP maintained power through every election because it cultivated its rural base and chose not to reapportion voting constituencies to reflect the population's postwar drift towards the cities. As a result, one rural vote can be worth as much as three urban votes.

The advantages of the system are obvious. Thirty-eight years of *de facto* one-party government greatly simplified relations between Japan's three key elite groups: the bureaucracy, big business and politicians. The same system, however, made the LDP beholden to well-organized interest groups at the expense of unattached urban voters. The old dictum "all politics is local" is nowhere truer than in Japan. Up to 70% of the rural population belong to associations and vote as a block according to association instructions. This, and an electoral system which allows two or more members of the same party to run for a single seat, make individual LDP diet men very vulnerable to requests from association leaders for roads, hospitals and other amenities. Similar pressures coming from other associations representing small shop owners, doctors, wholesalers, and farmers reduce political life to an exchange of votes for special favors. If ordinary people get involved at all, it is as recipients, not participants.

Asking them for contributions was out of the question; the money passed down from him to them. People from back home make trips to the capital and must be dined and given tours. A politician must attend every wedding and funeral, at heavy personal cost – the cash gifts and flowers typically run to ¥50,000 (US$333 in 1990) each. Sometimes there are four or five weddings a day and an equal number of funerals. The chores are exhausting, expensive and time-consuming. "Some days," said Watanabe, " you do nothing but ride around in your limousine in a black suit, with a white tie (for weddings) in one pocket and a black tie (for funerals) in the other." He must attend between 200 and 300 year-end and new year parties every season in Tokyo, each costing ¥10,000 to 20,000 (US$67-US$133) in gifts. Requests from temples, shrines, local festivals, and schools *are endless. "These days, whenever a new school opens in your district, you get a stream of requests for cash gifts. They want you to buy the school a new piano, a statue, or even a library. And you cannot be the only one not to donate. So politics costs more and more money."*

Source: *Inventing Japan* by William Chapman, Prentice Hall Press, 1991, p. 166.

Daniel Okimoto, the author of *Between MITI and the Market*, divides interest groups into four categories, each seeking different things from the LDP:

- **Votes for favors** The largest number of associations fit the pattern described above, exchanging votes for specific legislation, subsidies, and public works.The ministries most involved in these transfers at the behest of the LDP are Agriculture, Fisheries and Forestry, the Agency for Small and Medium Enterprises, Post and Telecommunications, and Health and Welfare.
- **Reciprocal patronage** Companies directly benefiting from specific legislation or contracts often share profits with the LDP. Most of the many scandals which have tarnished the LDP since the '50s have come in connection with this group. The main ministries involved are Post and Telecommunications, Construction, Transportation, Defense, and Local Autonomy.
- **Untied financial support** To maintain good relations with the LDP and reward its pro-business policies, all of Japan's export champions, banks and financial institutions make donations untied to specific requests. The size of these contributions is determined by very objective criteria such as the donor's size. Not surprisingly, the ministries overseeing these companies – mainly MITI and the Ministry of Finance (MOF) – enjoy a great deal of autonomy from direct LDP interference.
- **The kids in the hall** The weakest group of all are unorganized urban voters: housewives, white collar "salarymen" and the self-employed. The LDP seeks to maintain their support by crafting non-controversial policies aimed at improving the quality of life in general. Usually apathetic, this group occasionally monopolizes the LDP's attention when certain issues suddenly galvanize public outrage. Environmental pollution and healthcare were such issues in the '70s; political corruption took their place in the '90s.

Two private sectors

Business never spoke with a single voice when it sought government assistance. Big business, especially the highly competitive and modernized export sector, sought a direct consultative relationship with the economic bureaucracy that bypassed the provincialism and short-term bias of the political parties. What it wanted was maximum freedom for itself on the assumption that what was good for big business was good for Japan. And that is what it got in the main. Economic policies were shaped almost entirely by the bureaucracy or within big business and then rubber-stamped by the Diet with little debate. Big business welcomed *bureaucratic* involvement in the economy as long as it came with a minimum of *political* meddling.

Japan's millions of small and medium enterprises had very different aspirations. They make up a surprisingly large part of the economy. By the mid-'80s, 30% of the total labor force worked in micro-enterprises with one to four workers, including the proprietor. Within manufacturing, almost 50% of the labor force (women and older men especially) work in enterprises employing less than 50 workers. The proportion is similar in Italy, but much smaller (roughly 15%) in America and Britain. As a group, these businesses – the sheltered and inefficient service sector especially – enjoyed a special relationship with the LDP because they served as a surrogate welfare system, absorbing millions of workers who would have otherwise been unemployed because of automation in the efficient export sector. What small business wanted was protection from big business, domestic or foreign, and lax tax enforcement. That meant plenty of *political* patronage and freedom from *bureaucratic* meddling. It was all part of an unwritten social contract: massive tax evasion by small business was tolerated because it was compensated by massive over-employment. The average consumer also shared the burden in inflated prices. Nevertheless, opposition was muted because almost everyone had a relative benefiting from the system. The social role of the service sector has a lot to do with resistance to its reform.

Expensive farmers

A different kind of social contract between Japan's political class and its farmers also has a dampening effect on consumer spending. Rural support is so crucial to electoral success that half of Japan's non-mountainous land is set aside for the production of very expensive rice. In Tokyo, for example, 8 million inhabitants are squeezed into 60,000 acres of housing land while some 89,000 acres, or 10% of the city's total area, is reserved for farmland. Cramped housing means high land prices, small households and less space for consumer purchases.

GLOBALIZATION

MITI again

The turbulence and slower growth of the '70s and '80s forced MITI to redefine its development strategies. For one thing, the export sector included a crop of younger companies – Matsushita, Sony, Seiko,

Figure 1-5

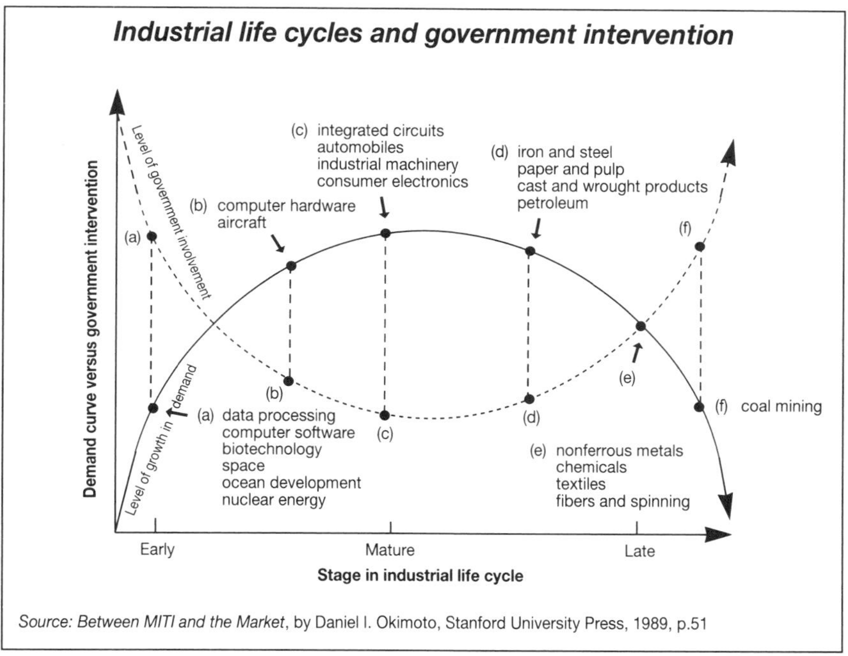

Source: Between MITI and the Market, by Daniel I. Okimoto, Stanford University Press, 1989, p.51

Honda, YKK, Kyocera – large enough to acquire technology, raise capital, enter new sectors and market their products without direct government assistance. There was a shift from largely public to largely private industrial targeting. MITI was now more coach than quarterback.

What emerged was a pattern of bureaucratic intervention based on industrial life cycles (see Fig. 1-5). The consensus was that Japan's future lay in non-polluting, knowledge- and capital-intensive industries such as semiconductors, computers, electronics, robotics, aerospace, biotechnology and telecommunications. These sectors were therefore targeted and protected. Because foreign, especially U.S., competitors were already established in these fields, MITI used every means possible to block threatening imports and FDI, facilitate technology acquisition through licensing, and finance joint precommercial R&D. Mature industries such as automobiles and consumer electronics, on the other hand, were given less protection because they were strong enough to take care of themselves.

As Japan's comparative advantages shifted, labor-intensive sectors and industries strongly affected by high oil prices – textiles, shipbuilding and petrochemicals – declined and shriveled. MITI's goal in such cases was not to buck overall market trends, but to promote an orderly and quick retreat. In the short term, this meant more government assistance: financial aid, tax relief, sponsored cartel arrangements and mergers, and occasionally higher tariffs to reduce the effect of foreign imports.

Price competition exported

The combination of slower growth and government targeting also accentuated the differences between the competitive behavior of big business inside and outside Japan.

Within the domestic market, Japanese-style market share rivalries eventually reduced the key players in mature industries to a half-a-dozen in each sector (see The Birth of a Growth Machine: 1945-1970). The members of these stable oligopolies saw no point in cutting prices further; the cost of gaining greater market share had become too prohibitive. Competition was therefore limited to quality and service, *not* price. Indeed, domestic prices came to exceed export prices because they subsidized the export effort and financed the exporters' over-staffed and captive domestic distribution networks.

For newer high-tech industries, this process of market concentration developed even more quickly, often in tandem with government targeting. Whenever MITI picked a sector, existing players were quickly joined by new ones created by *keiretsu* and leading manufacturers. Soon the chosen sector would be plagued by over-capacity and one round of intense market share (i.e., price-cutting) competition would follow another until bankruptcies and withdrawals reduced the number of contenders to a small cluster of firms, a stable oligopoly. These cycles of over-capacity and predatory competition were exacerbated by the "one set" mentality of horizontal *keiretsu*: they all wanted one member company represented in each major industry and were willing to weather heavy losses to achieve their goal.

Domestic bouts of competition inevitably spilled over into foreign markets. Companies such as Sony or Honda, not happy with their market share at home, sought desperately to achieve economies of scale through exports. Their Japanese competitors, fearing that they might be outflanked abroad, responded in kind. The result was intense price competition everywhere but in Japan. Domestic rivalries of this kind often became so obsessive that the participants hardly noticed the foreign industries they were crushing.

How elephants dance

At first, achieving economies of scale entailed the adoption of "focused" manufacturing. Production efficiency was maximized by specializing in product lines where market demand was strongest, thus undercutting more over-extended, full-line foreign producers.

The product life cycle of Japan's most successful exports, however, got increasingly shorter. The markets for automobiles and consumer electronics quickly subdivided themselves into hundreds of niches where product quality and variety counted more than price alone. This trend precipitated a shift to "flexible" or "lean" manufacturing. Going beyond the economies of scale associated with focused manufacturing, lean manufacturing cuts costs by means of synchronized parts delivery systems (just-in-time or JIT), the assembly of different models on single production lines, and the rapid introduction of new models and styles produced in small batches.

The impact of this trend on small manufacturers, 60% of which exist primarily on parts production, was gradual and profound. The relationship between large manufacturers and their primary suppliers became much more coordinated and interdependent. An automobile, for example, incorporates between 10,000 and 20,000 individual parts. Frequent model changes requires that both sides invest heavily in formal and informal mechanisms for coordinating design, engineering and production. With the proportion of external manufacturing costs rising well above 50% for many exported products, skill in managing subcontracting networks came to play a crucial role in a manufacturer's overall competitiveness. (See Industrial Purchasing for a more detailed examination of Japanese subcontracting.)

THOSE LEFT BEHIND

Production first

Visitors to Japan are often struck by the contrast between its corporate opulence and the cramped circumstances of most Japanese. There is no question that ordinary people gained a great deal from an economic system which had pulled them out so quickly from postwar misery. Between 1950 and 1990 real income per head rose from $1,230 (in 1990 prices) to $23,970, a growth rate of 7.7%. Over the same period America, her erstwhile victor, achieved growth in per capita incomes of just 1.9% a year.

But the same system which worked so brilliantly to achieve export success subordinated everything – people's savings, government capital, corporate profits – to promote corporate expansion while ignoring the amenities that make ordinary lives easier. Japan became the world's greatest creditor nation during the '80s even as half of all Tokyoites lived in areas liable to flooding and two-thirds of all Japanese resided in homes lacking flush toilets and sewage systems. There are only five yards of road per car in Japan. A third of that is not paved. The average Japanese commuter spends a whole month each year in overcrowded trains, where two people stand for every one who gets a seat.

Silence of the lambs

This production-first ethic not only restricted public service expenditures; it also undermined the profit-sharing pact labor had struck with management in the early '50s. At that time, labor accepted management's right to introduce new technology as it saw fit in exchange for lifetime work in large companies and annual wage increases tied to productivity (see The Birth of a Growth Machine: 1945-1970). This system worked very well in the high growth '50s and '60s, but it began to falter after the two oil shocks and collapsed in the mid-'80s. The rate of annual wage increases fell below that of productivity gains and stayed below throughout the eighties, even as corporate profits soared. As a result, Japan's manufacturing workers, among the world's most productive, were poorly rewarded in comparison with workers in other advanced countries.

The same pattern was evident in the number of hours spent at work. Throughout the '60s and early '70s, working hours declined sharply from a peak of 64 hours per week only to bounce back after 1975 and stabilize in the '80s at 2,150 hours per year, 500 hours more than West German workers. This was despite public opinion surveys showing a near unanimous desire for more leisure time. According to *The Economist*, Japan's per capita income was the world's highest in 1990 even though average hourly wages were among the lowest in the industrialized world at US$8.15. High incomes were due to long working hours and overtime, not high wages.

Demographic shifts and lower growth are undermining two other labor gains of the '50s: lifetime employment and the "escalator." In the pre-oil shock days of heady, almost automatic growth, large numbers of university graduates were recruited for life by large businesses on the assumption of continued expansion. Entry level pay was low, but new employees accepted this because seniority eventually conferred high rank and good salaries. In a rapidly expanding economy, the seniority pay system made sense to employers too because young recruits greatly out-numbered better-paid older workers. This reduced average wage costs per employee. Now, after 20 years of slower growth and lower recruitment levels, employees hired during the '60s are all crowded in middle management and their high salaries are pricing employers out of the market. Many are therefore being pushed out before the retirement age of 55. Those who resist are often shunted off to distant offices or to suppliers when they are not simply fired.

Middle managers, the group most vulnerable to sudden termination, are not unionized and have nowhere to go. Even if they had a union, things would not be much different. After achieving labor peace in the early '50s, most unions sat back and became part of company management. By the '90s, they had compromised for too long and could not regain their old bargaining clout with employers.

THE BUBBLE

Funneled savings

Until the mid-'70s, Japan's system of finance remained fragmented, highly regulated and protected from foreign competition. This reflected the Japanese government's development priorities right after the war when savings were minuscule and everyone was worried about their next meal. A free market in savings at this point would have raised interest rates to cripplingly high levels, choking off investment. The financial system was therefore deliberately designed to funnel deposits exclusively to priority borrowers at officially dictated low interest rates. That meant that depositors received even less in interest, of course, but their thriftiness could nevertheless be counted on in the absence of any kind of old-age security. That too was part of the unwritten social contract. Massive tax evasion by farmers, small business and the self-employed was tolerated, but government scrutiny was kept severe enough to prevent tax dodgers from spending their elicit gain too openly. What then could they do? Most put their money into tax-exempt small savings accounts. Big industry therefore paid its taxes and enjoyed access to the savings of tax-dodging small farmers and businessmen.

Liberalization

This system worked very well during the high growth '50s and '60s, but reform became necessary during the oil shock recession. The government tried to shore up the economy and its popularity through expanded public works and increased social security expenditures. To pay for this, it issued bonds in increasingly large amounts until the banks and other financial institutions, limited as they were to narrow exclusive segments of the industry, could not buy government debt in the required quantity. This forced the government to liberalize the system partially and sell its bonds directly on the open market at interest rates dictated by supply and demand, not regulations. What followed was a classic domino effect where one liberalized financial sector created anomalies and opportunity costs for other more regulated sectors, prompting demands for further reforms. This awoke the small savers' appetite for higher returns than those to which they had grown accustomed.

More important, liberalization weakened the close relationship between borrowers and lenders which had been the norm during the high growth years. The pressure on city banks became overpowering: they not only lost small deposits to other institutions willing to offer better terms, corporate clients were also looking elsewhere. With more options available, many manufacturers shifted from indirect financing (borrowing from the banks) to direct equity financing. As a consequence, banks extended a decreasing share of their loans to manufacturing: from 50% in 1970 to 16% in 1990.

Fortunately for Japan's banks, President Reagan's tax cuts both deepened the U.S. Federal budget deficits and required a tough monetary policy to prevent the economy from overheating. The result was an overabundance of cheap money in Japan and capital scarcity in America. By the mid-'80s Japan became the world's largest capital exporter. Foreign governments, the U.S. government in particular, were frequent borrowers.

Massive lending on this scale depressed the yen and strengthened the U.S. dollar, making Japanese exports extremely competitive and crippling foreign imports. Japan's surplus savings were thus translated into a rapidly rising trade surplus, much to the despair of American exporters who claimed that low interest and poor returns in Japan explained Japanese capital flows abroad. Political pressure from Washington led to an agreement in 1984 to reevaluate the yen *vis-à-vis* the dollar. The next five years were a period of financial instability at home and abroad: first the yen almost doubled in value from ¥260 to the dollar in 1985 to ¥140 in 1987; then world stock markets crashed in 1987; finally, Japan went through five years of manic speculation.

Zaitech

The yen's rapid rise (called *endaka*) and the October 1987 crash caused panic within the business community, leading them to cut back severely on investment even though the government was making credit cheap and plentiful. Financial speculation (called *zaitech*) seemed respectable in the short term for it was one way among others to improve one's balance sheet in the face of lower export growth. *Zaitech* operations soon proved irresistible. Convinced that the price of land and equities would continue rising, firms borrowed to invest in them, thus causing their expectations to come true. More valuable stock portfolios and land could be used as collateral for more borrowing and the cycle would feed on itself. Hence the name "bubble economy."

NEW MONEY

Great divide

Rising land values and a soaring stock market created a sudden asset gap between those who owned property and those who did not. Land prices increased so quickly, first in the business districts and then in residential neighborhoods, that middle-class families saving for a home were priced out of the housing market, unable to compete with corporate capital for land. Landowners, on the other hand, became instant millionaires whose land could be used to borrow cash for the stock market, where revenues were subject to almost no capital gains tax.

The swiftness of this social shift was stunning. In the late '70s, the income of Japan's wealthiest one-fifth of the population, was only 2.9 times that of the poorest fifth. By the end of the '80s, the richest fifth owned more than 10 times as much in assets as did the middle fifth. For the first time, more than 20% of Japanese considered themselves as lower class.

New consumer

If marriage ceremonies can be considered a social barometer, the last half of the '80s saw a shift away from traditional Japanese thriftiness to conspicuous consumption on a grand scale. In 1965, only 6% of engaged women received diamond engagement rings. Seventy seven percent of them had diamonds two decades later. The cost of a ceremony, reception and honeymoon soared to an average of US$30,000 in 1989, roughly equivalent to a worker's yearly salary.

This trend was not limited to public ceremonies. High-end department stores such as Takashimaya did a brisk business in expensive baubles such as gold putters (US$9,000), golf bags (US$3,750), crocodile purses (US$2,500) and mink toilet seat covers (US$1,500). Drab was out. Opulence was in.

Not everyone bought these things of course. Ordinary workers saw no evidence in their lives that Japan had become the world's most affluent society. The spending spree was concentrated in certain groups:

- **Young, unmarried women** could afford lavish spending on clothes and foreign holidays even on a modest working income because they still lived with their parents.
- Many **young married couples** who gave up the dream of owning a house one day, acquired a most un-Japanese "spend now" consumer ethos. They spent what they earned and assumed the future would take care of itself.
- **Corporate executives** belonging to large prosperous companies were usually expense-account rich. Total corporate expenditures on entertainment in Japan are at least three times that of the United States, a country with twice its population. This spending not only covered expensive restaurants and trips abroad, but also subsidized high-priced housing.
- Japan's **asset rich** had the collateral to borrow money and spend lavishly if they wanted. Otherwise, their wealth existed mostly on paper because few properties were sold. Many of these asset millionaires actually lived on modest incomes if they were retired.
- **Service industry entrepreneurs** who made fortunes during the '80s when Japan's manufacturing economy transformed itself into a service economy, were the most visible "new rich." Construction, travel, consultancy, business services and restaurants are just a few sectors where the quick and daring could amass fortunes. Like the *nouveau riche* anywhere else in the world, they sought consumer trophies that would mark them as successful.

HANGOVER

Rupture

As long as the bubble lasted, *zaitech* operations were a wondrous money-making machine. By 1989, however, the authorities had begun to worry that asset-price inflation might spill over into more general inflation throughout the economy. The Bank of Japan's move to higher interest rates led to a shift in market psychology and the ensuing stock market decline became a crash when Iraq's invasion of Kuwait in 1990 precipitated fears of another oil shock. Within six months the Nikkei index had fallen 50%. The property market also declined, though not as drastically. The collapse of asset price inflation hit property companies, banks and securities houses particularly hard. Many companies which had gambled on property found it difficult to service their debts. After 1990, the number of bankruptcies increased sharply.

Keiretsu crunch

Japan's **horizontal *keiretsu*** will likely weather the recession because the benefits of membership still outweigh the constraints. Large industrial groups provide member firms with far more clout in elite business and political circles than they could enjoy on their own, guarantee basic sales levels and give access to sufficient capital for promising long-term projects, especially in high-technology industries. The horizontal *keiretsu* are here to stay.

The same cannot be said about the **vertical *keiretsu***. At the manufacturing level, low consumer spending and the inability of many Japanese subcontractors to accommodate further cost-cutting measures are forcing top companies to bypass their inflexible production pyramids and subcontract to the NICs. As a result, some Japanese subcontractors with good technology and modern equipment are beginning to seek work outside their *keiretsu* network. Closed production systems are breaking down.

The same trend is evident within the vertical *keiretsu*'s captive distribution networks. With problems in the manufacturing pyramids as severe as they are now, major suppliers are increasingly reluctant to subsidize their thousands of tied wholesalers and retailers facing stiff competition from new discount chains. By the end of the decade, only a small fraction of today's *keiretsu* stores will still be around. The retail distribution of most goods will be much more open.

Low growth

Looking ahead, the government is still hoping for 4% growth a year, but this seems unlikely. Japan's high growth years, like those of its East Asian neighbors, were the product of a well-educated population catching up after the war with the technological progress made in the West during the previous 30 years. Now that Japan's stock of capital equipment is modernized, her population is no longer growing, and her exports are constrained by foreign demands for reciprocal market access, long-term increases in her GNP will have to rely almost entirely on rising domestic demand.

Reassessment

Unfortunately, domestic demand is now very sluggish. In the short term, Japan has the means to spur growth by spending tens of billions to put its roads, bridges, and housing on a world-class footing. Soon the postwar order – whereby her advanced export sector and her consumers shouldered the cost of inefficient and protectionist farmers, shopkeepers and small businessmen – will have to be drastically reformed or domestic demand will not grow and trade friction will only increase. For the past decade, the Japanese government has tried to steer a middle course, reforming the system as far as it dared back home, while hoping this would impress her trading partners. But time is running out.

THE ODD COUPLE

Like spouses in any marriage of convenience, Japan and the United States are forever quarreling with each other. The Cold War deal was very simple: Japan became a member of the Western Alliance and accepted American bases on its territory in exchange for access to the U.S. market. With the fall of the Soviet Union, there is greater recognition in Washington of Japan's unique brand of communitarian capitalism and of the inadequacy of free market models to explain their lopsided trading relationship. The trend in Japan therefore is towards negotiated sector-specific import market shares, not deregulation for its own sake.

WITH FRIENDS LIKE THAT...

America as #1

Although the United States emerged victorious in 1945 from her war with Japan, the spread of communism in the late '40s forced Washington to reassess the role of her erstwhile enemy. The Soviet Union had to be contained and Japan was an ideal bulwark for the Pacific region. America's interest in her new ally was therefore primarily strategic and military. Japan was admitted into the worldwide trading and currency system created by the U.S., and in exchange, she provided a home for the air and naval bases that were the cornerstone of America's forward defense strategy in Asia.

Lopsided trade

Equal market access was not a priority at the time because America's dependence on imports was minimal. What mattered in the short term was to counter the spread of communist ideology by fostering economic growth in Europe and Asia. As a result, allies were allowed to export to the United States even as their own markets remained fiercely protectionist.

Japan was no exception. During the '50s and '60s MITI used every possible measure to protect its rising export champions from foreign imports and investment (see The Birth of a Growth Machine: 1945-1970). Unfortunately, its targeting efforts eventually had a devastating effect on US industry. Japan's export strategy was peculiar in many respects, compared to that of most other trading nations.

- **Focus** Instead of covering a broad range of items growing gradually through time, Japan's exports were almost always concentrated in a small array of products in very large quantities. Once an item caught on, sales could increase 20-40% or more a year until the most lucrative segments of the market had been occupied. American manufacturers referred to this strategy as the "laser beam" approach.

- **Pricing** Japanese exporters were so intent on market share that they frequently made use of low prices to grab the low end of the market first and then move up the value-added chain until local manufacturers either dropped out or were restricted to luxury niche products. Predatory pricing (or dumping), as this practice later came to be called, was considered unfair in the U.S., but it was common practice in Japan's domestic market where competition was market-share driven, not profit-driven (see The Birth of a Growth Machine: 1945-1970).
- **Hollowing** Most damaging of all was that the same product linkages which formed the basis of MITI's industrial targeting strategies at home – start with steel and then produce automobiles; export radios and then move on to televisions – undermined America's industrial structure. The loss of market share by its auto industry weakened its steel industry. The virtual obliteration of its consumer electronics industry dragged down American semiconductor manufacturers. Ultimately, this could reduce an industrial country to the status of a service economy unless special measures were taken.

Borderless world?

On the import side of the equation, Japan's protectionism was the logical outcome of an insecurity few North Americans cared to understand. Now an industrial latecomer stripped of her colonial possessions, postwar Japan depended on foreigners for all of its vital raw materials. The first priority therefore was the acquisition of foreign currency. Powerful export champions and trade surpluses so large that they could pay many times over for necessary imports of food, energy and raw materials were viewed as crucial to Japan's national security. Nothing was allowed to interfere with these goals, least of all abstractions such as free market competition.

In time, security concerns shifted from foreign currency reserves to high technology. The pressure was on to use the characteristics of high-tech industries – the high cost of entry and R&D, ever shorter product life-cycles, rapid product development, and the manipulation of complex alliances and industrial structures – to secure independence from foreigners. The impact of these anxieties on Japanese import policies was profound and persist to this day.

- **Production first** Whereas U.S. economic policies emphasized the consumer's right to buy everything at the cheapest possible price, the Japanese system was designed to favor producers over consumers. Wages were kept low, rising only half as fast as productivity in the past 15 years. At the same time, consumer prices were kept high to help exporters build war chests for competition overseas. Japanese consumers were forced to save a high percentage of their income even though the interest they received was very low. The system very effectively raised investment at the expense of individual consumption.

- **Intra-industry trade**, the fastest growing type of international trade since World War II, is generally high among advanced countries but very low among developing countries because their economies are commodity-driven. However, Japan's overall rate is unusually low for a developed economy. Its propensity to import manufactured goods from other developed countries – i.e., manufactured imports as a percentage of GDP – is one quarter that of the United States and 1/12 that of Germany. Until the early '80s, this meant that the Japanese imported only goods they either could not make, such as raw materials, or had not yet developed. This attitude is now disappearing quickly.
- **FDI** Because the overseas subsidiaries of multinational corporations penetrate foreign markets much more effectively than arm's-length exporters can, foreign direct investment (FDI) usually has a profound impact on a country's ability to trade with another. At present, the overseas subsidiaries of U.S. multinationals report foreign sales three times the value of American arm's-length exports. And yet, FDI has played a relatively minor role in promoting exports to Japan because majority foreign ownership was prohibited for decades after the war until Japanese industrial muscle and the high cost of land made it prohibitively expensive for all but the largest of foreign multinationals. The result is a huge disparity between FDI in Japan and Japan's direct investment in the rest of the world. Although 10% of the U.S. economy is now foreign-owned, the corresponding figure in Japan is only about 1%, and is virtually zero in many crucial industries.
- **Technology** As explained earlier, Japan's aversion to relying on outsiders is reflected in the "one-set" mentality of her most powerful industrial groups. *Keiretsu* and large corporations all try to control their own technology and maintain independence by producing a full range of products within their industry sector. The urge to be the best at every level, rather than concentrate on some and leave the rest to competitors, is extremely strong among them. Importing is therefore an unwelcome admission of failure for many Japanese managers.

Blinded

America was slow to recognize the new challenge it was facing. Cold War rhetoric led most people to believe that there were only two clear visions of how society could be organized: democracy and free markets on the one hand, or totalitarianism and Marxism on the other. In short, everyone assumed that there could only be one form of capitalism once "protectionist" features were stripped away. As a consequence, the emphasis in trade negotiations involving GATT was on process not outcomes: reduce tariffs, abolish quotas, remove trade-blocking regulations and the market will take care of the rest, so the argument went.

The unprecedented burst of growth and prosperity in North America after 1945 also shielded the general population from the ruthless cut and thrust of international trade. The United States could easily pay for all of its imports because it did not have to earn foreign exchange; it could print it. Moreover, America's high relative productivity compared to that of its war-torn trading partners created a huge pool of well-paid, low-skill jobs which raised family incomes to unheard of levels. But the golden age could not last. Somewhere around the early '70s family incomes stalled and the Bretton Woods system of fixed exchange rate collapsed. An economy that had been virtually self-contained for 25 years after 1945 suddenly found itself severely challenged by international competition.

The loss of economic hegemony was understood by very few Americans because Washington's military and geopolitical power remained unchallenged until the Warsaw Pact, and finally, when the Soviet Union, disintegrated in 1989-1991. With the collapse of its old enemy, Cold War certainties evaporated and Americans were forced to re-evaluate their traditional market-access-for-anti-communist-solidarity trading relationships, especially those with Japan. The pressure was on to recapture the prosperity they had come to consider their birthright.

BILATERAL TANGO

Phase I

Actually, bilateral trade negotiations with Japan had been a fact of life since the early sixties. But they were either concerned with lowering Japanese import tariffs on specific items or, more often, with the imposition of "voluntary" export restraints (VERs) on certain Japanese industries. Fully two-thirds of Japan's manufactured exports to the U.S. now come under some form of managed trade.

By 1983, however, quotas and import tariffs accounted for only a minuscule portion of the market access complaints lodged by the United States and Japan's other trading partners. Japan's formal import barriers were now on an equal level with those of other industrial countries.

Phase II

Unfortunately, lower tariff barriers seemed to have little impact on the U.S. trade imbalance with Japan. A new dimension in U.S.-Japan friction opened in 1982 when a little-known company, Houdaille Industries, sought protection from certain machine tool imports because of the Japanese government's "tolerance of international cartels". In effect, some of Japan's industrial policies were being put on trial in Washington.

There was a corresponding shift in the bilateral dialogue in 1985 with the advent of the Market-Oriented Sector-Selective (MOSS) talks. The purpose of this new negotiating format was to avoid case-by-case disputes and focus on non-tariff barriers affecting industries where the U.S. was competitive everywhere else but in Japan.

On the Japanese side, a string of market-opening measures were announced during the '80s. However, Japanese concessions were often so little, so late and so grudging that they were poorly received in the U.S. The Japanese press, on the other hand, always portrayed them as "yet another concession to American threats of retaliation."

Phase III

The increased focus on Japanese domestic business practices and attitudes was formally recognized with the advent of the 1989-90 Structural Impediment Initiative (SII) talks. Six areas of the economy were discussed: domestic predatory pricing, the distribution system, Japan's high savings rate, the application of antitrust legislation to the *keiretsu*, discriminatory land regulations, and other exclusionary business practices. These talks are now considered to have been successful, but achieving meaningful results over such broad issues proved difficult.

Sector-specific "framework" talks continued, as always, on a separate track. There was a shift at that level towards "quantifiable results-oriented" trade. Specific, quantitative targets for U.S. export expansion would be set, leaving the Japanese to decide among themselves how the demands would be implemented. This drift towards managed trade was a shift from process (the "level playing field") to outcome, and was reinforced when American semiconductor exporters unexpectedly captured 20% of Japan's chip market in 1993 just as MITI had promised in the 1986 Semiconductor Trade Agreement. Now the Clinton Administration is pushing for similar targets in five separate sectoral negotiations:

- **Automobiles and auto parts** This sector accounts for three quarters of the U.S. trade deficit with Japan.
- **Government procurement** The targets here will likely be computers, supercomputers and construction contracts.
- **Regulatory reform** This will cover banking, insurance and other financial services.
- **U.S.-Japan economic integration** The focus is Japan's implicit barriers to foreign investment.
- **Compliance with existing agreements** A review of thirty U.S.-Japan bilateral deals that

have been negotiated in the past and are still in force.

As new liberalization measures will apply to all of Japan's trade partners on an MFN basis, exporters should pay attention to whatever benchmarks come out of these negotiations.

BLACK SHIP SYNDROME

Slow reforms

To portray this whole negotiation process as the imposition of "fairness" on a dishonest country would be a gross oversimplification of reality. Some of America's problems *vis-à-vis* Japanese competition are self-inflicted, not the result of foreign trickery. That being said, many of Japan's corporate and government leaders are beginning to recognize that the old "export or die" trade regime cannot nor should not continue forever because it isolates Japan, leaving it with virtually no reserves of goodwill with which to defend itself against fair or unfair foreign complaints and demands.

Nevertheless, trade reform in Japan remains a painfully slow process in part because groups normally associated with dissent elsewhere – unions, consumer groups and universities – are relatively apathetic. The bureaucracy is unwilling to forsake the power it exercises over big business through its complex maze of permits, licenses and informal requests ("administrative guidance"). The deregulation of retail distribution, for example, has been promised for years, and yet supermarket chains must still spend ¥160 million (US$1.6 million) on average to obtain all the permits required to open a single store. Given their operating profit margins, this implies that sales of US$75 million are needed to recoup that expense.

At the same time, many big businesses favor arcane regulations because they create an effective barrier against foreign and local upstarts intent on grabbing market share from them. Complex rules foster stable cartels; create secure private-sector positions for retired officials (the well-known practice of *amakudari*); and provide inside tracks for the well-connected. They also attract the support of millions of small businesses seeking protection for labor-intensive and inefficient sectors.

Gaiatsu

Who then wants trade reform? Mostly foreigners who are pushing from the outside, just as Commodore Perry did 140 years ago with his "black ships." Consequently, "managing" foreign relationships, especially those with the U.S., is now a major state industry in Japan. Even more peculiar, the Foreign Ministry and MITI have become very adept at using *gaiatsu* (pressure from abroad) to bring about painful, if gradual, reforms that no Japanese individual or institution can openly support because of possible retribution from affected interest groups.

Two things can be said in conclusion:

- Talk of cataclysmic change in Japan, whether due to an aging population, a consumer revolt or lazy children, regularly surfaces in the media every 10 years or so and should be greeted with extreme skepticism. Gradual change, yes; revolution, very unlikely. Never underestimate the flexible conservatism of the Japanese.
- The trend towards managed trade with Japan at the macro level is probably inevitable. That may be a good thing for powerful American industries enjoying strong political support. But it may make things more difficult for smaller players, depending on the product category, because managed trade gives a whole new lease on life to Japan's regulators.

UNDERSTANDING JAPANESE CUSTOMERS

THE JAPANESE CONSUMER

DENTSU BURSON-MARSTELLER

Japanese consumers are among the most discriminating in the world. Existing in a huge, competitive market (second only to the U.S.), they are inundated with temptations and pleas from marketers who seem to be able to fulfill every possible product need. As a result, the Japanese consumer is demanding and sophisticated, and unlikely to settle for second best.

In this challenging environment, what kinds of products can make it? Many say the key attributes are originality and high quality. Dentsu Burson-Marsteller is a communications consultancy based in Tokyo. A joint venture between two of the world's leading advertising and public relations firms, DBM has been operating in Japan for more than 20 years.

DEMOGRAPHICS

Especially to most foreigners, Japan seems to be a remarkably homogeneous market, given its size. School children across the country learn from a single curriculum. A few national daily newspapers reach a vast majority of the population and TV programming is fairly consistent. News, fashion and trends move rapidly across the country. Men exhibit very similar work patterns. Distribution of most products is fairly even nationally. Household incomes, too, are quite even. The difference between the highest and lowest income brackets is smaller than most countries; in a recent survey, 90% of Japanese described themselves as "middle class."

Given this homogeneity, the Japanese population is highly segmented, especially by age and region.

Regional segmentation

About 60% of the Japanese population lives in the urban belt extending from Tokyo to Osaka and Kobe. Within this region, consumer tastes and habits vary to some extent. Some food companies, for example, vary seasoning by locality. Nonetheless, the trend is toward greater homogeneity.

Ownership of durable goods (e.g., refrigerators, televisions) for example, varies little throughout the country, except for heating/cooling appliances.

In terms of spending habits, expenditures for food, housing, education and entertainment tend to be higher in urban areas. Clothing expenses, on the other hand, vary little from region to region.

As in many countries, successful marketers in Japan have effectively assessed local market conditions, watching for demographic shifts relevant to their marketing strategy and

JAPAN 1991

Total population:	124,043,000
Number of households:	41,797,000
Average family size:	2.96
Population density:	327 people/km^2
Average income:	¥463,862 (US$3,445)/month
Spending per capita:	¥345,473 (US$2,566)/month

Population ranking of cities

City	**Population (unit 1,000 persons)**
Tokyo (23 wards)	8,006
Yokohama	3,211
Osaka	2,512
Nagoya	2,098
Sapporo	1,663
Kobe	1,448
Kyoto	1,401
Fukuoka	1,193
Kawasaki	1,153
Hiroshima	1,062
Kita-Kyushu	1,020

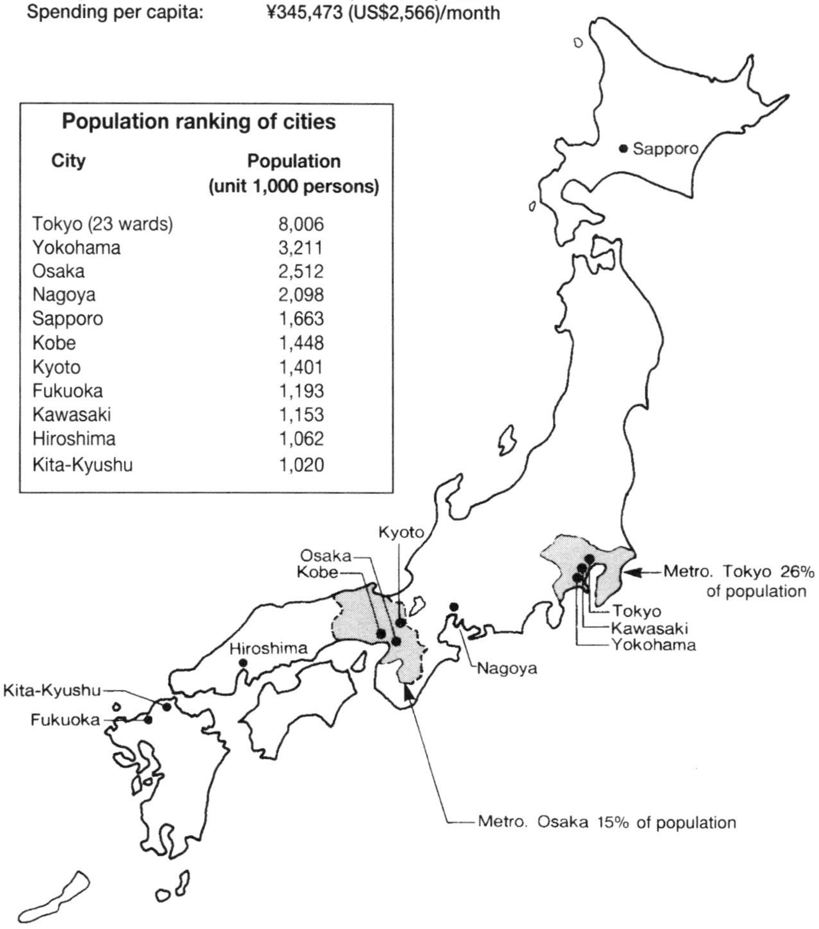

• Cities with populations of more than one million

product. For example, although populations of Japan's largest cities have plateaued, certain regional cities are growing, evolving into dynamic markets for new products.

Age segmentation

The most striking trend in Japanese demographics is the aging of the population. Japan has the highest life expectancy in the world (1989 figures are 75.9 years for men and 81.8 years for women). By the year 2000, 25% of the population will be over 65 years old.

This has enormous implications for many industries, especially travel, healthcare and leisure services.

As changes in Japanese society and culture continue, differences in lifestyle choices may vary strikingly between age groups. Nonetheless, within each age category, consumer behavior and tastes are quite consistent and some segment-specific generalizations may be made.

Students

More than 96% of the population attend senior high school, which follows a compulsory nine years of grade school. Through high school, Japanese students lead hectic, pressure-filled lives, as they strive for admittance to a prestigious college. Full days of classes are generally followed by attendance at special "cram" schools that prepare students for difficult college entrance exams.

More than a third make that next step to college, where the grueling schedules and academic pressures of the preparatory years are gone. In college, it is said that only about a third are diligent about their studies.

The remainder pursue social interests, hobbies, sports, music, etc., activities often subsidized by part-time work. About 21% of college students own a VCR, 34% a mini component stereo, 15% a compact disc player, and 14% a personal computer.

Generally, students have both the time and the income for a level of discretionary spending of interest to marketers. On average, 20-year-old students in Tokyo and Osaka report they spend ¥42,000 per month – about half their income from parents and part-time jobs – on leisure, including drinking/eating out, clothing/accessories, hobbies and holidays. Sixty percent have at least one credit card.

At this age, the patterns among males versus females begin to diverge.

Most students at two-year colleges are women, whereas only 17% of girls graduating from high school go on to a four-year university (versus 37% of boys who attend university and 23% of girls will go to a two-year college). After high school or college, most young women find employment in the service sector or a clerical position in manufacturing, and are referred to as "office ladies" or "OLs."

Twenty-somethings: women

The typical path for young Japanese women after school is to work as an "OL," living in her parents' home until marriage at about 26 years old (92.5% are married by the age of 39). Most stop working after marriage or the first child, although many resume part-time work once children have reached school-age. Only a small percentage continue to work through marriage and childrearing; only 20% of those who take a hiatus from work return to the same "career."

During their early 20s, Japanese women often save to help pay for their wedding and first home. But they also spend more on clothing, accessories and cosmetics than any other age group, and also on sports, eating out and travel – especially to resorts and abroad.

This group – with considerable discretionary funds, an acute fashion sense and desire to establish a household – is a prime target of many marketers. Wedding-related products and services, for example, are in high demand.

Twenty-somethings: men

After school, men generally join the workforce and become "salarymen," becoming more and more involved in work and business relationships as they progress through their twenties.

Men marry slightly later than women; at 28.4 years, on average. Not surprisingly, men in their twenties exhibit a relatively high ownership of automobiles and stereos. In addition, they spend their discretionary funds on sports, and, to a lesser degree, travel.

Leisure time is increasingly important to this group. Although their fathers' lives – in terms of time investment, life focus and even social life – revolved around work and business relationships, the newest working generation is beginning to put greater emphasis on a more balanced lifestyle. As a result, changes in their behavior as consumers are just beginning to emerge.

Consumption of leisure items – sporting goods and services (e.g., health clubs), travel, arts and crafts, electronics – by this group will likely continue to grow as the trend toward a balanced work/leisure lifestyle takes hold.

Married life: through middle age

Once married, the goal of most young families, though not attainable by all, is to purchase their own home. More families buy a home while their children are aged 6 to 17 than at any other time. Since real estate prices in the center of most cities are extremely high, most will opt for homes on the outskirts, or postpone purchase.

The term "housewife" would not be anachronistic in Japan. As noted earlier, most women quit work when they marry or have children, and turn their focus to the home. Many will take on a part-time position later, for purely economic reasons (i.e., to supplement the household budget) rather than out of personal ambition.

Husbands work long days at the office, and usually have limited time for family activities, leaving their wives to be the driving force in the family. Mothers are closely involved with their children's lives, especially their education.

In addition, wives handle the family finances – including managing the household budget and monitoring savings and investments. Usually, Japanese men give their full paycheck to their wives, reserving only an allowance for themselves.

Most of the family spending, therefore, is at the discretion of housewives.

Outside the home, housewives are active on a community level. Grassroots women's groups – both privately organized and ward- or city-sponsored – are booming. Although a benefit of these groups is sociability, most have a focus, such as addressing family, community or women's issues. Activities usually include monthly meetings, symposia, newsletters and study sessions on such topics as the environment, educational trends/needs and children's and women's health issues.

Marketers of household goods should keep in mind that local women's groups have become a powerful force, inspiring various consumer movements in Japan.

Men in their 30s and 40s, on the other hand, are concerned with moving up the corporate ladder: salaries, cost of living and position become more and more important. Although their wives tend to purchase underwear, socks, liquor and household necessities, men usually purchase their own work clothes, sporting goods and books or hobby items (e.g., audio equipment, personal computers). Couples often make larger purchases together (e.g., living room sets, large appliances, etc.)

Like the twenty-somethings, changing attitudes toward the postwar Japanese work ethic can be seen among middle-aged men (35 to 59). More and more regret about working too hard, at the expense of an active family life, has been documented in consumer surveys. Values are shifting; an unwillingness to sacrifice personal identity, needs and goals for "the good of the company" are more in evidence.

Nonetheless, whereas the twenty-somethings seem to be acting on this shift in values, male baby boomers remain the most hardworking demographic group. Marketers should be aware of this dichotomy in attitude versus behavior, as it gives valuable consumer insight into this group.

Age 60+

Mandatory retirement age is between 55 and 60 years old. Not surprisingly, many retirees move on to another job, sometimes with the assistance of their former employer. A full third of those over 65 are still working, not surprising in a country with a substantial, healthy older population.

Post-retirement activity usually includes leisure pursuits such as watching TV, reading, working on hobbies and visiting friends and family. Almost two-thirds of those over 70 take two or more trips annually.

Many companies are taking marketing aim at this group, offering tours and activities for seniors. Also, retirees are showing a greater interest in spending considerable time abroad. Especially with a strong yen, many are choosing to own homes overseas or move to retirement communities in foreign countries.

COMPENSATION/SPENDING

Some of the particulars of the unique Japanese employment and compensation system have direct effects on consumer spending patterns, so should be addressed here.

Bonuses

Twice a year, in mid-summer and December (coinciding with the gift-giving seasons), Japanese employees are given a bonus equal to about one to three times their regular monthly paycheck, depending on business performance. This acts as enforced savings for the employee, who usually uses the bonus for savings, large purchases and loan repayments. A higher percentage of the summer bonus is traditionally saved, whereas the winter bonus often goes to purchase consumer goods.

Consumers typically spend about half their bonuses, making these seasons prime marketing periods. For themselves, as well as others, consumers spend on high-quality foods, accessories and other gifts, plus major durables, such as cars, televisions, VCRs and refrigerators.

Compensation system

Traditionally, the larger Japanese companies offered their employees "lifetime employment," a system under which job security was bartered for company loyalty. An employee was hired straight from university and remained with the firm until retirement. Although this has been eroded somewhat by post-bubble economic pressures, and will continue to evolve, many of its aspects remain in place. For example, under the related seniority system, pay increases with age and length of service, rather than performance.

Therefore, disposable income and consumer spending still tend to increase with the age of the consumer, making the timing of major expenditures somewhat predictable.

Savings and consumer finance

Japan has one of the highest savings rates in the world – almost 17% in 1992. This percentage has declined somewhat in recent years, as income growth has slowed and savings goals have shifted. For example, although many still save to buy a house or apartment, the cost of buying a conveniently-located home has moved beyond the aspirations of may urban residents. Also, attitudes toward consumer credit have changed. While major durables always were once paid for out of savings, use of consumer credit is increasing, especially among those 40 and younger.

With use of consumer credit has come a recent increase in personal bankruptcies – from 26,000 in 1991 to 43,000 in 1992 – among individuals who are not accustomed to the rights and obligations associated with personal credit. As a result, outstanding consumer credit as a proportion of disposable income rose to 22.5% in 1990, significantly higher than that of the supposedly spendthrift Americans (18.8%).

Despite these available savings, personal asset management – including investment in equities, bonds and in overseas real estate – is a growing specialty in Japan, and represents an opportunity for financial services marketers. Only in recent years have Japanese begun to shop around for the highest-yielding investment vehicles. Many continue to keep funds in low-yield accounts administered by the postal system – a favorite savings vehicle.

Household expenditures

Average monthly disposable income among non-farming Japanese households was ¥463,862 in 1991. Of this, more than 70% was spent on goods and services, including food (at 17.7%, the largest category of expenditure), transportation (6.6%), housing (3.6%), utilities (3.9%), clothing and footwear (5.1%) and household furnishings (2.9%). Leisure and services represents a growing percentage of spending (about 7%).

The percentage spent on housing may be deceptively low. About 62% of households own their homes, so pay only utilities; in addition, many households are in company-subsidized or public housing. Naturally, for those who pay rent, housing expenses are a dramatically larger expenditure.

With the yen's steady appreciation against many international currencies since the 1985 Plaza Accord, the relative buying power of Japanese households, especially for imports, has increased substantially.

LIFESTYLE

Japanese homes

It is difficult to compile a single description of the typical Japanese home, since styles are evolving constantly. However, two generalizations would be generally accurate. Most are some combination of Western and Japanese style; almost all provide limited space.

Style Traditionally, the Japanese home was characterized by its floor covering – *tatami*, or tightly woven straw mats, held in place by wooden frames, about 90 x 180 cm. Room size and shape was defined by the *tatami*; indeed rooms still are measured by number of mats. Furniture in a *tatami* room is limited. One sits on cushions on the floor and at night, *futon* are taken from the closet and laid out for sleeping.

More and more, however, apartments are fitted with Western-style space, with linoleum or wooden

Figure 2-1

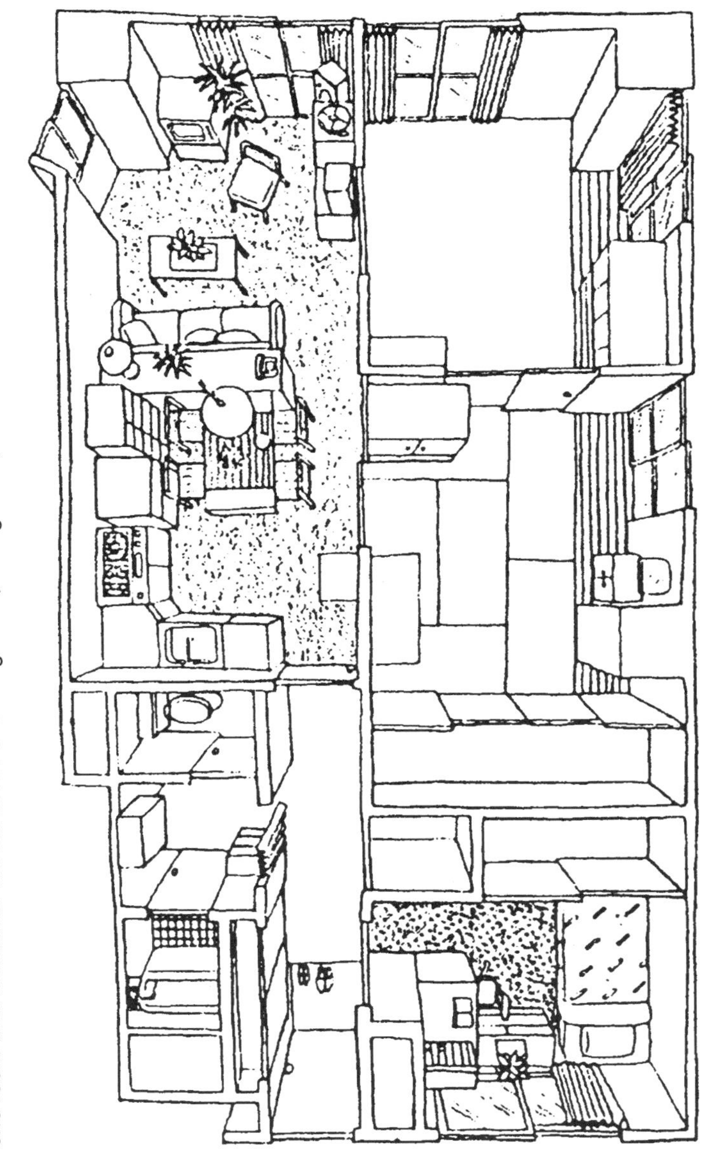

The typical new Japanese home consists of two or three small bedrooms, a Japanese-style tatami room and one room that combines the functions of a living room, dining room, and kitchen.

Source: JETRO

flooring sometimes covered with carpet or rugs, and Western-style furniture. Today, most homes have both *tatami* and Western-style rooms.

Ownership of beds, living room sets and dining sets correlates directly with income level – increasing with higher income groups. This suggests that higher income households have adopted a more Westernized living style, perhaps due to the expense of Western-style furniture as well as the larger living spaces needed to accommodate.

Nonetheless, interest in home improvement products and interior design is on the rise among a wide income segment.

Home size One aspect of the typical Japanese home cannot be overemphasized, especially to North Americans used to large spaces: space is at severe premium in Japan. Lifestyles are impacted profoundly, as a result. The average size of families continues to decline. Entertaining at home is unusual, though more likely among young adults; and houses are furnished functionally, for family use.

Owned homes average 117 square meters; rented homes, 44 square meters. In apartments, six-mat rooms are standard and the smallest might be only 3 mats. Larger homes may include eight and 12-mat rooms (see Fig. 2-1).

Using this limited space effectively, without sacrificing comfort, is truly a challenge. Refrigerators are smaller and kitchen cabinet space limited, so housewives shop more often, a practice which further reinforces consumer demand for freshness and quality foods. Many apartments have small balconies, which are often used for extra storage. A favorite feature of women's magazines is new ideas on planning use of space.

Many successful household products provide space solutions in some respect, whether it be with scaled-down product and package sizes, multipurpose functions or innovative storage solutions.

Quality of life

Although Japanese enjoy high incomes, fine education and health-care systems and a relatively crime-free environment, some aspects of living standards – amount of leisure time, size of homes and proximity to employment – are not at the same level.

For example, most Japanese homes do not have central heating (space heaters being the norm). The average commute for Tokyo workers to their job is one and a half hours (usually by subway). Vacation allotments are the lowest in the industrialized world and overtime work is standard.

There is an increasing amount of discussion in all quarters – government, media, academia, business – about improving quality of life among Japanese. Young people, in particular, are looking for improvement, and are open to marketing messages offering a "better way."

One result of interest in a better quality of life is the increasing expenditure by consumers on services, convenience items and health-related goods. Young women tend to spend on international travel and "culture centers" (self-improvement courses in traditional arts, language, and dancing). Housewives buy more and more convenience items (prepared foods, home improvement items). Young men, especially, spend on sports and health-related goods and services.

Tradition

For years, the trend in attitudes about traditional versus modern lifestyle tended toward greater and greater liberalization. Between 1989 and 1991, however, that trend was modified; the inclination among younger age groups moved toward a renewed appreciation of and return to Japanese style and tradition.

This may be a result of a changing Japanese perception of their place in the world. Recognizing shortcomings of other cultures, plus a decline in the sense that Japan needs to "catch up," young people are exhibiting a new appreciation for their heritage.

Traditional rites, gender roles, family relationships, tastes, plus a feeling of association with one's home town, interest in history, etc., are receiving greater regard.

Environmentalism

Concern for the environment and preference for a more "natural" lifestyle are influencing behavior of Japanese consumers.

Ninety-three percent of Japanese consumers in a recent survey report that they are probably more concerned about the environment now than before. Most recycle; 60% say they would choose the more environmentally friendly of two equivalent products. Sixty percent say they avoid, to some extent, buying throwaway goods.

It might be useful to note here the difference in the Western and Japanese meanings of "environmentalism," which perhaps have as their bases a divergent attitude toward the value of the untouched natural world. Whereas Westerners think of the "environment" as the world in its wild state, the Japanese perception integrates the manmade and natural worlds. The Japanese appreciate nature in its managed form; nature that has been improved by man to be more safe, ordered, convenient, sociable, tidy, etc.

Thus, in Japan, "environmental" concerns are not limited to protection of natural resources. Japanese think in terms of the state of their private environments (e.g., size of homes), public environments (e.g., city spaces) as well as the worldwide environment (e.g., the ozone).

CONSUMER TASTES

Standards

Successful marketers have learned that Japanese consumers are among the most discriminating in the world. Although their predilection for brand names -- among imports, usually the most famous and elite of international names -- has subsided somewhat, the Japanese still demand high quality in style and function. Products must be reliable and durable; their manufacturer must offer good after-sales service. The importance of appearance – style, package design, product uniformity and flawless condition – cannot be overestimated.

Some pitfalls that foreign companies have faced:

- Damage, even very slight, to packaging: a scratch on the package or other damage not affecting the product (which might go unnoticed in the West), will cause a Japanese consumer to reject it.
- Difficulty in providing efficient customer service: consumers often fear less-than-perfect service from a foreign company.
- Freshness of food products: no matter if an item "will still taste the same." Food must look fresh as well as be fresh. Some food companies have had to develop new packaging just for Japan.

Japanese consumers want a wide selection to choose from. Small lot sizes, of varied selection of size, color, product type, are recommended over large lots of less diversity.

Value pricing

Since the burst of the economic "bubble," Japanese consumers are going "back to basics."

A trend toward value pricing has developed and quickly accelerated. Big names are no longer a guarantee of big sales. Expensive goods still demanded are those that offer indisputable quality and style.

In addition, generic products that inexpensively fill basic needs are beginning to be introduced, and couponing, banned in Japan until very recently, is beginning to be used by manufacturers.

With consumer spending at its lowest level in a decade, competition among retailers is becoming increasingly aggressive. Department stores are suffering; discount stores selling myriad consumer goods – clothing, liquor, cosmetics and even automobiles – are booming, altering consumer buying habits and price expectations.

Fashion

The tastes of Japanese consumers are becoming ever more sophisticated, by international standards.

Appearances have always been important to the Japanese. Standards for personal appearance continue to be high. Dress is fairly conservative in this society where pressure to conform is great; yet, equally strong is pressure to be fashionable, especially among young adults.

As a result, fads come and go with particular fervor. What is "in" often catches on so quickly that within a short period of time it loses uniqueness and is replaced with a new fashion. As a result, product lives can be much shorter than in many other countries.

In Japan, successful products attract imitators on a scale and at a pace dizzying to many Western companies. Japanese marketers tend to use the introduction of new products to defend their market share (vs. discounting and promotion in the U.S., for example), often launching new products in rapid-fire succession. Thus, they are poised to quickly duplicate competitors' products – often incorporating improvements while matching or beating price.

To be successful, therefore, foreign companies, must remain flexible, open to quickly modifying marketing strategy or even product itself, to keep up with this very fluid marketing environment. Indeed, such forceful and swift competitive response should be anticipated long in advance of entering the market, so no time is lost in reacting when the inevitable occurs.

Color

Color preferences in Japan can be traced to traditional influences. For example, kimonos for older women were black silk, with a family crest in white, whereas garb for younger women were a mixture of bright colors. Still, today, a taste for subtle hues as well as bright primaries persist; and, as women get older, they tend to gravitate to neutral colors. Men's colors usually run from blue to earth tones.

Colors in the home were defined by building material. Straw mats, wooden beams and exterior, plus a sand mixture on the walls created an environment of earth tones.

Until recently, interior design and clothing fashions tended toward these monochrome influences. More and more, however, as marketers use color to differentiate their products, and as the world's fashions increasingly influence tastes, Japanese are embracing bolder use of color. Even cars, which were previously mostly white, are being marketed in new palettes of customized colors.

In addition, some color and style combinations, or juxtapositions of patterns that might not be attractive to Western tastes, are fully acceptable and used in Japan.

Seasons

Japanese are very attuned to the changing seasons. Traditions and activities (and therefore consumer demand for related products) change to suit seasonal nuances. Vacation times, gift-giving, various outdoor activities and foods are closely associated with certain times of year.

Seasonal advertising campaigns are a cornerstone of many marketing calendars in Japan. New campaign themes are constantly turned over as each new season begins.

Also, the climate itself has implications for marketers. Summers are generally hot and humid; winters, cold and dry.

Products must be durable under both extremes, and take varying consumer needs into account. Clothing, for example: in winter, Japanese usual wear a light overcoat and warm indoor garments. For the sticky Tokyo/Osaka summers, jackets should be unlined and clothing exceptionally light.

Diet

Japanese diets continue to diversify, with the ongoing influence of various cuisine's internationally. Consumption of alcohol, coffee and juices continues to rise, as does use of frozen and other prepared foods.

Nonetheless, the Japanese diet can still be characterized by high consumption of cereals (especially rice) and fish, and relatively little dairy product. Also, the traditional inclination for subtle flavors and attractive presentation (colors, design, appetizingly fresh) persists.

The trend toward processed foods continues, as consumers search for convenience (ease of preparation), without sacrificing good taste or healthfulness.

For specific inquiries, please contact:

Dentsu Burson-Marsteller
Sogo Kojimachi No. 3 Bldg.
6 Kojimachi, 1-chome
Chiyoda-ku, Tokyo 102
Tel: (03) 3264-6701
Fax: (03) 3234-9647

THE RETAIL ENVIRONMENT

Structural problems neglected for decades, government deregulation and sluggish "post-bubble" consumer spending have heightened competition between retail sectors formerly coexisting peacefully in legally-sanctioned retail "preserves" (see Japanese Distribution Management – the outside view*). Whether this will force Japan to adopt more American or European patterns of distribution will only become apparent in a decade. For the moment, the pace of change varies greatly across different product categories and different retail groups. The focus in this chapter is on these groups.*

BACKGROUND

Cramped

Japan's 124 million people live in a country physically the size of California, only 70% of which is inhabitable because of mountains and volcanoes. The resulting population pressures are often hard to understand for North Americans. Imagine what the social consequences would be if half of all Americans were forced to live, with their farmers, in the flat parts of southern California.

Small stores

In this cramped environment, small stores have a decided advantage in meeting consumer needs. For decades after World War II, Japan's roads and housing conditions were rudimentary, and most consumers did not have the means to transport and store large quantities of goods. Consumers, moreover, needed credit, something Mom and Pop stores were willing to provide because buyers and sellers both belonged to tight-knit neighborhoods where reputation was important. Even now, when money and roads are not a problem, many consumers still prefer to shop in small local stores because of their convenience, good service and "community atmosphere." Japan consequently has more than twice as many retailers per 1000 people (13.2) than does the U.S. (6.1). In other words, Japan has more retailers than the U.S. even though it has half its population.

Dual structure

Working alongside the small shops is the "modernized" segment of the retail sector: department stores, supermarkets, convenience store chains and discount stores. Overall, the market share of retail stores with 30 or more employees is slightly short of 30% (see Table 2-2). Only 2,300 outlets in Japan, mostly department stores and supermarket chains, employed 100 or more people in 1991. These large stores with their advanced retail techniques coexist amazingly well with the traditional sales practices of the small shops.

Table 2-2

Japanese retailing by size of business 1988/*1991*

Number of employees	Number of stores (000s)	Total employees (000s)	Annual sales (¥ billion)	Sales area (sq m)
1-2	874 / ***847***	1,438 / ***1,381***	12,832 / ***15,224***	25,967 / ***26,996***
3-4	422 / ***417***	1,424 / ***1,404***	19,246 / ***23,006***	20,982 / ***22,345***
5-9	214 / ***214***	1,337 / ***1,336***	24,095 / ***28,877***	16,883 / ***18,657***
10-19	70 / ***72***	924 / ***948***	16,948 / ***21,408***	9,571 / ***10,564***
20-29	19 / ***20***	452 / ***477***	8,446 / ***10,673***	4,465 / ***4,713***
30-49	12 / ***13***	458 / ***479***	8,552 / ***10,478***	4,818 / ***5,177***
50-99	5.4 / ***5.8***	353 / ***384***	7,494 / ***9,216***	5,405 / ***6,195***
100+	2.1 / ***2.3***	467 / ***525***	17,226 / ***21,754***	13,961 / ***15,255***

Source: Census of Commerce/MITI

Table 2-2 (cont.)

Japanese retailing by size of business 1988/*1991*

Number of employees	Annual sales (¥ billion)	Share of sales (%)	Sales per employee (¥ 000)
1-2	12,832 / ***15,224***	11.2 / ***10.8***	8,924 / ***11,023***
3-4	19,246 / ***23,006***	16.9 / ***16.4***	13,515 / ***16,386***
5-9	24,095 / ***28,877***	20.9 / ***20.5***	18,022 / ***21,615***
10-19	16,948 / ***21,408***	14.7 / ***15.2***	18,342 / ***22,582***
20-29	8,446 / ***10,673***	7.3 / ***7.6***	18,685 / ***22,375***
30-49	8,552 / ***10,478***	7.4 / ***7.4***	18,672 / ***21,874***
50-99	7,494 / ***9,216***	6.5 / ***6.6***	21,299 / ***24,000***
100+	17,226 / ***21,754***	15.1 / ***15.5***	36,886 / ***41,436***

Source: Census of Commerce/MITI

DEPARTMENT STORES

Definition

MITI's Census of Commerce defines a department store as any retail outlet with more than 50 employees, selling a wide variety of product lines none of which account for more than 70% of its total sales. Most department stores are classified as "large" under the revised (1992) version of the Large-Scale Retail Store Law (LSRSL) because their sales area frequently exceeds 6,000 square meters in major cities and 3,000 square meters in the rest of Japan. This forces them to go through certain procedures whenever they wish to open new stores (see Japanese Distribution management – the outside view).

Top Department Stores
Seibu
Mitsukoshi
Takashimaya
Daimaru
Marui
Matsuzakaya
Isetan
Tokyu
Hankyu
Sogo

What's in a name?

Department stores or *depato* are among the most traditional retail institutions in Japan. Many date back a century or more when they were set up at the end of major railway lines and run by railroad companies. Gradually thereafter, the largest among them positioned themselves at the medium to high end of the retail market. They became cultural centers exuding an aura of high class and taste where customers could expect luxurious surroundings, depth and breadth of product range, flawless quality, and a large number of salespeople in attendance to greet them, serve them and carefully wrap their purchases.

Wrapping is particularly important for gift items because the department store's name often confers great value to the donor's selection. Gifts are such an important means of social communication in Japan that a gift market of enormous proportions has grown around certain set occasions (see Table 2-3). It has been estimated that US$90 billion – split 60-40 between personal and business – is spent annually on gift items. As a market, this equals two-thirds of the entire revenues of the restaurant and catering industries.

Squeezed

Gone are the roaring '80s when department stores could stock $2,500 crocodile-skin purses in their "casual accessories" corner. Cuts in overtime and high personal debt have dampened consumption and rekindled the traditional thriftiness of many Japanese. The result has been a reduction in department stores' sales of 5.7% in 1992 to ¥9.5 trillion (US$76.4 billion) – the first annual decline in 27 years. For the first time, discounters are emerging nationwide, forcing department stores to hold sales of their own.

Table 2-3

Gift-giving occasions in Japan	
Jan. 2-3	*Otoshidama (pocket money is given to children)*
Jan. 15	*Coming-of-Age Day (receiver: 20-year-olds)*
Feb. 14	*St. Valentine's Day (receiver: men)*
March 14	*White Day (men reciprocate St. Valentine's gift)*
March/April	*School/University entrance and graduation days*
May	*Mother's Day*
June	*Father's Day*
Early July	*Ochugen (mid-year) gifts*
Sept. 15	*Respect-for-the-Aged Day*
December	*Oseibo (year-end) gifts*
Dec. 25	*Christmas*
Others	*Birthdays and Weddings*

Costly debts incurred during the '80s and sky-high rents in their prime downtown locations are reducing their room to maneuver. Their biggest problem, however, is a tradition of purchasing by consignment.

Purchasing

A department store such as Takashimaya, for example, sells goods "acquired" in three ways:

- Twenty percent of its products are non-returnable in the sense that Takashimaya assumes the loss if they are not sold. The breakdown by source of these goods is 70% Japanese, 30% imports.
- Forty percent are acquired on a consignment basis either from local suppliers or from import houses.
- Forty percent are sold through Japanese or foreign suppliers who rent a spot on one of their floors, set up and staff a booth, and share the proceeds with Takashimaya. This is sometimes referred to as "the shop within the shop system."

The percentages change from one department chain to another.

Weakness

On the surface, this sounds like a great deal for department stores. Their suppliers take back unsold stock, pay the salaries of nearly half of their sales clerks and still have to share a percentage of their revenues with the stores.

However, consignment forces suppliers to pad their margins and leaves little to the department store because prices have to be kept as low as possible to maintain sales. Even so, high overhead still drives prices too high and makes them vulnerable to competition. More important, consignment effectively isolates these stores from consumer trends in an age when growth depends primarily on one's ability to access and interpret sales data. Department stores are essentially real estate operations whose tenants select much of the merchandise they display. As such, department stores have little in-house purchasing expertise and limited data on consumer preferences. This leaves them very vulnerable to discounters who buy directly from manufacturers and make money even during a recession because their computerized information networks keep track of what sells.

SUPERMARKETS

Definition

MITI defines a supermarket as any self-service store open for less than 12 hours a day with a sales area larger than 500 square meters. There are two types of supermarket chains. Some, such as Fuji Super, rely on food for 70% or more of their sales. Others – Daiei and Seiyu, for example – are closer to general merchandise stores in that pharmaceuticals, electrical appliances, household goods and other sundries limit food to less than 40% of sales. The first type as an average sales area of 1,000-1,500 square meters, the second averages 4,000 square meters.

Efficient

Along with convenience stores, supermarket chains are among the most efficiently run retail sectors today. Their many outlets, POS computer systems, and strong purchasing power give them a lot of leverage over their suppliers. Requests for rebates and high listing fees (called "promotional expenses" to make them GATT-compatible) are therefore the rule.

Top Supermarket Chains

Daiei
Ito-Yokado
Seyu
Jusco
Nichii
Uny
Nagasakiya
Izumiya
Chujisuya
Maruetsu

Diversified

To make the most of their information systems and stay on top of shifting consumer trends, many of the largest supermarket chains have acquired discount chains and convenience stores. Daiei, for example owns both Topos (a discounter) and Lawson (convenience). Similarly, 7-Eleven (convenience) and Daikuma (discount) both belong to Ito-Yokado.

Purchasing

Most of the large chains have purchasing offices in Asia, Europe and the U.S.

CONVENIENCE STORES

Definition

MITI defines convenience stores as any self-service outlet open for more than 12 hours a day, with less than 50 employees and a sales area between 50 and 500 square meters.

> ***Top Convenience Stores***
>
> *7-Eleven*
> *Family Mart*
> *Lawson*

Youth and food

Most of Japan's 38,000 convenience stores are located in large cities and surrounding suburbs where land prices are high and young people are concentrated. Each outlet carries on average 3,000 items in a 100 square meter sales space, 75% of which are food products, including fast foods. This stands in marked contrast to U.S. practice where beverages and tobacco account for 50% of convenient store sales and food only 20%.

Convenience stores are particularly popular with working singles, young two-income couples and students. 7-Eleven estimates that 60% of its customers are either teens or in their 20s.

Slower growth

High growth is no longer possible for all the convenience store groups. Of the top 100 chains, one to two go bankrupt every year and only four to five are still expanding. One of these is 7-Eleven with 5,058 stores as of February 1993. Due to high land costs, the easiest way for it to grow is by converting old Mom and Pop stores and incorporating them under a franchise system. Over 80% of its stores were acquired in this way.

Competitive tools

The most successful chains such as 7-Eleven, Lawson and Family Mart, rely on two basic tools to succeed over the competition. The first is to capture as many good locations as possible and blanket the market. In typically Japanese fashion, the chains prefer distribution push tactics (improve accessibility; get the products on the shelves) over consumer pull strategies (lower prices; advertise). Indeed, there is far less price competition between the chains in Japan than there is in the U.S.

The second tool is computerized POS information systems and their attendant JIT delivery schedules. A typical 7-Eleven store averages about 1,000 customers a day who generate a minimum of 4.9 million items of POS data to be analyzed. This gives them enormous leverage over suppliers because they have a much better idea of what sells and why. It also binds suppliers very tightly to small-batch delivery schedules determined by each chain.

New Trends

To increase traffic, the best Japanese chains are incorporating services unusual in North America. Box lunches (called *bento*) are now commonly prepared every day for office workers. Other services include faxing, photocopying, dry cleaning, parcel delivery, theater ticket sales, photo development and the processing of utility payments.

7-Eleven has created a catalog purchasing system called "Shop America" promoting high-end foreign imports. Catalog sales average ¥15,000 per order compared to ¥670 per purchase inside their stores. Direct marketing tools such as catalogs are becoming increasingly popular among all retail chains as a way to expand sales volume and product assortments without investing in retail space (see Direct Marketing in Japan).

Purchasing

Convenience store chains can be an excellent entry point for certain product categories because 70% of their items are changed every year. Listing fees, stock returns and introductory margins are not the common practice. Supply contracts are reviewed every three months, however, and the chains often ask for six months of exclusivity if the product is new to Japan.

DISCOUNT STORES

Weak start

Until the late '80s, discount stores – also called wholesale clubs, home centers, and DIY (do-it-yourself) outlets – were bit players in Japan's retail scene. They were and still remain essentially a suburban phenomenon, clustered in areas close to road junctions, convenient to car drivers.

When everyone felt wealthy before 1990, the appeal of discount stores was weak. They carried a limited range of products, their staff was part-time and uninformed, and their appearance was very much "bare bones." Two types of discount stores, widely reported in the Western press as the death knell of the Japanese distribution system, flopped. One concept was "box stores" where products were displayed in their original cardboard cartons and customers brought their own bags. The second was "NIEs Super Shops" (NIEs for newly industrialized economies) focusing on electronic products imported from Taiwan, Hong Kong and Southeast Asia.

Top Discounters

Yodobashi Camera
Bic Camera
Sakuraya
Kimuraya
Doi
Topos

Expansion

By 1993, the prospects for discount stores, especially those selling menswear or electronics goods, looked much more positive. The "post-bubble" slump in consumer demand has left unsold goods stacking up at every level of the distribution chain, forcing some weaker manufacturers to bypass traditional channels and sell to discounters for whatever price they can get. Bankruptcies are also a major source of supply. Sales growth for the top 134 discount chains averaged

9.5% in the 12 months leading up to March 31, 1992, making them the fastest growing retail segment in Japan.

Some established discounters such as Aoyama Trading have even ventured out of their suburban base and opened stores on the Ginza to compete head on with the major department stores. They have also taken advantage of Japan's surging yen to source directly from overseas, bypassing the multi-layered domestic distribution system. The immediate reaction of most department stores was to offer discounts as well, but their high fixed costs make such tactics unsustainable. Seibu's response has been to come out with cheaper "no brand" goods, mostly clothing sourced in China, South Korea and Southeast Asia.

Weakness

The abiding weakness of Japanese discount chains remains their source of supply. Not one of them is big enough to do in Japan what a Wal-Mart does in the U.S.: force major suppliers to offer them much deeper discounts than are already offered to ordinary wholesalers. Unless that happens, their market power will evaporate when consumer demand picks up again and they will be left with two alternatives: either accept the no-discount policies of the main manufacturers and become specialty stores, or remain discounters and be reduced to selling hand-me-down products the specialty stores cannot sell, precisely what they were doing in the '80s.

SPECIALTY STORES

Definition

MITI defines specialty stores as retail outlets with more than 90% of its sales coming from one product line. According to the Census of Commerce, there were 1,000,166 specialty stores in 1991 (16% clothing, 28% foods and 56% household goods). Although small outlets with one to four employees account for 80% of specialty stores, 46% of total sales in this retail category are generated by the 18% of shops that are mid-sized (five to twenty-nine employees).

Specialty stores actually include many very different subgroups whose growth rates vary depending on product, store size and location. In general, mid- to large-size stores situated in the suburbs and developing areas are doing very well. Many group themselves into small shopping centers; others escape single-product categories and become "concept stores" where sundry items (clothing accessories, food, dinner sets, etc.) are presented in a unified ambiance to a targeted market segment defined by life style or consumer sensibility.

We will focus on two specific subgroups: specialty chain stores and family-owned (or Mom and Pop) stores.

Chain stores

The chains are a good example of how retail groups seeking customers through the discount route can end up being co-opted by Japan's "producer-driven" distribution system. Most of them started out believing that their bulk purchases could be used to challenge the manufacturer's control of pricing, only to give up when suppliers offered rebates and free staffing services too good to refuse. With their heavy reliance on manufacturers for management expertise and generous credit terms, most chains have become tied landlords renting out shelf space for goods.

Their biggest competitors, especially in electronics goods, are the discount chains. Another important group are the Mom and Pop stores. Family-owned outlets have more rigid pricing than the chains and offer less choice, but their closer connection with vertical *keiretsu* entitles them to certain special services from their parent manufacturers, such as free gifts for customers or sponsored athletic and other events in areas near the small shops.

Family stores

For years now, the demise of Mom and Pop stores has been predicted on account of one "distribution revolution" or another. And yet, it is amazing how resilient and cost-effective these small outlets can be. Dad often has a part-time job outside the shop and the rest of the family is willing to work so many hours that they hardly recognize any difference between private life and shopkeeping. Indeed, most live directly above or very near their shops. All in all, they are more accessible to shoppers living in the same neighborhood than the larger outlets, and can operate on relatively low margins. Compare that with the large shops where good employees are hard to find, salaries and overtime are high, rent in prime locations are astronomic and the difference in cost efficiency is not *that* great.

Family shops are best understood as a government-sanctioned social safety net for latent unemployment. Some shop owners were once the beneficiaries of "lifetime" employment in large firms, but had to retire at 55, ten years too young to receive a state pension. Many more were discharged from small and medium enterprises because of an economic downturn or new labor-saving equipment. All leave with a network of contacts built up during the years and try to slot themselves into their former employers' networks of distributors and suppliers. The transition is made easier because small-scale wholesaling and retailing is relatively easy for amateurs to run.

Nevertheless, many family-owned shops are losing out to discounters and convenience store chains. Where a typical Japanese housewife in the '70s knew that the local shop was the cheapest and most reliable place to buy anything, her children now view it as among the most expensive places to buy anything. Family shops also tend to disappear when the owners retire or die. Few of their children want to continue the business and inheritance taxes are high.

INDUSTRIAL PURCHASING

"Industrial" here refers to business (as opposed to consumer) end-users. Two distinct relationships between foreign exporters and Japanese buyers are prevalent in this area. The first is a simple purchasing transaction requiring only timely delivery and good after-sales service from the exporter or his representative. The second type, subcontracting, involves much closer, more long-term ties with Japanese buyers. Readers wishing to know more about the manufacturing techniques mentioned in this chapter should refer to Annex 1's reading list.

ARM'S-LENGTH TRANSACTIONS

Coal to Newcastle

Japan's R&D efforts during the past 20 years and her private sector's continuing innovations in process technology have raised domestic production capacity to such a level that sales opportunities for foreign manufacturers in this market have gradually become limited. Successful industrial exports tend to be either of a type and quality not yet achieved in Japan or extremely price competitive; middle-of-the-road products generally lose out. These exports must, in addition, be customized to the specific requirements of a precisely targeted customer base. This requires not only accurate information about the end-users' needs, but also an infrastructure which can guarantee faultless service over the long term and a reliable supply of spare parts.

That bubble again

Japan's bubble economy of the late '80s fostered more than a speculative boom in the property and equity markets: the availability of cheap financing led to a massive binge of capital spending. Capital investment accounted for two-thirds of GNP growth between late 1986 and early 1991. Quite usable older factories were often scrapped to make place for costly brand new ones burdened with excessive capacity and too much sophisticated paraphernalia. This raised the break-even point for many manufacturers (operating costs as a percentage of sales), so that they had to run factories close to capacity to maintain profits. The break-even ratio of the electronics and automobile sectors, for example was higher than 90% in 1992. Weaker demand in the '90s, however, made such production levels unsustainable and Japan's capacity utilization rates plunged to 71% in 1992, their lowest level since 1976. Many manufacturers are therefore glutted with capital stock. Most analysts feel that Japanese capital spending will decline or stay flat during the next two to three years at least.

Niche marketing

Compared to consumer products, the distribution systems used in capital goods are not as multi-layered and complex, and there are very few remaining tariff and non-tariff barriers to the import of capital goods. Yet, domestic competition in Japan is such that it is as good as impossible for foreign manufacturers to capture mass markets in that country. Rather, the best strategy is usually to study the market thoroughly and concentrate one's efforts on clearly defined niche buyers. It is also important to understand some peculiarities of Japanese industrial purchasing – decision-making, customization, payment, and after-sales service.

Decision-making

Except for small companies where president-owners frequently have great discretionary power, decision-making within Japanese organizations tends to be collective and conservative. Proposals, even for equipment widely regarded as excellent, are discussed in informal meetings (*nemawashi* or consensus-building) until a decision is made and it gets the stamp of approval from everyone concerned (*ringi* system). This form of decision-making is especially common when the seller is new to the purchaser, when the equipment in question is expensive, or when a purchase has repercussions affecting several departments. Decisions are collective to minimize individual responsibility. Attempts to locate "the man in charge" or to put someone on the spot for an immediate decision are therefore futile, even rude. The usual response is: "We will get back to you when we have an answer." It is therefore important to enlist the help of a Japanese agent or advisor who knows the industry, whom to contact and how to interpret the ambiguous messages sent to him by potential buyers.

Customization

Niche marketing unfortunately means customization with all the extra costs that entails. Japanese buyers are the most demanding in that respect; expect requests for alterations from nearly every potential buyer. Exporters offering a wide range of models or with an in-house capacity to modify their products according to customer requests have a definite competitive advantage in Japan.

For more complex or high-tech equipment, customization can become so expensive as to require joint development, either with the end-user, as is common in the semiconductor industry, or with a Japanese trading company. The latter case often arises when a large trading company asks a group of manufacturers to jointly produce a system comprised of several machines which it markets as a set afterwards.

Payment

Payments are made either in cash through bank transfers or via promissory notes. Foreign exporters usually deal only with bank transfers. Nevertheless, it is important that they understand the role of promissory notes because they bear a direct relationship to the margins requested by Japanese trading houses.

Promissory notes or *tegata* are still widely used by purchasers of industrial equipment, especially for large payments. A *tegata* is essentially an IOU redeemable for cash 60, 90, 120 or 180 days after it is issued. The recipient has three options: he can keep it until maturity and exchange it for full value; he can sell it to a bank or financial broker for a discounted price before it matures; or he can endorse it and pay a third party willing to accept it as cash even though it has not yet matured. That is where trading houses become important. If, for example, a foreign exporter insists on being paid 90 days after delivery even though the end-user only issues 180-day *tegata*, business only becomes possible when a trading company is found willing to assume 90 days of debt for a fee.

After-sale service

Japanese buyers insist on written warranties covering every aspect of the equipment's performance: efficiency, speed, accuracy, reliability, energy consumption, and tolerance. Warranty periods usually extend to one year, starting with the day the installation inspection is completed. These warranties tend to be very vague about the supplier's maximum liability because Japanese purchasers prefer to negotiate mutually agreeable solutions with their suppliers when problems arise. These "solutions" reflect the balance of power between the parties concerned.

Generally speaking, the Japanese tend to feel that the buyer enjoys a "superior" status in any buyer-seller relationship. At their worst, these feelings can lead a purchaser to revel in his position and lord it over any salesperson petitioning him for attention. Even when a buyer is not arrogant, however, custom dictates that a supplier accept his complaints without question and make every effort to rectify the situation even when he still does not understand what went wrong. Foreign exporters may find these expectations foolish and unacceptable, but their Japanese agents must conform to them. Exporters who succeed, therefore, pay prompt and serious attention to complaints because repeat business comes from servicemen not salesmen. It is no exaggeration to say that a company's reputation in Japan depends largely on the way it deals with complaints.

SUBCONTRACTING RELATIONSHIPS

Ties that bind

The focus, thus far, has been on the export of capital equipment to Japanese buyers, arm's-length transactions where both parties remain very independent of each other. Japanese-style subcontracting implies a continual flow of products and services, a more long-term (less transaction-to-transaction) relationship, and greater interdependence between buyer and seller. Before explaining what this means for an exporter, we will examine how it functions among Japanese companies in the automobile industry, one of the most highly integrated in Japan.

Automobile overview

For a variety of historical reasons, Japan's auto manufacturers in the '50s chose not to directly operate their parts factories – the standard U.S. Big Three practice – and opted instead to tap into the entrepreneurial vitality of independent suppliers. At present, most of Japan's 11 auto manufacturers rely so completely on their subcontract networks that manufacturing has taken a back seat to R&D and design, marketing, production coordination and final assembly. As clusters of interdependent manufacturers, they are prime examples of vertical *keiretsu* in action (see The Birth of a Growth Machine: 1950-1970).

Subcontract families are organized hierarchically with each supplier relying on a "parent firm" directly above it for most of its sales (see Fig. 2-4). Auto assemblers are served by "first-tier" suppliers, each one kept supplied by a network of "second-tier" suppliers, down the line to smaller and smaller companies. This allows the assemblers to take advantage of Japan's tiered labor market; the smaller the company, the lower the salaries generally (see Fig. 2-5).

Figure 2-4

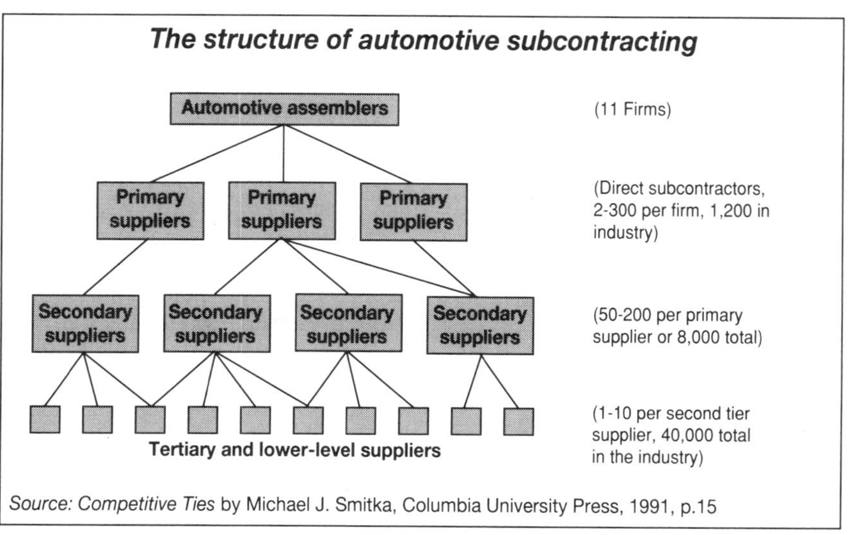

Source: Competitive Ties by Michael J. Smitka, Columbia University Press, 1991, p.15

Figure 2-5

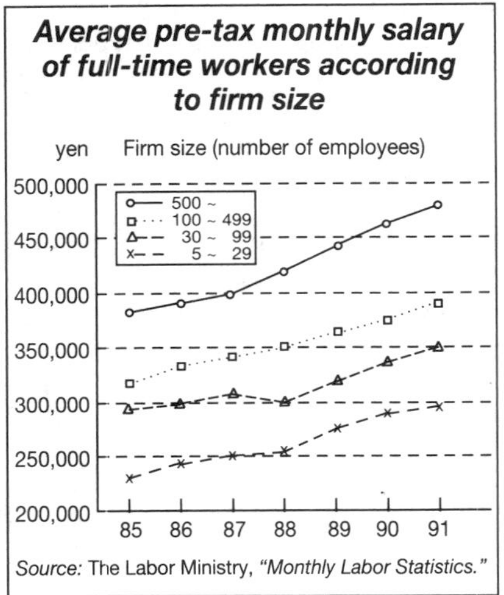

Average pre-tax monthly salary of full-time workers according to firm size

Source: The Labor Ministry, *"Monthly Labor Statistics."*

With approximately 50,000 suppliers in any given family, how is coordination and quality maintained? More important, is there not a conflict between the core manufacturer's natural desire to cut costs, and his dependence on profit-seeking suppliers to go beyond simple order-taking and develop new and better parts? The answer is twofold, according to Michael Smitka, a specialist on Japanese subcontracting. First, a transparent evaluation system is instituted throughout the network. Second, communication between existing suppliers and the admission of new members into the network is regulated to limit the role played by subjective feelings such as trust. Both merit closer attention by foreign exporters.

Evaluation techniques

The most contentious issues faced by subcontracting networks usually center around pricing, delivery schedules, quality control and profit-sharing with respect to innovations. Japan is no exception.

Pricing, of course, can easily lead to trouble because assemblers and suppliers are caught in a zero-sum game where one side's gain is the other's loss. To get around this problem, auto assemblers avoid bidding wars based on final unit prices. Instead, bidding suppliers are asked to break their expenses down into components – material costs, purchases from suppliers, tooling costs, direct manufacturing costs and gross margin – and compare them with their earlier bids to see whether cost reduction targets applied to all suppliers have been achieved. Note that gross margin (overhead, salaries and profit margin) is standardized and not subject to haggling. This forces suppliers with above-average labor costs to compensate with higher productivity or see their profits squeezed.

Assemblers have greatly reduced the space and working capital normally tied up in inventory by requiring frequent, small and pre-scheduled deliveries from their supplier networks. **Just-in-time (JIT) delivery systems** force each supplier to tune his production to harmonize with that of his parent firm. It also increases the whole network's sensitivity to production bottlenecks, quality problems, and lax equipment maintenance because breakdowns without buffer stocks quickly affect downstream operations.

There are two opposite approaches to **quality control**. The first inspects goods after production, checks them against a static set of norms, and filters out whatever is not up to standard. This is still the normal practice for most North American producers. Its main drawbacks are that it accepts some level of waste as normal and establishes an adversarial "we-they" attitude between inspectors and workers, and between suppliers and buyers. The second approach, the one commonly in use in Japan, uses statistical process control (SPC) to gradually decrease the failure rate at each step of the production process. Improvement thus becomes a continuous, quantifiable process, eventually canceling the need for post-production inspections. More important, from a supply network point of view, the price bidding process described above – suppliers divide their cost into components – becomes much more transparent and easier to implement when SPC procedures and documentation are standardized across the whole network.

It is sometimes said that the first 20% of the design process determines 80% of a product's cost. Japanese auto manufacturers measure the value of their suppliers' **innovations** and cost-saving designs by using techniques, called value analysis (VA) and value engineering (VE), originally developed in the U.S. during the '40s. Any savings generated are split 50-50 between the assembler and the supplier-inventor. The latter, however, has to share his new idea with the rest of the network. Here again, the technique's transparency encourages initiative while avoiding the appearance of favoritism.

Communication

Evaluation techniques foster transparency but they are not by themselves a positive incentive to cooperate. The control mechanisms most commonly used in the West – direct ownership, the courts, threats of severance – are not really available to the Japanese car industry. Ownership was not an option in the '50s when the industry's growth rate exceeded its capacity to buy suppliers. Contracts are no better when lawyers and courts are so few in number that cases take years to resolve. Cutting a supplier off, on the other hand, is possible, but can easily wreak havoc in a production network unless other suppliers agree the punishment is deserved.

Japanese manufacturers must hold their supplier families together by other means:

- Until the early '90s, assemblers urged their suppliers to design parts and components that were different from the competition's. Only a fifth of Japan's car parts went into more than one model. This locked suppliers into **closed systems** (the Toyota group, the Nissan group, etc.) where cross-purchasing was extremely rare.

- Suppliers are grouped into **associations** to improve communications within the network and keep everyone (including the assembler) in line through peer pressure.
- Regardless of ups and downs in the market, suppliers have a **long-term bond** with their parent firm. A poor performer may get smaller orders as a signal of displeasure, but he is always given time to redress the situation. Only if he fails consistently will orders gradually drop to nothing.
- **Personnel transfers** Parent firms' managers frequently take temporary or permanent executive positions within their suppliers' organizations. This greatly facilitates communication between different levels.
- **R&D** among suppliers is often done with their parent firms' support. Specialized personnel may be exchanged and money lent.
- **Concrete steps** Commitment to suppliers is made visible when the assembler gives up his internal manufacturing capacity to produce parts. In exchange, suppliers must improve their productivity in line with norms established by the assembler.
- **Supplier profitability** over the long term is a responsibility shared with the assembler, hence the Japanese manufacturer's obsession with market share.
- **Gradual admission** New suppliers are only gradually incorporated in the family. Initial orders will be small and seemingly not worth the effort. More important orders come later along with requests to share sensitive SPC and pricing information.

How relevant?

Of course, not all supply networks in Japan are as tightly integrated as the car industry. Japanese subcontracting relationships run from simple one-shot agreements to complex long-term arrangements. This has obvious implications for foreign exporters seeking a long-term supply relationship with a Japanese firm.

- Low sales growth, rising costs and a stronger yen are forcing many Japanese manufacturers to achieve economies of scale by reducing model variations, standardizing parts and dumping less effective suppliers. This trend **creates opportunities** for foreign suppliers with competitive products.
- Japanese buyers think in terms of **long-term relationships**, not deals. What interests them when initial contacts are made is your company history, your track record in Japan, your future business plans, and the degree to which you complement the network. Being introduced by a Japanese member of the network is a great advantage because the one doing the introductions becomes responsible for your actions.

Insisting on talking business immediately at this stage is a sure sign to them that you are an impatient self-seeker who will likely drop the relationship as soon as you encounter the first inconvenient obligation.

- The **first orders** will probably be small and cost you more than they are worth on their own. Again, initial orders are designed to test your attitude as much as your production capacity. Quality and service at this stage is particularly important.
- As orders grow, a greater degree of **customization** may be required. Requests will also be made, sometimes at this stage sometimes at the very beginning of the relationship, for extremely detailed information on your costs, your production processes, your present sales volume and production capacity, all of which are highly confidential in normal North American practice. This is often a major shock for Western suppliers used to cost-oriented rather than quality- or cooperation-oriented component buyers. Nevertheless, Japanese subcontracting has its own norms, and the decision is yours as to whether the added business is adequate compensation for the loss of confidentiality.
- Because of the buyer's JIT system, there is a definite preference for **frequent deliveries in small lots**. It is up to you to negotiate minimum order sizes and extra charges when anything less is requested.
- In cases where your skills or products could play a critical role in the buyer's future plans, money and personnel could be made available for **joint product development** projects.

JAPAN'S DISTRIBUTION SCENE

JAPANESE DISTRIBUTION MANAGEMENT – the outside view

The core distribution problem in any country is that manufacturers usually produce a limited number of products in large quantities, whereas consumers want a large number of diverse products in small amounts. Japan's solution reflects the "production-first" development strategy adopted in the high-growth years after the war. It is probably no longer sustainable. The focus in this chapter is on the highly influential manufacturer-controlled channels and independent wholesalers, the sogo shosha, *and wholesalers tied to powerful retail groups.*

BACKGROUND

Channels "Я" social

Supermarket managers negotiate special eye-level displays with their suppliers, salesmen get pep talks from their managers and share information about what products are moving, and retail product development teams design store-name imitations of best-selling brands. Consumption appears so "natural" to us that we forget the social values and institutional power plays that structure our shopping environment. Japan's own development in this respect has been unique in many ways.

The pre-war scene

In common with most developing countries today, Japan's pre-war distribution system was dominated by wholesalers. The small size of most manufacturers, the small retailers' financial weakness and the poor quality of most roads meant that everyone depended on multiple layers of wholesalers for financing, information, storage and distribution services. The system was "efficient" as long as manufacturers could not develop cheaper private distribution networks.

PRODUCER-DRIVEN

The game preserve

Japan's government and large manufacturers took this pre-war system and shaped it to fit their own priorities. What the politicians wanted was protection for an important voting constituency – small shop owners and wholesalers – against the onslaught of large department stores.

The result was a string of laws, culminating in the Large-Scale Retail Store Law (LSRSL) of 1974 designed to maintain harmony between big and small retailers. This law defined large stores as any outlet with sales space of 3,000 square meters or more in the 10 largest cities, and 1,500 square meters or more in the rest of the country. More important, a 1978 amendment to LSRSL gave small shop owners a *de facto* veto right over the creation or expansion of retail outlets with sales space of 500 square meters or more in their neighborhoods. There were ways, both legal and illegal, to get around LSRSL, but it effectively blocked the rapid growth of large department store chains during the '80s. LSRSL limited competition by segmenting the retail sector into self-contained pockets, each with its own customer base and business traditions. It was typical of the many laws created by the Japanese government to protect small business (see The Dual Face of Globalization: 1970-1995).

Producer-driven

Contained competition undoubtedly allowed small shop owners to resist market forces favoring the growth of large retailers, but it also left them very vulnerable to pressures from large suppliers. In certain sectors especially, such as consumer electronics, home appliances, cosmetics, non-prescription drugs, automobiles and motorcycles, most small retailers gravitated towards the exclusive distribution networks of large vertical *keiretsu* (see The Birth of a Growth Machine: 1945-1970). Matsushita, for example, organized a network of 27,000 stores. Toshiba has 15,000; Hitachi 10,000. Given the tendency of most Japanese to shop locally, the geographical spread and density of a manufacturer's distribution network determines its market share and effectively bars easy entry by new competitors.

In the '50s and '60s, for example, most Japanese households became brand loyal by default. No one made a conscious decision to rely on a single maker's appliances for the next 20 years, but most consumers drifted into it because the neighborhood electronic shop owners lived nearby, everyone knew them and they were always ready to take back faulty products.

With manufacturers at the helm, certain distribution practices gained wide currency, even outside the vertical *keiretsu:*

- **Consignment selling** To facilitate the acceptance of new products, retailers and wholesalers can return unsold merchandise to the manufacturer. This makes retailing a low-risk business.
- **Resale price maintenance** In exchange for accepting returned goods, manufacturers demand the right to set the retail price for their products. Discounting or unauthorized third-party sales are severely punished.
- ***Tegata*** To further assist small retailers, manufacturers allow them to pay with 60-120 day promissory notes (called *tegata*).
- **Rebates** Inasmuch as Western distribution incentive schemes are based on discounts, Japanese suppliers prefer to supplement rigid margins with flexible kickbacks. These come in three forms: compensation for promotional expenses, performance-tied payments, and rewards for

general loyalty. Rebates are such a big part of the profit levels achieved by small retailers that they effectively force most of them to comply with their suppliers' wishes. They also play a central role in the volume- (as opposed to profit-oriented) sales methods commonly used in captive distribution chains (see Japanese Distribution Management – the inside view).

- **Small-batch deliveries** High land prices limit the storage space channel members can afford even for products sold on consignment. Retailers want tertiary wholesalers to shoulder storage costs; tertiary wholesalers expect the secondary level to do the same, and so on up the chain to the manufacturer. As a result, there is an emphasis on frequent and timely small-batch deliveries throughout the system. This requires that the last wholesaler in a chain be physically close to his retail clients, hence the multiplicity of wholesale layers required to serve Japan's many small shops.
- **Personnel sharing** To assist their retail outlets and make sure they offer no unauthorized discounts, manufacturers and wholesalers often provide free sales personnel to retailers for limited periods of time. This practice is especially popular in the apparel and home electrical appliance industries, and will likely continue for a long time to come, despite its official "abolition" in March 1991 pursuant to the U.S.-Japan SII talks (see The Odd Couple). Many retailers have simply become too dependent on it to make ends meet.
- **Exclusivity** Wholesalers and retailers belonging to vertical *keiretsu* are usually only allowed to carry their parent manufacturer's own products unless otherwise authorized. Smaller manufacturers do their best to mimic this system through exclusion clauses in their distribution contracts, equity ownership of their most efficient wholesalers, and a variety of less reputable pressure tactics.
- **Special deals** In all the practices described above, Japanese manufacturers prefer to create a sense of mutual obligation within their distribution networks by making very "special," private deals with each wholesaler and retailer. Agreements are therefore verbal and reflect past business dealing together. Transparency and standardized offers are usually avoided.

What these practices all have in common is the dependency relationship they engender between retailers and their suppliers. Tied retailers are not value-added intermediaries selecting products and determining prices for a specific customer base. Rather, they are landlords renting out shelf space to a single customer who also happens to be a creditor.

Advantages

Such tied distribution networks have a profound influence on the domestic pricing and marketing strategies adopted by large Japanese manufacturers. By controlling much of its wholesale and retail network, a supplier can impose high fixed prices and avoid price competition. This is common practice in product categories dominated by manufacturing oligopolies (see The Dual Face of Globalization: 1970-1995).

Tied networks also fit in well with Japanese-style product development. American firms strive for "giant leaps forward" innovations based on costly market research; Japanese producers typically aim for incremental improvements to already successful products. Continuous adaptation – also called product churning (see Prospecting in Japan – product mapping) – speeds up new product introductions, captures market share and maintains distributor/retailer loyalty. Guaranteed shelf space makes launching these new products extremely cheap. It also reduces the need for pre-production market research. New products are simply churned out as fast as possible and put on display to see which ones catch on. Shelf space is determined by the manufacturer's leverage over its retailers, not how well a given item sells. Consumer "pull" is created by the manufacturer's name and the service reputation of its distribution network, not product brands.

Not easy

It would be wrong to conclude from the sheer number of small shops (see The Retail Environment) and the marginal nature of discounting that competition in Japanese retailing is weak. On the contrary, competition is fierce even when it extends only to quality and service, not price. Japanese consumers are among the most demanding in the world. Freshness of produce, a precise product-need fit, the absence of even the smallest defects and perfect packaging, especially for gift items, are expected as a matter of course. Retailers go one step further by organizing purchasing clubs and adding extra services to build a relationship with each customer. A large department store might, for example, create a sports club or hire a famous athlete to teach golf to its regular clients. Small shops will make small deliveries and perform personal services that supermarkets are unwilling to provide.

Nature or nurture?

Japan's high prices are often explained away as a logical consequence of the Japanese consumer's willingness to pay for excellent service, and so they are to some extent. It is also fair to say, however, that Japan's producer-driven distribution system has never allowed them to do what American consumers take for granted: pay less for fewer services (see "Three American Snapshots" in this chapter). To use an analogy proposed by the well-known market analyst George Fields, the Japanese market is like a jumbo jet filled with first class seats; economy class is simply not available. With limited price competition until recently, Japanese retailers could only distinguish themselves by offering more services, which went a long way towards skewing the consumer's perception of value: their true cost was hidden and there was nowhere else to go to forego bowing elevator attendants for lower prices.

THREE AMERICAN SNAPSHOTS

1890s

The cornerstone of American retailing 100 years ago was the village general store. Small and crammed to the rafters with whatever bags of flour or kegs of nails the shopowner could get on credit, general stores served so few customers on average that profits derived from high margins, not volume. What consumers expected in return was credit and services, such as home deliveries and prompt attention from clerks standing behind the counter. Since products were undifferentiated commodities and supply was sporadic, the store policy was more "push" (sell aggressively whatever is in stock) than "pull" (increase demand through advertising). The most powerful players in the distribution chain were the wholesalers because they both extended credit to shopowners and told small manufacturers what customers were buying.

1950s

Despite fierce legal and political opposition from small shopowners and wholesalers in the 1930s, the fastest growing retail segments thereafter were the chains. Their formula for success was simple: centralize purchasing to cut out the middleman; build bigger stores located in low-rent districts accessible to automobiles; reduce service levels (credit and delivery especially); and, most importantly, raise profits by aiming for high volume and low prices. An essential "pull" element of this strategy was something new in American marketing that radio and television had made possible, the nationally advertised brand, a kind of supername which simplified the buying process because it conveyed information about products and the people using them. Distribution power was therefore concentrated in the manufacturers who created brands and in the retailers who bought in vast quantities for a mass market.

1990s

The splintering of the "mass market" into hundreds of consumer groups, a slow growth economy, the escalating costs of labor, capital and construction, and new computerized POS technologies have made retailing a very fluid, vulnerable business. Indeed, the market has polarized into distinct "high-touch" and "high-tech" segments. The fastest growing chains either offer depth of selection within a single product category to a highly targeted customer group willing to pay more for personalized attention and knowledgable staff, or they are large merchandising operations selling a wide variety of goods at low prices to customers willing to accept minimal services. To distinguish themselves from the competition and increase their leverage with manufacturers, both of these groups have successfully established private brands based on their POS data. This has undermined the national brands, forcing once-powerful manufacturers such as Heinz and Campbell to cave in to pressure and make private brand goods for the chains. Media fragmentation – from three networks to hundreds of television channels – is further weakening manufacturer brands by making audiences harder to reach.

OTHER WHOLESALERS

Lots of middlemen

So far we have focused on marketing channels dominated by manufacturing oligopolies, an influential part of the distribution system, but still only a part. Left out are hundreds of thousands of relatively independent wholesalers (called *tonya*) serving as intermediaries between small manufacturers and retailers, the general trading firms (*sogo shosha*) belonging to horizontal *keiretsu*, and distribution channels tied to large retail groups.

According to MITI's latest Census of Commerce, there were 475,983 wholesalers in 1991, 75% of which employ fewer than 10 employees (see Table 3-1). Most are specialized by function (primary, secondary, and tertiary wholesalers), geography (national or regional) and product category. Product specialization is often the result of regional strengths in the manufacture of certain product categories such as textiles or pharmaceuticals, reminiscent of Amsterdam's diamond district or Manhattan's garment district.

- The defining characteristic of **primary wholesalers** is not size, but an "open account" with manufacturers or large retailers who buy in large quantities. As such, this category includes the giant *sogo shosha*, intermediaries for about half of Japan's exports and two-thirds of its imports. Most primary wholesalers, however, are much smaller and owe their unique position to very strong personal and financial ties with their purchasing clients, ties that transcend short-term profit considerations.

Table 3-1

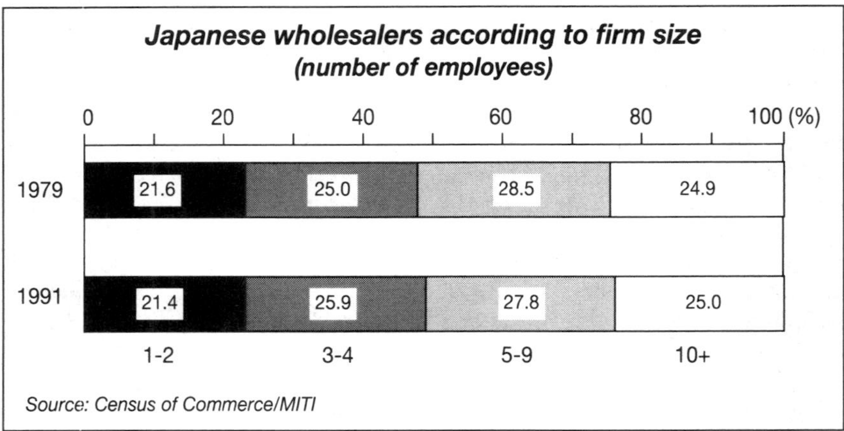

Source: Census of Commerce/MITI

- **Secondary wholesalers** greatly outnumber primary ones and often outstrip them (excepting the *sogo shosha*) in size and technical expertise. Indeed, whereas primary wholesalers are best thought of as their clients' exclusive agents, secondary ones are more like diversified trading firms balancing the conflicting requirements of several manufacturers and many product lines. The fastest growing among them consolidate their business networks by using data derived from electronic ordering systems (EOS) and their sales force to advise clients both at the manufacturing and retail end.
- **Tertiary wholesalers** are usually tiny family businesses with a few trucks and lodgings directly above the warehouse. Most serve Mom and Pop stores in small geographic areas, a very time-consuming and unprofitable market. (See Fig. 3-2 for an example of how all three levels interact.)

A key difference between the North American and Japanese wholesaler is the latter's higher burden of risk due to its retail financing (i.e., consignment selling), marketing and inventory responsibilities. Depending on its size, a wholesaler may have to provide next-day delivery for certain retail groups while others may insist that he repackage products in smaller, more attractive ways. It is often the wholesaler who travels around with manufacturers' sales reps to promote products to retailers. He may even be responsible for setting up point-of-purchase displays for small shop owners.

Sogo shosha

At the center of Japan's global economic web are her general trading

Figure 3-2

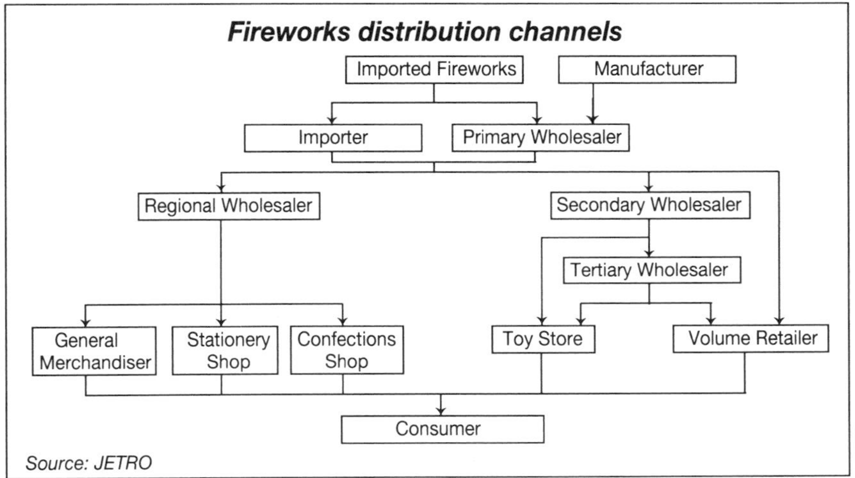

Source: JETRO

companies (called *sogo shosha*), organizations whose comprehensive business capacities, information gathering networks and ample funds make them unique. The six largest *sogo shosha* all rank among the ten largest non-U.S. firms in the world. Total domestic and external activities for the top nine are equivalent to more than one-quarter of Japan's GNP.

Top Nine *Sogo Shosha*

Sumitomo
Itochu (formerly C. Itoh)
Mitsui
Marubeni
Mitsubishi
Nissho Iwai
Tomen
Nichimen
Kanematsu

Although many of the *sogo shosha* date back to the Meiji Restoration when they were key trading units within family-run *zaibatsu* (see The Colonial Path: 1867-1945), their greatest growth years came after World War II. At that time, Japanese manufacturers focused primarily on solving production problems and raising domestic market share. They therefore came to rely on *sogo shosha* to shop around for raw materials and foreign technology worldwide, and sell their finished products. This cozy division of labor began to erode in the '70s and '80s when large manufacturers and big retail chains took advantage of their greater access to money and information to start exporting and importing on their own. This has left the *sogo shosha* over-reliant on a handful of low-margin commodities, making them very vulnerable to business cycles.

The *sogo shosha*'s core competence has always been the creation and coordination of global product systems for the horizontal *keiretsu* to which they belong (see Fig. 3-3). In a steel system, for example (see Fig. 3-4), goods, services and resources are supplied to a string of separate processing units transforming raw materials into finished products. Such controlled systems are particularly common in multi-stage process flow industries such as chemicals, steel, synthetic fibers and petrochemicals. All were high-growth industries in the '50s and '60s, but demand has since slowed with the maturing of Japan's economy and the drift of production overseas.

These structural problems received wide attention during the mid-'80s, but were then promptly forgotten as stock speculation made up for losses elsewhere. For example, *zaitech* operations accounted for nearly 30% of

Figure 3-3

Functions of General Trading Companies

Basic Trading Services

Conduct of Transactions
Providing a link between buyers and sellers, arranging for trade documentation and satisfaction of various legal requirements, plus collections and payments

Physical Distribution
Arranging for optimal transportation and distribution, including insurance coverage, warehousing, distribution systems, and related services

Financing
Financing services range from the provision of trade credits for facilitating international commerce to equity investments, direct loans, and guarantees

Providing Information
Using a worldwide network of offices and familiarity with market trends, Mitsui is well positioned to provide up-to-the-minute advice to clients on trading opportunities

Integrated Services

Investment
Drawing on Mitsui's capabilities in fund-raising to provide financial resources for equity investments, loans, and other forms of finance to facilitate major projects

Organizing Business Ventures
Using all of Mitsui's resources and know-how to organize major projects and set up businesses around the globe

Resource Development
Investing in development of raw material resources and making contractual commitments to market the output of these projects in Japan and elsewhere

Technology Transfer
Providing new technologies for the establishment of business ventures and promoting development of competitive industries on a worldwide basis

Source: Mitsui & Co. Ltd.

Figure 3-4

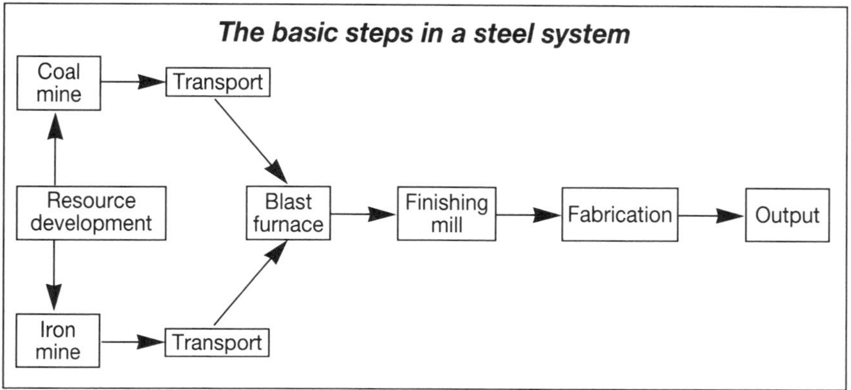

Mitsubishi's recurring profits at the height of the bubble economy (1988-89). Collapsing stock prices have since put restructuring back on the agenda, presenting foreign exporters with certain opportunities (see Defining Relationships).

Tied retail wholesalers

Some large retail groups, especially supermarket and convenience chains equipped with POS tracking systems, do not return goods nor need financial assistance from wholesalers. To simplify procurement, they have, therefore, appointed certain buying agents called ***choai* wholesalers** and ask that all their suppliers go through them.

This system often confuses foreign exporters because these primary wholesalers get their 3-4% margin even when, as often happens, products are shipped directly to the retailer (see Fig. 3-5). The practice is inefficient, but dates back to pre-war days when wholesalers were more powerful than manufacturers and retailers. Its continued use, even at a time when large retailer groups control their supply channels, illustrates the conservatism of Japanese distribution practice.

RECENT TRENDS

Deregulation

As of January 1992, LSRSL has been amended pursuant to the U.S.-Japan SII talks (see The Odd Couple) to limit the veto power of small shop owners over the opening of large stores in their neighborhoods. It seems doubtful, however, that this will quickly reduce distribution costs in Japan. Dismantling LSRSL in the early '80s might have led to rapid reform, but land prices have since skyrocketed greatly limiting the possibility of many new large store openings.

Figure 3-5

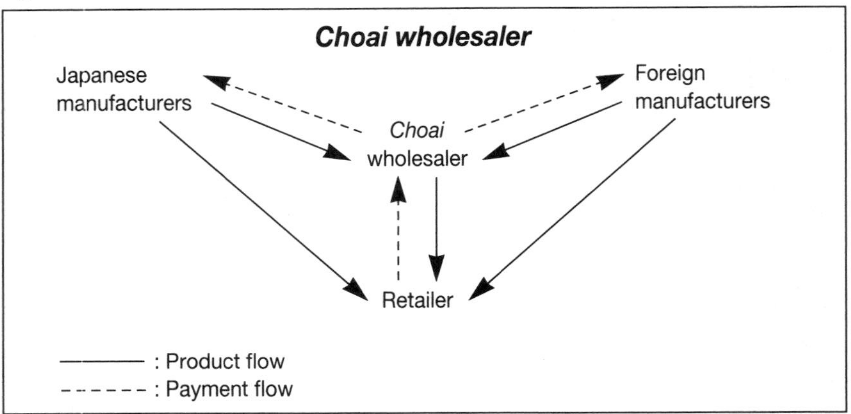

A more likely scenario is that deregulation and sluggish "post-bubble" consumer demand will gradually do three things to help make shopping cheaper in Japan:

- Resale price maintenance (RPM) will become too costly to operate even for large manufacturers. In 1990, five Japanese drug firms voluntarily abandoned RPM precisely for these reasons. The same trend is apparent in toiletries and household products where discounting is now widespread.
- Mom and Pop stores will likely give way to computerized chains of small- to medium-sized outlets. Fewer, bigger retailers unfettered by government-sanctioned RPM schemes means larger economies of scale and more independence from manufacturers.
- Lower growth will force Japanese manufacturers to reduce the size of their tied distribution networks because rebates and product buy-backs are making them very costly to operate. Smaller, more efficient retail networks entail fewer new products and longer product life cycles; well-run stores cannot afford to stock goods that do not sell.

These changes will be gradual. Japan is a consensus-building society receptive to evolution, not revolution.

Wholesale trends

Wholesalers tied to **manufacturer-controlled networks** are now under greater pressure than ever from their suppliers.

- The increasing retail market share of supermarket chains and discount stores has forced some large manufacturers to deal directly with them with offers of large volume rebates, thus by passing their own distribution networks.

- Large manufacturers are increasingly making use of value-added information network (VAN) systems to control inventory and collect market information directly from their retail network, both wholesale functions originally.

The ability to amass and interpret market information for suppliers and retailers is increasingly becoming as important to wholesalers as their original storage and delivery functions. Being tied to a major manufacturer is no longer a guarantee of survival.

The trend towards value-added information processing services is even more apparent among the fastest-growing **independent wholesalers**. There is also a gradual movement away from the volume selling characteristic of "mainstream" distribution practice (see Japanese Distribution Management – the inside view).

- Breaking bulk and order-taking are no longer enough. Wholesalers must also aggressively sell the products they carry.
- This requires a much closer analysis of sales and service costs, and a more careful selection of products and customers.
- Instead of rendering similar services and charges to all their customers (the volume-selling approach), some wholesalers are customizing service levels and charges to reflect the requirements of different retail segments.
- To gain some independence from powerful retail groups, larger wholesalers organize smaller retailers into voluntary chains and integrate backwards into manufacturing and private branding.

The late '80s saw the appearance of **cash-and-carry wholesalers** in Japan, a new breed of middleman with very un-Japanese business methods. Cash-and-carry wholesalers buy and sell on a transaction-to-transaction, best-offer basis, not according to pre-existing business relationships. Their main competitive tool is price. Typically, they seek out small local manufacturers or foreign exporters whose products are price competitive and resell them to small retailers requiring no financing or delivery services. No product returns from retailers are accepted; they will simply have to discount slow-moving items. This shuts cash-and-carry wholesalers out from the major domestic brands because large Japanese manufacturers disapprove of their methods. Their annual inventory turnover rates are nevertheless as high as 30, while conventional consumer goods wholesalers average turnover rates of seven.

JAPANESE DISTRIBUTION MANAGEMENT – the inside view

As we saw in the last chapter, manufacturer-controlled channels played a central role in shaping Japan's "mainstream" distribution practices after World War II. The same holds true with marketing and sales management, the subject of this chapter. Our first concern is therefore with large organizations: major manufacturers, the general trading firms (sogo shosha), *and large captive wholesale and retail networks. The main challenge to their volume-oriented sales approach is coming from retail groups equipped with sophisticated information systems.*

WHITE COLLAR

Two worlds of management

Business visitors to Japan are often struck by the differences between the management styles used in factories and offices. Modern Japanese factories are world-famous for their efficient use of machinery, space and manpower to achieve high productivity. Work spaces are spotless; machinery layout is carefully thought out; statistical process control (SPC) techniques are used at every step of the production process to measure quality levels; parts are delivered by suppliers "just-in-time" (JIT), exactly when they are needed. Japan's global manufacturing success was built on her achievements in managing things and blue-collar workers.

Factory-style productivity seems to be a secondary consideration in the white-collar world of offices. Work rooms are wide open with rows of desks pushed together and facing each other (see Fig. 3-6). Each row constitutes a group or section with its manager sitting at one end or nearby. Even with all the space available, every inch is crammed full. Desks are often cluttered with books and papers, leaving little space for writing. Partitions and carpeting are notably lacking, making noise levels very high and concentration difficult.

Working in this atmosphere are salarymen, clerks and office ladies (OLs) divided into small, closely-knit groups. The task and time planning so evident in the factories are obviously absent here. Work responsibilities are not clearly defined. Office time is slower than in America; clocks are rarely seen on the wall and two-month calendars are preferred. Overstaffing is so common that an estimated 2.5 million office workers in Japan are effectively unemployed on the job. As long as salarymen show up for work, do whatever their managers want done at the moment and

Figure 3-6

Typical office layout

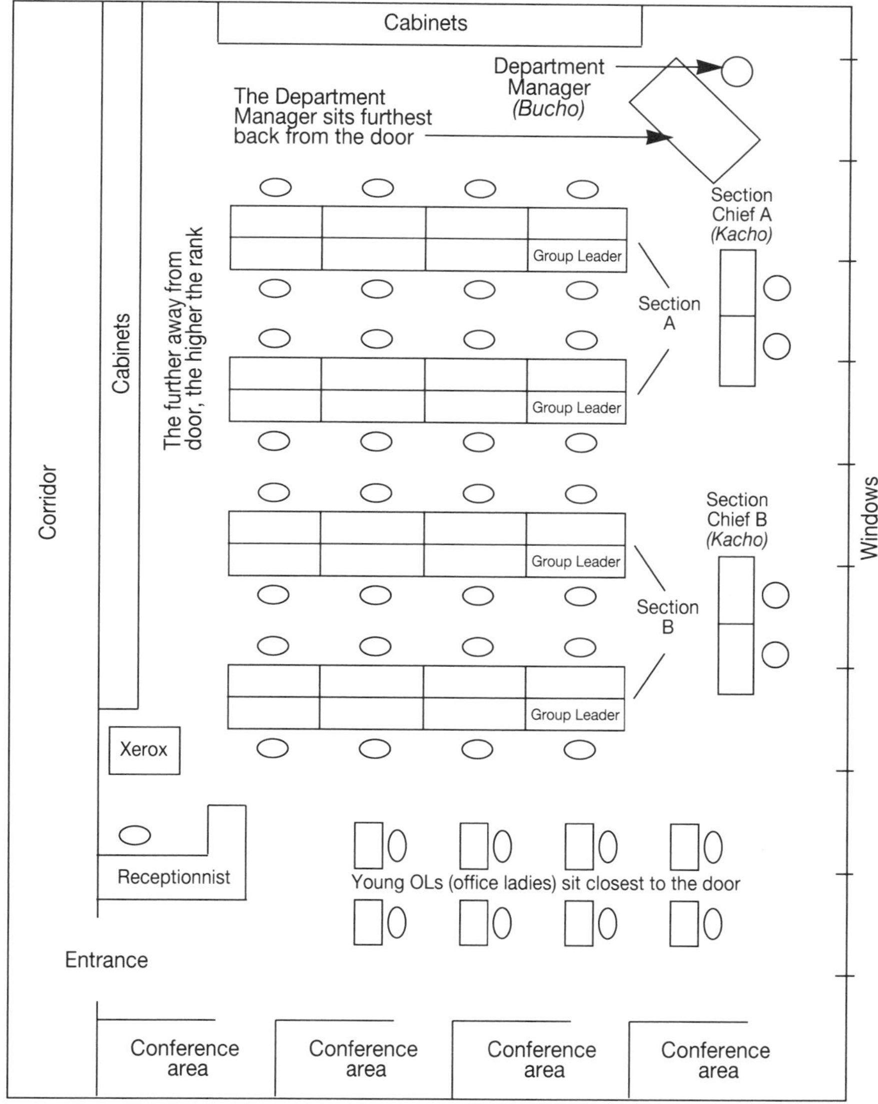

don't cause trouble, they can count on seniority-based promotions to push them forward. Loyalty, not ability, is what counts. Their productivity as a group is therefore surprisingly low. And their managers are not much better: over 70% of their time is spent in attending meetings (*nemawashi* or behind-the-scenes consensus-building) and collecting data. From the foreign exporter's perspective, the best way to understand white-collar management is through its hiring, training and leadership practices: Who am I dealing with? How much does he know? What motivates him?

Recruitment

Western business practice is to hire personnel to fill pre-defined positions requiring certain specialized skills. It is the rarity and market value of these skills which determine an employee's remuneration. The underlying assumption, especially in Anglo-Saxon business cultures, is that a company is a goal-oriented machine whose parts (specialist-employees) are held together by universal principles (contracts) and come fully formed (require minimal training).

The practice among large Japanese corporations is to hire their core staff (excluding clerks and OLs) in batches once a year from a small number of elite universities directly after graduation. The result, even in a highly homogeneous society such as Japan's, is that new recruits in any given company tend to be even more homogeneous. They also tend to be generalists because employers prefer to do their own training. What companies are looking for are capable and loyal long-term employees whose networks of friends acquired in university – now working in other elite institutions – could eventually become very valuable. They are not primarily interested in skills at that stage or in filling specific positions. Remuneration levels are therefore identical for all new recruits.

Training

Corporate training methods build on values instilled early on by the Japanese educational system; group identity, nurturing relationships with older mentors and unquestioning obedience. After a very solemn welcoming ceremony presided over by all members of top management, recruits are bussed away to a remote company training center where group discussions, sports activities and Zen meditation techniques are used to build comradeship and instill a strong sense of the company's history, traditions and greatness.

Ranking System

Kaicho	Chairman
Shacho	President
Fuku-shacho	Vice President
Yakuin	Director
Bucho	Department manager
Kacho	Section chief
Kakaricho	Supervisor
Hancho	Foreman

A month later, the recruits report to their assigned sections where they attend courses and are rotated around to expose them to as many areas of the firm's activity as possible. Most real training takes place on the job. A recruit may assist an older colleague for a couple of months until he can accomplish everything asked of him and then moves on to someone else. These elder-junior (*sempai-kohai*) mentoring relationships can create strong vertical bonds of loyalty between employees at different seniority levels. Indeed, the seniority system fosters harmony by protecting the relative position of older employees in relation to trainees who may be more capable.

For the first 10 to 15 years after recruitment, until they reach their late thirties, younger employees are strongly discouraged from competing with each other. Talent and diligence nevertheless attract more responsibilities and confer more authority in group discussions even though salaries and ranking remain identical for employees hired in the same year. It often happens therefore that work is unequally apportioned within a group, with some overburdened members sitting alongside others who chat and drink tea. This is possible because there are no job definitions; responsibilities are allocated to groups, not individuals.

An employee who has won the approval of his colleagues through his various lateral transfers at home and abroad can expect to be promoted *Kacho* (section chief) in his early forties and *Bucho* (department manager) five to seven years after that. If he fails to impress sufficiently at this crucial stage, he will be pushed aside and become a *mado-guchi*, a subgroup of managers who have fallen off the promotion track until they are retired at 55 or 60. Only senior managers who have reached or surpassed the position of director can stay longer.

Decision-making

Earlier on, we compared Anglo-American firms to machines. From an employee's point of view, a large Japanese firm is more like a dense network of obligations beginning with his group and growing weaker as it spreads to departments and divisions, beyond the formal boundaries of the firm to networks of suppliers, wholesalers and retailers, and other firms belonging to the same *keiretsu* (see Fig. 3-7). Insiders or *uchi* people are treated with consideration; outsiders or *soto* people are ignored, if possible. The *uchi/soto* distinction is very clear for most Japanese. It explains why polite and deferential salarymen become pushy and inconsiderate as soon as they leave their offices and board crowded trains.

Japanese decision-making tends, therefore, to be a consensus-building exercise among a wide variety of generalists belonging to several departments rather than the sole

Figure 3-7

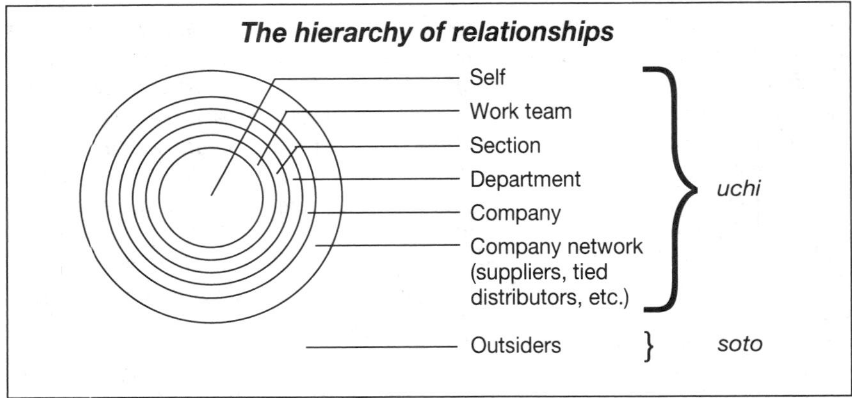

responsibility of Western-style specialists (like engineers or marketing experts). It also tends to be incremental (bold innovations are avoided) and very sensitive to pre-existing relationships. ("Let's give the job to Tanaka because his father helped us 20 years ago!") Japan is no place for one-minute managers and loners.

White collar group leaders, unlike Japanese factory foremen, are not there to give orders and check on everyone. Rather, their main task is to create a harmonious family atmosphere within the group where everyone can do his best. Personal brilliance is not a precondition to leadership. Indeed, there is a general preference for bonds of mutual dependence where a leader takes his subordinates' unexpressed feelings into consideration, and they make up for his or any other group member's mistakes, especially with regard to outsiders. Whether it is the president of a company or a simple section chief, Japanese-style leadership consists of setting general goals and embodying group values; creative problem-solving comes from below. This system gives subordinates plenty of leeway, so much so that extremely capable followers sometimes take all the key decisions. This is acceptable as long as they always defer to their chief in front of third parties and never make him lose face.

Sensitivity to group dynamics and the passive nature of leadership make for very conservative decision-making. Assertiveness of any kind is frowned upon.

The times they initiated a conversation their sentences seemed curiously punctuated. Although I waited to hear them out, they never seemed to finish a thought. The longer they spoke, the more hesitant they seemed to get. Sentences were left dangling; it was maddening.

Every other sentence seemed to end with a question: "Ne?" *"Right?" It eventually dawned on me that the appropriate response was,* "Soo desu ne." *"Yes, it's true."*

I also began to add the hesitant "ne" *to my assertations, and to reply with* "soo desu ne" *to observations made to me. Thus I slowly learned* "aizuchi" *such as: "I see...I hear you." "Is that so?" "Right". This is to show involvement. Hearing an* "aizuchi" *word interrupting him, the speaker knows the other person is attentive and listening. Not being interrupted makes the speaker think the listener isn't following or is upset. [....]*

These were all small ambiguous expressions that allowed others to participate. They were invitations to partake that made communication a group endeavor. Their ambiguity also robbed sentences of any possible aggressive tenor, rendering them curiously oblique, and their passive construction made it seem as if no one person was ever solely responsible.

I understood perfectly as I discussed with several co-workers some simple office arrangements. Bits and pieces of a sentence would be supplied by three or four people. It was as if everyone was finishing the sentence for the other person, only to have someone else pick up the sentence and continue. The group was speaking. The group was harmonious; the speakers, content.

Source: *Funny Business: An Outsider's Year in Japan*, by Gary Katzenstein, Soho Press, 1989, p. 45-47.

Living within their own closed circle, Japanese salarymen often have very limited horizons. Relations with "outsiders" (other departments or companies) tend to be managed through hierarchical ranking systems and a limited number of time-tested intermediaries. This leads many Japanese institutions to strive for self-sufficiency as a way of simplifying internal relations.

Recent trends

As we mentioned earlier (see The Dual Face of Globalization: 1970-1995), slower growth is forcing many large Japanese companies to rethink their "lifetime" employment system. The pressure to resign is especially strong on middle managers recruited in the high-growth '60s. However, this trend will have a limited influence on the recruitment, training and decision-making practices just described, at least for the next decade. Lifetime or not, the conservatism of Japanese businesses is such that long-term employment will remain the goal of most employees and employers.

What are the consequences of Japanese white collar management at the marketing and sales level?

MARKETING

Strategists?

Japan's awesome export success was built on carefully thought out marketing strategies. Market analysis, entry strategies, product improvement, aggressive pricing, distribution policies, and advertising; nothing was left to chance or kept static for very long. Japan's top export firms are considered master marketers.

And yet, American-style marketing as a research discipline subordinating sales and product development to target domestic consumers (as opposed to foreign ones) is rare within large Japanese companies.

- Decisions which would be left to marketing departments in the U.S. are the product of wide-ranging consultation (sales, R&D, and production) in Japanese organizations. Japanese executives look down on specialists.
- In-house market intuition is thought more reliable than quantitative research and deductive reasoning.
- Marketing can be a fast-track career to the top in the U.S. Not so in Japan.
- Sales is subordinated to marketing in the U.S. The opposite is the case in Japan.

Tacticians

Captive distribution channels are an important reason why large Japanese firms distrust "big" marketing strategies when targeting their own market. The preferred strategy has been to develop as many new products as possible to see which ones catch on. With guaranteed shelf space from their retail network, Western-style marketing research with its emphasis on consumer needs was never as important as exhaustive competitor analysis. No expenses are spared to know what the competition is up to, even including details on how many trucks leave their warehouses every hour or what their confidential floor prices are.

The Japanese approach in their domestic market is therefore more tactical than strategic. What really counts are solid relationships, a thorough grasp of the competition's operations and the ability to respond quickly to the whims and requests of important wholesalers and retailers. This is primarily the responsibility of the sales department.

SALES

Volume-oriented

Sales management is one area where Japanese practice seems to contradict sound business principles, at least in the West. Lifetime employment means that labor becomes a fixed rather than a variable cost. Consequently, surplus personnel tend to be dumped with sales, especially when business is slack. These salesmen are under such strong pressure to move product and create cash flow that related costs are often ignored even as margins are squeezed to win sales. Also, high volume is associated with high market share.

This volume-orientation (as opposed to profit-orientation) is transmitted throughout the distribution channel by the rebate system. Rebates are based in large part on sales volume. Wholesalers and retailers must therefore sell in large volume even when gross margins are reduced to zero, because the manufacturer's rebates are huge. In addition, bank credit, which is so important to the majority of financially weak retailers, tends to be given according to sales volume. The result is sloppy attention to the bottom line at every level of distribution and gradually higher prices to consumers.

Relationship selling

The Japanese company's attitude towards distribution is therefore simple: get the sales force out and push the product through the system. The traditional and still the most common way of doing this is through personal connections, obligation-building entertainment, and rebates. Playing with price, quality and delivery alone is not enough.

The business of selling is further complicated by a residual feudal contempt among most Japanese for sales as an occupation. In Japan, buyers are kings and salesmen are beggars. Approaching purchasers without a proper introduction usually leads only to humiliating rejections. The simplest sales call requires elaborate diplomatic overtures to see if the client is in the mood. Pushy sales pitches are especially counterproductive. This frequently limits a salesman's conversations with clients to sports news and family inquiries. Stress levels are particularly high with foreign products because unless their manufacturers are already well known, they are often not accepted.

To minimize the humiliation and lay a solid foundation for future sales, Japanese salesmen tend to accept the buyer's opinions uncritically. They never argue with the customer or even ask for clarification, believing that their job is to relay and defend what they hear in the field to their head office. The fact that commissions reflect group, not individual, sales performance no doubt encourages this attitude.

"Services" designed to build up a weight of obligation that has to be repaid are another common sales tool. These can go much further than current North American practice. A drug salesman, for example, might have to drive a doctor's wife around to do some shopping or regularly take his children to kindergarten. The common belief is that there is a direct relationship between the amount of time physically spent with the customer and the amount sold. Frequent visits, perseverance (*gambare*) in the face of indifference and passive-aggressive persuasion techniques usually win sales in the end.

INDEPENDENT CHANNELS

The stragglers

Our emphasis so far has been on sales and marketing practices common within distribution chains tied to the large Japanese *keiretsu*. There are a multitude of small wholesalers and retailers unhampered by lifetime employment subsisting outside of these systems. Most, however, are also wedded to volume selling and time-consuming "services" because the rebate system is so pervasive. Their profit levels are therefore very limited. As they carry virtually no imported products, they are of no interest to foreign exporters.

Information leverage

The greatest challenge to producer-driven sales practices is coming from retailers with sophisticated POS computer systems: supermarkets, convenience stores and the discounters. Instead of the traditional arrangement whereby manufacturers determine what consumers want, retailers with POS systems now have sufficient data to decide on their own what to carry or even create their own brands. The system is slowly becoming more consumer-driven.

DEFINING RELATIONSHIPS

North American exporters investigating potential partnerships in Japan are often handicapped by a poor grasp of the different options open to them. Although we will refer to "agents" and "distributors" throughout this book, it is important to note that these terms describe relationships rather than organizations. A given general trading firm, for example, can act as an import firm for one supplier, a manufacturer's representative for another, and a distributor for a third. Nor are these relationships mutually exclusive. A supplier could export his product to Japan simultaneously by way of an import firm designated by a department store chain and through an independent distributor targeting other segments of the market.

LICENSING

To avoid all the hassles associated with exporting to Japan – heavy transportation costs, import quotas and regulations, exchange rate fluctuations – some exporters choose to sell their know-how along with the right to use their trademarks and designs to Japanese retailers, manufacturers or trading companies. Licensing is a low-investment, low-return option.

Advantages

- Instant market access.
- Few payment problems, good up-front cash flow.
- Minimal risks and start-up costs.
- May be the only feasible choice for a small start-up company in need of money.

But check for...

- Little control over the licensee, including sales outlets and customer service.
- Limited opportunity for direct customer feedback.
- Brand image may be hurt if the licensee floods the market with look-alike products.
- Once the licensee has absorbed the technology, he often becomes the licenser's greatest competitor. This has been a recurring pattern in U.S.-Japan trade relations.

A major shirt manufacturer, Van Heusen, found direct export impracticable because most large Japanese retailers would accept its products only on a sale-or-return basis. It therefore opted for a licensing agreement with a trading firm. Japanese production of Van Heusen shirts expanded to half-a-million units by 1990.

IMPORT FIRMS

Most foreign exporters of commodity goods and products with little brand recognition depend on Japan's general trading firms (*sogo shosha*) or her thousands of specialized trading firms (*senmon shosha*) to penetrate the market. Import firms typically match buyers with sellers on a commission basis, warehouse and transport the goods they import, and assume neither financial nor credit risks. While some are large, wealthy and well-established, others may be new to the business or one-man operations. Some specialize in specific geographical markets; others trade only in a small number of products. Others may be controlled by or have ownership interests in a particular wholesaler while some may be sufficiently independent to find the best wholesaler for a given product. The main point to remember about import houses is that they are transaction-oriented volume businesses. Anything which detracts from volume selling usually gets short shrift.

Advantages

- Handles import documentation and provides short-term warehousing.
- Assumes the cost of physical distribution to the wholesaler.
- Saves the supplier the time and expense required to find a buyer for his product.

But check for...

- The supplier loses control over pricing and thus over long-term market share.
- Brand identity remains undeveloped.
- The supplier is cut off from the Japanese customer, and cannot react effectively to market trends and opportunities.
- Because they are deal-oriented, import firms are rarely interested in developing markets for new products or in providing after-sales service to end-users of capital equipment. Claims to the contrary in a given deal usually mean the import firm intends to subcontract this work to someone else.

AGENTS

An agent is a person or firm that is granted a carefully circumscribed right to sign sales agreements in the supplier's name to secure orders. Accordingly, agents rarely keep an inventory except on a consignment basis for demonstration purposes. As long as they do not overstep the limited authority originally granted to them, they have the power to bind their suppliers contractually. A great source of confusion is the incorrect application of the term "agent" to all trade intermediaries, i.e., distributors, sales representatives, manufacturer's representatives, and import firms. What are referred to as **sole import agents** in Japan, for example, are general or specialized trading firms which have the exclusive right to import and sell certain goods. As such, they are more like distributors because they maintain an inventory and actively market their products.

Advantages

- In matters of marketing strategy, pricing and sales methods, a supplier has more control over his agent than he has over an import firm or a manufacturer's representative.
- Agents allow a supplier to get increased feedback from Japanese end-users, wholesalers and retailers.

But check for...

- Although this is open to negotiation, most agents do not assume credit risks; the supplier must investigate the credit-worthiness of every customer.
- According to Japanese law, a local agent may render his supplier liable for certain taxes depending on whether he negotiates and concludes sales contracts or simply solicits orders (see Taxation in Japan).

ABC, a small family operation, specializes in the marketing of Italian shoes and leather products. To secure orders, ABC's sales team regularly visits specialized stores selling luxury goods in Tokyo to investigate what items are most successful and, at the same time, to convince the owners to stock up on their suppliers' shoes and handbags.

To insure the sales force is motivated and well informed, most of ABC's suppliers have agreed to pay the cost of sending the best salesmen to Italy for a thorough introduction to their manufacturing and design processes. However, the suppliers insist on regular reports from ABC on its sales activities and on Tokyo market trends. They also exercise tight control over ABC's marketing activities.

Because most specialized shops only buy on consignment, ABC does not buy the Italian products it sells. It consolidates and transmits a multitude of small orders to its suppliers and takes a commission on everything that is sold. ABC keeps no inventory except on a short-term consignment basis.

MANUFACTURER'S REPRESENTATIVES

The manufacturer's representative is an independent person or firm that maintains a stable of suppliers specialized in a narrow range of products. Some are so small that they merely arrange sales and facilitate the flow of information between supplier and purchaser. Others, however, bid for government contracts or participate in one-shot deals connected with infrastructure projects, military hardware or heavy equipment. Manufacturer's representatives are like agents in many respects, except that they have no authority to sell goods in their suppliers' name. They are paid on commission and do not buy from a supplier on their own account or maintain an inventory. They may or may not provide after-sales service.

Advantages

- For products that are bulky, expensive or made to order, manufacturer's representatives may be the logical way to successfully export.

But check for...

- Suppliers have very little control over the sales methods and marketing activities of their manufacturers' representatives.
- The supplier is still responsible for assessing the customer's credit worthiness.
- For products requiring extensive buyer education or high levels of after-sales servicing, manufacturer's representatives are not the ideal solution.

XYZ, a well-known German manufacturer of high-precision lenses and industrial measuring equipment, has had an office in Tokyo since 1911. By now, it has a whole network of regional sales and servicing reps to take care of its industrial clients. Many sales opportunities, however, depend to a considerable extent on public sector procurement policies which are rarely very open. For this market, XYZ relies on a small group of manufacturer's reps well-connected with local governments. It is well understood that these reps are professional bidders who "represent" a large number of Japanese and foreign suppliers because they want to make sure they can quote good prices for every item included in government tenders. They do not actively market a given product. Rather, they respond to government requests and leave after-sales servicing to the supplier. The degree of exclusivity XYZ grants to them is therefore quite limited.

DISTRIBUTORS

A distributor is an independent company which takes ownership of its suppliers' merchandise, maintains an inventory, and deploys its own sales, marketing and after-sales service staff in passing the goods down the distribution chain. In other words, he is a wholesaler.

Advantages

- Because a distributor buys and imports on his own account, suppliers need only concern themselves with his credit standing, not that of his downline wholesalers and retailers.
- Using a distributor limits the supplier's exposure to tax, product and warranty liabilities in Japan.
- Distributors are more capable and willing than agents or manufacturer's representatives to provide warehousing, servicing and market intelligence.
- Compared to import houses and agents, distributors are more willing to invest in market development work for new products and after-sales service for capital goods.

But check for...

- Because distributors are independent foreign businesses, suppliers often have less control over or even information about their distributor's downline intermediaries, marketing methods and pricing practices than they would have with an agent. Supplier influence depends on what has been agreed to in the distribution contract and the degree to which the supplier's support helps the distributor earn money with that product line.

- The support required by most distributors to push a supplier's products in Japan does not come cheap. In addition to the travel and legal expenses required to locate a distributor, do a credit check and make a contract, success also requires sales training, follow-up visits, promotional support and sales materials.
- The short-term profit orientation of most distributors might not suit exporters aiming for market share. "Sole import agents," for example, dominate the importation of foreign consumer products and are the ones most responsible for the wide price differences between imports and domestic products. This reflects their preference for low sales with high prices, a bias shared by most distributors of foreign products.

LQ is a Japanese distributor specialized in software products. His biggest problem at the moment are the conflicting demands of two different groups of foreign suppliers. The first group exports commodity-type shrink wrap PC software packages. What they want is quick access to a large dealership network, high name recognition and volume selling.

The second group supplies sophisticated packages requiring ongoing customer support. What interests them is a small number of strategic alliances with a few important clients and close relationships with end-users. Unfortunately for LQ, acceding to their request would put him in head-to-head competition with another distributor selling similar products, a distributor with whom he has had a long and profitable business relationship. That conflict of interest and LQ's preference for a simple volume business will lead him to put the second group's products on the back burner for the time being.

REPS AND SALES OFFICES

Unlike a distributor who is retained by a group of suppliers, a sales representative is usually the employee of a single supplier and represents only his employer. As a result, most of his work revolves around selling: paying regular visits to existing clients, relaying orders to head office, finding and investigating the credit worthiness of new clients, and informing his employer of market trends. In time, and if his office is upgraded to a sales branch, his job may orient itself around the supervision and support of third parties, such as agents and distributors.

Advantages

- Motivation. One or two of the supplier's own employees selling full time are worth a dozen distributor salesmen who feel no personal connection with the supplier or his products.
- Better after-sales service. Foreign suppliers selling high-priced equipment to a demanding clientele almost always aim to set up their own sales and servicing centre as soon as possible. This does not exclude the possibility of using other Japanese intermediaries to take care of minor repairs.

But check for...

- Higher costs. Exporters choose to go through distributors for a simple reason: the level of available business is not substantial enough to justify the high initial cost of setting up their own offices.
- More tax problems for foreign exporters. Basically, in business transactions involving money, a Japanese company is required to withhold taxes if the recipient is not a Japanese-incorporated company.
- Good sales reps are very difficult to find. Most are native Japanese with a solid network of contacts built up through years of distribution work in a narrow range of products.

After several years of lackluster sales in Japan, PX, a major American mountain bike manufacturer, decided to cancel its Japanese distributor and set up its own sales office/warehouse. The site chosen was Osaka because of its lower costs, its port, the availability of workers, and because most of Japan's bicycle manufacturers and component makers are based there. Moreover, next-day deliveries are easy to arrange from Osaka for almost every part of Japan.

Running its own small sales office had one immediate benefit for PX: it was not stuck with poor dealers simply because they belonged to a Japanese distributor's network. Over 30,000 retail outlets call themselves "bike shops" in Japan, but most look too ratty to fit PX's high-end image. After some investigation, the list of potential dealers was reduced to 2,000 and then to 1,000. This allowed PX to focus all its marketing and training efforts on a manageable number of outlets willing to offer excellent after-sales service.

JOINT VENTURES

Until the early '70s, foreign companies interested in the Japanese market only had three options: licensing, arms-length exporting or joint venturing. Licensing was certainly MITI's preferred option, but in certain cases where targeted technologies were involved, 50-50 joint ventures with Japanese partners were allowed. The situation is much freer now. Nevertheless, many foreign investors still opt for joint ventures because they give instant access to existing distribution channels. Body Shop, for example, franchised its cosmetic shops in Japan through a Jusco subsidiary which imports Body Shop products. But the problem with most joint ventures is conflicting priorities. All too often, what the Japanese partner really wants is a licensing agreement whereas the foreign investor is looking for a tied distributor. The number of break-ups among existing joint ventures is therefore high after a decade of operation. By that time, foreign partners already have established distribution networks while their Japanese participants have absorbed their technological and marketing know-how.

Advantages

- Reduced risk of failure because of burden sharing.
- Immediate access to an established distribution network. Joint ventures are most useful when the market for the product is mature and almost saturated. The only way to get in at that point is by choosing a partner who already has a strong presence in the market.
- Easier market acceptance because joint production and a local sales force "Japanizes" the product.

But check for...

- Reduced risk also means reduced potential rewards.
- Joint ventures tend to be poorly integrated into the foreign partners' worldwide operations because the Japanese side insists on doing things in its own way.
- Japanese companies, like their Western partners, often create joint ventures because the preferred options (licensing or a wholly-owned subsidiary) are not possible. The result is poor motivation on both sides and lackluster performance for the joint venture.
- Joint ventures often require more sustained attention than Western firms are willing to offer. U.S. and European managers tend to sit back once the joint venture agreement is signed, expecting it to run on its own. This gives the Japanese a *de facto* right to run the show and cuts their Western partners off from customer feedback, potential contacts and joint product development opportunities.
- Japanese partners sometimes dump their incompetent employees into joint ventures because the lifetime employment system makes firing them impractical. Good personnel, on the other hand, are more concerned with HQ than with the joint venture because they are soon called back. Control over personnel matters is crucial to the success of joint ventures, but few foreign partners ever achieve it.

- Western partners insist that the joint venture be profitable on its own, but the Japanese often expects it only to help the parent companies become more competitive. These conflicting expectations have a direct bearing on the way each side goes about defining and solving problems.
- Joint ventures can be very hard to get out of when things go wrong.

WHOLLY-OWNED VENTURES

Multinationals that have been successful in Japan usually choose to become wholly-owned enterprises eventually because of the increased control it gives them. The two most common paths used to get there are local distributor → sales rep/office → subsidiary, and joint venture → subsidiary. Either way, wholly-owned ventures are increasingly easy to arrange in Japan even if "partnerships" with local firms are almost always necessary to reduce land and distribution costs.

Advantages

- It is easier to tap into a broader range of distribution channels
- More control over local production options and local R&D.

But check for...

- Land costs can be extremely high. So are utility, telecommunication and advertising expenses.
- Finding good personnel can be very difficult because foreign companies are not considered long-term employers. Established Japanese firms also offer more prestige.
- Distribution supervision without an experienced Japanese partner can be very time-consuming.

TYPES OF DISTRIBUTORS

If an exporter, after careful study, is convinced that his products have a sufficiently large potential market in Japan, the next step is to select the best distributor or agent to do the job. Distributors in Japan can be divided into groups, each with their own strengths and weaknesses.

SOGO SHOSHA

As we saw earlier (see Japanese Distribution management – the outside view), the strength of Japan's huge general trading companies lies mostly in the bulk distribution of commodity products for processing industries such as steel and chemicals. Unfortunately, commodities are low-margin goods highly vulnerable to business cycles.

Attempts in recent years to change this situation through diversification (retailing, plant exports, high-tech ventures, foreign joint ventures, and merchant banking) have not yet produced a clear breakthrough for any of them. Pressures to find new sources of revenue remain nevertheless very strong. Heavy exposure in speculative stocks during the bubble years (1985-90) has left most *sogo shosha* overexposed under a mountain of debt and portfolio losses. Moreover, labor costs are becoming especially onerous because their seniority system is pushing the large numbers of employees hired during the high-growth '60s into well-paid middle-management positions. By some estimates, most of the top nine *sogo shosha* have over 800 redundant managers.

To cut costs and encourage in-house entrepreneurialism, senior management has asked each division to spin off small, specialized, affiliated companies, between 400 to 500 per *sogo shosha.* About 20% of these new companies are 50-50 joint ventures. The rest are wholly-owned subsidiaries headed by former section managers *(kacho)* who will not be welcomed back if they fail to succeed on their own.

Advantages

- Well-established and financially strong. Getting paid is rarely a problem.
- *Sogo shosha* can assume responsibility for the entire process of importing and distributing goods in Japan, from advertising to customer service.
- They give foreign exporters instant access to the horizontal *keiretsu* to which they belong.
- Easy communication because of their network of foreign offices and their large pool of English-speaking managers.
- They may have good bargaining clout with specific retail chains. They also may be able to get

around tied distribution networks.

- Easy access to sales information and to the sales force for training programs.
- Capable of extending sales to Asian markets outside of Japan.
- Better able to coordinate large-scale projects involving many suppliers. Can provide access to banking and insurance services on more favorable terms.

But check for...

- The *sogo shosha* are so huge that your leverage over them is almost nil. In most cases, they have no incentive to pay special attention to any single exporter's products.
- Pre-existing commitments often limit what they can import, under what terms imported manufactured products can be sold, and how much market share they can seek for those products. Initial sales growth, therefore, tends to be brisk, only to flatten out at an early stage. There are even widespread rumors of a "10 and 20" rule whereby foreign imports cannot capture more than 10% of the market unless they are at least 20% cheaper than their Japanese competitors.
- *Sogo shosha* have such high fixed costs that they tend to concentrate on high-volume products. Building up a business from scratch, except for products with extraordinary potential, is not cost-effective for them.
- Their "general" nature limits what they can do. They are weak on items requiring carefully planned sales strategies, extensive buyer education or sophisticated after-sales service.
- Some suppliers find them bureaucratic and unassertive. For niche markets in particular, they are often too slow to react effectively.
- Since they are so few in number and carry thousands of items, it is difficult to avoid *sogo shosha* carrying competing products. Also, the leverage any single supplier has over them can only be very limited. Weak leverage and product neglect go hand-in-hand.

SENMON SHOSHA

Another option are Japan's tens of thousands of smaller, specialized trading companies (called *senmon shosha*). The hundreds of newly-created *sogo shosha* subsidiaries mentioned above also belong to this group.

General trading companies are primarily interested in high-volume items; specialized trading firms concentrate on marketing expensive specialty goods to a certain group of industrial or retail buyers with which they have good personal relations. High margins achieved through sole import arrangements are what they seek.

Advantages

- They assume responsibility for the whole process of importing, advertising, distribution and customer service.
- They are very hungry for business and are likely to give the supplier's products close and individualized attention.
- Their small size also give suppliers more leverage over their decision-making.

But check for...

- They often over-promise the extent to which they are capable or prepared to provide national market coverage for a given product. Many of them are fully occupied with the high service expectations of a small client base. Going further afield to satisfy a supplier may therefore seem counter-productive.
- Since they tend to accumulate complete lines within narrowly defined product categories, you must especially watch out for competing products.
- There are so many of them that potential suppliers must spend more time investigating which ones are competent. Lack of transparency and conflicts of interest are also a problem because many of them own production companies or are dominated by local manufacturers.
- Their generally weak technical and marketing capabilities often forces suppliers to supervise and support their efforts more closely than would be necessary with larger trading firms. Accordingly, liaison offices and temporary on-site reps are frequently involved as soon as business volume justifies it.

FOREIGN TRANSNATIONALS

There are a number of American and especially European trading firms with subsidiaries in Japan offering a wide range of distribution services to foreign suppliers (see Annex 11). Some were established in Japan decades ago and are almost regarded there as Japanese firms.

Most of the foreign transnationals are specialized in industrial (business-to-business) products. However, some more recently established firms deal with imported consumer goods, mostly from Europe.

Advantages

- Easy access to Western-trained managers who know the Japanese market well.
- Easier communication because they have a good grasp of Western marketing concepts. English is also widely understood.
- Compared to Japanese distributors, foreign transnationals tend to be more open, less secretive.
- Many of them have excellent reputations for after-sales service.

- Easy access to the sales force for training and incentives programs.

But check for...

- Their small number and specialized product lines make it very difficult to find a transnational which does not already carry competing products.
- Some of them are especially loyal to products originating from their home country. Outsiders have less leverage.
- Their popularity with foreign suppliers sometimes leads to product clutter among less well-run transnationals. Too many franchises are accepted, leaving many products unattended unless they take off on their own.

SECONDARY WHOLESALERS

Secondary wholesalers by definition do not import directly from abroad (see Japanese Distribution Management – the outside view). However, the largest and fastest growing among them can sometimes become "channel leaders" for certain product categories in specific regions of Japan. A foreign exporter of toiletry products might, for instance, find out that a given toiletry wholesaler is heavily relied upon by key retail groups in a certain region. If that wholesaler is interested in his products, import formalities could be left to a trading firm selected by the wholesaler. The wholesaler would play the distributor role, not the trading firm.

Advantages

- Can be very effective to reach a certain set of retail clients in a given region of Japan. Good wholesalers do much more than warehouse stock; they also act as merchandising consultants for their retail circle.

But check for...

- Secondary wholesalers rarely market products outside their network or region. Their existing clients' high service demands leave them no time for it.
- Wholesalers have to accept returns. The same might be expected of their foreign suppliers. They also may want to "buy" on consignment.

JAPANESE MANUFACTURERS

Many Japanese manufacturers with established distribution networks look for foreign products complementing their own lines. Piggybacking can be an effective way to penetrate the Japanese market.

Advantages

- Domestic manufacturers are often more focused and entrepreneurial than the trading firms.
- Instant access is possible to a product-specific network of contacts, expertise and distribution channels.

- Within their own narrow specialty, these manufacturers have the in-house expertise required for buyer education and good after-sales service.

But check for...

- Certainly more secretive than the large trading firms. Unless the piggyback arrangement is part of a larger joint venture agreement, they do not, in general, see themselves as "working" for the interests of foreign suppliers. They are merely completing their product line. This can complicate communications.
- They are likely to give priority to their own products at the expense of their suppliers'. Every possibility of product conflict should therefore be investigated by suppliers interested in this distribution option.
- Like joint ventures (see Defining Relationships), foreign parties to piggyback arrangement often acquire very little in-house Japan expertise from these deals because they tend to sit back and let the Japanese manufacturer run the show. As difficult as it can be sometimes, foreign exporters with ambitions to expand in Japan must acquire the right to meet with end-users, servicing personnel, the sales force as well as downline wholesalers and retailers.
- Japanese manufacturers carrying unexpectedly popular foreign products are often tempted to knock off own-label clones if licensing agreements are not forthcoming.

THE REST

Smaller versions of the above may be worth considering for exporters new to Japan, whose products are completely unknown, and those targeting a geographically restricted area (the city of Osaka, for example). Products with a successful track record in Japan, even on a limited scale, soon attract offers from stronger distributors willing to invest more resources.

Advantages

- All the advantages of small business: hunger for new opportunities, good supplier leverage, close and individualized attention to products.
- For small and medium exporters, more opportunities to find a partner whose business methods complement their own. Japan has thousands of small distribution companies run by local or foreign managers with years of experience in certain product categories. Finding a motivated partner with whom communication is easy is always possible if you are willing to look around hard enough.

But check for...

- Finding good, small-sized distributors requires more thorough research from suppliers. Many small firms make inflated claims that are difficult to verify.

- Most of these distributors have too few resources to commit themselves to a product that does not take off quickly. Products requiring after-sales service should only be entrusted to them after careful evaluation of in-house expertise and excess capacity.
- Small distributors frequently require more training, promotional and inventory support from their suppliers than large firms do.
- They also tend to be financially weak. Suppliers using them often learn to live with consignments selling and greater credit exposure.

DIRECT MARKETING IN JAPAN

Exporters of consumer products are showing increased interest in direct marketing (DM) as a way to bypass Japan's byzantine distribution system. Their eagerness is shared by Japanese consumers seeking wider choices and lower prices than are available in department stores. And yet, direct marketing in Japan is still in its infancy, hampered by high postal rates and a poor image. How DM fits into the scheme of things, and how to make it work for your firm, is the subject of this chapter. *I wish to thank Thomas Ainlay Jr. (McCann-Erickson Hakuhodo Inc.) and F. Alan Moore (Dentsu Wunderman Direct Inc.) for their many insights. Any errors or omissions are the author's responsibility.*

NON-STORE RETAILING

Definition

MITI defines direct marketing as the sale of merchandise through non-store channels. This blurs the difference between marketing methods based on segmented customer lists – the North American definition of direct marketing – and non-store retailing, a far larger marketing category which also includes distribution through the use of vending machines and consumer cooperatives (see Fig. 3-8). Before moving on to direct marketing, it is worthwhile to know a little about these two other non-retail channels even though they are not significant players in the foreign import scene.

Vending machines

Looking for ice cream, pizza, whiskey, video cassettes or bouquets of flowers? They can be bought from the many vending machines throughout Japan. With one for every 22 people, it is the country with the greatest concentration of vending machines in the world. America, by comparison, has one for every 46; the EEC has only one for every 200.

Japanese vending machines are also more productive, selling high-value products such as wine, as well as the usual soft drinks and gum. Sales per machine are 60% higher than in America.

Seventy percent of all vending machines are owned and serviced exclusively by the product manufacturer who pays a "location fee" and a percentage of the profits to whomever owns the land on which the machine is placed. Everything is done to maximize the PR/advertising impact of these vending machines, especially those clustered in busy shopping arcades and train stations. The remaining 30% are loaned, leased or sold to small shop owners. These owners purchase the goods at wholesale prices, maintain machine inventory and make a profit from the money collected.

Appearances notwithstanding, the Japanese vending machine market is not yet saturated. Declining birth

Figure 3-8

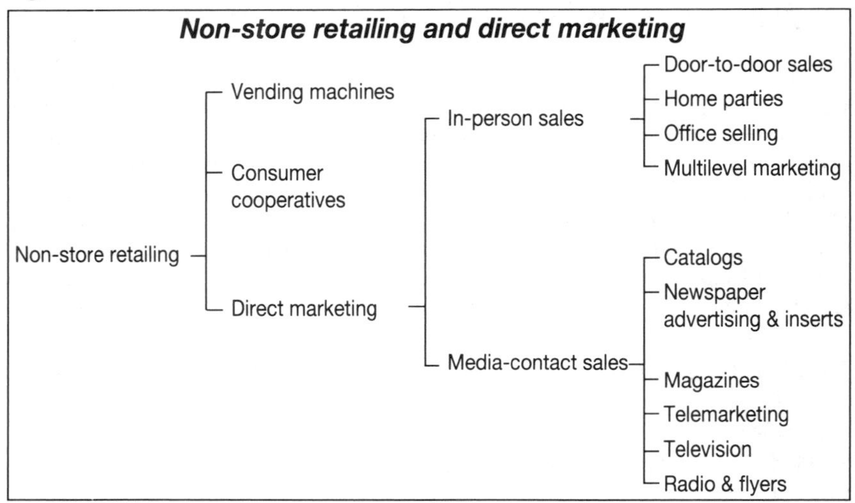

rates, low immigration levels and an aging population are making them ever more necessary. One of the fastest growing sectors is food, especially microwave-heated meals (pizza, spaghetti, curry dishes, and so forth).

Consumer cooperatives

There are two types of consumer cooperatives (or *seikyo*): regional cooperatives serving housewives primarily, and employee cooperatives set up in work places and universities. Almost all *seikyo* belong to the Japanese Consumer Cooperative Union, an umbrella organization which purchases in bulk over 7,000 food and household items for its members. Consumers join *seikyo* not only to save money, but also to avoid foods with chemical additives.

Japan's politically powerful rural population has its own government-sponsored cooperative movement called the *nokyo*. Like *seikyo*, *nokyo* has its national federations and local co-ops, but it is far bigger and more politically active than its urban counterpart.

It is worth noting that the cooperatives have often been the most vociferous opponents of market liberalization. The *nokyo*, for obvious reasons, fiercely opposes the importation of competing agricultural product, rice especially. Food imports are also questioned by *seikyo* for different reasons related to the spread of harmful food additives. As a result, both groups have convinced many Japanese consumers that expensive domestic prices are acceptable if they guarantee their food's safety.

DIRECT MARKETING

Definition

Direct marketing is an interactive marketing system utilizing one or more information media to elicit measurable responses or specific actions from selected consumer segments. It has at its core a database of names, addresses and selected information about individuals.

There are two major direct marketing approaches recognized in Japan: in-person sales (*homon hambai*) and media-contact sales (*tsushin hambai*).

In-person sales

If "segmentation" is what distinguishes direct marketing from the mass marketing concept commonly applied in retail sales, most Japanese in-person selling is still too haphazard to qualify as direct marketing. One reason for this is the traditional preference for service-oriented and face-to-face driven relationship selling. Another is volume selling by overstaffed sales departments belonging to large corporations (see Japanese Distribution Management – the inside view).

Despite its long history in Japan, **door-to-door sales** in its traditional form – cold calls, random visits with product samples, and so on – is quickly growing obsolete. Questionable marketing methods gave it a bad reputation during the '70s, but its greatest problem now is the increasing difficulty of catching housewives at home because so many of them are out working. The best known examples of foreign firms using door-to-door sales in Japan are Electrolux (vacuum cleaners) and HomCare Japan (detergent). Household products purchased on a regular basis, such as detergents, are the bread and butter of the industry. Luxury items designed for women like cosmetics, kimonos, and jewelry are also marketed door to door.

Home parties were introduced to the Japanese market by Japan Tupperware in 1963. As a marketing method, its image is much better than that of door-to-door sales because the hustle element is largely absent. Most "home party" salespersons are housewives seeking extra income by introducing new products to their friends and neighbors in the privacy of their homes. Very few try their luck outside of their small network. The products which dominate in this field are lingerie and household goods.

Office selling is conducted either according to agreements with companies/labor unions or directly to individuals. The first method is extensively used by manufacturers, wholesalers and large retailers to test-try products and expand sales among their own employees and those working for companies belonging to the same *keiretsu*. The second is most common among small entrepreneurs and food manufacturers selling lunches to office workers. Yakult Honsha, for example, has 57,000 "Yakult Ladies" across Japan selling its fermented lactic drinks to office workers and housewives. Because the

Japanese are group-oriented buyers and office consumption is so public, the likes and dislikes of key opinion leaders in each office tend to precipitate chain-reaction purchasing decisions among their colleagues for or against certain products. Given the lack of space and time available to promote sales in offices and the large number of players exploiting this small niche, this is a marketing method with relatively limited sales potential for new entrants.

Multilevel marketing or MLM (also called network marketing) is a form of direct marketing which relies not on a salaried sales force but on private individuals who both sell the product and sponsor other people willing to do the same. In this way, by a process of duplication, a "down-line" of distributors is created who sell by word-of-mouth promotion. The best known example in Japan is Amway with its 870,000 distributors selling household products, kitchen aids and personal care products. Launched 13 years ago, Amway Japan earned US$135 million in 1991 on revenues of US$1 billion. Sales of Amway Japan make up more than one-quarter of Amway's worldwide revenues and nearly equal sales in the U.S., where it has had a foothold for 33 years. Other American companies successfully using MLM in Japan include Shaklee Japan (nutrition, personal care and household products), Noevir (beauty aids, nutrition and clothing) and Japan Life (health and lifestyle products).

Media-contact sales

In this area, everything in Japan revolves around mail-order sales, a true form of direct marketing because it rests squarely on segmented consumer lists. Before moving on to specific marketing channels, here are a few basic facts that put mail-order into perspective.

- It is now a ¥1.8 trillion-a-year (US$15.5 billion) business with an 11.9% average growth rate during the last decade (see Table 3-9).
- Even so, it only accounts for 1.25% of the overall Japanese retail market. Compare that to 2.5% for mail order in Europe and 3.2% in the U.S.
- Only 30% of Japan's 44 million households have tried mail order.
- Some 90% of all Japanese mail-order customers are female, most of whom are either between 20 and 35 years old or in their 60s. Few men have ever ordered anything by mail.
- In Japan there are two types of businesses active in mail order: those specialized in mail order (see the "Top 10" list) and those that use it as a sideline. It is the second type – department stores, credit card and insurance companies, trading firms, and the media – that are the biggest players.

- Mail order looks deceptively cheap, but costs in Japan are very high and competition is fierce. The average customer gets 5 to 6 different catalogs at any one time.

Table 3-9

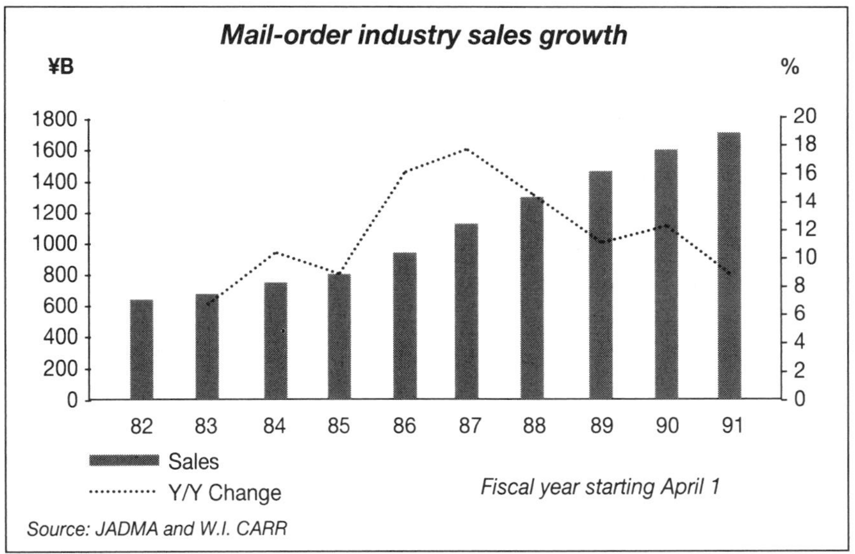

TOP 10 MAIL-ORDER COMPANIES

Company	***Major Products***
Cecile	*Women's clothing*
Senshukai	*Clothing*
Shaddy	*Household goods*
Fukutake	*Correspondence courses*
Takashimaya	*General merchandise*
Nissen	*Clothing*
Mutow	*Clothing*
Mitsukoshi	*General merchandise*
Kinki Nippon	*Travel*
Simree	*Underwear/clothing*

Catalogs are by far the most powerful channel, accounting for approximately 50% of mail-order sales and 75% of mail-order customers. It is also the most popular channel for imported products because of lower promotion costs compared to other mail-order media, and because unknown foreign brands are much more sellable in Japan when established catalogs vouch for their quality. Most products sold by catalog are in the ¥5,000 to ¥30,000 range. They mostly include men's and women's clothing, fashion accessories, interior decorating items, appliances, books, furniture, jewelry, food and correspondence courses.

Thirty percent of mail-order sales come from **newspaper advertising** and **inserts**. Their relatively wide readership make them ideal media for retail chains, department stores and supermarkets. They are also extensively used by companies soliciting customer feedback to improve their database. Overall, however, there has been a gradual shift away from newspaper advertising towards inserts because column space is getting very expensive.

Magazines by their very nature target audiences with narrowly defined interests and sensibilities. They are therefore often used by firms which, unlike department stores, are specialized in mail-order sales. Magazines account for less than 10% of mail-order sales, but this could change as they are a relatively inexpensive medium.

Telemarketing in Japan is still in its infancy because customers react very negatively to unsolicited sales calls from strangers. As a result, telephones tend to be used as adjuncts to larger mass-marketing or mail-order systems rather than as sales tools in their own right. The marketing of cars, for example, might involve a series of customer-relation programs, all feeding into a common database (see Fig. 3-10). Because the potential market for new cars is very broad, traditional mass marketing techniques (Program A) might be used to create interest and attract inquiries. At the same time, a mail-order campaign in newspapers and magazines (Program B) is launched to generate a more detailed customer database. It is only at that point, when someone's response has created a relationship, that telephone operators feel comfortable in calling potential clients. And even then, it takes a tremendous training effort to get them to sell effectively on the phone because the Japanese are by nature extremely shy and non-confrontational. In Program C, showroom salesmen make use of database information on individual customers' lifestyles and preferences to facilitate the one-on-one selling process during demonstrations. Finally, in Program D, telephone calls and personalized mailings are kept up to ensure after-sale customer satisfaction.

Figure 3-10

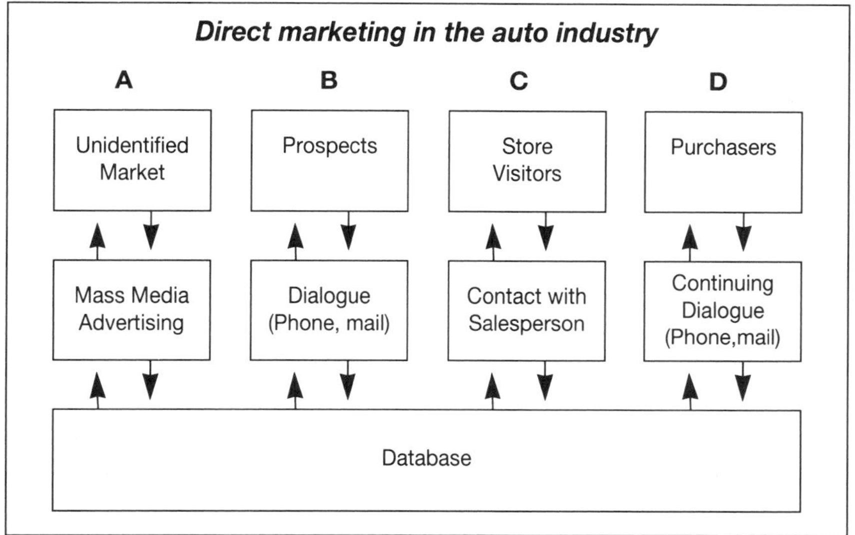

Due to its high cost, only the largest mail-order companies – those with annual sales exceeding ¥10 billion – actively use **television** for direct marketing. They use it less to boost sales than to increase their database and raise their image. TV shopping sales make up a little over 10% of mail-order sales. Its effectiveness as a marketing channel has decreased with the number of women staying at home during the daytime.

Radio and **flyers** are used for less than 2% of mail-order sales. Because consumers give them little attention, they tend to be used to impart simple information (e.g., the address of a new restaurant), remind listeners of a well-known name (e.g., a department store), or advertise commodity-like products (e.g., electrical appliances). They are not the ideal medium to explain something new or change people's minds.

STRATEGIC CHOICES

Why mail order?

Foreign exporters are attracted to direct marketing (or DM) because it helps them get around the complexities and inefficiencies of Japan's distribution system. In particular, they want to avoid three problems inherent in traditional multi-layered distribution arrangements.

- **Weak starting position** Japanese importers and distributors demand product novelty, products which, by definition, have no track record in Japan. This leaves foreign exporters in a weak bargaining position.

- **No control** This initial weakness also translates into large price jumps in Japan, designed more to enrich sole import agents than to secure a long-term position for foreign products in that market. Most exporters lose control over the marketing of their products in Japan because there are too many intermediaries involved.
- **No feedback** Japanese middlemen are often so taken up with their own needs and complex arrangements that they effectively cut foreign suppliers off from end-users. As a consequence, exporters find themselves unable to react in time to changing Japanese consumer trends or to local imitations.

Frost International (USA) Inc. started marketing an American home exercise system called Soloflex in Japan eight years ago. They first paid a large amount of money for a market research study from a Japanese advertising agency and their conclusion was that their product was unsellable in Japan. That report was filed in the nearest round file.

They contacted a number of fitness equipment distributors about marketing their product. But it took 50% margins to arouse even minimal interest among them.

So they went direct to the consumers, bypassing the normal distribution channels. In less than three years, they sold 10,000 of the US$1,400 units by using direct response ads in magazines and newspapers.

Once they had an established track record in direct marketing, they had plenty of distributors knocking on their door. They turned Seibu Department Store down once who persisted, accepting a 5% dealer's discount.

Direct marketing can be used to make believers out of unbelievers. It creates a sales history in Japan, allowing one to enter regular distribution routes, if one decides to do so, on much more favorable terms.

But Japan is a very expensive place to learn DM. Foreign exporters who do well at it almost always start off with DM infrastructures that are already effective in their own domestic markets.

Setting up successful and cost-efficient DM programs for the Japanese market involves certain necessary steps like market research, product adaptation, partnerships, and channel selection – all of which are interdependent. Weakness in any single area can negate your strength in other areas.

Market research

The first step in DM is to define your target market as accurately as possible. For example, it could be: "Males, university graduates, 40-years-old or more, home owners, presidents of companies, annual incomes exceeding ¥20 million, living in the greater Tokyo area."

Market research often uncovers Japanese government regulations or consumer preferences which conflict with what you have to offer. Make sure your product is adapted to Japan, but don't go so far as to hide its national origin. Too much adaptation can hurt, too. Remember that many Japanese direct marketing customers enjoy the feeling of importing distinctive products not commonly available in stores.

Finally, targets have to be set. Remember: the main advantage of DM is that it creates a direct relationship between a supplier and his consumer base where measurable responses are possible. To use DM simply "to sell more" leaves you groping in the dark, unable to measure the return on investment (ROI) of your various programs. Always define your sales goals in quantitative terms so that results can be measured against your goals.

Channel selection

Your market research must help you select the most cost-effective way to elicit responses and information from your target customers. Will you use a one-step program, sending a complete set of sales materials to every potential customer? Or will you rely on a two-step system where detailed sales information is only mailed to people who respond to shorter, cheaper ads? Suppliers selling low-cost, low profit margin items generally stick to one-step mailings. Two-step mailings are more appropriate for expensive products or in situations where the seller wants to find out more about his customers. The quality of the name lists produced by both programs also differ. One-step sales and especially impulse-purchasing television advertising often attract one-shot buyers. This is a far less reliable group than catalog buyers, for example, a consumer segment that brings a lot of repeat business to direct marketers who know how to analyze their purchasing behavior.

Another strategic choice you have to make is between different DM channels. Which ones reach your prospects most effectively? Will you rely on catalogs? What about magazines or newspapers? Is TV really cost-effective?

Mailing lists

According to Kerry Kennedy, president of Direct Marketing Services Japan, the factors most affecting the success of a mailing are the mailing list (50%), the offer (40%), and the season the package was mailed (10%).

Unfortunately, acquiring usable lists is one of the thorniest problems facing DM beginners in Japan. Magazine subscriptions played a crucial role in the creation and growth of a sophisticated list industry in the U.S. In Japan, however, most magazines are bought at newsstands, not through subscriptions. This fact creates special difficulties. Whereas there are from 25,000 to 50,000 lists for rent in the U.S., Japan has only 400 to 500 computerized, commercially available lists. Accessible DM responder lists are virtually unheard of. This forces all Japanese direct marketers to either slowly build up their own lists from scratch, buy some commercially available lists, or acquire better-quality lists by purchasing bankrupt mail order firms.

Among the commercially available lists, the information available for segmentation is extremely limited. Most include only names, addresses and telephone numbers compiled under a single heading such as occupation or income level. Most exporters of consumer goods need much more information, such as type of residence (house, apartment, condo), how the residence is financed (owned, rented, loaned), and family member lifestyle (income, car ownership, hobbies).

Another difficulty with these lists is that they are sold to many companies and often have poor response rates. It is therefore very difficult for foreign exporters to become competitive and profitable at the start with them. Exporters thinking of buying such a list should answer some basic questions:

- *From what source were the names on the list compiled?*
- *How current is the list?*
- *How often is it updated?*
- *What is its response rate?*
- *Should I rent or buy? (There is no point in buying a list unless you have the infrastructure required to keep it up to date.)*
- *Do I want to use segments of various lists to test their response rates or do I want to limit myself to a single list?*
- *If I acquire more than one list, are they all compatible for computer merge/purge operations?*

Getting around these problems is possible if your target consumers are clearly defined and your advertising channels are well targeted. The speed with which you build up a good database also depends on your entry strategy and local "partnerships."

Market entry

There are four ways to approach the Japanese mail-order market:

- The simplest approach is to **become a supplier** to established Japanese or foreign direct marketers, be they specialist firms or the large retail chains. The only competitive advantages in this market are novelty and price, two areas where the newly industrialized economies (Taiwan, Hong Kong, South Korea, etc.) are quickly outperforming traditional European and U.S. suppliers. The top five import categories for Japanese DM firms are clothing and accessories, interior decoration items (furniture, carpets), personal products (watches, eye glasses, cameras), tableware, and home electrical appliances (including air conditioners). The catalog life span of most products tend to be short because successful items soon attract copies.
- The **airmail route** is the most popular entry channel among

small exporters with their own catalogs because U.S. and Canadian postal rates to Japan are often cheaper than Japan's domestic rates. In addition, MITI and its affiliated agency, the Manufactured Imports Promotion Organization (MIPRO), have been pushing "individual importing" since the late '80s as one way of reducing Japan's trade surplus. Unfortunately, using the international mail system is not a very effective channel in terms of large-scale market penetration.

- **Setting up shop in Japan** is the third route, one used by large U.S. and European DM firms with extensive supply networks around the world. Building up one's own customer lists is an expensive process requiring a long-term commitment to the Japanese market because losses are bound to pile up with plenty of returns and complaints in the early years. Still, the payoff can be high because Japanese consumers are very loyal once they are satisfied.
- **Mergers and acquisitions** make up the fourth market approach. This has been going on in both directions: foreign firms buy up Japanese companies which get into the mail-order business too quickly while large Japanese retail chains absorb American or European DM corporations to acquire their expertise and software. Remember that a joint venture arrangement without a proactive foreign partner is essentially a Japanese company regardless of what the contract says. Too many North American firms sign expensive partnership agreements only to see their influence slip away because they see it as a division of labor allowing them to forget about Japan and concentrate on their domestic concerns. Either adopt an export strategy where you stay out of Japan or get in and become fully involved. Avoid expensive fence-sitting situations.

Partnerships

Companies considering the use of direct marketing as part of their export strategy for Japan almost always depend heavily on outside assistance to accelerate the process and improve their chances of success. For the sake of clarity, I will describe under separate headings services frequently sold in combination as package deals. With DM consultants and service firms proliferating in Japan, foreign exporters who do not know what they are looking for have more opportunities to lose money and become confused than they ever did before.

- **Market research** firms can give you easy access to secondary market reports on your product category: Who are your main competitors? What are Japanese buyers looking for in that area? Is demand growing or stagnant? Two or three focus groups can be set up for between US$10,000 and $20,000 to find out how Japanese consumers react to your product and what changes should be made.

- **Creative services** include advertising, graphics, headlines, special offers, and so forth. Don't make the mistake of confusing general advertising with effective DM copy. The first is geared towards changing attitudes and television. DM copy tries to create an immediate response to a specific offer. Leave DM copy to DM specialists.
- Companies with offices in Japan often make use of **letter shops** to stuff their direct mail pieces into envelopes, seal them, put address labels on and zip code sort them. For mailings of a 1,000 pieces or more, letter shops can be very cost-effective. A good relationship with the **local post office** is equally important to shorten the approval process for bulk mail rates.

- Fulfillment means tracking items that are ordered, making sure that customers are satisfied and returns are dealt with, collecting payments and creating final reports. Many foreign exporters relying on the "airmail route" to send their catalogs to Japan, team up with **Japanese order-processing companies** for fulfillment because a local presence is important for many consumers. **Trucking and warehouse companies** often offer such services, but their reputation for follow-up is generally poor. Restrict yourself to partners with a good order-processing infrastructure and track record.

A DIRECT MARKETING CASE HISTORY

WAYNE STEINHAUER

Austad's sells high quality golf equipment, clothing and gifts through direct marketing and retail stores. A privately-held family business, it was founded in 1963 and employs 450 people. In 1991, Austad's fulfilled over 700,000 catalog orders and responded to over 340,000 customer service requests. Austad's four retail stores accounted for 13% of sales. Catalog sales accounted for 87% of total sales; of these, 97% were from sales in the U.S. and 3% from international sales. Austad's maintains nearly three million golfers on their mailing list worldwide. They started marketing overseas in 1990 and now have seven different international catalog editions.

Please note that the following account was a presentation made by Austad's vice president and general manager, Wayne Steinhauer, at the American Direct Marketing Association's Annual Catalog Conference in June 1992. The situation it describes, both at Austad's and in Japan, has developed since then.

DM industry information

Japan's direct marketing industry has been estimated to be about US$12 billion annually. Conservative numbers show a growth rate of about 12 percent. The average Japanese individual will receive about 166 letters in one year compared to about 600 or more in the U.S., which means that your mail will receive attention and be read when it reaches a Japanese home.

The average order for Japanese direct marketing companies is about US$100. Austad's average order is almost double. For international marketers, especially if orders are being shipped from the U.S., the average cost of the order will exceed US$100.

The average return rate is about 5.7 percent. Austad's is much lower.

In Japan there are two types of businesses that are active in direct marketing: those solely in direct marketing and those that are in it as a sideline. And it's really companies that are in it as a sideline that are the biggest players.

Businesses like department stores, credit card companies, and the media are doing a big job in direct marketing in Japan and own many of the larger lists.

If you are using telephone services, free dial is becoming very common in Japan; however, no discounts are available as is the custom in the U.S.

About 50 percent of your orders will come in by phone, and that number seems to be increasing.

Phases to international growth

In our planning process we initially thought we would need four phases to achieve our growth. The last one would be physical presence.

We started out in 1987 by gathering information from our customers. Our customers and expatriates in many countries helped us identify which markets to enter and who the competition was.

To complete our research, we relied on the U.S. Department of Commerce and several other information-gathering sources.

We then decided to increase our house mailings into Japan; at this stage we were still mailing our domestic catalog, but we included an order sheet in Japanese, which was a literal translation, to break down some of the barriers of placing an order.

Looking back on the first order form that we produced, we made our share of mistakes. But at the time of execution we thought we were right. We used a local firm to translate our English copy, word for word. When the Japanese became more comfortable in dealing with us, we were told that we had done some things wrong. It was a learning experience, and it helped us move ahead.

In the third phase, which is where we are now, we produced a fully adapted catalog in Japanese with yen pricing. We have a partner in Japan who handles our customer service.

We were able to accomplish this phase because of testing that we conducted in phase two. We were able to identify what the average weight and size of the order was going to be. We were able to break down some of the barriers to placing an order by simplifying our shipping and ordering methods.

All along, our goal was to have a catalog concept that gave the customer in Japan the same comfort of dealing with a local firm, but still left the excitement of direct import.

The Japanese have a strong affinity for American-made golf products. So we decided to retain our U.S. identity, and at the same time offer our customers the comfort of dealing with a local firm to take their orders.

To achieve this, we established a partner relationship, and basically what our partner in Japan does is provide market research, i.e., pricing and competition, translation, and typesetting. He also handles our banking and customer service, when customers phone or write. In addition, he helped us build our mailing list which is an important asset to our growth.

All of this is very costly, especially when you are adapting a catalog to meet the needs of a specific market. To keep our catalog unit costs down, we decided to enter several markets at the same time by using the same four-color but doing a black plate change. By printing offset, we reduced our costs. We first rolled out a Japanese, British, and Swedish catalog. We also produced another English version which we mailed throughout the world.

The copy used in the English worldwide version was basic in order to break down the barriers of placing an order in the smaller markets where we didn't have a partner relationship. Having several versions lowered our costs, and it helped us figure out which market had the most potential.

Due to some difficulties in our Swedish operation and marketing errors in the U.K., we have since discontinued these versions. We are reworking things and expanding our customer base before setting up physical presence in Japan.

In Japan, from an operational/procedural standpoint, the orders are collected by our service partner. He sends them to us on a nightly basis by fax, so the orders are waiting in the morning. We send back an acknowledgment, any information about product problems, back orders, etc. Then we enter the order in U.S. dollars in our computers at Austad's, although the catalog is expressed in Japanese yen. We take care of the conversion to yen through a manual spreadsheet system. This eliminated the need for heavy programming in the initial stages. But eventually we will have to make some changes. We ship the orders twice weekly from the U.S. on a consolidated freight basis. We guarantee a two-week delivery.

In Japan, the returns come back to our partner, who sells them to local shops. This eliminates the expense of transporting them back to the US, and we basically recover our manufacturing cost.

Catalog delivery

From a catalog delivery standpoint, we learned that it's definitely cheaper to mail from the U.S. Our catalog, which weighs a little over 3 ounces, would cost about $1.17 to $1.20 if a Japanese firm mailed it in Japan. Our costs are nearly half. We've tried a variety of different re-mailers and there's an abundance of them out there offering a variety of levels of service. Currently we're satisfied with the U.S. Postal Service (ISAL).

There are several different ways to write a Japanese address correctly. This has been one of our main difficulties, and I think it has caused some high undeliverable rates. Our computer will only allow four-line addresses, and addresses can be quite lengthy.

The Japanese post office won't necessarily guarantee all deliveries, because it officially only recognizes one address format. The different postmasters have a lot of authority, however, and they will go the extra mile to get it delivered. But it still is a very big concern for us at Austad's.

On average, about 20 percent of a list in Japan will move annually, and this is another concern because there is no national change of address service as in the U.S.

We have not been able to locate an English translation of the Japanese postal regulations, although many people have been helpful in explaining them to us.

Postal discounts can be negotiated if you are mailing from within Japan, but you are only eligible if, in a given month, you mail 50,000 catalogs. We found that mailing our catalogs from the U.S. is cheaper. If you polly-bag them, it's to your advantage to leave a white strip on the polly-bag, which allows the postal carrier to make notations about delivery address changes.

We've also found that getting the catalog to the homes around the 20th of the month tends to increase responses in Japan because it's closer to pay day. You need to be aware of all the holidays and avoid mailing during certain ones. However, if you are in the gift business, you will want to mail during certain holidays.

Product delivery

We find it convenient to fulfill our orders from the U.S. We're located in Sioux Falls, South Dakota, the golf capital of the world. But you can deliver products into Japan within a two-week period from anywhere in the world.

In fact, with DHL we're getting a six to eight day delivery on a consolidated freight basis.

Japanese firms promise two to three week delivery, but deliver in 8 to 10 days, because they feel it's crucial not to disappoint the customer.

Occasionally, things will go wrong with your delivery, and we've experienced that too. But a small gift to atone for any delivery deficiencies will really go a long way.

Austad's has been offering guaranteed two-week delivery since 1990. We used to refund for shipping and handling if our customers did not receive the product within two weeks' time. We now send a dozen golf balls instead, which is a lot cheaper and has saved us a lot of money. The average customer in Japan will spend about $41 in postage and handling.

If you're in the gift business, you should be aware that the Japanese post office offers a fixed-day delivery service that you can take advantage of. It is critical that the packing of your product is very presentable when it is delivered.

List industry

The list industry is probably the biggest hurdle that we've encountered. In the U.S., we've grown a great deal through magazine subscription lists. In Japan magazine subscription lists are very small, only five to ten percent of magazines are distributed by subscription. Most are sold through newsstands.

You therefore have to be a little more creative in finding your lists. For most of the public lists that are available, typically large compiled lists, there will be more than one list manager, owner, broker marketing the same lists, so you need to be cautious when buying them. There is typically not a lot of information attached to the list. As I mentioned earlier, since 20 percent of your list will move in one year, you need to make sure that the list is up to date to avoid deliverability problems.

The services of merging list and addresses, and address-up-dates, etc., are basically unsophisticated. A lot of this stems from a reluctance to share information with other Japanese firms or even international firms.

A list usually can be obtained in hard copy rather than on mag-tape for fear that it might get stolen, and there is no monitoring or decoy service to prevent that from happening, which makes the problem worse.

So there's a great opportunity for someone to get into the monitoring and decoying business in Japan, and I think that will make things run smoother.

You have to use caution when testing a list. We've found that even though the test results may be good, the roll-out may not be successful.

There are rumors that sometimes the list owners will pick the better names rather than doing an nth name selection. Expect to spend about $185 per 1000 or more on a list rental.

The advantage of having a partner is that you can arrange to set up cooperative programs with other companies, ride-alongs, and other methods to help develop your own names in-house.

You need to be aware that the standard practice in the U.S. is that your buyer's name belongs to you, which is not always the case in Japan. You need to clarify what you intend to do with the buyers' names.

Creative

The key here is to remember that language will strongly affect your creative. When we produced our first order form, we translated it from English word for word. If you are translating in the U.S., make sure someone in Japan sees it before printing. Japanese creative is typically blocky with few drop-outs and little copy. Since we wanted to be perceived as an American firm, we haven't made attempts to copy the Japanese creative.

We've been told that you can afford to have a longer letter when you're doing a solo mailing because there's not as much mailbox clutter. However, avoid sounding too folksy or too friendly. What usually works in the U.S. can be offensive in Japan.

We have found that in space ads, you don't always need to include a cut-out response vehicle. You can simply show a picture of it and the respondents will actually fill out and return their own cards.

We translate and adapt the main text of our catalog and leave the headings in English to give an international flavor. We feature a photograph of the Austad family. We position Austad's as a family-owned business ready to serve its customers. We also feature a photo of our service partner in the lower right hand in black and white. It's in black and white so that we can do a plate change when mailing to other countries. We also show airplanes to communicate the speed of delivery.

Product positioning

You should be aware that products used in daily necessities tend to be priced lower, whereas if they represent a brand name or if they are meant to improve your lifestyle, they will be priced higher.

Don't make the mistake of basing your pricing on U.S. costs and converting to yen. Do the market research. Find out what a comparable product sells for.

If you have more than one channel of distribution, it could affect the pricing of your product, so be careful that it doesn't happen.

Be prepared to accept other payment methods besides credit cards like bank transfers, open accounts, etc.

With all of these measures, what could possibly go wrong? We've made our fair share of mistakes, and it's normal to stumble in the beginning. We're in our second year, and we're taking a slow-growth approach.

I encourage others to also explore the Japanese market.

PREPARING THE GROUNDWORK

SOME FUNDAMENTALS

Despite its many obvious advantages, Japan is not a potentially profitable export market for everyone. Would-be exporters must check how their products compare to competing items, whether Japanese consumers are likely to be receptive, and, most important, what returns are possible given the high cost of marketing foreign goods in Japan. Unfortunately, many small and medium exporters skip this basic research and are forced to withdraw even when their products are competitive. The reasons for these failures mostly fall under three headings: no plan, no time, and inadequate sales back-up.

IS JAPAN RIGHT FOR ME?

Yes...

The case for exporting to Japan has so often been made that I don't need to belabor the point.

- Japan now has the second largest economy in the world.
- That means that a relatively modest market share in Japan can translate into a very large sales volume.
- Japanese per capita income is higher than that of the U.S. and much of Europe.
- For exporters of high-tech products especially, some involvement in the Japanese market is becoming necessary to keep abreast of technological developments and global investment trends. Waiting for the Japanese competition to reach your shores before reacting usually spells disaster.
- Finally, the Japanese are under pressure to increase their imports, especially imports of manufactured products.

But...

What is true for exporters in general may not be true for you. Each industry, each product category has its own dynamics; moreover, you face your own unique set of circumstances as a seller. Your firm produces a specific product, of a specific quality, at a specific price, for a specific market segment, and so on. You must thoroughly understand your firm's present limitations and your product's chances of success in Japan before selecting anyone to represent you over there. Japan is not the right choice for everyone.

- For exporters looking to go beyond hit-or-miss opportunities in Japan, the cost of travel and market research and the time required to build up a network of trusted advisors can seem prohibitive. Japan is an expensive place to make mistakes.
- Japan's market is highly structured compared to that of the U.S. or Canada. Long-term relationships, industrial groups (*keiretsu*) and seemingly-irrational distribution practices complicate the market entry process

for every foreign exporter. Success requires more networking skill and more time-consuming research than almost anywhere else. "Winging it" rarely works.

- Japanese customers are accustomed to high quality and excellent service.
- Half-hearted export campaigns get short shrift. Japanese distributors are the world's most export-oriented traders and expect no less from foreigners trying to enter their market.
- As the world's premier "new product laboratory," Japan is extremely difficult to export to unless your products are either very price-competitive – and there you are competing with the likes of China and Taiwan – or very distinctive. And price is playing an increasingly important role for all imports because the post-bubble "recession" has made the Japanese feel less wealthy.

That being said, one should not allow oneself to be overawed. Total American exports grew by 76% in five years to reach nearly $450 billion in 1992, and most of this success, even in the Japanese market, appears to stem from smaller companies. Such figures bring us into line with countries such as Germany, where smaller firms lead the way into foreign markets.

Three categories

These new small and medium exporters can be broken down into three categories: born exporters, gradual exporters, and – unfortunately in the majority – reluctant exporters.

Born exporters think globally from the very first day. In some cases, ethnic background may be the reason. A Chinese-Canadian entrepreneur working out of Vancouver probably finds Hong Kong buyers as easy to deal with as Americans. For many others, however, the very nature of their product forces them to look abroad. High-tech products, for example, have increasingly shorter shelf lives and are only profitable when targeted at narrow niches in a worldwide market.

Some small firms slowly grow and export business one step at time. At first, they know nothing about foreign markets. Then, they become aware of export opportunities, but do nothing. After some time, they might send staff members to conferences and start exporting through a few trial contacts. It is only when export sales expand sufficiently to account for 15% of total sales that they really acquire an export mentality.

Reluctant exporters turn to foreign markets because domestic demand has turned sour. It is this category of exporters that is most prone to make costly mistakes because they eagerly tackle demanding foreign markets without a plan, without sufficient time and without adequate sales back-up. This is what I call blind exporting.

THE PERILS OF GOING BLIND

No plan

Sales reps targeting the Asia Pacific region frequently receive only ambivalent support from their superiors. The attitude of many senior managers is: "Bring me an interesting offer and I will approve it." This leaves the sales rep with no basis for a plan. As a consequence, Japanese retailers and distributors have grown used to a daily parade of visitors on a fishing expedition, hoping something will fall in their lap, never to be heard of again. With no preliminary sales promotion plan, inadequate background information on the Japanese market, and no idea as to which distribution mechanism is more likely to bring the best overall results, these representatives lack the basic tools required to attract and select good distributors.

A more useful approach would be to say: "I want to get into Japan. I have set aside X dollars to do it. Find out how." This gives the sales rep sufficient resources to effectively plan his distribution strategy.

No time

Ambivalent support from senior management also creates pressures for quick pay-backs, the result being a shotgun approach to distributor selection which can be very costly in the long run (see Weak Points and Trouble Spots). For lack of time, one finds sales reps accepting at face value data fed to them by distributors; initiating negotiations with distributor companies at trade shows without first completing any independent research in the marketplace; and seeking advice from the uninformed while junketing with trade missions. The classic mistake is the whirlwind tour of Asia by marketing managers who spend a few days in each of the main capitals, talk to two or three potential distributors, and make a decision before leaving town, often granting exclusive rights to the candidate who places the largest initial order.

Inadequate sales back-up

Some manufacturers succeed in locating a competent distributor only to see their relationship slowly go sour because their export sales departments are too disorganized to respond adequately to the distributor's requests. The best efforts to identify, screen and select good distributors will likely be in vain if responsibilities for certain vital functions are not clearly defined and placed in capable hands. These key functions are:

- **Management** An experienced export manager is a must.
- **Sales coordination** Export planning, labeling and packaging, development of promotional material, etc.
- **Accounting** Maintain timely product cost estimates; deal with L/Cs and other trade-related bank instruments; advise management about expenses, new product launches, etc.

- **Transportation** Negotiate, schedule and supervise land, sea and air transportation.
- **Field sales liaison** Keep direct contact with field reps and distributors.

This may seem trivial, but one of the main complaints Japanese agents and distributors have about North American suppliers is the number of messages they send which somehow fall through the cracks. Suppliers who do this once too often lose the battle for distributor attention. No amount of correspondence after the fact will change this.

DOING YOUR HOMEWORK

In the last chapter, I mentioned some of the negative consequences faced by exporters who base key decisions on chance meetings and friendly tips. A plan is needed, one based on research both at home (the subject of this chapter) and in Japan (see Prospecting in Japan*).*

PRE-DEPARTURE RESEARCH

Crucial

Research is very necessary at this stage for four basic reasons:

- You have to decide whether market conditions in Japan at present and in the near future are sufficiently encouraging to warrant the time and expense of further market research over there. Market conditions, in general, are not enough; what you want to know are market conditions as they affect your product category.
- If you do decide to go, you have to accumulate a list of promising contacts – ideally, people referred to you by mutual acquaintances. This has to be done before leaving because cold calls rarely get you very far in Japan.
- It saves time. Given the high cost of traveling to and living in Japan, you don't want to waste days over there looking for basic information you could have acquired at home.
- It saves money. You don't want to hire a consulting firm and spend tens of thousands of dollars for information you could have obtained free of charge from JETRO or your government.

Salespeople, especially those working in small and medium enterprises, are understandably obsessed with contacts at this stage. They want the names and addresses of good importers or distributors interested in their product category. And there is nothing wrong with that as long as they supplement this data with answers to the questions listed in Table 4-1. Regardless of the importer's competence or level of interest, sales reps who skip this kind of preliminary research are in a very weak negotiating position once in Japan.

Market overview

The best place to start is with your government because it can give you far more individualized attention than JETRO can. Visit your nearest federal and provincial or state trade promotion offices (see Annex 4) to acquire their country overviews and off-the-shelf industry and product information. Most of it is available free of charge or for a nominal fee. Also, learn all you can about their various export assistance programs.

Table 4-1

PRELIMINARY QUESTIONS

Market Overview

- *What is the overall market size of my product category?*
- *Has it been growing or shrinking during the last 3-5 years? If so, at what rate and why?*
- *Who are my Japanese competitors and what is their market share?*
- *What percentage of the market is taken up by imports? Has this market share changed during the last 3-5 years? How does this affect trade volume?*
- *Where are these imports coming from?*
- *Who are my foreign competitors, and what are their sales level and market share?*
- *Who are the end users? What do they look for in imports?*
- *What are recent market trends affecting my product?*

Regulatory environment

- *What import tariffs, if any, exist for my product category?*
- *Are there special customs procedures associated with my product?*
- *What standards and certification systems apply in my case?*
- *If certification is needed, what ministry office should I contact in Tokyo? What is the address, fax and telephone number of the relevant bureau?*
- *Are patents advisable in my case? What are the costs involved?*

Distribution

- *Who imports my product category? Who are the top 15 importers (names, addresses, etc.) in both Tokyo and Osaka?*
- *Who distributes my foreign competitors' products? Where are they sold?*
- *What distribution margins are current in my product category?*
- *What are the most common distribution arrangements (licensing, sole import agents, joint ventures, etc.)?*

Travel preparations

- *Names, addresses, telephone and fax numbers of trade officials or business people considered especially knowledgeable.*
- *List, dates and locations of related exhibitions or trade fairs coming up in the next two years. Which ones bring together the people I want to meet?*
- *List and addresses of organizations (trade groups, chambers of commerce, consultants, etc.) associated with my product category.*

The second obvious place to go is your nearest JETRO office (see Annex 2). JETRO stands for Japan External Trade Organization, an agency originally set up by the Japanese Ministry of International Trade and Industry (MITI) to assist their own exporters, but which now also helps inform foreign manufacturers about market trends and export opportunities in Japan.

Many of the more general questions listed in Table 4-1 will be answered if JETRO has a recent *Your Market in Japan* report on your product category (see Annex 3). If not, you should consult their trade libraries for industry-specific annual review, such as *Japan Pharmaceutical Reference*, *Japan Electronics Almanac*. See Annex 1 for other industry-specific titles.

For more precise import figures, Japan's trade statistics are classified according to the *Harmonized Commodity Description and Coding System* or *Harmonized System* (HS) for short. If you check out your product's HS number in the *Japan Exports & Imports* series (Commodity by Country), you can find out how much of your product category is being imported into Japan and where these products are coming from. Compare these for the three to five previous years to find out whether the market for imported products in your category is growing and, if so, by how much.

To go beyond country of origin and find out what German companies, for example, are exporting products similar to your own, you may have to contact the German embassy or go to Japan. For Japanese companies, Yano Research Institute annually publishes *Market Share in Japan*, listing the top players in each product category. If these companies are listed in the Tokyo Stock Exchange, you can find out more about them by referring to Toyo Keizai's two-volume *Japan Company Handbook*.

Finally, it is worthwhile to take advantage of JETRO's Import Products Specialist Program. Every year JETRO sends Japanese product specialists from trading companies, manufacturers and distributors around the world to locate products suitable for the Japanese market and advise exporters interested in Japan. A specialist in your product area could visit your plant free of charge to look over your production and advise you on your chances of success. Products judged marketable in Japan are exposed to potential importers in JETRO's New Imports Showcase at no cost to the foreign manufacturer. All you have to do is apply at your nearest JETRO office.

Regulatory environment

Imported goods are either free import items, products requiring authorization, products restricted by quota, or products requiring notification. Each category has its own procedures; only the first is exempt of tariffs. Both JETRO and MIPRO (Manufactured Imports Promotion Organization) have published easy to understand procedures for imports in English.

For information on tariffs, refer to the Japan Tariff Association's *Customs Tariff Schedules of Japan* under your HS number. The regularly updated *Exporter's Encyclopedia* by Dun's Marketing Services is also worth consulting on all import regulations. Most trade libraries have a copy.

Special import procedures, quarantine and labeling regulations are explained succinctly in a series of booklets titled *Procedures for Importing and Selling...in Japan* published by the Japan Standards Association. Japan's use of the metric system, for example, usually means that American packaging has to be modified. Other book series explain the application of Japanese agricultural standards (JAS) to "natural" products (food, wood products, raw materials, etc.) and Japanese industrial standards (JIS) to manufactured products. All are available in JETRO trade libraries.

The problem with Japanese standards is that they are often very theoretical. The Japanese government seldom does testing, preferring instead to rely on standards set by their trade associations. Fortunately, Japanese regulations increasingly conform to international standards. Your own government is probably the best source of information on regulatory problems which have affected products similar to yours in the past. There are also accredited laboratories in Canada and the U.S. capable of evaluating your product's compatibility with Japanese standards. Lists are available from your government offices.

If JETRO cannot answer your questions with regards to standards, contact:

Standards Information Center
Ministry of International Trade and Industry (MITI)
1-3-1 Kasumigaseki, Chiyoda-ku, Tokyo 100
Tel: 03-3501-1668
Fax: 03-3501-5983

Japan Standards Association (JSA)
4-1-24 Akasaka, Minato-ku, Tokyo 107
Tel: 03-3583-8001
Fax: 03-3586-2014

The question of patents can be discouragingly complex (see Weak Points and Trouble Spots). Here again, our government trade officials are probably the best source of advice.

Distribution

Getting a list of importers and wholesalers active in your product category from JETRO or your government is relatively easy. Written sources include the *Standard Trade Index of Japan*, the very comprehensive studies done by Dodwell Marketing Consultants (see Annex I) and JETRO's own *Japan Trade Directory*. JETRO also has a computerized database which can be used both to list your firm as one seeking a Japanese importer (JETRO TOPS) or to get lists of Japanese importers active in your product category (TRADE WINDS).

Evaluations are another matter. JETRO doesn't give any and your government's expertise in these matters is probably concentrated in Tokyo or Osaka. Remember, too, that a given importer may be ideal for large exporters and totally inadequate for small and medium suppliers. It all depends on what you expect the importer to do for you and your degree of involvement in the whole Japan marketing process.

Information on your competitors' distribution channels is also hard to come by outside of Japan. What is available from many JETRO market reports are ballpark estimates of distribution margins.

Travel preparations

Refer to JETRO publications and to the *Japan Yellow Pages* for a complete list of upcoming trade shows and exhibitions. JETRO also has pamphlets on each conference. Written evaluations of these conferences are not available, but knowledgeable JETRO product specialists will very willingly tell you which ones they think would best serve your purposes.

The most complete list of Japanese business and trade associations is *The Economic and Industrial Organizations* compiled and updated every year by the Tokyo Chamber of Commerce and Industry. Copies are usually available for consultation in every JETRO office. Remember, however, that these associations exist primarily to serve their Japanese members, and that references from someone who is known to them will attract a lot more attention to your requests than they would merit otherwise.

This question of referrals is crucial. Business life in Japan is primarily based on personal relationships. Make a point of visiting your local chamber of commerce, world trade center, universities, banks, *sogo shosha* branch offices, Japanese consulates and so on, to present yourself and get referrals from people with friends in Japan who could help you with information or other contacts. Do the same with all your suppliers and clients. Read through the list of names in the most recent American Chamber of Commerce in Japan (ACCJ) *Membership Directory* or that of the Canadian Chamber of Commerce in Japan (CCCJ). Find as many connections and mutual acquaintances as you can. Market data is vital, but by itself it will not get you very far unless you quickly build up a network of friends and contacts willing to advise you.

Cultural information

With so much research to do, you may think that cultural information is not as important, and you are partially right. Being able to talk intelligently about Japanese history or cuisine is certainly an asset, but knowledge of "high culture" is not really needed to do business successfully in Japan. What you do need, however, and this goes back to the importance of networking and relationships, is a feeling for Japanese non-verbal communication and some understanding of the institutional and personal straight jackets (by Western standards) they live with every day. If I had to recommend five books on these issues from the list contained in Annex 1, it would be Collins (1992), Fields (1985), Japan Travel Bureau (Vol. 8), Rowland (1985) and Woronoff (1991).

Another pleasant way to learn about Japan is to borrow videos in the series *Nippon: The Land and its People Video* from your nearest JETRO office. The two I recommend most are *The Japanese Businessman* and *The Japanese Family*.

KNOW THYSELF

More?

Isn't all this enough? No, unfortunately not. Exporters visiting Japan can expect many questions about their companies (see Table 4-2), especially if they are seeking subcontracting relationships (see Industrial Purchasing). Glossy brochures are not enough; they want to assess your level of professionalism. Part of it is simple curiosity, but many Japanese importers also want to avoid dealing with poorly organized companies promising more than they can deliver. As a result, they tend to be far more impressed by clear and precise answers than by sales bluster. Be prepared.

Table 4-2

KNOW THYSELF

The basics

- *Your company's history.*
- *Its location and size.*
- *Your product: what needs does it serve?*
- *Your major customers.*
- *Your major competitors.*
- *Market trends in your domestic market.*
- *Your export track record.*
- *What are your strengths and weaknesses?*
- *Your estimate as to your product's sales potential in Japan, the ideal kind of distribution arrangement, etc.*
- *Your product's CIF price to the nearest Japanese port or airport. What are your minimum order levels beyond which extra charges are necessary?*

Internal matters

- *Past financial performance indicators, including monthly sales figures.*
- *Information on how you distribute your product.*
- *Your allocation of personnel for administration, production and storage.*
- *The size and preferred (as opposed to rated) capacity of your various facilities: output per hour, units per day, etc.*
- *Capacity utilization: estimate the percentage of the capacity of each facility (administration, equipment, storage) being used at present.*
- *Age: how old is your machinery? When do you plan to replace it?*
- *Key proprietary technology in your possession.*
- *How do you maintain quality control?*

The basics

The list of questions in Table 4-2 is self-explanatory. The reason why knowing your CIF price to Japan is so important before leaving is that you must be able to calculate how different distribution alternatives affect your product's final price in Japan, its competitiveness and your profit picture. (See Prospecting in Japan – channel mapping for examples.)

Minimum orders are very important because Japanese importers prefer frequent small orders that cut down the cost of warehousing. If you don't have a firm grasp of your costs, you can't discuss the issue intelligently.

Internal matters

These questions are mainly of concern to foreign companies seeking long-term supply (i.e., subcontracting) relationships in Japan. Even so, ordinary exporters are often asked questions about capacity utilization especially if they are small and medium enterprises.

Foreign suppliers new to Japan are often shocked by the sheer quantity of information Japanese buyers feel entitled to. They frequently insist on visiting plants and demand to know everything about your production techniques, all highly confidential information in normal North American practice. This is why companies understanding these requirements and still willing to go through with it if the right Japanese partner can be found, must sit down with their sales rep and carefully plan how much information can be made available during the market exploration phase. Things should not be left to chance, or too much may be given away for free.

SOME OBJECTIONS

No time

Sales managers who postponed reading this chapter until their flight to Japan can be forgiven if they shake their heads in disbelief. Who other than trade analysts has the time to pursue this kind of research?

Misleading

Isn't it misleading to focus on books of regulations when Japanese customs officials and government bureaucrats commonly interpret the rules in a very discretionary fashion? As for the HS classifications, are they not still too broad to tell you much about a given product's true market situation? Don't the Japanese importers take care of any certifications or patents required?

Useless

Are trade statistics and market surveys really that useful? While they may agree at the general level, they frequently contradict each other when you narrow your focus to a single topic. Worse still, they can engender a form of paralysis by providing you with a wealth of intelligent-sounding excuses for doing nothing.

Our position

It is very true that market studies will only get you so far. If the trade statistics seem to indicate that there is a worthwhile market for your product in Japan, the next step is to go there for a visit. The real data – the solid market information – can only come from talking to people with experience. This does not deny the value of statistical data; indeed, a good understanding of Japan's trade statistics and import procedures as they relate to your product will give you the self-confidence to talk to those who really know what is going on.

An important reason to master as much secondary information as possible about the import channels for your product category is that it puts you in the driver's seat from the very beginning; you can select the channels best suited to your needs, agree to discounts that reflect real services (as opposed to tradition) and know when to pull out if nothing worthwhile materializes. Don't be put off by the apparent success of exporters who avoid this work and trust in luck. Most of them don't care to admit how much time was wasted in blind alleys or pulling out of bad partnerships.

JAPAN'S BANKING SYSTEM

HONGKONG BANK OF CANADA

This is a brief overview of the banking system of Japan and some of the technical terms relating to trade finance. The author is chief economist at Hongkong Bank of Canada, a member of the HSBC Group, which is one of the world's largest banking and financial services organizations, with offices throughout Asia, including Japan.

OVERVIEW

Structure

The banking system in Japan is, in many ways, similar to that in Canada. There are a small number of very large nationwide retail operations with branches in numerous locations. Indeed, Japanese banks are among the largest financial institutions in the world. As in Canada, the structure of the financial sector and the activities of each of the participants has been changing rapidly. While they may have different names – city banks, regional banks, trust banks, or long-term credit banks – like their counterparts in Canada, they all essentially engage in the full line of banking services.

For the purposes of a Canadian business which is non-resident in Japan, the traditional banks – city banks (*toshi ginko*), regional banks (*chiho ginko*) and the specialized foreign exchange bank, The Bank of Tokyo, which was established under a special law to concentrate on foreign exchange and trade finance – would be most able to provide the financial services required.

While there are a number of specialized institutions catering to small- and medium-size business, they are domestically oriented and would be unlikely to deal with non-resident firms. However, were a joint partner resident in Japan to be involved, these institutions might prove to be a source of finance.

With the opening of The Hongkong and Shanghai Banking Corporation branch in 1866, foreign banks have been established in Japan for more than 125 years. Still, they constitute only a small portion of the domestic market. In recent decades, as the result of strenuous pressure on Japanese authorities, many more foreign financial institutions have been granted licenses to enter the Japanese market. The results have been of mixed success.

The extensive domestic branch system has inhibited the growth of foreign bank retail operations. Consequently, most such operations are located in the major cities such as Tokyo, Osaka, Kobe, and Nagasaki. Collectively, these foreign banks have concentrated primarily on provision of trade finance and foreign exchange dealings and have provided the normal banking services for both Japanese and foreign clients. Some recently have entered into primary securities distribution and the provision of trust services; but these activities constitute only a small portion of total activity.

Deposit products

Most corporations hold current accounts which bear no interest and are payable on demand. In addition, there are time deposits which are also payable on demand but only upon presentation of a pass book and a registered seal or by means of a bank card. These deposits are used for automatic transfer services such as payroll, pension and dividend payments, payment of public utility bills, taxes and insurance premiums and installment credit payments. The bulk of these deposits are held by individuals.

Time deposits, deposits left with an institution for a fixed term, have rates of interest related to the length of term. These time deposits are subject to interest rate regulation while newer time deposit forms (including certificates of deposits and non-negotiable large sum time deposits) are not.

One other type of deposit is worth noting. Foreign currency deposits are available at banks authorized to deal in foreign exchange, and the terms and rates paid on such deposits are subject to negotiation.

Loan products

Lending activities involve either the discounting of bills or straight loans. Discounting is the purchase of an outstanding bill at its face value less the amount of interest that accrues by the maturity date. Most such purchases are of trade bills, which are issued to settle the payment in commercial transactions and are normally of about three months maturity. Those of the highest quality, usually only the largest corporations, can be used as collateral by the banks when seeking accommodation at the central bank.

Straight loans are not unlike those obtainable in Canada. The bank agrees to lend money usually for a fixed period at a predetermined rate though conditions and terms are subject to negotiation. Commercial mortgage financing is also available from these institutions as are over-draft facilities. The granting of over-draft facilities, however, is not as common as it is in Canada.

Obtaining banking accommodation

While approaching virtually any foreign bank operation in Japan would be similar to approaching a Canadian bank, obtaining financial assistance, i.e., loans and/or trade finance from a Japanese bank might best be done in conjunction with a Japanese partner. Knowledge of the language is one consideration as is familiarity with normal commercial and legal concepts.

METHODS OF IMPORT SETTLEMENT

There are five main methods of import settlement:

1. Documentary letter of credit (DC)
2. Inward collection
   - Document against acceptance (D/A)
   - Document against payment (D/P)
3. Import consignment
4. Advance and Interim Payments
5. Cash, including advance payment by telegraphic transfer, demand draft or mail transfer. Cash settlements are used for small orders or as alternative to DC when the parties trust each other for settlement risk.

Below follows a brief description of the major items:

Documentary letter of credit (DC)

In Asia, the DC is the most widely used method of facilitating payment to the supplier after shipping his goods. When the buyer opens a DC, he arranges with the bank to act as the importer's agent who will transfer funds to the exporter once certain documents, according to specific terms, have been presented. The issuing bank undertakes to make payment to the exporter's account via his own bank or another bank once the exporter satisfies the documentary requirements and conditions of the DC. Deadlines are always attached to a DC regarding latest shipping, expiry and presentation dates.

Documentary letters of credit are almost always irrevocable as revocable credits can be amended or canceled by the person who opened the credit without prior warning or notice to the beneficiary. Irrevocable credits can be amended or canceled only with the agreement of all parties concerned, if the amendment is derogatory to the beneficiary. It is important to specify that the credit is "irrevocable" otherwise it will be deemed to be revocable. Reverse in ICC 500 came into effect January 1, 1993.

Letters of credit can also be confirmed. An **unconfirmed credit** means that the issuing bank is the only party responsible for payment to the supplier. The negotiating bank may choose to purchase bills with or without recourse but is obliged to pay only after it has received payment from the issuing bank. A **confirmed credit** means that the issuing bank requests a second bank to add its own confirmation to the credit so that the confirming banks is responsible to make payment upon presentation of conforming documents in advance of reimbursement and with recourse to the beneficiary. If the beneficiary is unfamiliar with the buyer's bank, confirmation allows the risk to be transferred to a bank he is comfortable with.

The exporter is not obliged to accept the terms of the buyer's DC. The exporter can ask for correction and amendments and should check it for changes from the original version.

A review of draft DC terms is preferable before the DC is issued as amendments after a DC is issued may lead to delays in shipment.

When the buyer applies for a DC, he will need to supply the following information:

- The correct name and address of the supplier.
- The exact amount of the credit to be opened, or when drafts are to be drawn and the tenor, if any, of the drafts.
- The type and terms of the credit, and whether it can be transferred to another beneficiary.
- A brief description and the quantity of merchandise ordered. Usually, plus or minus 5 percent of the quantity is acceptable, depending on the items ordered. It is unusual to have a letter of credit requiring shipment to exactly 100 percent of the order amount.
- Who will arrange for shipment, the port of shipment and port of discharge, whether freight costs are to be prepaid, whether partial shipments are allowed, and the latest date when shipment will be allowed by the buyer.
- The method (telex/mail) that the credit is to be advised to the supplier, the place where the credit will be negotiated and the expiry date. The importer can advise the exporter that he has opened a DC by short telegraphic transfer notice, receipt airmail, or full text authenticated cable.
- The types of documents required, whether third-party documents are required (e.g., inspector certificate), whether the documents should be copies or originals, and the period of time after shipping within which the supplier must present the documents to the advising bank for negotiation, acceptance and payment.

All of this information is normally recorded on DC application.

Inward collection

Under inward collection, when the importer's bank in Asia receives the waybill and draft sent by the overseas bank, it must first advise the importer holding the import permit to come to the bank to have the documents checked. The time taken in settlement varies according to the method used, which may be either:

- **Document against acceptance (D/A)** The exporter agrees to extend some credit terms to the importer with payment being made a stipulated number of days after the acceptance of the document or another date stipulated in the draft, such as so many days after the date on the bill of lading. This implies considerable risk for the exporter, as he will not be paid until after the buyer has taken title to the goods.
- **Document against payment (D/P)** The exporter does not release the documents relating to the transfer of title until payment has been made. This case also

involves less risk for the exporter because he is expected to produce and ship the order before tendering the required documents for payment. If the buyer does not accept the documents and title to the goods at the order of the exporter, the supplier still controls the documents and may dispose of the goods.

Import consignment

The foreign supplier ships the goods to his Asian lawyer, places them in a customs designated bonded warehouse and entrusts a local agent with their sale subject to certain preconditions. After deducting a commission and other expenses, the agent makes payment for the goods to the foreign supplier.

Advance and interim payments

This simply means the exporter pays the importer through a series of installments, and is a method often used for large-scale machinery and equipment imports. Payment may be partly in advance and partly by credit, but in most cases, it is made by means of a fixed number of payments after delivery. This has advantages for the importer's cash flow. When a series of bills are guaranteed by a bank, they may be sold for cash (forfeiting). Default on a bill or refusal to accept a bill when presented is a serious matter. It is common practice for refused bills to be protested to enable a summary judgment according to local laws regarding Bills of Exchange.

GLOSSARY OF FINANCE AND DC TERMS

Back-to-back documentary letter of credit *A back-to-back or subsidiary credit is a commonly used method to help finance orders by middlemen. On receipt of the buyer's DC (the master DC), the trader opens a new DC mirroring the first (with some modifications as to the price and delivery time) for the benefit of the producer. The master DC is used as partial collateral to open another credit in favor of the producer, enabling the middleman to buy goods from that company and sell them to the buyer.*

Back-to-back DCs achieve the same result as transferable DCs but involve another DC and hence additional credit risk. The main differences are that under back-to-back DCs, the buyer might be unaware a second DC is issued against his master DC, and the second beneficiary (producer) cannot tender his own documents against the master DC, assists in the protection of the identity of the actual manufacturer.

Some banks require the applicant for a back-to-back DC to supply a pre-signed act of documents (draft, invoice, and other available documents) and Power of Attorney at the time of application so that in an emergency, the bank staff can type in all the specifications and details for the documents (based on the information in the documents submitted by the factory under the second DC) and negotiate the master DC straight away. This precaution is taken by the banks to avoid the possibility of a time default, which may occur because of delays between the time when the factory tenders its documents for payment under the back-to-back DC and the middleman substitutes his own draft, invoice and other documents for payment under the master DC. In this way, the banks reduce the risk of paying the exporter and then not being able to collect under the master DC because the middleman failed to comply with the documentary conditions of the master DC.

When documents do not conform to the credit, delays are inevitable. It is therefore important for the middleman to inform the buyer as soon as possible if the manufacturer is unable to comply with terms of the credit so that the necessary amendments to the DC can be negotiated.

Bill of exchange *A draft or check drawn on a party or bank which can be drawn at sight or demand, or be a usance draft (time draft) payable at a later date as stipulated on the draft.*

Deferred payment letter of credit (usance DC) *Under this arrangement, the importer takes delivery of the merchandise by accepting the documents and agreeing to pay after a fixed period of time (usually 30 to 120 days after the date on the bill of landing or date documents are "sighted at sight"). The issuing bank makes arrangements with the negotiating or third party bank to purchase the bills to finance the transaction or supplier often discounts the DC with the negotiating bank to obtain funds in advance of maturity of the bills. On maturity, the issuing bank reimburses the negotiating bank the full face amount of the credit plus any interest agreed upon. The fees and interest charges are negotiable and can be to the exporter's or the importer's account.*

Drafts *A bill exchange or bank check, which can be drawn at sight or demand, or be post-dated (usurance draft).*

Packing credits *An exporter who has a credit line with the bank can take the importer's irrevocable documentary letter of credit and get "packing credits" from his bank – a type of advance is used to pay for cost incurred to production of the goods.*

Packing credits involve an agreed-to arrangement between the supplier and his bank once the firm order is in hand. Packing credits perform a similar function to "Red Clause" letters of credit except that the importer is not necessarily aware of the arrangement and is not directly involved with it.

Red clause letter of credit *A Red Clause DC is sometimes used to provide an exporter with funds prior to shipment to enable the exporter to tool-up, purchase raw materials or hire workers. The credit includes a special clause that authorizes the advance of some funds to the beneficiary prior to presentation of final documents.*

To receive the advance, which can be for the full amount or any stipulated part thereof, the exporter presents a sight draft to the negotiating bank and signs a statement of receipt that the advance is drawn when the required documentation is tendered within the stipulated time. If documents are not presented to the advising bank, the advising bank can still claim reimbursement from the issuing bank for advances made.

Revolving documentary letters of credit *A revolving letter of credit is one that can be automatically restored to its original amount without requiring an amendment to the DC. Such credits can revolve in relation to "time" or "value."*

A revolving credit based on time means that the amount may be automatically available to the supplier during a stipulated period of time. For example, the credit may be used for US$25,000 for six months (allowing for five incremental shipments). The US$25,000 covers the first shipment, with the stipulation that upon successful negotiation of the documents the credit is restored to US$25,000 for another 30 days to cover the second shipment, and so on for a total of five shipments within six months. The value of the credit does not become cumulative unless expressly stated as such in the credit terms, but from the bank's perspective, the liability is the sum of the individual amounts available. Also, the importer can state in the conditions of the DC that, if the chain is broken and a shipment is not made on time, the credit will stop.

A revolving credit based on value means that the amount of the credit may be automatically reinstated upon utilization within a specified period of time. The funds are restored to the original amount upon presentation of the documents by the exporter, or after receipt of the documents by the issuing bank, whichever is stipulated by the buyer. For example, a revolving credit is opened for US$10,000 for four separate shipments to be made within a period of six months. This does not mean that each shipment must be for a value of US$10,000, for the value may fluctuate. The supplier ships US$7,000 worth of products one month; two months later he ships US$10,000 worth; and the next month US$6,000, etc. The value of the credit is restored to the original US$10,000 after each shipment is made within the time period and in compliance with the number of shipments stipulated in DC.

Revolving credits are always for less than the full value of the order (otherwise that would be a documentary letter of credit available by installments). This method is often used when a buyer is dealing with a buying agent, or direct with a manufacturer for a large order that will enable multiple shipments. Revolving credits are also used when buying merchandise that is prone to fluctuating raw material costs or when the export price is negotiated on an ongoing basis due to fluctuating foreign exchange rates. A revolving credit allows the importer to purchase goods when the market situation is favorable and save time and effort by not having to arrange new DCs for every shipment. Time is saved because the exporter does not have to wait for new DCs to be opened for each shipment.

However, there is considerable risk involved with revolving letters of credit because not all of the terms and conditions can be precisely stipulated at the time of opening the credit, such as the exact shipping dates or value of the shipments. Consequently, revolving DCs are usually not entered into unless both parties know each other well.

Standby documentary letters of credit *This is essentially a guarantee by another party or another bank giving the issuing bank the assurance that payment will be made for the DC the buyers wants to open. The main difference between the standby DC and a regular DC is that it may be drawn against by the execution of simple statement by the beneficiary for non-performance under a contract or agreement. "We, the beneficiary, do hereby certify that the buyer's outstanding with us as to date are X amount, and we hereby claim for payment of that amount."*

A standby letter of credit is a financial substitute. If anything should go wrong with the order, the buyer and his guarantor would be liable for any advances paid to the supplier.

Transferable documentary letters of credit *A transferable letter of credit allows the supplier to transfer all or part of the original DC once only to a second beneficiary. This second beneficiary cannot transfer the DC again to a third party. The second beneficiary (usually the manufacturer) can ship the merchandise ordered and then tender his own documents and invoice (commonly for an amount smaller than the value of the master DC to allow for the middleman's commission) to receive payment. Transferable letters of credit give the bank the right to draw documents from the secondary beneficiary to negotiate the DC straight away in the event the first beneficiary (the middleman) does not produce, or is unable to produce, the required documents to negotiate the master DC.*

Transferable DCs are issued only at the buyer's instruction, and any letter of credit that does not expressly permit transfer is considered as non-transferable. Furthermore, a transferable credit means only that the DC may be transferred and not necessarily that it will be transferred.

The use of transferable DCs is quite common when purchasing goods through a buying agent. The buyer can restrict the transferability of the DC by nominating the second beneficiary, when the name of the actual manufacturer is known. It should be noted that many buyers prefer to pay their buying agents by other methods rather than directing their finances through the middleman.

When using a transferable DC, the buyer is accepting the fact that the supplier he is dealing with may not be the actual manufacturer of the goods being purchased. The middleman will instruct the negotiating bank to substitute his name and address for the buyer's name and address on the DC to be transferred so that the second beneficiary (the factory) does not learn the identity of the buyer.

Trust receipts *These are sometimes called "bridging loans" or "merchandise loans" whereby the buyer and his bank enter into an arrangement as to how they will repay the bank for merchandise ordered that will be shipped under letter of credit, D/A or D/P payment terms. A trust receipt is a document signed by the buyer, on the strength of his credit line, with his bank. His bank obtains a security interest in the goods, and he obtains possession of the goods on a sort of consignment basis.*

When the merchandise arrives in his country, his bank allows him to take possession of the goods for resale, but the bank retains title to the goods. The buyer acts as a trustee of the bank and is required to keep the identity of these products, and the proceeds from their sales, separate from his other assets and to properly care for and insure the merchandise until it is sold.

In practice, however, this is generally not the case. Many buyers who negotiate trust receipts do not keep the merchandise and proceeds from their sales separate from other assets, such as the case with department stores where all the merchandise in the store is mixed and payment is made to the bank out of general funds when the receipt is due. Some banks, therefore, will only grant trust receipts for merchandise over which they can exercise some control.

When using trust receipts, the buyer is required to pay back the bank within the period stipulated in the arrangement, along with any interest charges due, or the bank can repossess the merchandise.

PROSPECTING IN JAPAN – product mapping

If you want to be in control during the distributor selection process, you have to know what end-users you intend to target, what they look for in products such as yours, what the competition has to offer, and what standards are expected of you. Then, and only then, analyze your channel options (see Prospecting in Japan – channel mapping*).*

THE BASICS

Goals

Your main goals with respect to product are threefold:

- Define the end-user: who, what, when, where and why do they buy?
- Study the competition: Who exports to Japan products similar to your own? Who are the main Japanese producers? What distribution channels do both of them use? What is the pricing structure?
- Evaluate what standards your product must satisfy to succeed in Japan: adaptation, distinctiveness, delivery, price, quality, service and transparency.

These goals may seem daunting and you will almost certainly have to rely on a market research firm to get some answers; but successful exporters often recommend that you do as much of the research as you can to build up a network of useful contacts. I will discuss market research firms in the next chapter. (See Prospecting in Japan – channel mapping.)

Market entry

End-users, competition and standards have to be analyzed in the context of your overall market entry goals. Put simply, are you aiming for a niche market or a mass market?

Most successful exporters, small and medium ones especially, aim for a **niche market** and grow from there. Niche marketing means that you concentrate your firepower. You don't market all your products; you only push the one or two items with the biggest edge over the competition. You don't launch your product across Japan; you aim instead for a portion of Tokyo, a regional market such as Kyushu, or the city of Osaka. And once the target is set, you give the launch all the backup you can to insure a good foothold. That is how Japan's export champions penetrated the U.S. market, starting first with California and only expanding further afield when an acceptable share of that market had been acquired.

Some North American managers are uncomfortable with niche-oriented strategies because they involve more market study, limited market shares, small-batch production and accelerated product development. Their ideal is a Universal Product – Big Macs, M&Ms, Coca Cola – aimed at a **mass market**. Only the wealthiest of multinationals can afford this strategy in Japan because it invites immediate countermeasures from the competition.

- Competition for a mass market in Japan is much more intensive than the North American norm because it is market-share driven, not profit-driven (see The Birth of a Growth Machine: 1945-1970).
- Japanese companies routinely rush out instant imitations of the competition's newest products, a process known as product covering. This is actually part of a larger phenomenon – called product churning (see Japanese Distribution Management – the outside view) – whereby new products are introduced in a "shotgun" fashion that cuts out the need for advanced market research. For instance, over 1,000 new soft drinks appear every year, 99% of which vanish within a few months.

Unless your product is wildly successful, niche marketing sidesteps or at least postpones these problems. It is therefore the strategy I focus on in this book.

Language

In most cases, language will not be a problem during the early stages if you concentrate on foreign contacts working in Japan or on organizations set up to serve foreigners. Interviewing end-users or wholesalers, on the other hand, often requires the services of an interpreter. The best way to minimize this added expense is to gather as much information as possible from English speakers before approaching other groups, and limit your Japanese interviews to a few key points. Whatever happens, don't let language stand in the way of getting the information you need.

WHERE TO GO

Government

The first stop for many is to visit their country's embassy in Tokyo or its trade office in Osaka (see Annex 6). In most cases, this is a very wise step. Foreign trade commissions advise thousands of business visitors every year and have enough clout to open many doors. Distribution is usually the responsibility of the local staff because of their knowledge of Japanese and local business practices. Make a point of befriending these local officers; their advice can be very valuable.

JETRO

Reference has already been made to the services available from JETRO's worldwide network of offices (see Doing your Homework and Annex 2). Their head office in Tokyo is definitely worth visiting for information on competing products and foreign import channels. Their market studies of popular import items are as good as anything available from most market research firms. Where consultants do a better job is with complex, specialized products requiring tailor-made reports.

Two other report-producing Japanese organizations worth visiting are MIPRO and the ASEAN Center:

Manufactured Imports Promotion Organization (MIPRO)
World Import Mart Bldg.
6F, 1-3 Higashi-Ikebukuro
3-chome, Toshima-ku, Tokyo 170
Tel: (03) 3971-6571
Fax: (03) 3988-2791

ASEAN Center
Central Bldg.
4-10-3 Ginza
Chuo-ku, Tokyo 104
Tel: (03) 3546-1221

Because of the large number of business visitors these three organizations receive everyday, you cannot expect from them the same level of individualized attention and follow-up that your country's embassy can provide.

Foreign business associations

Whether the individuals heading these organizations (see Annex 9) have expertise in your product category depends a lot on the person involved. Chambers of commerce and trade associations are first and foremost networking forums designed to inform and defend their members by exchanging data and acting as industry-watchers. Used with care, they can be a good source of contacts.

Japanese business associations

Although many of these associations (see Annex 8) claim to be willing to help foreigners, they are rarely organized to do so efficiently and often refer you back to JETRO. It is wise therefore to concentrate first on what JETRO and your trade officials have to offer and refer to Japanese associations only for very specific items like some data or a contact when someone known to them has given you an introduction.

Banks

Foreign banks, especially those heavily involved in trade financing, can be a very useful source of advice and contacts. Japanese banks have excellent reports on various industries. Unfortunately, most are only available in Japanese.

Sogo shosha

As long as you steer away from any negotiations and cross-check what you are told, Japan's general trading firms can be a very useful source of data and advice, particularly if your product is compatible with the ones they already carry. To meet the right people, make sure you visit their North American branch offices nearest to you before going to Japan in order to get proper introductions.

Foreign transnational distributors

Much of what is said about the *sogo shosha* also applies to this group (see Types of Distributors and Annex 11).

To find out more about them, check the most recent ACCJ Membership Directory or those of the European Business Community in Japan (EBC) and the Canadian Chamber of Commerce in Japan (CCCJ). Most of these distributors are specialized in industrial products.

Small distributors

Small distributors should be avoided at this stage because they have no time to waste offering free information. Worse still, if they are interested in your product, they will urge you over lavish meals to stop wasting your time with research and entrust everything to them. Accepting such offers amounts to playing Russian roulette with your product.

Retail chains

Department stores, supermarkets, convenience stores and specialty store chains (see The Retail Environment) all have purchasing departments filled with people willing to look over your product and offer advice. Tell them beforehand that you are there to study the market, not negotiate a deal. Make a point, too, of visiting their stores to see what products similar to your own are selling and at what price.

Market research firms

Consultants (see Annexes 12 and 13) are willing to tolerate a certain amount of brain picking by prospective clients and you should take every opportunity to meet as many of them as you can. They are an especially good source of off-the-record information on consumer products and trends.

Law and accounting firms

Another good source of contacts are law and accounting firms, especially if your lawyer or accountant has some pre-existing connection with them. Accountants generally have a deeper understanding of their clients' business activities than lawyers. Pay most attention to lawyers and accountants who do the deal-making for the firm: they are the best-informed sources.

Academia

Universities and technical institutes can often be an excellent source of information on industrial purchasing and occasionally on consumer products and trends.

DEFINE THE END-USER

The only way to ensure that you remain in the driver's seat throughout the distributor selection process is to have a firm grasp of who your target customers are before the negotiation process begins. Done well, it should leave you with a good idea of which distribution mechanism is best for you and provide a short list of distributors who are perceived to do a good job with products similar to your own.

The textbook way to classify their behavior is still the best: who, what, when, where and why do they buy?

Who?

Who purchases products similar to yours? What is their age, income bracket, educational level, mobility, etc.? If you target industrial buyers, is decision-making highly centralized or is there plenty of *nemawashi* across several departments? Which companies have shown an interest in imported products similar to yours?

What?

What are the attributes Japanese end-users look for in a product similar to yours? Prioritize them. What is the trade-off between cost and quality or cost and brand image? What lot sizes are most popular among buyers?

When?

What is the near-, mid- and long-term outlook on the economy by end-users? How might this influence purchasing? What are the seasonal sales variations for your product category? When and how frequently do end-users prefer to buy? Every day, twice a week, once a month?

Where?

Where do your target customers do their purchasing? Are they willing to go some distance to find what they want or will they take whatever is available in the neighborhood store? Do they like to buy from general stores or do they prefer to purchase products similar to your own from smaller specialized retailers? Is the store's location in an upscale part of town important? The same type of questions can be asked of industrial buyers. Are they bound by *keiretsu* ties to always purchase from a short list of potential sellers? Do their purchasing managers prefer to source certain products from certain countries for reasons other than price?

Why?

What is the most cost-effective stimulus to purchase? Editorials in specialized trade journals? Certain trade fairs? Personalized visits? Mail order? The right shelf space in supermarket chains? Why do industrial buyers purchase Product X out of a list of "equivalent" offerings? Image? Long-term business ties? Better after-sales service?

The middlemen

Don't let end-users' preferences, important as they are, blind you to the fact that importers, wholesalers and retailers have their own reasons for rejecting certain imported products before they even reach their intended target. As a result, "trade perception studies" have become an increasingly important part of knowing the Japanese market. These are normally conducted by market research firms (see next chapter) who question a sample group of middlemen about their perception of your product's strengths and weaknesses compared to those of competing Japanese and foreign products already on the market.

STUDY THE COMPETITION

If you have followed my advice so far, your diligent efforts will have uncovered plenty of data on your main Japanese competitors and the overall size of the market for your product category. It is their products and the service levels they provide that will determine how distributors and end-users perceive what you have to offer. Take the time to study them thoroughly.

If you conclude that your product is still competitive on its own, you still face the issue of representation and service, both of which put you at a great disadvantage compared to Japanese competitors with established distribution networks. To improve your chances of success, it is more instructive to investigate how foreign exporters in your product category have solved the problems now confronting you. After all, they once were as handicapped as you are.

- How large is their market share? What is the saturation rate?
- Who are the major players? How long have they been there?
- Is their market share (as opposed to that of Japanese competitors) growing? How fast?
- What are their distribution strategies? Why? Which ones seem to be working? What role does distribution play in differentiating their products?

PRODUCT EVALUATION

Evaluating a foreign product's potential for the Japanese market involves much more than the product alone. Marketing failures frequently happen because foreign marketers think they are selling one thing, while the Japanese feel they are buying another. The most contentious issues usually center on seven factors: product adaptation, distinctiveness, delivery, price, quality, service and transparency. If you wonder how successful exporters make a profit after paying for all of these things, the answer is simple: they charge for it! The Japanese do it. So should you.

Adaptation

It's been repeated to death, but many exporters fail in Japan because they refuse to alter their products to better fit local needs and customs.

Generally speaking, most Japanese are physically smaller than North Americans. Their houses and apartments are also tinier. Western furniture and household appliances stand a better chance to succeed, therefore, if they occupy less space and are multipurpose. Remember, too, that voltage and water pressure may differ and that Japan uses the metric system, not feet and inches.

Japanese sensitivities to colors, fabrics, odors and tastes are also different. Where else can one find squid pizza or seaweed-flavored French fries? They also lavish a great deal of attention on boxes and wrappings, especially for gift items. Poorly designed packaging will kill the best of products.

Distinctiveness

It has often been said that your product has to be unique to stand a chance in the Japanese market. This is an obvious exaggeration; Japan's trade statistics are filled with thousands of examples of commonplace imports doing very well in that market. Indeed, how many products in this world are truly "unique"?

What is true is that successful imports generally have a competitive advantage. The advantage may be price in the case of products coming from developing countries; it may be a tied distribution network; it may be snob appeal arising from extensive advertising; or it may be technical or design superiority. It is rarely one single factor.

The point to remember for North American exporters is that their manufactured products generally lose out when pitted against similar products coming from the Asian NICs unless they are distinctive in some way: more advanced, more efficient, better designed, and so on. Competing on price alone, except for certain product categories where we have a natural comparative advantage, is very hard and rarely worth the effort.

Delivery

No matter how impressed Japanese manufacturers and distributors are with your product, your relations with them will quickly sour if you fail to maintain prompt and regular deliveries. The reason is simple. Most manufacturers and wholesalers have very little storage space and depend on just-in-time (JIT) delivery to run their businesses. Indeed, this is one reason why there are so many wholesalers in Japan; retailers like to have them nearby for quick small-batch deliveries. Given the relatively underdeveloped state of Japan's transportation and warehousing infrastructure, exporters have to investigate the costs – money and time – inherent in different transport options.

Delivery of North American products are often hampered by exporters' sloppy attention to transit and customs documentation. Vague product descriptions attract higher tariffs, more inspections and expensive delays. These situations are particularly common with first shipments. Take the trouble to visit ports and shipping agents to find out what is required. Remember that customs bureaus in Japan's ports and airports are little independent kingdoms with wide discretionary powers when interpreting the law. Showing up before your first shipment to show your product and get advice is time well spent.

Price

This is an area where big exporters have a definite advantage over small ones in the Japanese market. The best approach, according to most marketing specialists, is to adopt a price – not necessarily a low one – that gives you an advantage over the competition, and then accept whatever is left after the middlemen (importers, wholesalers, retailers) have taken their customary margins. Penetration pricing is a big company strategy. Its goals are rapid growth in market share and cost advantages arising from large-volume production. Small exporters, on the other hand, use cost-plus pricing. Prices are determined not by the market, but by tagging on an acceptable profit to the cost of manufacturing and shipping. That leaves very few options other than licensing when prices are too high for the Japanese market.

Pricing has also become a problem for exporters of high-end consumer products. During the "bubble" years (1985-90) Japan was a bonanza for many exporters of luxury items. Sole import agents were doing everything possible to increase the snob appeal of their foreign products. The result was prestige pricing and parallel imports (see Weak Points and Trouble Spots) in the short term and a big drop in sales volume during the '90s.

Quality

Conflicts over quality between Western suppliers and Japanese buyers reflect different manufacturing traditions. North American manufacturers think in terms of volume production out of which customers select – and pay for – the quality level that suits their needs. Japan's production ethos is much closer to its roots in traditional craftsmanship. Everything has to be custom-made for the buyer and of consistent high quality. Products are an extension of the maker's "face," objects whose degree of perfection reflects the producer's moral character. To perform substandard work is to be shamed before one's peers.

The Japanese are therefore fanatical about quality not only with respect to the product's ability to function but also its cosmetic qualities. Buyers are turned off by machinery or consumer goods with scratches, uneven painting or other blemishes. Whole containers of beer have been shipped back because of labels scraped in transit. The Japanese believe that such seemingly superficial defects point to deeper product flaws or at least show the producer's lack of commitment to them – a moral failing. As a result, one bad shipment can erase the positive impression of a dozen good ones. Regularity is very highly valued.

Service

The distinction between manufacturing and service industries has always been blurry in Japan. Every product, no matter how humble, carries with it certain expectations of service. A good consumer item, for example, might sell poorly in nondescript stores and do much better in the plush surroundings of a department store surrounded by uniformed sales personnel. Note, too, that Japanese-style service might not be what North Americans would spontaneously go for. For instance, a sales girl might be taking all the time required to wrap a given item perfectly, oblivious to the line of customers with purchases in hand waiting for their turn. You have to find out for yourself what is expected.

The notion of hierarchy implicit in Japanese-style service is even more difficult for many Western exporters to accept. As I explained earlier (see Japanese Distribution Management –

the inside view), the Japanese believe that sellers, be they Japanese or foreigners, owe their living to buyers and, as such, are further down the social ladder. Sellers are a rung below buyers and two rungs below end-users. The exporter's first instinct to ask "why?" whenever there is a complaint is therefore all wrong. You had better apologize profusely and show the right attitude before inquiring discreetly what went wrong. Assurances that it will not happen again are not enough. You have to apologize first.

Transparency

Depending on how one views Japanese-style subcontracting (see Industrial Purchasing), this section could just as well be titled "trust" or "dependency." Whereas price, quality and delivery are the only factors at play in North American subcontracting, Japanese buyers insist on knowing everything possible about their suppliers.

After developing our own anti-rust processes, we contacted Honda and Toyota. Both companies told us that we had to choose between them. Supplier relationships had to be exclusive. Moreover, the price of entry was complete transparency; our technology had to be shared with other suppliers in exchange for guaranteed orders.

We manufacture particle wood boards used by Japan's construction industry. To be accepted, however, we had to let their technicians visit our plant and answer all their questions, even with regards to glue composition, one of our most closely guarded technologies. In exchange, their technicians were willing to make suggestions on possible improvements, many of which were very useful. At present, we are very closely tied into our buyer's supply needs across the Pacific. We fax him production reports three times a day. It's uncanny sometimes because they know so much about us that they occasionally warn us of upcoming and unanticipated production problems.

Supplier relationships have many advantages, but they do also entail some squeezing when demand takes a downturn.

PROSPECTING IN JAPAN – channel mapping

Assuming that the product-mapping process described in the previous chapter has convinced you that your product could be successful in the Japanese market, your next step is to check out what your distribution alternatives are. Channel selection is extremely important in Japan. Indeed, talk of "value-added" products often blinds exporters to the fact that a well-selected and well-managed distribution channel can sometimes give you more bang for your buck than product originality alone could.

TRADE-OFFS

This same product-mapping process will also have provided you with a short list of highly-regarded importers and wholesalers, as well as some estimates of possible sales targets for the first year. None of these makes any sense, however, unless decisions have been taken with respect to some of the trade-offs involved.

Large vs. small distributors

As we saw earlier (see Types of Distributors), large distributors such as the *sogo shosha* have plenty of trained personnel, money and clout. Unfortunately, their very size frequently condemns your product to neglect and leaves you powerless to change the situation.

Smaller distributors, on the other hand, may have the enthusiasm, but their limited contacts and disorganized marketing methods often require plenty of support from exporters – training, communication, longer payment periods, travel, and so on – to keep them on track.

Large vs. small territories

This is not an issue for exporters whose target market is small, dispersed and highly demanding. In such cases, exclusivity for the whole of Japan is usually granted to a single distributor. Many other exporters, however, have the option of limiting their entry to a geographically defined niche market. Osaka Prefecture, for instance, could be an excellent target for an exporter's initial foray into the Japanese market. It has a population of over eight million people and lies at the heart of the Kansai, a region with a Gross Regional Product (GRP) greater than Canada's GNP.

Aiming for the whole of Japan from Day One obviously has great appeal; but unfortunately, most distributors are strong in one region only and even then, only within a certain network. Moreover, a smaller geographical target allows you to focus your support in a much more powerful way than you could for the whole country.

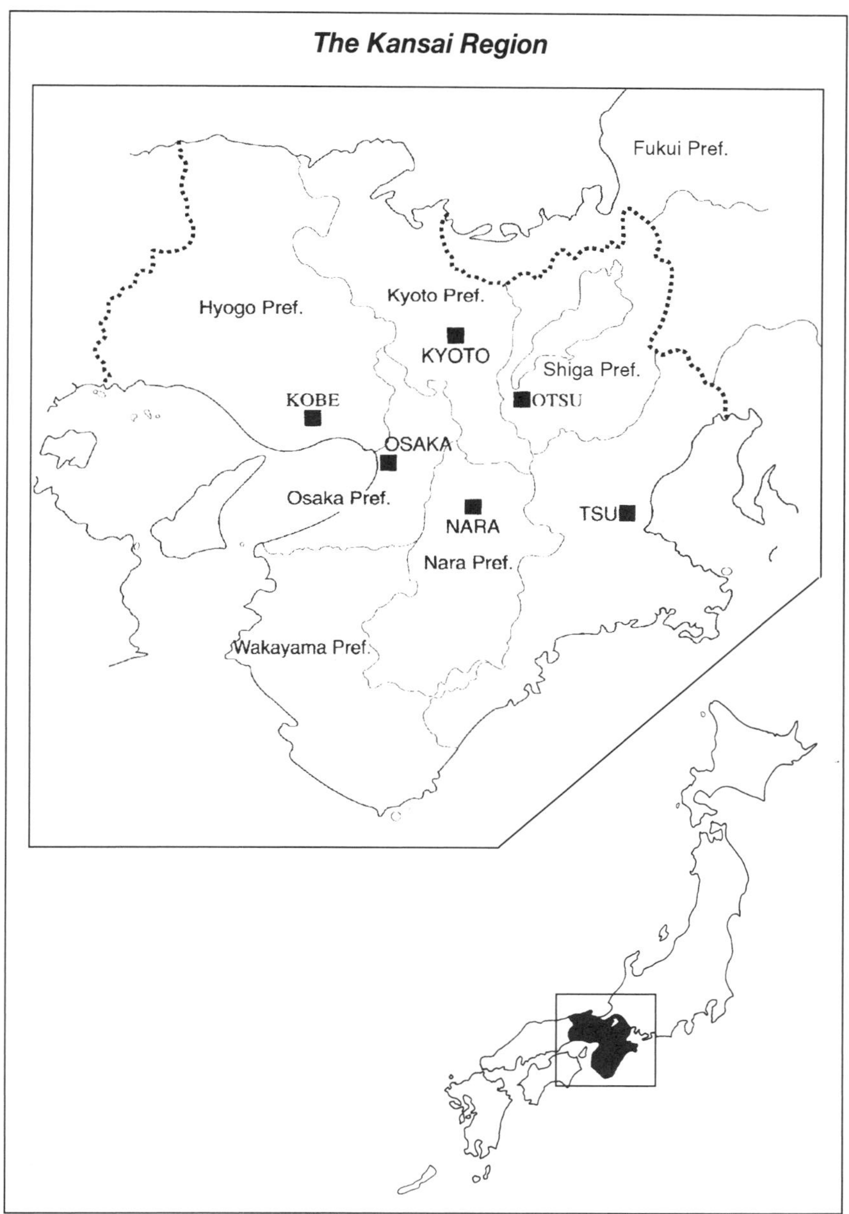
The Kansai Region
Fukui Pref.
Kyoto Pref.
Hyogo Pref.
KYOTO
Shiga Pref.
KOBE
OTSU
OSAKA
Osaka Pref.
NARA
TSU
Nara Pref.
Wakayama Pref.

Push vs. pull

You will have to find a balance between push and pull strategies that is right for your product and your pocketbook. **Push** refers to margins, rebates, discounts, minimum order quantities, and encouragement – whatever can be done to get importers, wholesalers and retailers to promote your product instead of simply stocking it. **Pull** refers to incentives, such as advertising, directed at end-users to increase demand. Both are needed for most products, but a balance has to be struck.

Both will cost you. Push requires market study, careful channel selection, constant vigilance, more travel and communication. Pull may increase demand, but it can also be very expensive as distributors rarely chip in.

Degree of involvement

This is perhaps the most fundamental trade-off of all. Do you see your relationship with the distributor as a division of labor allowing you to forget about Japan and concentrate on your domestic market, or do you want to remain active in Japan with a distribution partner helping you go further and faster than you could on your own?

As we saw earlier (see Some Fundamentals), exporting for many small and medium companies is treated as a stop-gap measure designed to pick up slack when domestic demand is weak. Consequently, the kind of distribution partner they hope to find in Japan is one who can make do with whatever margins the market will allow after the exporter has been paid. Talk of product alteration, distribution strategies or even of market study is distasteful to them. Many, therefore, willingly "throw their product over the wall" and turn to Japan's large *sogo shosha* for help even though such intermediaries end up pocketing much of the profit.

This book is not written for them. I am concerned with exporters interested in building a long-term business presence in Japan – step by step.

CHANNEL ANALYSIS

First principles

It is easy to be sidetracked by details and wishful thinking when considering distribution options. The key principles to keep in mind always are:

- **There is no such thing as *the* Japanese distribution system**, a single tube through which every product must go through. Distribution channels, margins, rebates, product flows, and buyer-seller relations can differ markedly from sector to sector and product to product. The distribution channels for capital goods, for example, are generally far shorter and less complex than those associated with consumer goods.
- **Middlemen** (importers, wholesalers and retailers) **are independent businesses**, not hired links in a chain forged by foreign exporters.

- **Few Japanese middlemen actively market anything.** They act primarily as purchasing agents for their downline customers, and only secondarily as selling agents for their suppliers.
- A Japanese middleman's competitiveness comes from welding a family of items into a packaged assortment for a specific group of customers. **His selling efforts are therefore directed primarily at obtaining orders for the assortment, rather than for individual items.** For instance, hybrid pricing is common among middlemen because Japanese buyers like to purchase multiple products as a group from one supplier. As a result, middlemen often meet this need by bundling different products and services into units and later work out the profitability allocation to various departments or product lines within their own organizations. Similarly, the return of unsold items by retailers is best understood as a trade of goods. Competition for shelf space is such, that a wholesaler must replace what isn't selling well or risk losing space to products from other wholesalers. Hence his focus on a family of goods, as opposed to individual items.
- **You can eliminate the middleman but you cannot eliminate his functions.** Except in the case of direct marketing, attempts by individual exporters to bypass intermediaries usually prove futile because of the services over a wide assortment of products each distribution level performs for channel members directly above and below them. Whatever the future may hold for Japan's distribution system, don't waste your time trying to change it; rather, learn to use it to your own advantage.
- **Most successful exporters, therefore, seek to piggyback on entrepreneurial distributors who already call on their target customer groups.** They have no illusions that Japanese distributors will stray far from existing accounts because of a single new product.

Margins

The first thing to look for is the margin breakdown for your product category in a few target markets because they have a direct bearing on how much money you will be making. Figure 4-3 and Table 4-4 give a hypothetical example with two toys sold in Tokyo, one imported and one domestic. These margins might differ in other cities such as Osaka, but they are often fixed by custom, give or take 5 percent. Other factors influencing margins are the size and frequency of shipments, the current sales situation and buyer-seller relationships. In many cases, the margin increases the closer the product gets to the end-user.

If you examine Table 4-4, you will notice that the whole distribution margin for imported toys (67%) is higher than that of domestic toys (45%). Why is that? One important reason is that wholesalers of foreign goods must assume marketing functions Japanese manufacturers keep for themselves. The same rationale applies to sole import agents who advertise and apply for patents.

Product flows

The second important factor to look at when analyzing distribution options is product flows both at the sector level and for each of your main competitors.

Assume, for example, that you hope to export a processed food to Japan. Assume that your product category, like most processed foods, is sold both to retailers (supermarkets, department stores) and to institutional users (restaurants, office cafeterias, food caterers). A sector-level product flow breakdown might give you Fig. 4-5, a useful tool when analyzing similar data about individual companies. It also says something about the relative power of channel members with respect to your product category; the larger the percentages bypassing secondary wholesalers the greater the domination exercised by a few large retail chains or institutional buyers.

Figure 4-3

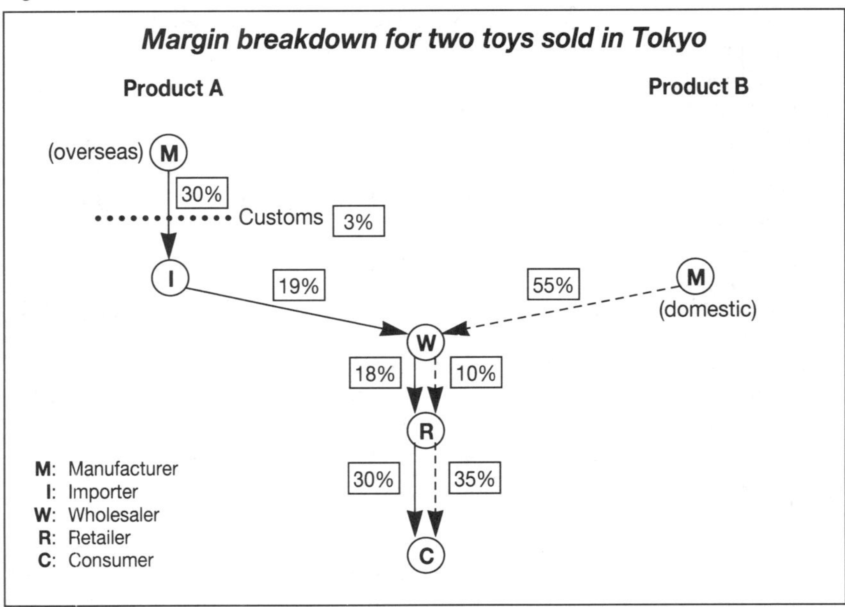

Table 4-4

MARGIN BREAKDOWN

Product A: Imported toy retailing for approx. ¥ 8,000
Product B: Domestic toy retailing for approx. ¥ 10,000

		A	B	
CIF		*30%*	—	
Customs duty & excise tax		*2%*	—	
Customs related expenses		*1%*	—	
TOTAL	*(x)*	*33%*	*55%*	*(Maker's price and shipment expenses)*
Sole import agent margin		*19%*	—	
Wholesaler(s) margin		*18%*	*10%*	
Retailer margin		*30%*	*35%*	
RETAIL PRICE	*(y)*	*100%*	*100%*	

Whole distribution margin = y–x = 67% for A
45% for B

A similar breakdown of your main Japanese competitor's distribution flow could produce Fig. 4-6. Manufacturer A's strategy obviously targets high-volume cost-conscious retail chains and institutional buyers. Department stores, restaurants and hotels purchase only negligible amounts. With this kind of information about your key competitors in hand, distribution becomes less of a mystery, and you are much better placed to plot your own niche strategy intelligently.

Channel leadership

Distribution channels can vary greatly from one product category to another. Some may be very stable and conservative – fixed margins, little turnover in personnel, and an unwillingness to explore alternative channels. Others may be contracting because of excessive discounting (i.e., price wars) or a growing gray market. The situation for most products is somewhere in between.

The third factor you must focus on, after margins and product flow, is channel leadership: Which intermediary should you focus your attention on? Who has the greatest ability to "push" your product within the geographical limits you have set for yourself? The channel leaders for many products in Japan have usually

Figure 4-5

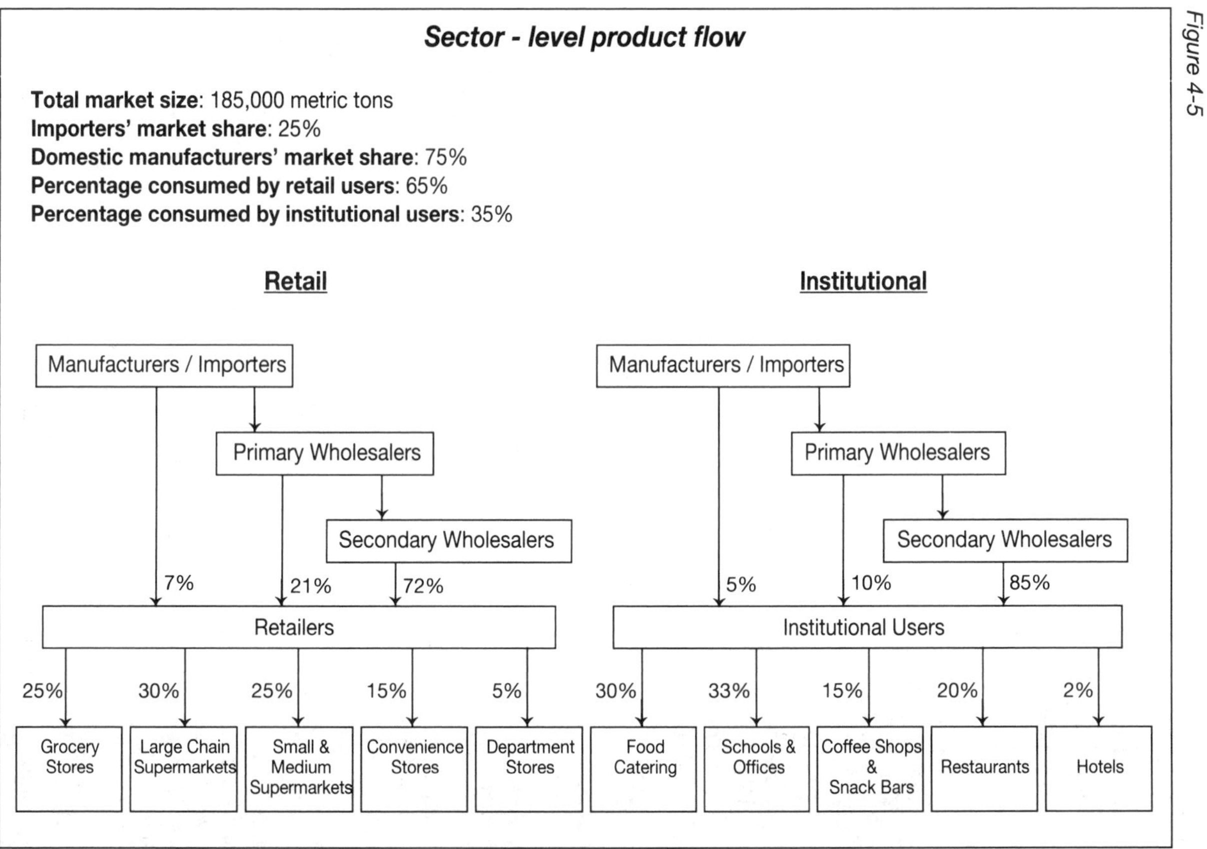
Sector - level product flow
Total market size: 185,000 metric tons
Importers' market share: 25%
Domestic manufacturers' market share: 75%
Percentage consumed by retail users: 65%
Percentage consumed by institutional users: 35%
Retail
Institutional
Manufacturers / Importers
Primary Wholesalers
Secondary Wholesalers
7%
21%
72%
Retailers
25%
30%
25%
15%
5%
Grocery Stores
Large Chain Supermarkets
Small & Medium Supermarkets
Convenience Stores
Department Stores
Manufacturers / Importers
Primary Wholesalers
Secondary Wholesalers
5%
10%
85%
Institutional Users
30%
33%
15%
20%
2%
Food Catering
Schools & Offices
Coffee Shops & Snack Bars
Restaurants
Hotels

Figure 4-6

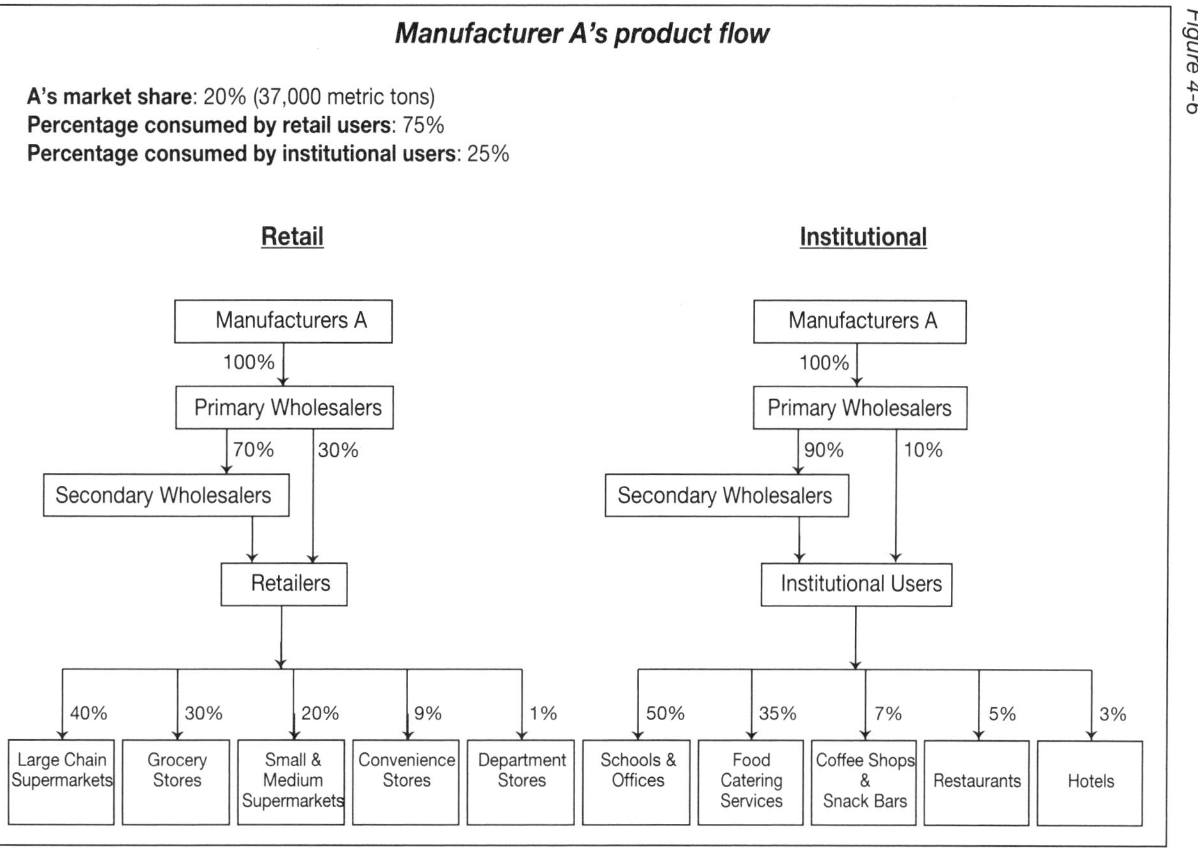
Manufacturer A's product flow
A's market share: 20% (37,000 metric tons)
Percentage consumed by retail users: 75%
Percentage consumed by institutional users: 25%
Retail
Manufacturers A
100%
Primary Wholesalers
70%
30%
Secondary Wholesalers
Retailers
40%
Large Chain Supermarkets
30%
Grocery Stores
20%
Small & Medium Supermarkets
9%
Convenience Stores
1%
Department Stores
Institutional
Manufacturers A
100%
Primary Wholesalers
90%
10%
Secondary Wholesalers
Institutional Users
50%
Schools & Offices
35%
Food Catering Services
7%
Coffee Shops & Snack Bars
5%
Restaurants
3%
Hotels

been well-established domestic manufacturers. It is they who establish support systems for wholesalers and retailers: rebates, in-channel promotions, etc. (see Japanese Distribution Management – the outside view). Foreign exporters are by definition absent, and importers usually cannot create support systems that can match those of domestic manufacturers. The result is that imported products are often sold on a spot basis in very small batches, strictly as either very high-end or low-end products or for niche markets.

Some of this is unavoidable unless you set up a sales office in Japan and create your own distribution support system. Until then, you will have to focus your special incentives on channel members willing and capable of offsetting the power of local producers with imported products. That is what I mean by channel leaders.

The simplest leadership situation is the **retail-dominated channel**. For instance, a supermarket or convenience store chain might give you an acceptable offer, in which case your product will be shipped through importers and wholesalers determined by them, not you. In other cases, your relationship with institutional buyers might resemble subcontracting (see Industrial Purchasing).

We export chilled beef to restaurant chains. The timing of our negotiations is largely driven by their menu changes every six months. And, each time we do our best to put a Canada Beef logo on the menu to create some brand loyalty among the restaurant's customers. Whenever an agreement is settled, we ship our product trimmed to their specifications via import firms specified by them.

High-volume exporting is not possible with all retail-dominated channels; the large department stores, for example, are notorious for small orders, consignment selling, frequent requests for deep discounts and slow payments. The point to remember about retail-dominated channels is that your support and incentives should all be directed to the retail or institutional buyer, not their upstream import and wholesale firms.

The second option is rarely used by foreign exporters: **wholesale-dominated channels**. In certain cases, you may find that a secondary wholesaler is aggressively expanding in the geographical area you have targeted and that he is very interested in your product. Any deal with him would mean that your product would go through the import firm of his choice and be sold through smaller retail chains with whom he is connected. Selecting distributors at this level is not always easy because information on them is sometimes hard to verify. The two most common pitfalls exporters face are insufficient volume and expertise.

- It is vital that you choose a wholesaler whose network of retail clients can sell your product in sufficient volume. Low-volume sales make margins meaningless and force retailers to sell your product as an eye-catching discount item. Discounting in a few stores forces everyone else to do the same. Very soon, no one wants to carry your item. Remember, too, that long years of resale price maintenance among Japanese manufacturers (see Japanese Distribution Management - the outside view) have fostered the belief among many consumers that discount items are in some way inferior.

- You must consider your wholesaler's product specialty. Exporters ignorant of the wholesale industry sometimes select an inexperienced party or, worse still, choose several distributors at random. Poor wholesalers produce low sales volumes and scare away the really competent ones because of the discounting problem just mentioned.

The most common option by far is **importer-dominated channels** because most exporters assume that the firm importing an item does so because it intends to market it wherever customers can be found. In most cases, this is simply not possible because importers, like other Japanese intermediaries, buy for a pre-existing set of customers (see "first principles" above) and sell packaged assortments, not individual items. Many exporters seem blissfully unaware that in choosing an importer, they usually lock themselves into a particular wholesale and retail network which may or may not serve their niche strategy.

Multiple channels

The final factor exporters should look into is the possibility of multiple channels. The basic arguments against granting exclusivity are quite obvious. Multiple channels:

- give you a basis of comparison;
- protect you in the event of a distributor's bankruptcy or poor performance (you don't have to start at zero again);
- broaden your customer base because you are not limited to a single distributor's network.

On the other hand, many exporters claim that multiple channels rob distributors of any incentive to commit significant resources to a new product and this can harm you in a market such as Japan where service expectations are very high.

There is no absolute right or wrong answer here. Many factors have to be considered: products whose sales potential appears small and those requiring extensive market development or after-sales servicing all tend to fall into the hands of sole import agents. Multiple channels also raise the specter of channel conflict. Japanese wholesalers spend a large percentage of their time checking out who in their network has been approached by other wholesalers, matching offers, and generally warding off poachers of all kinds. Avoiding this is impossible, even with a good grasp of market dynamics before distributor selection and frequent travel afterwards to smooth out disputes. Most exporters therefore reject multiple channels as counter-productive and too burdensome unless they have a permanent presence in Japan capable of managing channel relations, such as a sales office.

Direct marketing is one alternative channel often acceptable to traditional intermediaries such as wholesalers and retailers (see Fig. 4-7). Some exporters use it to build a track record in Japan before selecting distributors (see Direct Marketing in Japan) and keep it up afterwards in part because of the leverage it gives them in negotiations.

MARKET RESEARCH FIRMS

Necessary

Product mapping (see previous chapter) and especially channel mapping in Japan is rarely easy. Language is one barrier. No less challenging is the evasiveness of most Japanese businessmen during interviews. Sharing information with strangers simply does not have a win-win image among the Japanese. Hence the need for hired research help (see Annex 12).

Most sales reps seriously looking for opportunities in Japan eventually turn to market consultants to save time and because their questions are too specific for JETRO. Their range of options at this point are very broad. All can be divided into three basic tiers.

Top tier

At the top end are management consultants and think tanks such as Booz Allen or Boston Consulting. These firms are interested in the broader strategic issues confronting large multinationals willing to pay US$100,000 and up for their advice. The quality of what they have to offer is now questioned by many companies because they are weak where it counts the most: the interpretation of industry-specific data and implementation. This is the kind of work they subcontract to the second tier.

Second tier

Sandwiched between the top and bottom ends of the consulting spectrum are a large number of Japanese firms and a few foreign ones largely concerned with industry-specific data. Both are very different.

The Japanese firms are generally much better at gathering data than at analyzing it to suggest specific actions. This is due in part to their many Japanese clients wanting numbers, not advice, from outsiders. Another factor at work, however, is the conceptual gap between Western marketing thought and the more tactical, more relationship-oriented Japanese approach to sales (see Japanese Distribution Management – the inside view). What percentage of women between 20 and 25 are buying product X? What new products is the competition coming out with? Who is my main rival playing golf with? Indeed, most domestic Japanese market research is either number crunching or industrial espionage. Grand strategies get short shrift.

Figure 4-7

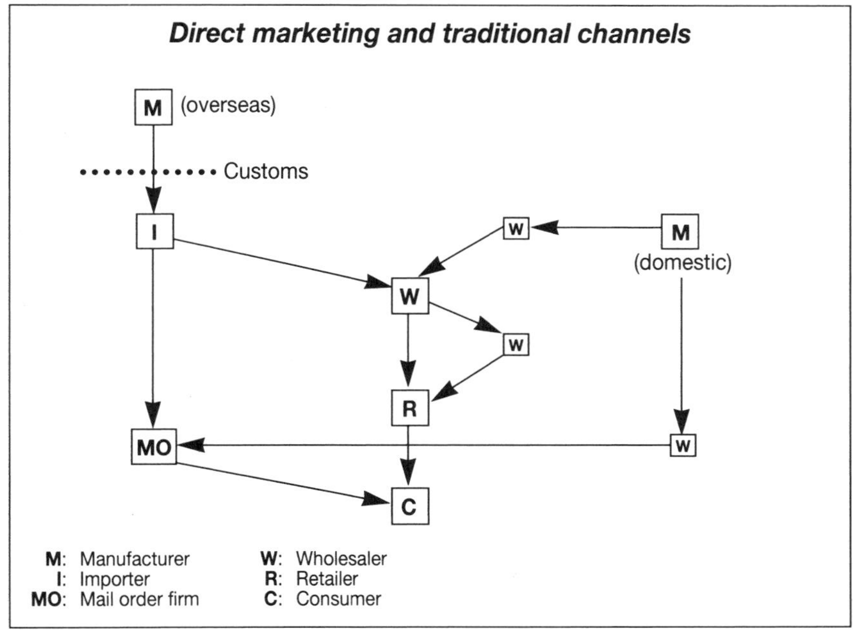

The Western firms, of course, are much more attuned to the requirements of foreign marketing executives and the best among them have almost 50% Japanese staff. Their price range for research projects is between US$40,000 and US$70,000.

Third tier

This last group is a miscellaneous collection of the superb and the ghastly. It includes translation firms and publishers as well as solo players, like lawyers, accountants and some retired foreign executives. Some of the Japanese firms are very popular with small foreign companies because they have plenty of English-speaking staff members, but their data may only be a rehash of old clippings. Some retired executives know a great deal about the industry they specialize in and can act as incubators for promising products. Most admit that detailed market research is something they farm out to others. Unlike second tier consultants, third tier firms mostly rely on published Japanese-language data; product-specific interviews in the industry are rarely thorough or may be skipped altogether. The price of research at this level varies between US$10,000 and US$35,000. The amount charged depends on the complexity of the research and the speed with which you want it done. That is true of all three levels.

Recommendations

As stated earlier, many exporters recommend that you do as much of the research and interviewing on your own as possible because it gives you a network of contacts and a "market sense" no report, however excellent, can give you.

Acquiring some contacts of your own has special value if you decide to hire a Japanese consulting firm to do your research. The Japanese are superb researchers and their services cost less than those of Western firms. However, their weakness in analysis makes it next to impossible to get a good usable report – as opposed to raw data – from them if you simply sit back and wait. To get the most out of a Japanese firm, you have to contribute to the research process and ask the right questions. It is very difficult to do that if you have not already done some basic spade work on your own.

More for less

The process of product mapping and channel mapping can take months, sometimes a year, because who you know in Japan is at least as important as what you know. Some exporters accomplish it by sending the same person to Japan for a series of visits. Others find more imaginative solutions.

You could, for example, set up a small joint office in Japan with four other North American companies whose products are compatible, not competitive, with your own. Finding the right person to do your common research and paying him for two years can be very cost-effective when the final bill is shared by five participants. Japan is full of highly competent Japanese managers with extensive international experience who have been forced to retire because of the demographic crunch now hitting middle management (see The Dual Face of Globalization: 1970-1995). There are also retired Western managers who speak Japanese and have lived there for many years. This kind of project only works, however, if all participants guarantee two years of support. One year is too short because such offices not only coordinate market research, but also select distribution channels and give them some support during the first crucial eight months when your product's fate is being decided.

DEVELOPING A SHORT LIST

By this stage, if you have followed my advice, the process of learning more about the end-user's needs, of product mapping and of channel mapping will have also produced a list of distributors in your product category who have a reputation for doing a good job. Everything you have learned so far, every contact you have made, will be of great value when negotiation starts in earnest. Now you need to have a closer look at your list of candidates.

PERILS OF PARTNERSHIP

A recap

Any kind of market research in Japan simultaneously generates so much information that it is easy to put the cart before the horse and forget what questions have to first be answered:

- Determine who your target end-users are and their service requirements.
- Examine your product to see what alterations if any are needed. Remember that every product, no matter how humble, has service expectations associated with it. Can the whole package be exported profitably?
- What channel alternatives do you have that can reach your target buyers and provide the required service levels? Are there elements within these channels sufficiently powerful to drive the rest of the system and attract most of your support?

The order is important and must be respected or you will drown in a mass of claims and meaningless figures.

The last two chapters were largely concerned with these three issues. It is time now to focus on the selection criteria you should use in evaluating potential distributors interested in your product. I assume that these importers or wholesalers are "channel leaders" (see previous chapter) in the sense that they have more power to "push" foreign products such as yours than any other channel member. If, like most exporters, you can only offer limited support, there is no point in wasting it on powerless or passive channel members. Reserve it for players who can make a difference.

Two approaches

Advice on how best to approach supplier-distributor relationships is frequently contradictory. Depending on who is speaking, exporters may be told that cultural norms in Japan make long-term relationships based on trust a precondition of success. Other experts believe that distributors, like used car salesmen, have a vested interest in starving their suppliers of information. What, then, is the attitude exporters should adopt when evaluating prospective distributors?

To clarify the issues involved, we can divide advice of this kind into two theoretically opposed, yet practically compatible, schools of thought: partnership versus carrot and stick.

The partnership school

Distributors, Japanologists and academic theoreticians of competitiveness are strong partisans of this approach. It encourages suppliers to aim for very close and long-term alliances with the distributors they select based on common goals and complementary strengths. They therefore deny any fundamental conflicts of interest between suppliers and distributors and point to the benefits of trust, early admission of mutual vulnerability, a win-win approach to negotiation, an open exchange of information, and active sharing of resources by both partners at every level (technology, personnel, promotion and advertising). Some will also add a cultural dimension to this line of reasoning by stressing that Japanese distributors have a cultural preference for long-term, highly personalized relationships.

The carrot and stick school

The opposite view holds that distributors should be kept at arm's length because their interests are, in some ways, fundamentally at odds with those of their suppliers.

- Distributors have a vested interest in limiting their suppliers' access to information. Information, after all, is ammunition the supplier can use to criticize his distributor's performance. Moreover, the less a supplier knows about the market, the more indispensable is the distributor.
- From the distributor's perspective, he is caught in a black widow relationship with his supplier: not only can he lose the account if he does poorly, he can also lose it if he succeeds too well and makes it worth the supplier's while to set up his own direct sales operation. The best defense therefore consists in stretching out his useful life by doing the bare minimum to keep the supplier happy and no more.
- From the supplier's perspective, his main competition may not be the Japanese products similar to his own being sold in Japan, but the many unrelated products being carried by his distributor. It is them, not the domestic competition, that limit his share of distributor resources. One of his key tasks, therefore, is to motivate his distributor's sales team to push his product as much as possible. As long as this does not negatively affect the distributor's network relations, no one in management should have any objections.

These and other conflicts of interest have led many successful exporters to apply a carrot and stick approach to distribution. The first rule initially is to be wary, not trusting. They accept the fact that information and opinions provided by distributors must be largely discounted because they are incomplete and self-serving.

They know that there is a basic conflict between their goal of rapidly increasing sales and the distributor's desire to keep them dependent as long as possible. Above all, these exporters believe that above-average performance from distributors does not happen spontaneously because both parties are "partners." It depends on performance-based, *quid pro quo* incentives for every level of the distribution team, and active courting by the supplier to insure that his products absorb more than their share of distributor resources. Hence the term "carrot and stick".

Our findings

The partnership model comes closest to the truth when a foreign firm enters a subcontracting relationship with a Japanese buyer (see Industrial Purchasing) or when the product being sold is complex enough to require a lot of pre-sale and after-sale coordination between an exporter and his distributor.

Apart from these situations, the carrot and stick approach is far more realistic, especially for small and medium enterprises new to Japan. Unless their products are so innovative as to offer extraordinary growth potential, large distributors will probably not be interested because the funds required to build up sales to profitable levels *for them* cannot be justified by the eventual returns. This means that small, hungry and (perhaps) naive players will almost always be better in the early days to painstakingly develop a niche market for new products because small distributors must get out and sell to survive. At the same time, they require more supervision and support by their suppliers, and respond very well to the carrot and stick approach.

However, scale does make a difference. Large overseas companies planning to eventually set up a wholly-owned subsidiary in Japan often try to penetrate the market in a big way during the early "arm's-length" phase (see Fig. 4-8) only to find that carrot and stick methods exercised from an overseas base cannot compete with the support packages devised by Japanese manufacturers to control distribution channels in their own market:

- Many of the most efficient wholesalers are already tied in with powerful domestic manufacturers. A superior foreign product at a superior price is not enough to make them switch overnight.
- The fact that so much distribution in Japan is based on credit diminishes wholesaler responsiveness to discounting by foreign exporters.

These companies are therefore most anxious to get over this phase as soon as possible and establish a local presence. As long as they remain overseas, Japan's peculiar combination of lethargic distribution and rapid product matching (see Weak Points and Trouble Spots) can make arm's length exporting very dangerous. As a result, their first set of distributors are chosen with modest performance

Figure 4-8

The goal is control

	Phase I Arm's-length exporting	**Phase II Initiate local presence**	**Phase III Consolidate local presence**
Objectives	• Test-try the company's products in Japan. • Establish an initial set of contacts in Japan. • Begin to build in-house Japan expertise.	• Internalize Japanese business practices. • Alter existing product lines to better fit Japanese requirements. • Build resources and skills to support an independent distribution strategy.	• Establish an independent business position. • Produce customized products for Japan. • Integrate Japanese R&D in worldwide business.
Operational consequences	• Sell products through one or more Japanese distributors. • Possibly a small 1-2 person branch office. • Possibly a joint venture.	• Initial investment in wholly-owned subsidiary *Sales* *Marketing* *Distribution* • Reevaluation and fine-tuning of joint venture	• More investment in wholly-owned subsidiary *Distribution* *R&D* *Manufacturing* • Phase out joint venture • More alliances with Japanese partners.
Time frame	2 - 5 years	2 - 5 years	5 - 10 years

expectations to last until a branch office is set up a year or two later.

DISTRIBUTION EVALUATION

Criteria

Selection criteria are not equally important for all products. Sales strength, for example, is crucial for consumer products and less so for capital goods where technical know-how and after-sales servicing facilities are key. The list of criteria used by successful exporters can be summarized as follows:

- **Market coverage** Remember the piggyback principle explained on page 185. What is his geographical coverage? How much of this is served by his sales force directly and how much is subcontracted to associated organizations? What is his industry coverage? Industrial buyers only deal with distributors who have an account with them. Who can't he sell to? Anyone who claims he can sell to everyone is almost certainly lying. How often do his salesmen visit clients?

- **Financial strength** Enough to insure that bills are paid but not so much as to kill their appetite for new products. Financial health is particularly important in Japan because credit is the backbone of its distribution system. Credit checks can be made through organizations such as Dun & Bradstreet (Japan) K.K., Nishiazabu Mitsui Bldg., 6F, 4-17-30 Nishiazabu, Minato-ku, Tokyo 106, Tel: 3-5485-0451, Fax: 3-5485-0646. (See Annex 15 for more firms.)
- **Sales strength** Number of sales agents (full- and part-time). Technical competence of its sales force. Given the face-to-face nature of Japanese-style selling (see Japanese Distribution Management – the inside view) numbers count for a lot.
- **Product lines** Any competing, compatible or complementary products? Avoid distributors with competing products. Compatible or complementary products are a definite plus because Japanese buyers like one-stop shopping. Consequently, distributors tend to sell packaged assortments rather than individual items.
- **Advertising and sales promotion programs** How much promotion is the distributor willing to pay for based on his margin? What level of advertising support does he expect you to provide? Do his exhibits stand out in trade fairs? Do his salesmen at these fairs know their products? What is the quality of his press releases and ads in national or industry magazines?
- **Warehousing and delivery** How many warehouses does he have? Where are they located? How big are they? Can they handle shipments efficiently? What is his strategic response to rising transportation costs and Japan's severe labor shortage? What size inventory does he keep for your product category? Is there an inventory minimum? How are his products delivered to wholesalers or retailers? How are records kept? Per item or some other sales unit? The ability to deliver quickly and in small lots is so crucial a competitive advantage in Japan that warehousing and delivery capacity has to be carefully checked.
- **Installation and repair services** What is his after-sales servicing track record? How good are his repair facilities? How many technicians does he have? What is their familiarity with your type of equipment?
- **Sales performance** What is his general record? What about the performance of products compatible with yours? What are his growth prospects? How able or willing is he to open new accounts? Does he need your participation to do that? How successful is he in reaching your target customers?

- **Reputation** Is he a "channel leader" with respect to foreign products in your category? Who are his other foreign suppliers and what do they think of his services? How about his downstream distributors? To what extent is he an active marketer, as opposed to being a passive order-taker?
- **Exclusivity** Does he insist on being a sole import agent? Can you restrict him to a geographical area with high potential sales such as Tokyo or Osaka? What if you limit him to only a portion of your product line? Are his activities compatible with your direct marketing activities in Japan?
- **Good government relations** In some sectors this is very important.
- **Training programs** What training programs, if any, does he organize for his sales force? Can a foreign supplier participate?
- **Leverage** Given sales projections both of you agree are realistic for your product in the next year or two, how big a part of his business will you become? Is your product strategically important for him or is it a mere add-on item?
- **Transparency** How willing is he to share data on customers, the sales force, inventory levels or delivery schedules?
- **Sales compensation** What is it? Can you give special bonuses to high performers?
- **Ordering and payments** Do his procedures make sense to you?
- **Quotas** What is his attitude towards action quotas (visits per week, etc.) and sales quotas?
- **Resources** How willing is he to devote resources to your product? Can you jointly select a "product manager" for special training related to your product?
- **Enthusiasm** How enthusiastic is he about your product?

Partnership again

This last criteria bears repeating. Notwithstanding what I said about the limitations of "partnership," many experienced exporters, especially those who select small distributors because they are starting from scratch in Japan, will overlook certain organizational deficiencies if they sense that the distributor sales force and management are solidly behind the product. Their enthusiasm may be the result of the prestige the new product brings to them, the avenues to other business it opens, or the good human relations on both sides (between senior management, between the supplier's sales rep and the distributor's sales force). What accounts most for small and medium exporters breaking into the Japanese market is effective representation as soon as possible. Salesmen must be out there showing the product, exhibiting it and making the calls. Until that happens, there are no sales and no cash flow.

Creative snooping

Once you have narrowed your list of interested candidates down to three or four, getting complete answers to all of the questions listed above is not always easy. Direct interviews require a playful tolerance of hype and obfuscation. Barging into a distributor's office unannounced or adopting an inquisitorial line of questioning in the owner's presence will get you nowhere. The best approach is to appear less informed than you really are and use every opportunity possible to talk separately and informally to the owner and some of his salesmen after work. Trade fairs are another good avenue to initiate contacts and gather information because the distributor's salesmen are scattered around the room. All of the distributor's employees are fair game. Expect inconsistencies and do not adopt an outraged, self-righteous attitude. Some exporters even hire small investigation firms to get as complete a picture as possible.

SUPPLIER EVALUATION

Buyer's market

Don't let this long list of selection criteria deceive you into thinking that good Japanese distributors will be bending over backwards to please you. That only happens if your product has excellent sales potential. In many cases, it is the exporter who must convince them he is up to standards.

Their criteria

Here again, the relative importance of the following criteria can vary greatly depending on the product involved:

- Will your product appeal to end-users?
- Is your product unique or different from other products like it?
- Is your product quality high enough? Can you maintain it at the same level for as long as it sells in Japan?
- Is your product compatible with his existing lines? Does he have to rush around looking for new clients simply to sell your item?
- Is the price reasonable? Do you provide adequate margins on suggested list prices?
- Will your product attract new business or at least give him more prestige?
- Can you deliver on time and in small lots? Can he avoid a minimum order size?
- Will you accept damaged or unsold merchandise returns?
- Are you willing to sell on consignment? If not, how long are you willing to extend credit?
- Do you have a good reputation he can verify? Are you honest and trustworthy by keeping all your promises, large and small?
- Will you offer sufficient promotional support? This includes price discounts, rebates, in-store demonstrations and media support.

- Does he like you and your sales reps? Will you try to meddle in his internal affairs? Are your sales quotas completely unreasonable? Will you hurt his relations with existing clients?
- Will you try to get rid of him at the first opportunity? Are you planning to set up an office in Japan to increase pressure on him?

WEAK POINTS AND TROUBLE SPOTS

Most of the difficulties described below can be avoided or at least kept under control if an exporter has done his homework before beginning serious negotiations, has a preliminary promotion plan he can use to test the candidate's willingness to invest in a new product, and has protected himself with a well-drafted distribution contract.

WRONG ENTHUSIASM

In the best case scenario, the distributor accepts your line because he thinks he can achieve a respectable market share for you while generating good profits for himself. However, certain distributors may be interested in your product for reasons that have nothing to do with market share.

The vampires

These are generally small distributors devoid of sales planning and weighed down by a multitude of mismatched product lines whose survival depends on securing the rights to new products as fast as older ones are taken from them. Their cash flow is generated during the highly profitable early months of a franchise when inexperienced exporters are most willing to sell their goods at sampling prices or on credit. A few months later, the whole relationship ruptures when sales drop because the product's novelty has worn off and the exporter grows impatient with the distributor's excuses for non-payment – hence the distributor's perpetual quest for new suppliers.

Less competition

A distributor, large or small, may be interested in your product because he wants to limit competition. There are two common scenarios:

- The distributor may be sufficiently intrigued by your product's possibilities to want to prevent other distributors from getting their hands on it. His first instinct is to sign you up as soon as possible and determine your product's real value later. To increase his flexibility, he will also want the smallest possible initial stocking order and a favorable return of merchandise clause in his contract.
- Unbeknownst to you, the distributor may have the distribution rights for a competing product through a sister company. His goal therefore may be to bottle up your product in a useless distribution agreement to protect your competitor.

Professional bidders

Some trading and service industry firms which frequently compete for tenders are always on the lookout for "fillers" because their chances of success are far greater if they can quote for all items listed in a tender. One good way to secure access to products occasionally listed in tenders and at reasonable prices is to become the authorized distributors for these products. The trick is to recognize the business this kind of company specializes in and grant it the limited rights of a manufacturer's representative to secure a few orders for yourself when they do win tenders. Never, however, be under the illusion that they are true distributors interested in market share for your product.

PRODUCT MATCHING

Nasty surprise

Western firms work in a retail and consumer environment where new products are chosen and developed based on exhaustive pre-production marketing analysis. A single dud can damage a carefully nurtured image.

Japanese companies abroad are considered masters at this sort of thing. And yet at home, almost the opposite is the case as many foreign firms trying to compete in Japan have been shocked to discover. Products entering Japan with a large technical advantage over the competition have been quickly matched – not copied – and then left behind.

Maintaining loyalty

The reason for this is quite simple: large Japanese manufacturers are determined to maintain the loyalty of their tied dealer and distribution networks. As soon as a promising product is introduced into the market, instant imitations are rushed out by everyone else to make sure their networks are not left out. To survive in this environment, large manufacturers engage in parallel development – the creation of second- and third-generation products at the same time as the initial version so as to have something new ready to hit the market as soon as the competition catches up. It has been estimated that new product development in Japan takes a third to one-half the time necessary in the West, at a quarter to a tenth of the cost. How is this possible?

Engineers and information

Three factors help Japanese companies pull off this feat:

- **Education** Japan's enormous investment in education, especially in engineering schools, has made it the most technically literate society on earth. It has 5,000 technicians for every million people. The comparable figures for the U.S. and Germany is 3,500 and 2,500 respectively.
- **Catalog design** Instead of designing every component from scratch, Japanese engineers turn to their vertical *keiretsu*'s parts catalogue. With so much reliance on off-the-shelf components, the engineers can focus 90% of their creative energies on those aspects of the new product that are truly innovative.

- **Free flow of information** Within a vertical *keiretsu*'s supplier family (see Industrial Purchasing) the most sensitive information about future products can be freely exchanged with little fear of leakage because job-hopping among Japanese engineers is very rare. This dramatically widens the pool of talent available for any given project and keeps it very close to the technical requirements of efficient manufacturing, the supplier's chief priority.

Product matching affects all successful imports, but the reaction time can vary depending on your product category and your initial customer base. Exporters of cars and consumer electronics, for example, can expect very quick responses because these industries are notorious for their ability to rush out instant imitations. Similarly, exporters aiming for a mass market can expect a much faster reaction than those targeting niche groups.

WEAK MARKETING

Distributors as a group are wary of advertising because it is impossible to quantify its value. Consequently, promotional campaigns are often jointly planned and financed by suppliers and their distributors. With smaller distributors, other marketing problems gain prominence which may come as a surprise to some exporters new to Asia.

- Market research and planning as a discipline is alien to many small distributors used to relying on word-of-mouth information flowing through their network of friends and associates. Their tendency is to launch a product cheaply through their contacts rather than spend money on promotion. If the product does not take off quickly, they drop it.
- Small firms like to travel light, with plenty of loose change for deals and emergencies. They are often reluctant to tie up scarce financial resources to keep what the supplier thinks is sufficient inventory.
- Feedback is always a challenge with the Japanese, regardless of company size. For the sake of harmonious human relations, bad news can be held back until problems grow and become insurmountable. It is often only after work during an informal meal or drinking session that frank opinions finally come out.

What emerges loud and clear from this picture is that successful exporting to Japan through small distributors requires more scrutiny, more market research before selection, and close, sympathetic and ongoing marketing support once the distributor has been chosen. This may cost more in terms of travel and communications expenses; however, two or three eager and well-trained salesmen pushing your product full time in a niche market can often succeed where a half-dozen unmotivated salesmen from big distribution firms fail.

PARALLEL IMPORTS

In Japan, it is legal to grant exclusivity to a single importer, but you have no redress against another company acquiring your products legally anywhere in the world for resale in Japan. These "parallel imports" by unauthorized dealers in competition with your appointed distributor have become a serious problem for expensive and well-established brand name products such as neckties, liquors, golf clubs, bags, confectionery, high-end running shoes, chinaware and scarves. Other products such as perfumes and cosmetics would be ideal parallel imports but for the strict application of the Pharmaceutical Law.

The biggest buyers of parallel imports are department stores, supermarkets, the discount chains and small- to medium-size retailers. They appreciate the lower cost of parallel imports and especially the bigger margins they provide because they are sold at prices only slightly lower than properly imported goods. The parallel importer also does very well. He can free-ride on the sole import agent's marketing activities, hold as little stock as possible, and undercut authorized prices.

If parallel importing affects your product category, appropriate countermeasures must be implemented very early. Parallel imports, if left uncontrolled, prevent the authorized distributor from supporting his marketing activities properly and take away his incentive to work with you. The only cures are clear and enforceable agreements with your partners worldwide; a global pricing structure which takes into account Japan's peculiar situation; packaging unique to Japan which avoids the styles popular in known havens of parallel trade such as the U.K., Holland, Singapore, and Hong Kong; and close collaboration with your Japanese distributor.

INTELLECTUAL PROPERTY RIGHTS

Although Japan has reformed its laws to give better IPR protection to foreign manufacturers, exporters interested in Asia would be well advised to have a worldwide patent and trademark strategy. Leaving things to chance means that you are poorly prepared when, as is usually the case, the burden of proof for infringement is on you. The whole field is complex and changing every year. All I can offer is a short summary. Consult Japanese lawyers and your government officials for the most common IPR problems affecting your product category.

Patents

Japan's system for granting patents is different from that of Canada and the U.S. in two important respects:

- Whereas our North American systems are based on the "first to invent" principle, Japan employs the "first to use" rule in granting patents.

- From the date of filing the first patent application in your home country, you have a year to file it in Japan after which time it becomes un-patentable. Filing patents in Japan is a lengthy process. The Japan Patent Office (JPO) is inefficient and understaffed. The tendency of Japanese manufacturers to surround each new technology with a flood of patent applications also contributes to the tremendous case backlog. As a result, it often takes 6 to 8 years from the date of application to receive a final approval valid for 15 to 20 years after the date of application. The same process takes about 2 years in the U.S.

Trademarks

Here again, Western companies with famous trademarks are often shocked to find their trademarks being used by other companies in Japan. According to Japanese law, the person first to apply is entitled to the registration and protection of a trademark, whereas the first to use has priority in North America.

Copyrights

Under the Universal Copyright Convention, to which Japan is a party, copyright holders are granted automatic intellectual property protection of three to fifty years' duration depending on the nature of the work. No separate filing for protection in Japan is necessary.

Trade secrets

This nebulous area is far less well-defined in Japanese law. It includes such things as know-how, customer lists, sales manuals, experimental data and so on. Suing for breach of contract in such cases has one important disadvantage: the trade secret in question must be made public.

DISTRIBUTOR AGREEMENTS

COMMUNICATING WITH THE JAPANESE

Communication appears simple enough. It involves a sender, a receiver and a message. People, however, are not blank slates. They interpret messages through the prism of their own, mainly unconscious, cultural assumptions. It is these assumptions or communication styles I am concerned with in this chapter, not negotiation strategies per se. And the first place to start is with a little social history.

THE NORTH AMERICAN HERITAGE

Immigrant roots

The United States and Canada are unique in many respects. Both were influenced by waves of immigrants fleeing poverty and oppressive governments from around the world. Both belong to a handful of nations whose citizenship statutes are tolerant and embracing.

These immigrants came overwhelmingly from the lower classes and were mostly left to fend for themselves in a land unfettered by tradition or feudal class structures. Government was minimal at best. Indeed, the U.S. was more a state of mind than a European-style nation state. People were bonded together by powerful ideas like the Constitution, equality, independence, and progress rather than by leaders or the land they cultivated.

Frontier heritage

The concrete expression of these ideas took shape in a frontier environment. Millions of pioneers and their families headed west across a continent to seek a better life. Their struggles form the core of American cowboy mythology exalting rugged competition, freedom from government interference, and unfettered self-expression.

The long distances between people fostered a certain disdain for overelaborate social conventions. Straight talk and plain dealing were the preferred approach in any conflict. And in any case, one could always move on if the land became unproductive or if neighbors were inhospitable.

Word power

This basic approach to negotiation is still upheld by our educational system, especially in our law and business schools. Adversarial relationships and winning are essential themes of our socialization process, both in the classroom and on the sporting field.

Verbal combativeness is particularly appreciated by North Americans. From infancy to adulthood, our children are encouraged to succeed through relentless self-promotion. If this develops an ability to discuss and debate and a capacity for immediate and easy friendships, it also creates an insatiable appetite for signs of personal intimacy and evidence of social success.

THE NORTH AMERICAN NEGOTIATION STYLE

In their excellent negotiation handbook, *Smart Bargaining: doing business with the Japanese*, authors John Graham and Yoshihiro Sano point out how these unique historical circumstances produced the North American negotiation style.

Although the following characteristics are presented separately for the sake of clarity, it must be understood that all of them are based on a common set of attitudes and expectations most North American think of as part of human nature, not culturally acquired. Altering them to get your message across in Japan is not always easy.

- **Going it alone** Most North American executives, like Captain Kirk in a Star Trek episode, profoundly believe that leadership is best demonstrated when an individual grasps the whole situation on his own, makes a quick decision down to the last detail, and communicates what has to be done down a chain of command. This is not the Japanese approach. Their managers set general goals and leave specific problem-solving to their subordinates. As a result, North American companies often court disaster by sending a single individual to negotiate complex deals with a whole team of Japanese.
- **Warts and all** North Americans often strive to create as informal an atmosphere as possible in the belief that this will simplify communication. The effect is usually the exact opposite in Japan where clear ranking and a respect for social conventions go very far in putting everyone at ease.
- **Pardon my French** Our neglect of foreign language study hurts us during the negotiation process. First, the Japanese side is often much better informed about us than we are about them. Secondly, we tend to focus all our attention on the few Japanese who speak English well, believing that they must be the most influential people in their organization. This is rarely the case.
- **Get to the point** We like to get to the point quickly. Unfortunately, what is considered the point varies across cultures. Any negotiation can be broken up into four stages: rapport building, information sharing, persuasion, and finally concessions and agreement. Most North Americans rush through the first two stages because the whole point of the exercise, as far as they are concerned, is persuasion. The Japanese find this approach rather short-sighted. They believe that rapport-building provides plenty of clues as to the

quality of relationship to be expected with the other side.

- **Sequence and whole** This question of rapport building in Japan highlights another North American tendency. We often attack complex negotiations by bargaining over specific issues one by one in a sequential fashion and keep broader questions for the end (see Fig. 5-1). "Once the initial stocking order is agreed upon, we'll be halfway there." Approached in this way, progress can be easily measured. The Japanese, on the other hand, tend to discuss all issues together in the context of the whole and make concessions only at the end.
- **Here I am!** North Americans prefer to state what they are looking for early on and expect reciprocal treatment from the other side. If the Japanese side is a large company, however, it may take them some time to come up with a counterproposal because the decision is a group responsibility. And even if the answer is no, they may try to avoid embarrassment by claiming that there are "problems" and leave it at that.
- **Awkward silences** North Americans are made extremely uncomfortable by long pauses. They feel compelled to fill the silence with more appeals and concessions. Pauses are very common with the Japanese. Learning when to shut up and listen is a precious negotiation skill in Japan.

Figure 5-1

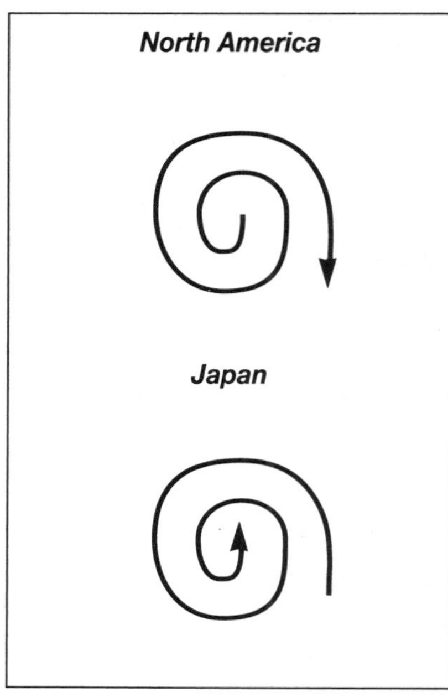

- **Deals and relationships** The North American business style is very transaction-oriented. We tend to believe that each deal or contract stands on its own and that there is a basic distinction between liking someone and wanting his product. The boundaries in Japan are rarely as clear. In their view, contracts grow from relationships, not the other way around. Proving that you can deliver the right product at the right price is not enough; you must also convince them that your two organizations have the potential to build a rewarding relationship over the long term.

THE JAPANESE HERITAGE

Insular geography

Japan is a crescent-shaped archipelago of four large islands and numerous smaller ones lying hundreds of miles off the Asian mainland. Historically, invasions of Japan from Asia have failed because the waters separating both land masses are extremely treacherous, more so even than the English Channel. Not only did maritime barriers keep foreigners out, but they also made Japanese emigration overseas very difficult. As a consequence, Japan's population was able to develop a highly homogeneous culture in relative isolation.

High density

Within Japan, the population was divided into extremely dense pockets by its mountainous geography. Only 10% of the land can be cultivated. This crowding has fostered a highly ordered society which values the group over the individual and stresses the importance of social harmony, hierarchy and cooperation.

Rice cultivation also played an important role in shaping Japanese social values. Rice is a finicky crop, demanding steady and individualized attention, whose yield varies in direct proportion to the farmer's efforts. At the same time, rice farming tied every peasant's fate to that of his village because help was needed twice a year: when rice seedlings were transplanted in late spring, and again in the fall for the harvest. Failing that cooperation, a farmer was ruined. It is no surprise therefore that Japan's two gift-giving seasons fall just after these two crucial times of the year. Maintaining good social relations was a matter of survival.

Belly talk

Most villagers lived under the authority and protection of a nearby feudal lord (*daimyo*) residing in a castle town. During the Tokugawa period (1615-1868), *daimyos* and their samurai had the power of life and death over ordinary commoners. One wrong word and heads could literally roll. There were no civil rights or legal codes. Social order depended instead on hierarchical and situation-specific relationships between superior and inferior. Plain speech was therefore highly dangerous. The result was "belly talk," an extremely vague and supportive speaking style where the listener had to guess at hidden meanings.

Things have changed a great deal since then. But most Japanese remain very deferential towards rules, particularly the unwritten ones which form such an important part of their social code. They also tend to seek long-term "protection" from powerful employers or individuals who provide nurturing stability in exchange for obedience. Problem-solving is largely a group effort. Individualism is frowned upon.

Postwar oligopolies

MITI's postwar industrial targeting practices (see The Birth of a Growth Machine: 1945-1970) favored large corporations in each of the important industrial sectors and the shaping of those companies into government-guided, market-share driven oligopolies. Competition remained fierce, of course, especially in new industries where relative market share had yet to be determined, but competition was never allowed to weaken an industry as a whole in relation to foreign competitors. The overwhelming priority was the creation of powerful export champions capable of serving Japan's national interests in a global trading system set up by the U.S.

The resulting economic system could not be described as socialism because there was very little national ownership of industry. Nor was it North American-style free-market capitalism. It was something strangely different, with stable oligopolies, life-time employment in big industry, and highly structured subcontracting and distribution networks reaching down into Japan's millions of small and medium enterprises.

The impact this had on Japanese negotiation methods was profound. Relations between companies in mature industries tend to be very hierarchical and long term. Large companies strive to become as self-sufficient as possible by surrounding themselves with a network of smaller firms exclusively tied to them. These firms in exchange expect that their protector will take care of them, not necessarily in this or that deal, but over the long run. Consequently, Japanese negotiations frequently involve participants who know each other very well. Contracts and lawyers are dispensed with. Implicit understandings and non-verbal communication come to the fore. Is it any surprise that foreign exporters barging into this closed world feel like bulls in a china shop?

THE JAPANESE NEGOTIATION STYLE

Here again, my focus is on basic perceptions and attitudes. It would be a big mistake to interpret what follows as a list of "strategies" the Japanese use or discard at will. I will get into specific tactics in the next chapter.

- **Hierarchy always** It is difficult for North Americans to understand how vertical relationships form the basis of Japanese social life. The origin of unequal status can be age, sex, place of education, occupation within a firm, the firm's rank among its peers, or even industry of employment. This is why business cards are so important in Japan; as soon as they are exchanged, everyone knows where they stand and how to act. And one source of inequality is the buyer-seller relationship. Being an exporter puts you a rung or two below in the eyes of most Japanese buyers. As such, a seller must be properly deferential when asking for information (a favor, not a right), providing services (exceed expectations) or responding to complaints (apologize first, inquire why after). That is what "the buyer is king" means in Japan. The size and prestige of your firm back home has no bearing on the issue.

- **Paternalism** The reverse side of this belief in vertical relationships is that superiors must take the needs of subordinates into account before making demands. This fosters a feeling of trusting dependency (called *amae*) where both sides perceive their fates as tied. *Amae* is the ideology underlying Japanese labor relations. Exporters interested in keeping their shirts should not get overly sentimental about *amae*, but it is worth noting that arguments based on your own needs may get a respectful hearing in Japan and should be raised whenever there is talk of long-term relationships.
- **Yes, but is it love?** In their own business dealings, the Japanese show a net preference for long-term relationships. Its impact on negotiations is two-fold. First, much more time is spent getting to know prospective partners: their history, future plans, the personalities making up senior management, etc. Secondly, deals tend to be evaluated as part of the overall relationship, not in isolation. If the relationship is weak or rudderless, the deal looses much of its appeal.
- **Jekyll and Hyde** During the initial rapport-building stage, the Japanese pay careful attention to off-the-cuff remarks and non-verbal clues betraying true intentions. The key distinction, as they see it, is between *tatemae* – one's public persona or official line – and *honne* or real purpose. When making that evaluation, most Japanese put their faith in gut feelings over logic.
- **One-way flow** One consequence of the vertical nature of Japanese social relationships is that information tends to flow in one direction only, from seller to buyer. Sellers describe what they have to offer, what they need, and then wait for a decision. If the buyer-seller relationship is a long-standing one, sellers don't even question a negative response because they trust that the buyer will take care of them in the end. Foreigners can, to a certain extent, get out of that loop. Japanese executives occasionally share market or company information with foreign exporters which they would never do with Japanese outsiders or sales reps.
- **All you need is *wa*** A universal complaint about the Japanese in business or negotiation is that frank assessments are hard to come by. Their preference for social harmony (or *wa*) often gets in the way of an honest answer. It may be also that they are putting you off because they

have not yet reached a group consensus. If the answer is no, some roundabout way will be found to communicate it. Watch out for apologies, claims that your request "causes difficulties." long silences, delayed meetings or responses, "Yes, but..." answers, or extreme ambiguity. They often signal a less than enthusiastic response.

- ***Ringi* system** The industrial marketing nostrums about "identifying key decision-makers" in North America often hit a brick wall in Japan. Remember what I said about our Captain Kirk fantasy earlier on in this chapter. Japanese managers in large companies don't work like that. Decisions typically require a seal of approval from many people working in several departments. The less they know you, the newer your technology or the more expensive your product, the greater the consensus required. The informal consensus-building process preceding a decision is called *nemawashi*. *Ringi* refers to the actual group decision-making.
- **More belly talk** North American sales reps are usually consummate extroverts from a land where buzzwords and verbal self-promotion make up for loose multi-ethnic social bonds. Japan, on the other hand, is filled with reserved introverts who function very well with non-verbal cues in an extremely homogeneous and isolated society. Is it any surprise that lack of feedback is a problem for us?
- **Introducers and mediators** Although everyone knows that third parties can occasionally be useful in business, it is important to understand that their role is virtually institutionalized in Japan. First of all, most business relationships are established with the help of a mutual contact. "Cold calls" usually get you nowhere. If a dispute erupts at some later stage, the same third party or another respected person may be asked to act as a mediator. Exporters who understand these social dynamics and create their own network of trusted advisors can avoid many small misunderstandings that may weaken a Japanese business relationship.
- **Many subcultures** It is important to note that Japanese executives do not adhere to a single negotiation style. Size makes a big difference. The owner-managers running small and medium enterprises can make up their minds on the spot without the time-consuming group decision-making characteristic of big firms. Regional differences are also important. Businessmen from Osaka and the Kansai region generally have a reputation for daring and an almost "Western" short-term profit orientation. Tokyo's business community, on the other hand, is

more conservative, ritualistic and long range in its approach. For that reason alone, many smaller foreign exporters focus their energies on the Kansai region first, before spreading out to other parts of Japan.

A CULTURE SHOCK DICTIONARY

Anger expressed publicly is a major social error. The Japanese consider it childish and uncivilized. Social harmony and a sense of decorum are highly valued.

Blowing your nose in public is considered very impolite in Japan.

Boasting is disliked. Don't belittle Japan by making unfavorable comparisons with North America. The same goes for your own abilities and accomplishments; always remain modest, even self-deprecating.

Business conversations with the Japanese can sometimes prove frustrating for confessional types anxious to "communicate." Hardly given to self-disclosure, Japanese businessmen often guide the conversation towards establishing relative status rather than intimacy. Do not expect the kind of instant friendships so common in North America.

Criticism of someone is a loss of face for him, especially if done in front of others. Avoid it if possible. If it is absolutely necessary, do it privately, balance it with praise and be very indirect.

Criticism of your company or management in front of the Japanese will not gain you high marks for independence. The effect achieved is often very counterproductive. They will wonder how long you intend to remain with your firm and whether your replacement will have other priorities with respect to Japan.

Dozing off is very common among the Japanese during meetings, in nightclubs or in subways. The lives of salarymen, in particular, are full of stress.

Dress is an expression of your status. Avoid clothes that are too informal, flashy or colorful.

Education is valued in Japan and the pressure placed on children to excel academically can be grueling.

Elderly people should be shown respect and kindness at all times.

Eye contact is much less frequent among the Japanese than among North Americans. Do not interpret its absence as a lack of sincerity and avoid using it insistently during negotiations. Pushed beyond a certain point, it is considered too aggressive.

Face is primarily the prestige and respect one has in the eyes of others, and is very important to the Japanese. It also has a collective dimension. If a group member wins a prize or commits a crime, the whole group (family, company, club) shares in his prestige or shame. Face can not only be lost or saved in Japan; it can also be given. Giving face means doing something to enhance someone else's prestige among his peers. Publicly thanking someone for his help or giving a gift with snob appeal carries great weight among the Japanese.

Favors are very important. Doing business in Japan is, first and foremost, a process of making friends, and favors are the currency of friendship.

First names should be avoided when speaking to the Japanese unless you are given a clear signal that they wish to be on a first-name basis. The Japanese are especially prone to interpret excessive familiarity as a lack of respect.

Frankness is not as important to the Japanese as a respect for appearances and human feelings. People prize social harmony, not always saying what they mean. Expect plenty of sugarcoating from those with whom you are not on intimate terms.

Generosity and ostentation are great sources of prestige and face; don't be cheap.

Hai in Japanese does not necessarily mean, "Yes, I agree with you." It can mean, "Yes, I understand what you are saying" or merely, "Yes, I am still listening to you."

Handing paper or business cards with both hands shows respect. Some Japanese businessmen, however, are sufficiently cosmopolitan to offer their cards with one hand, and when this happens, you can, of course, do the same.

Invitations by Japanese businessmen are usually to restaurants and nightclubs, not to their homes.

Networking in Japan is not an exchange of business cards; it is an exchange of favors. A good networker is one who listens carefully to find needs he can satisfy at no great cost to himself. Can he introduce the speaker to a prospective customer or supplier? His whole focus is on one simple question: what can I do to help this person? By working at this daily, he is developing a network of people who owe him favors.

Patience is highly valued. To flare up when things go wrong is to display a lack of self-control which the Japanese find unsettling.

Paying for meals is done by the person who did the inviting. "Going Dutch" is never done. If no one in particular made the invitation, the bill is fought over. Paying is considered a matter of pride.

Posture is important in meetings because it is an indication of attitude. Avoid slouching in your seat and crossing your legs in front of someone of higher status. It could be interpreted as disinterest or sloppiness.

Reciprocity governs the exchange of favors. Do not give gifts so expensive or favors so great that the recipient is unable to reciprocate. To do this is to invite refusal.

Recommendations are not given lightly in Japan for fear of cheapening the currency. If someone's introductions give you access to useful contacts, you now owe that person and are obliged to do everything possible to justify his good opinion of you in the eyes of his contacts.

Respect corporate chains of command. Once you have a contact in an organization through whom you have made proposals or arranged meetings, do not try to circumvent him unless you are explicitly told to do so by someone higher up. No one likes an outsider who mucks up organizational hierarchies.

The **sexism** of Japanese executives is mainly directed at Japanese women, not foreigners. Foreign businesswomen are perceived as foreigners first and women second. As long as one dresses conservatively and acts professionally, gender will remain a peripheral factor.

Social harmony (or *wa*) should be preserved at all costs, and may require small lies and indirect ways of communicating your message.

Status is very important. Acknowledging other people's status simplifies social relationships as does acting according to one's own status.

Touching in public. The basic rule is not to touch members of the opposite sex in public, except for handshakes. Among men, back slapping, putting your arm around someone's shoulders or physical touching make the Japanese uncomfortable.

Young foreign executives, however technically capable, must be particularly careful when dealing with older Japanese businessmen. Avoid anything that could be interpreted as a sign of arrogance, such as boasting, speaking to someone new on a first-name basis, belittling the competition or the competence of Japanese people, and so on. There is a cultural assumption in Asia that age connotes experience and that youth has everything to learn.

NETWORKING AND NEGOTIATIONS

Prospecting a short list of good distributors requires certain basic networking skills I describe in this chapter. As for the negotiation process itself, I concentrate on those aspects of the agreement which are most important from a business standpoint. The two chapters which follow, Elements of a Distribution Agreement *and* Taxation in Japan, *examine these same agreements from a legal and tax perspective, respectively.*

EXPLORATORY INTERVIEWS

What to bring

Here are some things you must have with you in Japan:

- Bilingual business cards
- Annual reports and/or one-page company descriptions
- Product brochures and specifications
- Small photo albums of your plant, offices, management and employees
- Company letterhead stationary
- A preliminary list of contacts along with copies of any correspondence with them
- A preliminary list of questions

Timing

Timing your visits is important. Avoid national holidays (see Planning and Reference). The longest are *Obon* (around August 15), when most Japanese visit their relatives and pay respect to their ancestors, and Golden Week from April 19 (Greenery Day) to May 5 (Children's Day). Any business visits that are timed for these dates are bound to fail.

Face-to-face

Information-gathering in Japan is a very personalized, face-to-face process. Swamping target contacts with phone calls and faxes usually yield very little. You have to get out there and meet people.

Door-openers

The most effective way to arrange a first meeting is through a mutual acquaintance. Except in rare cases, cold calling is just not the Japanese way.

As I explained earlier, people and institutions willing to give you good introductions can be found both in North America (see Doing Your Homework) and, of course, in Japan (see Prospecting in Japan – product mapping). Most exporters wisely turn to their own government representatives for contacts and guidance during their initial visits to Japan. Foreign embassies and consulates advise thousands of visitors every year and have enough clout to open many doors.

Confirmations

Visitors who already have contacts in Japan should set up their appointments 3 to 4 weeks before arrival; confirm by fax a week in advance; and reconfirm by phone the day before. Unconfirmed meetings are sometimes canceled without notice because the Japanese assume you are not really serious. Make sure to ask these contacts to fax you a map showing the exact location of their offices in Tokyo or Osaka. Faxed maps with addresses written in Japanese will help your taxi driver get you where you want to go.

Horse's mouth

Well-organized exporters usually start off with government bodies (like embassies and JETRO), move on afterwards to foreign expats already involved in some sort of related business in Japan, and focus on Japanese contacts last of all to explore specific points or partnership possibilities. The reason for this order is that you are moving from general to specific information and from very open to relatively secretive sources.

Government officials are contacted first because they are there to help you. Apart from introductions, they are very good at providing general industry surveys and advice with regards to Japan's regulations as they affect your product category.

To go further, however, you have to contact expats already experienced in your industrial sector, preferably people who have worked in Japan for many years. For the price of air fare and a hotel room, you can acquire filtered and processed information from contacts with actual business experience. They, more than anyone else, can help you decide what the statistics really mean for your business and whether Japan is right for you at this point in time. One word of warning, however. Such people are hard to find. In general, Americans are far more generous with market information than ethnic groups with long trading traditions such as the Europeans or Chinese. Salespeople with big egos or underlings working for transnational distributors looking for a product to start their own businesses can also be tapped. It is amazing how much valuable information can be obtained from a little wining and dining.

Last of all are the Japanese because they are often quite uncommunicative unless an actual business proposal is on the table. There are exceptions, of course. Finding good Japanese advisors is a lot easier if you rely on the locally-hired trade officers staffing your country's embassy or consulates.

JETRO's Business Support Center

Setting up meetings with Japanese executive can be quite a chore because most secretaries speak poor English. To facilitate the market research and networking process, JETRO introduced a new program in March 1993. Exporters can now apply for temporary office space in their new Tokyo-based Business Support Center (BSC) staffed with advisors and support personnel willing to guide them and arrange appointments free of charge. You are only billed for using the telephone, fax or photocopier on a use-basis. The length of stay can be between two weeks and two months. Application forms and flyers on the BSC are available in every JETRO office (see Annex 2).

Since Japanese executives are often much harder to reach than expats for language reasons, it is probably wise to use the BSC only when you have reached the stage where most of your interviewees are Japanese contacts. That way, you will be relying on the BSC's severely rationed free staff time when it is most needed.

Arrivals

Commuting from one meeting to another in Japan's major cities is relatively easy once you have learned how to use the subway. Most newcomers, however, rely on taxis because subways have few English signs. The street numbering system also makes it difficult to find addresses on your own. Look at any Japanese map; most streets don't have names, only city areas do. Moreover, buildings in Japan are numbered according to when they were built, not spatially, according to where they are located, hence the need for faxed maps or Japanese addresses if you don't want your taxi rides to become major exploratory expeditions.

On the day of the meeting, you must show up on time; it is considered extremely rude to be even a few minutes late. Make sure you leave plenty of time to get from one place to another. Getting stuck in a traffic jam is not an acceptable excuse because most Japanese take the subway. Indeed, most Japanese make it a practice to arrive fifteen minutes before a meeting, drink a cup of coffee in a nearby coffee shop, and show up no more than five minutes before the meeting is due to start.

Appearances

Your general appearance is both an expression of your status and your respect for the host's status, all very important in Japanese society. Being well-dressed and groomed (not necessarily expensively) is a must. The quality of your supportive material must also be up to standard. Finally, your hotel should reflect your rank. Presidents and CEOs should stay in first-class hotels; middle managers and sales reps can select business hotels. When relationships have solidified and people get to know you, the hotel you stay in will matter less.

Anxieties

Upon arrival, you will either be ushered into your host's office or, more likely, into a meeting room where you will be asked to wait. The ritualism of the whole situation is often striking for exporters new to Japan. Perhaps because of the homogeneity of their society, most

Japanese have grown up in an environment where human interactions are, and must remain, highly predictable. Committing *faux pas* is everyone's worse nightmare. This often makes them even stiffer and more formal with foreigners than they are among their colleagues.

Their first concern when meeting someone new is to find out where that person fits in their scheme of things. The urge is so strong that Chie Nakane, a well-known anthropologist, labels them *frame people*, while Westerners are *attribute people*. That is, the Japanese are primarily interested in knowing where you fit (the company you belong to, your rank, the extent of your business network) whereas Westerners tend to concentrate on who you are (your specialty, past experiences, interests). Their desire for predictability and context is apparent as soon as you meet: they want to exchange business cards.

Business cards

In North America, business cards sometimes only come out at the end of a meeting as a way to pass on an address or phone number. In Japan, cards (or *meishi*) are presented as soon as you meet because they are credentials and an extension of identity. To appear at a meeting in Japan without a card is tantamount to refusing to shake hands in the West – a major social blunder.

Your business cards should be bilingual, with English on one side and Japanese on the other. The Japanese side need not include a translation of your North American address because they will turn to the English side if a letter has to be sent.

In Japan, the actual mechanics of exchanging business cards is taken very seriously. Large companies even have "house styles" new employees must learn soon after they are hired. Foreigners are not expected to know all the rules, but you should be aware of basic courtesies. In general, junior persons or sellers like you present their cards first to the most senior person present and then to the others. Cards are presented with the Japanese side up facing your host so that he can read it. A small, quick bow should follow to show your respect.

After receiving a card, it is important to study its contents, bowing again as you read it. To ignore a card by merely stuffing it in a pocket implies that the host is of no importance. Memorize the name on the card and slide it into your wallet or card case. Why a case? Because business cards are extensions of their owners and should be treated with respect. Scribbling on a card or bending a card in front of its owner may be treated as an insult.

The Japanese side of a business card often includes information not apparent on the English side:

- **Titles** No two people can have exactly the same rank within one department of a Japanese corporation. The difference may only be one of seniority, but it all disappears in the translation.

- **Format** Characters printed in the traditional vertical fashion – as opposed to horizontal typeset – probably indicate a more conservative corporate culture. If there is no English translation, your host probably never deals with foreigners.
- **Address** Companies located in major office districts where land prices are high, often have a more "solid reputation" than those situated in the suburbs, residential areas or entertainment districts.
- **Ownership** Japanese businessmen can often discern from a card whether a company owns its building or simply rents office space. The first kind is thought more reliable.
- **Phone numbers** Two phone numbers, one for the main switchboard and the other for individuals, creates an impression of size.

These tests for reliability – large size, ownership, prestige locations – are typically Japanese. Your own may be different, depending on your goals.

Interpreters

No matter how good your product is, if you can't communicate you can't do business. Exporters making use of interpreters should brief them a couple of days earlier to make sure they understand the issues. They may also have advice on how best to get your message across.

During meetings, focus your attention on the person you came to meet, not the interpreter. Avoid slang words, speak slowly and keep your sentences short to simplify the interpreter's work.

Information gathering

Regardless of your title, you will probably be greeted by a junior person at first, unless the host is a small enterprise. Aiming for the top is not necessary when you are fishing for information because most of the hands-on decision-making is left to subordinates in Japan. Treat these junior people with respect as they are the ones who prepare the background reports upon which future decisions may rest.

Nor should you expect a great deal of respect because you are a small entrepreneur. The opposite is the case. Most Japanese salarymen (i.e., white-collar employees) are really conservative bureaucrats. Talk of samurai and economic warriors misrepresents reality. Like bureaucrats, salarymen are not hired for specific jobs but for membership in a given group. Promotions are gradual, one step at a time, just like bureaucrats. Team playing and smooth interpersonal relations are far more important than personal initiative or a willingness to buck the general trend. In that context, companies that are new, small, and foreign have a definite image problem to overcome. Japan's corporate culture tends to favor homogeneity and strength. Being very risk-adverse, they prefer big institutions with long histories over small ones.

Information-gathering meetings are generally quite straightforward with relatively little small talk. In some cases, you hit the wrong person and end up sitting through an hour of platitudes, but that is rare if you are proceeding methodically. Being prepared is essential; assume that most interviewees will only give you one hour to pick their brains because you are a foreigner. Extra sessions will only come if you have actual business to discuss.

Potential partners

As the research process nears completion and your focus shifts to a short list of potential partners, expect longer meetings with more probing questions on your company's facilities and track record. Arrange your schedule in consequence; no one is very impressed if you have to make an abrupt exit because of other meetings.

There should also be a shift in ranking. Junior people are perfect for information gathering, but for working relationships it is wiser to strive for contacts at the same level or at least in senior management.

Negotiations are always preceded by plenty of rapport-building rituals: information-sharing, mutual visits, golf and nightclubs, and so forth. This may seem an intolerable imposition to you, but the Japanese feel that the real waste of time is having a relationship go sour after one has spent 3 to 4 years nurturing it. See Communicating with the Japanese for more details.

Group presentations

While group presentations with distributors might seem a great way to save time, the consensus among experts is that the disadvantages of this approach outweigh the advantages. The main shortcomings with this approach are the loss of confidentiality as price lists and discount policies enter the public domain; an overemphasis on your product's weak points as everyone in the room evaluates how you react to criticism; and reduced flexibility during negotiations. Individual interviews may require more time, but they allow you to learn as much as the person being interviewed while limiting the negative effects of your inexperience.

NEGOTIATIONS

Shadows

Never give a distributor the impression he is your only choice. Indeed, if you have done your groundwork properly, you should have three or four good candidates. And even if one stands out, try to create the appearance that you are seriously considering other options.

Never allow a single distributor to meet you at the airport or otherwise control your schedule. Allude occasionally to competing distributors in your discussions; carry their business cards and literature in your briefcase; mention other meetings, real or imaginary. Look like a real prospect who should not be taken for granted.

Preparation

If the distributors on your short list are good and your product is new to Japan, you are in a buyer's market and must be prepared for plenty of skepticism. Good distributors fear the loss of focus which comes from unprofitable diversification, and the first questions you can expect to be asked will center on prices, margins, potential sales volumes, product compatibility with existing lines, inventory levels and after-sales service requirements.

Consequently, you must have a well-rehearsed sales pitch, one that gives a full and convincing picture without allowing your audience to get bogged down in misunderstandings. Some suppliers even suggest that inexperienced exporters deal with their best candidates last because the first presentations are bound to reveal many unanticipated shortcomings in their assumptions. Do this and, by the last one or two candidates, you should have a good answer for almost any objection. This is where your pre-negotiation groundwork really pays off.

Inventory levels

Inventory levels are best discussed during the final stage of the negotiation process, after you have both agreed on a sales promotion plan for the first year (see Launching Your Product). Indeed, it is best to keep details about training, payments, returns, and activity quotas until later, when management has had an opportunity to assess the product's potential in the light of your joint sales promotion plan.

Classic ploys

The Japanese are as tough during negotiations as they are honest once the deal is settled. Expect them to squeeze you with every trick they can use to their advantage. But most of these methods are standard fare in distribution negotiations around the world.

Below are some of the most common tactics used by buyers when asking exporters to lower their prices. Do not confuse them with the communication styles I explained in the last chapter (see Communicating with the Japanese). Communication styles are mainly culture-driven and unconscious. The following tactics, on the other hand, are selected very consciously.

- Confront the exporter with a competitor's prices.
- Probe his knowledge of the market and discredit his assumptions.
- Confuse the issues by concentrating on percentage figures instead of absolute figures, costs per unit not total costs, and rounded figures instead of exact figures.
- Set up a credible deadline which is not in the exporter's advantage.

- Present the exporter with a single take-it-or-leave it option.
- Keep the exporter off balance by putting off the final signing. Nibble away at his position with a thousand small concessions which individually cost little but collectively are interesting.
- Tell the exporter you are financially constrained by some credible larger force.
- Come in with high demands to give yourself some bargaining room.
- Do him some small favors for free, and then play on his sense of obligation later when negotiating major items.
- Get the third party who introduced the exporter to pressure him for concessions.
- Stall for time. The exporter has to show results and his hotel bills are piling up.
- If the exporter's position is strong, emphasize to him how much he has to lose (services, inventory levels, whatever) if he demands too much.

The effectiveness of these tactics in the final analysis depends on two things: your knowledge of the Japanese market with respect to your product category and the number of distributors on your short list who have shown an interest in your item. Both only come to those who do the groundwork before attempting to negotiate anything; otherwise, a seller is at their mercy.

Lawyers

Lawyers are best kept out of the negotiation process until the end when draft agreements have materialized. Their participation at the beginning is, at best, a waste of their time because the situation is too fluid to support a legal opinion. At worst, their presence communicates your distrust of the other side.

The phone

Phones are best used to arrange meetings. Never try to negotiate on the phone. Do it face-to-face.

INVITATIONS AND MEALS

Gifts

Gift-giving is an important part of social communication in Japan. Gifts are used to say thank you, congratulations, welcome, or even "I'm sorry." In a business context, they are often presented during the rapport-building stage, at signing ceremonies, or to commemorate business milestones.

The whole business of gift-giving can be fairly tricky and I strongly recommend that you ask your translator or a Japanese advisor what is appropriate on any given occasion. Here are a few principles to keep in mind:

- Keep gifts small at first. Pens, ties or desktop ornaments with your company's logo are appropriate.
- In Japanese eyes, brand names are important. Handicrafts, on the other hand, look cheap. Try to find brand-name items which

the Japanese associate with your country: whiskey from Scotland, golf clubs from the U.S. Don't forget too that the wrapping should be first-class. Bows are not necessary. Avoid funeral colors such as black or white. Stick to "business" colors: brown, blue, green and gray.

- Pay attention to rank always. Giving the same thing to a president and his vice president only causes embarrassment. The higher up you go, the more expensive it should be. At the same time, gifts that are too expensive may create an unwelcome burden of obligation. Finding the right balance for a particular occasion often requires advice.
- Except for liquor, don't give the same gift twice to the same person. Keep track of past gifts to avoid repetition.
- Avoid unlucky gifts. Sharp objects such as letter openers should be avoided because they symbolize severed relationships. Numbered items can be inauspicious. (The number four in Japanese sounds like the verb 'to die' and nine sounds like the verb 'to suffer.')
- Do not open a gift you have just received in front of the giver, nor pressure the receiver of your gift to open his in front of you.
- Use both hands to give or receive a gift.
- Never try to speed up a decision by giving money or unusually expensive gifts. Bribery in Japan is mainly associated with politics and the underworld, not purely commercial relations.

Meals

Unless time is pressing, meals are rarely a venue for serious negotiations. The main point of a meal together from the distributor's point of view is to know you informally, probe the extent of your network and understand your true intentions. Drinks in nightclubs push the process even further.

The seat of honor is generally the one furthest from the door. The first rule of table manners concerns the use of chopsticks. Don't...

- try to skewer food with one chopstick in each hand.
- point at anyone with your chopsticks or wave them in the air.
- poke at food you don't intend to eat.
- stick chopsticks into rice so that they stand up on their own. This is done when rice is symbolically offered to the dead.

There are many other rules connected with soy sauce, *sake* (rice wine), service attendant and so on. Most of them are very well described in Shelley (1993) and Rowland (1985). Refer to Annex 1 for more details.

Meals are relatively quiet occasions by Western standards. The Japanese rarely appreciate the cut and thrust characteristic of issue-oriented debates. Rip-roaring jokes also make them uncomfortable except in bars. The general feeling is that mealtime is for eating, not other distractions.

Drinking manners

Sooner or later you will be invited to a bar after the day's work is done. Bars exist in every category from the very posh "hostess" bar for executives on an expense account, to much more modest ones offering *karaoke* singing and food to go along with the drinks. The hostess bar, like *karaoke*, is a Japanese invention which is spreading to other countries (particularly in Asia). Beautiful young women are seated with a group of businessmen – their salary is included in the cover charge and drink prices. They are there to entertain with their conversation, to fill glasses, to dance with their "guests" – a hostess in the conventional sense. Their duties rarely go beyond that. *Karaoke* singing is both fun and embarrassing. If you are asked to sing, you can't really refuse even if your voice is terrible. Stick to old standbys such as *Yesterday* or *My Way* and don't sing too long.

The general rule when drinking is that everyone pours drinks for each other, so don't fill your own glass. It symbolizes reciprocity and friendship. Another rule is that young people pour for their bosses, sellers for buyers and women for men. Receive cups of *sake*, with both hands and do not empty your glass unless you want it refilled.

If you go bar-hopping with a group, expect a decline in self-discipline as the evening wears on. "Childish" misbehavior is accepted when people get drunk. After-hours drinking is a widely-used pressure valve among Japanese salarymen.

Business women

Given the importance of after-hours socializing and the fact that most hostess bars and clubs are geared to a male clientele, what should foreign businesswomen do? There is no "right" answer here. Some women adapt to the male role and follow the group. Others skip it and schedule informal lunches or early dinners in coffee shops or hotel restaurants.

Foreign businesswomen can both avoid the awkardness of hostess bars and obtain the benefits of after-hours socializing by suggesting a dinner at a traditional Japanese-style restaurant. These can often be long and drawn out events complete with drinks, depending on the style of food that is chosen. Showing interest in your host's superb cuisine will also go along way in the relationship-building process.

THE CONTRACT

Over-rated

Perhaps because contract drafting absorbs a good deal of time during the negotiation process, exporters again and again make the mistake of ascribing intrinsic value to distribution agreements. The core of any productive cooperation between you and your distributor is his willingness to work hard selling your product, and what motivates a distributor is your product's profitability. No contract, however iron-clad, can by itself rekindle that motivation if it is lost. What it can do, however, is make a separation easier.

The simple truth is that distribution contracts are divorce agreements, not marriage contracts, and function best if they give a supplier an easy exit when things go wrong and protect him during the termination process.

Of course, you don't say this to your distributor during the negotiation process. Whether you believe it or not, you speak the language of long-term relationships. And if it works out that way, fine. But it may not.

Two rules

First, **be specific**. Define in quantitative terms what you mean by performance standards, activities, payments and credit terms. List the names of the people who will be selling your product. Quantify what you mean by reasonable access to staff for training purposes. Don't sign a deal for all eternity; set a time limit based on your product category's procurement cycle. The more specific the contract, the easier it is to terminate if the distributor does not perform.

Second, **reserve a right of veto** in cases where distribution work is subcontracted to others and **an opting-out clause** in case your distributor is taken over by another company with whom you do not want to work.

ELEMENTS OF A DISTRIBUTION AGREEMENT

HAYASHIDA, KASHIWAGI AND TAZAWA

This is an overview of distribution agreements in Japan from a legal perspective. For a direct response to your particular needs, Hayashida, Kashiwagi & Tazawa can be reached at the Ozawa Bldg., 5th Floor, 21-18 Toranomon 1-chome, Minato-ku, Tokyo 105, Tel: (03) 3508-2271, Fax: (03) 3595-2657.

INTRODUCTION

There are two types of agreements by which a foreign supplier may promote and market its products in Japan: an agency agreement and a distribution agreement.

Under an agency agreement, an agent does not purchase the supplier's products but merely acts on his behalf; title to the products transfers directly to the customer of the products in Japan and never to the agent. Under a distribution agreement, a distributor purchases the foreign supplier's products for its own account, and the title to the products transfers to the distributor when the purchase is completed. In an agency agreement, while foreign suppliers may exercise a control over the sales conditions of the products in Japan, the foreign supplier has to assume full responsibility for the products sold. Conversely, in a distribution agreement, a foreign supplier may not have a control over sales conditions of the products in Japan but may avoid liability and financial exposure for the products sold by its distributor.

Since a distribution agreement is more commonly used as sales vehicle, this chapter will mainly focus on a distribution agreement.

MAIN ELEMENTS OF A DISTRIBUTION AGREEMENT

While clauses covered by a distribution agreement vary, typical clauses commonly provided in the agreement are discussed below.

Scope of products

The definition of the products to be sold should be described in detail.

Exclusivity

A foreign supplier may appoint a distributor either on an exclusive basis or non-exclusive basis. The term "exclusive" means that the supplier is prohibited from appointing any other distributor in Japan. Because of a lack of Japanese court precedence, it is not clear whether the appointment of "exclusive" distributor or "exclusive and sole" means a waiver of the right by a foreign supplier to make a direct sales in Japan. Thus, it should be explicitly spelled out in the agreement as to whether the supplier's right to make a direct sales to Japan is reserved or given up.

Territory

A designation of Japan or part of Japan as the territory will be covered in the agreement.

Trademarks

The protection clause for trademarks should be included. The distributor's right to use the supplier's trademarks should be limited to promotion and sales activities of the products and the distributor should acknowledge the ownership of the trademarks.

Distributor's duties

The distributor's duties should be specified in some detail, for example, scope and manner of advertisements, after-sale service, start-up activities or maintenance of stocks and spare parts.

Sales conditions

A distribution agreement itself is not a sales contract, but the conditions of sale such as price, risk of loss, title passage, shipment terms warranty should be fixed in the agreement.

Title retention

It is possible to provide for security interest so that the supplier remains the owner of the products sold until payment is made in full. However, it should be noted that such a clause is of no effect against bona fide third parties who have purchased the products.

Waiver of compensation upon termination

A waiver clause of all compensation, damages, or claims upon termination such as loss of profits, goodwill or the like is advisable. Although it is doubtful that such a clause will be given full effect by the court, it is at least of help as a "moral obligation."

Notice of termination

One should provide a reasonable prior notice for termination such as three-, six- or twelve- months' notice, depending on the length of the relationship.

Non-competition after termination

The validity of a non-competition clause is doubtful, in particular, if the period exceeds more than two years after termination.

Governing law

A governing law clause is customary and will be given an effect under Japanese law.

Settlement of disputes

Arbitration clauses are common in international distribution agreements. In Japan, there are two permanent arbitral bodies handling international commercial disputes; one is the National Committee of the International Chamber of Commerce, and the other the Japan Commercial Arbitration Association. The latter has concluded inter-institutional agreements with other permanent arbitral bodies of various countries.

An agreement to arbitrate is enforceable and a good defense to a suit. If one party brings a suit notwithstanding an arbitration clause, the court will dismiss the case without going into the merits.

Since Japan is a signatory country to the 1958 New York Convention on the Recognition and Enforcement of Foreign Arbitral Awards, Japanese courts will give recognition and enforcement on an arbitral award rendered in a member country of the Convention. With respect to the choice of the place of arbitration, the choice of home country is preferable, because it will save costs and discourage the other party from initiating arbitration.

Term

As explained later, a distribution agreement for an indefinite period can be terminated only by just cause, by paying termination compensation, and/or giving a reasonable prior notice. Thus, in order to avoid the agreement being interpreted as providing for an indefinite period, it is of importance that the distribution agreement have a definite and fixed term and that automatic renewal be avoided.

JAPANESE ANTI-TRUST LAW AND DISTRIBUTION AGREEMENTS

The Japanese anti-trust laws have an effect on certain provisions of the distribution agreement. The laws prohibit "unreasonable restraint of trade" and "unfair business practices." The term "unreasonable restraint of trade" is defined as such business activities by which entrepreneurs by contract, agreement, or any other concerted activities mutually restrict or conduct their business activities in such a manner as to fix, maintain, or enhance prices; or to limit production, technology, products, facilities, or customers or suppliers, thereby causing, contrary to the public interest, a substantial restraint of competition in any particular field of trade. The term "unfair business practices" is defined as any act coming under any one of the following paragraphs which tends to impede fair competition and which is so designated by the Fair Trade Commission: 1) Unduly discriminating against other entrepreneurs; 2) Dealing at undue prices; 3) unreasonably inducing or coercing customers of a competitor to deal with oneself; 4) trading with another party on such conditions as will restrict unjustly the business activities of the said party; and 5) dealing with another party by unwarranted use of one's bargaining position.

The following restrictions are those of major concern which are likely to constitute unfair business practices under the laws:

Resale price-fixing

A supplier may not fix resale prices. Any attempt by the supplier to control the resale price of the distributor is prohibited.

Restriction on distribution channels

A distributor is free to sell the products to whomsoever he chooses. A supplier may not restrict the distribution channels of the distributor.

Restriction on source of parts

A distributor's freedom in obtaining parts is protected under the law.

Restriction on termination

To impose an unduly disadvantageous condition for termination is restricted.

Restriction on competing products

In an exclusive distribution agreement, this restriction is deleted if a supplier will allow a distributor to continue dealing in competing products which a distributor has already handled.

NO PROTECTIVE LEGISLATION

In order to strengthen or protect a distributor, there are many countries which enact special legislation obligating the supplier to compensate the distributor for damages or loss caused by termination or by prohibiting unjust refusal of renewal.

In Japan, however, no special protective legislation has been enacted. Principal and distributor relations are governed by the principle of contract law and commercial law. Thus, parties are, in principle, free to agree on their relationship, and the terms and conditions of a distribution agreement are left to the agreement between the supplier and the distributor.

TERMINATION OF DISTRIBUTION AGREEMENTS

Terminating a distributorship agreement often raises legal disputes.

In a distribution agreement with a definite term, it appears that the court will recognize a principle of party autonomy. A fixed term of agreement will be allowed to expire at the end of the term as agreed, without any obligation to pay compensation for damages, if reasonable prior notice is made.

However, in a distribution agreement containing no fixed term or providing for successive automatic renewals, there is considerable risk that the court will hold the agreement to be intended to endure for an indefinite period, in which case just cause is required to effect a unilateral termination or refusal to renew. The notion of "just cause" is, needless to say, of a blank content. The courts look into all of the facts surrounding the termination of the agreement to see if there have occurred such circumstances or causes as are serious enough to destroy the good faith relationship between the two. Such a relationship is considered an essential factor underlying a long-term continuous agreement such as distribution agreements, leases for housing, etc.

In certain cases, adequate prior notice and/or compensation can be a substitute for just cause. The period of such notice and the amount of compensation will depend on the length of agreement, the amount of lost profits, the amount of capital expenditures invested by the distributor and other factors.

TAXATION IN JAPAN

SHOWA OTA & CO.

From a supplier's perspective, knowledge of Japan's tax regime is important at two fundamental levels: What are the tax consequences of choosing intermediaries who sell on one's behalf, such as agents or manufacturer's representatives, as opposed to a distributor who buys on his own account? And what are the tax consequences for suppliers who expand their role by establishing sales branches in Japan? These questions are addressed in the following overview. Showa Ota & Co., one of Japan's largest and most experienced audit corporations, has a staff of over 1,500 professionals serving more than 2,500 clients from 23 offices nationwide. As a member firm of Ernst & Young International, Showa Ota & Co. provides audit services to more of the top 100 companies on the Tokyo Stock Exchange than any other accounting firm in Japan.

PRINCIPAL TAXES

Taxes in Japan are assessed by the national government and by local governments at the prefectural and municipal levels. All three levels of government – national, prefectural and municipal – levy tax on the income of both corporations and individuals.

Direct taxes

Income taxes National and local (prefectural, municipal or both) income taxes are assessed on the income of corporations and individuals.

Inheritance and gift taxes Inheritance and gift taxes are assessed by the national tax authorities on the transfer of assets at death or by gifts (see below).

Per capita taxes Per capita taxes are assessed on corporations and individuals by both prefectural and municipal authorities as inhabitants' taxes.

Business office taxes Business office taxes are assessed by certain large cities. Calculations are based on both the space utilized for offices and the amount of salaries to employees. Corporations that own or lease 1000 square meters or less and employ 100 staff or less in the cities are not subject to these taxes.

Property taxes Taxes on property are assessed annually by prefectural and municipal authorities. The following property taxes are levied: fixed assets tax, at 1.4%; city planning tax, at 0.3%; special landholding tax, at 1.4%; and automobile and light vehicle tax, ranging from ¥1000 to ¥111,000 depending on the size of the vehicle's engine.

Taxes on acquisition of property Taxes on acquisition of property are imposed by the prefectural and municipal authorities when such property is acquired. Property acquisition tax is generally assessed at the rate of 4% of the value used to determine real estate tax.

Payroll taxes Social security taxes, assessed on compensation paid by employers, are payable by both employers and employees.

Indirect taxes

Consumption tax A 3% consumption tax on the transfer of goods and services is imposed by the national government. The tax is collected by sellers at each stage of the transaction, but the ultimate consumers of the goods and services bear the burden of the tax.

Securities transaction tax National securities transaction tax is assessed on the transfer of securities in Japan at rates of 0.01% to 0.3% of the sale price, depending on the nature of the transaction and the type of securities.

Registration and license tax The national tax authorities levy registration and license tax at the time corporations and property – real property, vessels, patents and so forth – are registered, recorded and licensed. For the registration of a new corporation, for example, the tax is ¥150,000 or 0.7% of paid-in capital, whichever is greater, and for the registration of real property the tax is 5% of the value used to determine real estate tax.

Stamp tax A stamp tax ranging from ¥200 to ¥600,000 (based on the type of documents and the amounts involved) is collected for affixing and canceling the stamps that must be affixed to an extensive list of documents, as detailed in the Stamp Tax Law. These stamps are sold by post offices, but in some cases, a company can pay the tax office directly.

Tax administration

Both the National Tax Law and the Local Tax Law were enacted by the National Diet. The administration of the National Tax Law is supervised by the Ministry of Finance and actually handled by the National Tax Administration Agency. The Local Tax Law is administered by local government authorities. Because the Local Tax Law is enacted by the Diet, local taxes are uniform throughout Japan, although they may be modified slightly by local governments.

Corporate income tax The system of collecting corporate income tax is based on self-assessment. Corporate tax payers are required to file tax returns with the national tax offices and with prefectural and municipal tax offices where the corporations have offices or places of business.

A corporation must file its tax returns and pay the tax due within two months after the end of its fiscal period. Corporations, other than newly-established corporations having fiscal years longer, than six months should file an interim return and pay interim tax within two months after the end of the first six months of their fiscal year.

Taxes must be paid on or before the due dates in the applicable laws. If taxes are paid after the due dates or insufficient tax is paid because of an understatement in the return, a delinquency tax comprising penalty and interest is assessed. In the case of national tax, the delinquency tax is made up of the following components:

- Penalty for understatement: If income was understated in the return, 10% to 15% (depending on the amount due) of the tax increment (the difference between the tax on the understated income and the tax on the accurate income) will be assessed as a penalty.
- Penalty for failing to file: If the return was not filed or filed after the due date, 15% of the total tax due will be assessed.
- Heavy penalty tax: In the case of fraud, 35% of the tax increment will be assessed.
- Interest: When taxes are paid after the due date, interest (which is not tax deductible) will be computed at annual rates of 7.3% for the first two months after the due date, and 14.6% thereafter. Interest for a legally authorized extension period is tax deductible and is computed at an annual rate of 7.3% for the period.

Individual Income Tax Since this book focuses on doing business in Japan, this section outlining individual income tax is presented only as a brief summary.

Individual income taxes are collected through a self-assessment system and a withholding system. Individual tax payers who are required to file income tax returns generally file their returns only with a national tax office and do not need to file returns with the prefectural and municipal tax offices.

If an individual's tax liabilities are settled entirely through withholding, no final tax return needs to be filed. Wages, salaries, bonuses, fees, interest and dividends are subject to withholding at source. In most cases, individuals are required to file a final tax return if:

- total employment income exceeds ¥15 million.
- employment income was received from one employer and the total of taxable income other than employment income was more than ¥200,000.
- employment income was received from two or more employers and the total of taxable income other than employment income, after the year-end withholding adjustment, was more than ¥200,000.
- employment income was not subject to withholding.
- employment income was paid outside of Japan.

Accordingly, a non-resident individual who is paid salary outside of Japan for services rendered in Japan is required to file a tax return, unless exempt from tax under treaty privileges.

Returns must be filed and the final tax paid between February 16 and March 15 for income accrued during the previous calendar year. Taxpayers who expect to incur a tax liability, after credits and withholding taxes, of ¥150,000 or more on their returns are required to prepay income tax during the calendar year in which the income is earned. Prepayments are due on July 31 and November 30. Each prepayment is normally one-third of the previous year's liability less amounts withheld at source. By filing a final return, a taxpayer may obtain a refund of any prepaid or withheld payments which exceed the total tax due.

If tax is paid after the due date for filing the return, interest is assessed at an annual rate of 7.3% for the first two months, and

14.6% thereafter. Filing after the due date will also be subject to a 5% or 15% penalty. If an individual leaves Japan permanently in the middle of the year, the individual must file a quasi-final tax return and pay the balance of tax due before departure, or the taxpayer may appoint a tax agent to file the final tax return between February 16 and March 15 of the following year.

Statute of Limitations The statute of limitations for tax collection by the tax authorities is five years from the due date of the tax payment or seven years from the due date in the case of fraud. The period during which the tax authorities will accept returns filed by taxpayers is generally three years from the original due date for filing the return or seven years from the due date in the case of fraud.

Tax examinations and appeals The National Tax Administration Agency has three levels: the Central National Tax Office, the Regional Tax Offices and the Local Tax Offices. Tax audit and examinations are handled by the Regional Tax Offices and the Local Tax Offices. If a taxpayer disagrees with an assessment resulting from a tax audit, the taxpayer may first submit an application concerning the dispute to the Chief Officer of either the Regional or the Local Tax Office that performed the tax audit. If the taxpayer disagrees with the Chief Officer's decision, the taxpayer may appeal to the National Tax Board, a semi-independent organization of the Central National Tax Office. If the taxpayer disagrees with the decision of the National Tax Board, the taxpayer may take the issue to court. Such a dispute is seldom brought to court in Japan.

RESIDENT CORPORATIONS

Domestic and foreign corporations

A domestic corporation is defined as a company that is incorporated or has its head office in Japan. A corporation that is incorporated or has its head office outside of Japan is considered a foreign corporation. The place of effective management has no bearing on the definition of either a domestic or a foreign corporation.

National and local taxes are assessed on the worldwide income of a domestic corporation and, for foreign corporations having permanent establishment in Japan, on income from sources within Japan. A fixed place of business, such as a liaison office or a representative office, does not constitute a permanent establishment as long as its activities are limited to those of an auxiliary nature. A Japanese branch of a foreign corporation, however, is considered a permanent establishment and may be subject to tax on its Japanese-sourced income. In addition, an agent of a foreign corporation who has authority to conclude contracts or habitually performs important activities in Japan exclusively for or on behalf of a foreign corporation are subject to tax on the income attributable to the permanent establishment.

Taxable income

Net income reported under generally accepted accounting principles does not constitute taxable income for corporate tax purposes, because special provisions in the tax law require the adjustment of net income when computing taxable income.

Gross income is broadly defined, and how it is generated is irrelevant. Expenses incurred in the conduct of business are allowed as deductions from gross income, except for some expenses limited by law, such as directors' bonuses, certain entertainment expenses (as specified in the regulations) and certain contributions.

Dividends distributed from a domestic corporation are subject to a 20% withholding tax on the gross amount of the dividends unless a tax treaty modifies the rate. A corporation receiving dividends from a domestic corporation can exclude from gross income the net amount of the dividends received, less any interest expense incurred for the acquisition of the shares. If the recipient corporation owns less than 25% of the domestic corporation distributing the dividends, 20% of the net dividend income must be included in gross income.

Deductions

Depreciation The cost of tangible fixed assets, excluding land, can be recovered using statutory depreciation methods, such as the straight-line or the declining-balance methods, over the statutory period established by the Ministry of Finance. The amount of ordinary depreciation deductible for tax purposes must agree with the amount of depreciation for financial accounting purposes.

Taxes The following taxes are deductible: enterprise tax, indirect taxes and interest on taxes unpaid during an extension period granted for the filing of a tax return. National tax, inhabitants' tax and any delinquent or penalty taxes, however, are not deductible.

Salaries and bonuses Salaries and bonuses paid to employees are deductible expenses. Salaries and other compensation periodically and reasonably paid to directors performing services for a corporation are also deductible, but bonuses to directors are generally not deductible. If a director (other than the president or managing director) is assigned duties as an employee, however, the portion of the bonus paid for those services rendered as an employee is treated as a deductible expense.

Entertainment expenses Entertainment expenses incurred by corporations may be deductible to the extent of the statutory limit, determined according to the amount of the corporation's capital. Any amount in excess of this statutory limit is not deductible for tax purposes.

Capital of corporation at fiscal year-end

Exceeding (¥)	Not exceeding (¥)	Annual statutory limit (¥)
———	10,000,000	4,000,000
10,000,000	50,000,000	3,000,000
50,000,000	———	None

Contributions Unless made to national or local governments, public welfare organizations designated by the Minister of Finance, or certain public organizations established by special law and listed in the government ordinance, contributions are not deductible to the extent that they exceed the sum of 1.25% of profits plus 0.125% of the amount of paid-in capital and capital surplus.

Retirement and severance benefits Retirement and severance benefits for employees are based on a company's work rules and are accrued by the company in accordance with an established formula. The tax law, however, allows only 40% of the accrual as a current deduction for income tax purposes. When the benefits are paid, the difference between the payment and the accrual is then deductible. Directors' severance benefits must be authorized at a shareholders' meeting and are therefore not necessarily determinable by an established formula. No portion of such benefits is allowed as a deduction for corporate tax purposes until paid.

Interest expense Japan does not have debt-to-equity requirements. Interest expense can generally be deducted on an accrual basis. Interest expense attributable to the purchase of land not utilized, however, cannot be deducted for four years after the date of the land purchase. If the land is utilized and the date of utilization is earlier than the fourth business year, interest expense can be deducted from that date. Capitalized interest expense can be amortized over a four-year period beginning after such capitalization period. This rule is applied to the purchase of the stock of a company on or after December 31, 1988 if the purchasing domestic company owns 30% or more of the stock in a company that owns land constituting 70% or more of its total assets.

Tax rates National, enterprise and inhabitants' taxes, in the aggregate, amount to approximately 52% of taxable income.

National tax For corporations capitalized at ¥100 million or less, the national tax rate is 28% on taxable income up to ¥8 million and 37.5% on taxable income over ¥8 million.

For corporation capitalized at more than ¥100 million, the rate is 37.5%.

Enterprise tax Corporate enterprise tax is levied by prefectures on all types of business conducted by a corporation in the prefecture in which a corporation has an office or place of business.

Corporate enterprise tax is levied on taxable income computed by deducting expenses from gross revenue in the same manner as taxable income for national income tax is computed, unless there are special provisions in the local tax law or other contingencies. Enterprise tax is levied on taxable income at rates ranging from 6% to 12.6%, depending on the prefecture in which the business is located. For national tax purposes, a deduction is allowed on a cash basis for enterprise taxes paid.

Inhabitants' tax Inhabitants' tax, assessed by both prefectures and municipalities, are computed as a percentage of the national income tax, at rates ranging from 17.3% to 20.7%. The assessment for per capita taxes, which range from ¥50,000 to ¥3,750,000 a year, is included in the inhabitants' tax return. The per capita tax is based on the company's capitalization and the number of employees.

Calculation of effective tax rates The following are the maximum tax rates as percentages of taxable income for the business year beginning on or after April 1, 1990:

	Large corporations %	Small-and medium-size corporations %
National tax	37.50	28 *
Enterprise tax	12.60	12.60
Inhabitants' tax (37.5% x 20.7%)	7.76	5.79

* on taxable income up to ¥8 million. The excess is taxed at 37.5%.

Because enterprise tax is deductible in computing the national and inhabitants' taxes in the following fiscal period, the effective tax rate (excluding the per capita levy) is 51.38% for large corporations and 41.19% for small- and medium-size corporations with income of ¥8 million or less.

Blue form tax returns

The blue form tax return system, which is used by most corporations, entitles a taxpayer to various tax benefits. A taxpayer using this system is required to keep a set of books that clearly reflects all transactions affecting assets, liabilities and capital in accordance with the principles of double-entry bookkeeping and to settle accounts on the basis of those books. A blue return may be filed if, in addition to keeping the required books and records, the taxpayer obtains the consent of the head of the taxation office for the appropriate filing district.

Blue return taxpayers are allowed the following benefits:

- A net operating loss for any taxable year in which a taxpayer filed a blue return may be carried forward for five years.
- A net operating loss may be carried back one year provided a blue return was filed for the earlier year as well as for the loss year.
- Reassessments are made only if an actual tax examination is carried out and mistakes are discovered in the computation of taxable income, deductible reserves or the additional depreciation deduction for the taxable year. Tax authorities do not have the discretion

to increase taxable income based on a finding that it falls below statistical guidelines.

Tax credit

Withheld taxes Income taxes withheld on interest income from bank deposits, and on dividend income can be credited against national and inhabitants' income taxes. If the income tax withheld exceeds the tax liability, the excess can be refunded with certain limitations.

Foreign tax credit A domestic company may be entitled to claim a foreign tax credit against both national tax and inhabitants' tax for foreign income taxes paid. The amount of the credit is the lesser of the creditable foreign income taxes or the foreign tax credit limitation. With certain limitations, creditable foreign income taxes for a domestic company include a direct tax credit (foreign income taxes paid directly by a domestic company and its foreign branches) and an indirect tax credit (foreign income taxes paid by a first-tier foreign subsidiary, at least 25%, or lower treaty percentage, of the voting stock of which is owned by a domestic company). In addition, a tax-sparing credit, applicable under a treaty where the foreign tax is not actually payable, is available to domestic companies with a branch or subsidiary in a developing country.

The foreign tax credit limitation is calculated as follows:

$$\text{Japanese corporate tax} \times \frac{\text{Foreign-source income}}{\text{Worldwide taxable income}}$$

Foreign-sourced income is generally limited to 90% of worldwide taxable income. Two-thirds of foreign-sourced income that is not subject to income taxes in a foreign country is deducted from the foreign-sourced income.

If creditable foreign taxes exceed the foreign tax credit limitation or if the limitation exceeds the creditable foreign taxes, the unused portion may be carried forward for three years.

Investment tax credit A corporation may claim an investment tax credit if, by March 31, 1992, it acquires or produces qualified machinery or equipment to improve its utilization of energy and uses the machinery or equipment within one year of the date of acquisition or production. The credit is the lesser of 7% of the cost of the qualifying properties or 20% of the corporations' national tax. The corporation has the option of taking the investment tax credit instead of using the additional depreciation.

Credit for research and development expenses A corporation filing a blue form tax return may claim a credit equal to 20% of certain incremental research and development expenses or 10% of the national tax before the credit, whichever is lower. Incremental research and development expenses are amounts incurred during the current fiscal period in excess of the largest amount incurred during any earlier fiscal period since 1967. Research and development expenses are defined as expenses incurred in research and development to develop new products, improve products, or design or invent techniques.

Credit for imported products A manufacturing corporation filing a blue form tax return may claim a credit if its imports increased 10% or more over the largest amount of imports in the preceding years since the fiscal year including April 1, 1990. The credit that can be claimed against its national tax is 5% of certain incremental imports or 10% of the national tax, whichever is smaller.

Transfer pricing legislation Transfer pricing legislation was enacted in 1986. The law stipulates that pricing between internationally affiliated entities should be at an arm's-length rate. "Internationally affiliated entities" are defined as entities with a relationship consisting of 50% or more direct or indirect share holding.

Treatment of groups of companies Groups of companies are not permitted to file a single income tax return on a consolidated basis. There is no special tax treatment for groups of companies in Japan.

Dividends, interest and royalties paid to foreign affiliates

Dividends Dividends distributed from a domestic company to foreign affiliates are subject to withholding tax at 20% (or lower treaty rate) on the gross amount of the dividends.

Interest A 20% (or lower treaty rate) withholding tax is imposed on gross interest payments. A domestic company can obtain a tax deduction for reasonable interest paid to foreign affiliates.

Royalties A 20% (or lower treaty rate) withholding tax is imposed on gross royalty payments to foreign entities. A domestic company can obtain a tax deduction for the withholding tax on reasonable royalty payments.

NON-RESIDENT COMPANIES WITH BRANCHES IN JAPAN

Non-resident companies with branches or agencies in Japan are subject to Japanese income taxes on their entire Japanese-sourced income regardless of whether the income is attributable to the branch operations. Foreign income attributable to the branch operations is generally not subject to Japanese income taxes.

Where a non-resident corporation is doing business through an agency in Japan, the Japanese-sourced income attributable to the agency is fully taxable in the general course of Japanese taxation and other Japanese-sourced income is subject to withholding tax. However, a consideration has to be made to the permanent establishment for doing business through an agency. Regarding this consideration, each tax treaty has to be read carefully, as this has a strong impact upon the tax treatment of the business. Advice from a professional tax consulting firm could be very helpful at the planning stage.

TAXATION OF FOREIGN-SOURCED INCOME

Japanese domestic companies are subject to national and inhabitants' income taxes on their worldwide income. Income attributable to permanent establishments of Japanese domestic companies in foreign countries, however, is not subject to enterprise tax. Foreign income taxes paid can be utilized either as deductions from income or as tax credits against both national and inhabitants' taxes.

PARTNERSHIPS

A partnership (*kumiai*) is not a legal entity and is not subject to any reporting requirements, nor is it subject to any income taxes. Each partner (*kumiaiin*) of the partnership is required to report its proportional share of the partnership income or loss in its own income tax return.

There are two types of *kumiai*. In a *nini kumiai*, each *kumiaiin* participates in the business and bears unlimited liability. In a *tokumei kumiai*, each *kumiaiin* contributes capital but does not participate in the business and incurs only limited liability. Non-resident companies without a branch in Japan that are *kumiaiin* of a *tokumei kumiai* are subject only to the 20% Japanese withholding tax on their share of the income derived from a Japanese source and are not required to file income tax returns if the *tokumei kumiai* has 10 or more partners.

INDIVIDUALS

Taxation on individual income consists of national tax and inhabitants' tax, which is a local tax. In addition, enterprise tax, also a local tax, is levied on individual income from business or professional activities.

Residence

Taxation of individuals in Japan is based on residence. Taxable income, tax rates and method of tax payment differ by category of residence. Individual taxpayers are classified as either residents (permanent residents or non-permanent residents) or non-residents under the income tax law.

Permanent and non-permanent residents Individuals who have a domicile in Japan or have resided continuously in Japan for one year or more are considered residents. If an individual does not intend to reside permanently in Japan, however, he or she is considered a non-permanent resident for the first five years of residence. Non-permanent residents who reside in Japan for more than five years then become permanent residents for tax purposes.

Permanent residents are subject to taxes on their worldwide income at progressive rates. Non-permanent residents are subject to taxes at progressive rates on Japanese-sourced income and on income from sources outside of Japan if such income is paid in or remitted to Japan.

When a foreign individual arrives in Japan on assignment, unless it is clear from the employment contract or other document that the period of stay will be less than one year, he or she will be considered a non-permanent resident from the time of arrival and will be taxed accordingly.

Non-residents Non-residents comprise all individuals other than residents. Individuals who have not established a domicile in Japan and have not resided in Japan for one year or more will be treated as non-residents. Non-residents are subject to Japanese income tax on income from sources within Japan, normally at a 20% withholding rate without deductions, or at a progressive rate, depending on the type of income. If taxes are withheld from payments to a non-resident and the amount withheld satisfies the Japanese tax liability, the individual need not file an income tax return.

Salaries and bonuses paid by Japanese companies are subject to a 20% withholding tax when paid to non-residents. Dividends, interest and royalties paid to non-residents are also subject to a 20% withholding tax, unless modified by the terms of the applicable tax treaties.

Under most Japanese tax treaties, a resident of a treaty country whose period of stay in Japan is fewer than 183 days in a calendar year is exempt from Japanese taxes on compensation for services rendered in Japan if the compensation is paid by an employer's office, branch or other fixed place of business located in Japan. If the stay overlaps two calendar years, the expatriate can still enjoy exemption if the period of the stay in each year is less than 183 days.

Income

The income of individuals is reported by calendar year using an accrual method of accounting. Interest on public bonds or corporate debentures in bearer form, however, must be reported on a cash basis.

Taxable income is divided into 10 categories. First, the net income in each category is determined. Gross receipts are aggregated and then reduced by the necessary and direct expenses attributable to that category. The progressive tax rates are then applied to compute the amount of income tax.

The following are the 10 categories of income: interest, dividends, real estate rental income, business income, employment income, capital gains, occasional income, retirement income, forestry income and miscellaneous income. These income categories relate primarily to the income of permanent and non-permanent residents.

Interest income Interest income includes interest on public bonds and corporate debentures, postal savings and deposits, distributions of earnings of joint operation trusts or public bonds, and debenture investment trusts. No deductions are allowed for expenses. Interest, taxed separately from other income, is subject to a 20% withholding tax at source (15% national tax, 5% inhabitants' tax). Interest on public bonds and debentures issued overseas is subject to a 20% withholding tax if it is paid through a dealer in Japan. The tax liabilities on interest income are satisfied by the withholding tax, and interest income need not be reported.

Dividend income Dividend income includes dividends and distributions of profits from corporations. Dividends are subject to a 20% withholding tax at source. Tax withheld and dividend credits may be applied against the total income tax liability. Dividends need not be included in dividend income if all of the following apply:

- The taxpayer elects to have tax withheld at a 35% rate.
- The taxpayer owns less than 5% of the shares of the company.
- Total dividends received from the company are less than ¥500,000 in the calendar year (¥250,000 if the company's fiscal year is six months).

Real estate rental income Net income from the rental of real estate consists of gross rental income less the necessary expenses incurred to generate such income, including depreciation, insurance and taxes.

Business income Business income includes income derived from business and professional activities. Net income consists of the gross receipts less the necessary expenses incurred to generate such income. Certain tax advantages – relating to depreciation, inventory valuation and so forth – are available to taxpayers who file a blue return.

Employment income Employment income includes salaries, wages, bonuses, pension payments and any other compensation for personal services performed in Japan, regardless of whether or not they are paid in Japan. Allowances for housing, schooling, tax equalization and similar items are included in employment income. Taxable employment income is computed by subtracting the employment income deduction from the gross amount of compensation.

Employment income paid in Japan is subject to a monthly withholding tax based on tax tables. The annual tax liability is normally settled through withholding if the gross employment income does not exceed ¥15 million and there is no taxable income from other sources.

If employers provide employees with benefits in kind that are essential to the discharge of the employees' duties, the benefits are excluded from taxable employment income. Such tax-free benefits include commuting allowances, travel and living expenses for business trips, home leave transportation and moving expenses.

The tax treatment of certain benefits applicable to expatriate employees is explained below.

- **Company housing** If the employer provides housing for the employee, the employee is assessed only the value of the economic benefit, instead of the actual cost to the employer. The formula to compute the economic benefit is based on the taxable value of the building and land, plus an amount for the floor space. The assessed amount is generally a small fraction of the actual rent paid for Western-style housing. The taxable rent for a director is substantially higher than that for an employee, ranging from 35% to 50% of the actual rental value. The 35% rate applies if the director periodically uses the residence for business purposes, such as entertaining customers.
- **Utilities** Utility charges borne by the employer, or the amount paid to the employee as reimbursement for utilities, are fully taxable to the employee.
- **Club dues** If club dues paid by the employer are for the sole benefit of the employee, the amount is taxable; if such dues are for the benefit of the employer, the amount should be included in normal expenses and not reflected in the employee's earnings. If the dues are part personal and part business, only the portion attributable to personal use is included in the employee's taxable income.
- **Education allowance** An education allowance provided to the employee, or borne by the employer, to defray expenses incurred in the education of the employee's children is taxable to the employee. Certain international schools have a program by which the employer makes a contribution instead of paying tuition for the employee's children. Such a contribution by the employer is not taxable to the employee. An education allowance paid to educate the employee in skills directly necessary to the performance of the employee's duties is not taxable to the employee.

- **Auto allowance** A company car used primarily for the employer's business is not treated as income of the employee, even if the employee sometimes uses the car for personal purposes; but money paid to the employee in lieu of a company car constitutes taxable income.
- **Home leave** Direct round-trip air fares paid by the employer for the employee and his or her family to travel once a year to their home country are not taxable to the employee. However, if payment by the employer includes indirect routing, such as a vacation trip en route, that portion of the fare is taxable to the employee.
- **Moving expenses** Moving expenses paid by the employer for the employee's relocation or transfer are not taxable to the employee unless the amount is excessive.

Normally, taxable compensation is reportable on an accrual basis; however, for items not paid on a regular basis, such as tax equalization payments, the payments are considered to have accrued as of the date they are paid by the employer to, or on behalf of, the employee and are therefore included in income in the year in which such payments are made.

Occasional income Occasional income includes income such as prizes, gambling winnings and life insurance proceeds received on a policy's maturity (excluding proceeds received by reason of the death of the insured and proceeds paid from a tax-qualified pension plan). After the deduction of expenses and the standard deduction of ¥500,000, one-half of the remaining amount is taxable.

Deductions

A resident individual is allowed a number of deductions in calculating net taxable income. These deductions include casualty losses, medical expenses, social insurance premiums, life and casualty insurance premiums, contributions and personal deductions. Non-residents are generally not allowed any deductions except for the basic personal deduction.

Casualty losses Losses from natural disasters, fire, theft and so forth incurred in respect to property in Japan owned by the taxpayer or the taxpayer's family are deductible up to the amount not covered by the insurance proceeds and in excess of 10% of the total income or ¥50,000, whichever is less.

Medical expenses Medical and dental expenses (less insurance reimbursement) for a taxpayer and dependents in excess of 5% of total income or ¥100,000, whichever is less, are deductible up to a maximum of ¥2 million. Receipts must accompany a claim for a deduction when the tax return is filed.

Tax rates

National individual income tax rates are progressive, ranging from 10% on taxable income of less than ¥3 million to 50% on taxable income of ¥20 million or more.

Tax credits

A resident individual may reduce the amount of tax payable by certain tax credits as well as by tax prepayments.

Credit for income tax withheld Income tax withheld at source – such as withholding tax on dividend income, employment income, retirement income and miscellaneous income – can be credited against national income taxes. If the income tax withheld exceeds the tax liability, the excess can be refunded.

Dividend tax credit If a taxpayer's aggregate income is ¥10 million or less, a tax credit of 10% of the amount of gross dividends received is allowed. If the aggregate income exceeds ¥10 million, the 10% credit applies to the amount of dividends received which, when added to all other ordinary income, brings the total income to ¥10 million. A 5% credit is allowed on dividends in excess of that amount. Dividends received from foreign corporations do not qualify for this credit.

Foreign tax credit Resident taxpayers are taxed on their worldwide income. To avoid double taxation, taxpayers can take direct foreign taxes paid as a tax credit, subject to a limit which is calculated as follows:

$$\text{Japanese corporate tax} \times \frac{\text{Taxable income from foreign sources}}{\text{Total taxable income}}$$

If creditable foreign taxes exceed the limit or if the foreign tax credit limitation exceeds creditable foreign taxes, the unused portion may be carried forward for three years.

Instead of taking a foreign tax credit, a taxpayer may elect to deduct the foreign tax from taxable income.

Credit for the purchase of a private residence If a taxpayer with an annual income not exceeding ¥30 million acquires a residence, he or she is allowed a tax credit. The credit is equal to the lesser of ¥200,000 or 1% of the year-end balance of the mortgage from a private financial institution plus one-half of the housing loan from a public financial institution. The credit may be taken for six years.

Inhabitants' tax

Residents are subject to inhabitants' tax, both prefectural and municipal, consisting of a per capita levy and an income levy. Inhabitants' tax is assessed as of January 1 of each year, based on the prior year's income. Accordingly, non-residents and non-permanent residents will not be subject to inhabitants' tax in the year of arrival but will be subject to inhabitants' tax in the year of departure from Japan on income accrued during the previous year.

The computation of taxable income for the purposes of inhabitants' tax is similar to the calculation for national tax, except that the amounts of the deductions and tax credits differ.

An individual who files a final income tax return is not required to file an inhabitants' tax return. Inhabitants' tax is payable in four equal installments in June, August and October and in January of the following year. Usually, however, salary earners paid in yen pay inhabitants' tax through withholding from their monthly salary during the 12-month period from June to May.

Enterprise tax

Enterprise tax is levied on the business income of individuals. An individual who files a final income tax return or an inhabitants' tax return does not need to file a separate enterprise tax return. The tax base is the net business income, as determined for national tax purposes.

No personal exemptions are allowed, but a standard deduction of ¥2.4 million is given. The tax rates range from 3% to 5%, depending on the type of business or profession. The tax is payable in two equal installments in August and November.

WITHHOLDING TAXES

Dividends, interest and royalties distributed by a domestic corporation are subject to a 20% withholding tax unless an applicable tax treaty modifies the rate.

INHERITANCE AND GIFT TAXES

Inheritance tax is imposed on heirs and beneficiaries on the value of the property they acquire by inheritance or bequest. Gift tax is imposed on the recipients on the value of property received as a gift. Individuals who have domiciles in Japan are subject to inheritance tax and/or gift tax on all property transferred to them as an inheritance tax and/or gift. Individuals who have domiciles outside Japan are subject to inheritance tax and/or gift tax only on property located in Japan. A domicile is defined as the place of an individual's principal residence at the item the inherited or donated property is transferred.

Japan's only inheritance and gift tax treaty is with the United States.

CONSUMPTION TAX

Consumption tax is a value-added tax similar to the GST in effect in Canada and the VAT in countries of the European Community. It is levied at each stage in the distribution of goods from manufacturing to wholesale and on retail sales and the provision of services; however, the tax burden is ultimately transferred to the consumer. The tax paid to suppliers in connection with the purchase of goods and services may be credited against the tax charged on sales. A business must fully transfer the tax to the next stage of distribution; otherwise, it may be forced to bear a portion of the tax, thus reducing its profit margin. Smaller businesses are given preferential treatment to alleviate the tax burden.

Credit for the tax paid to suppliers is calculated based on accounting records rather than on invoices. Companies must retain such records for at least seven years.

The main points of the consumption tax are outlined below.

Taxable transactions

Consumption tax is levied on the sale and lease of assets and provision of services in Japan by corporations or individuals operating a business. It is also levied on imported goods.

Taxpayers

Corporations and individuals operating businesses in Japan and importers (including individuals) are subject to consumption tax. Small businesses with annual sales of ¥30 million or less are exempt. They may, however, choose to report as taxpayers in order to reclaim the consumption tax they have paid. The period used to determine whether or not a business qualifies for the small business exemption is the fiscal year which falls two fiscal years prior to the current fiscal period.

Tax-exempt transactions

The following items are tax-exempt:

- capital, financial and insurance transactions, including the sale or lease of land, the sale of securities, interest on loans, guarantee fees and insurance premiums.
- government sales of postal services and revenue stamps for stamp duty and certain government handling charges that are not in competition with the private sector.
- international postal transfers and foreign exchange transactions based on international treaties.

As a matter of government policy, public medical insurance services, certain social welfare services, and school tuition and entrance examination fees are also exempt. Land rented for less than one month and land used for parking lots, tennis courts and playgrounds is taxed on use. Brokerage commissions are also subject to tax.

Exports

Export transactions, including export-related transactions such as the sale or lease of freight goods in bonded areas, international transportation and telecommunications are exempt. Services rendered to non-residents overseas are exempt as export-related transactions. Taxes paid to purchase goods that are subsequently exported can be deducted by exporters when calculating their tax liability.

Taxable base

The taxable base is the amount charged for goods and services. For imported goods, the amount charged includes customs duties and other excise taxes.

Tax rate

The consumption tax rate is 3%. However, a 4.5% rate applies to passenger cars (excluding small cars with an engine displacement of 550 cc or less) until March 31, 1994.

Calculation of tax

The amount of tax payable is calculated at 3% of taxable sales less taxes paid on taxable purchases. Taxable purchases include purchases from tax-exempt suppliers.

Taxes paid to suppliers may be deducted in full unless the value of tax-exempt sales exceeds 5% of the total sales, in which case the deductible amount is calculated using either of the following formulas:

- Taxes paid on taxable purchases made solely in conjunction with taxable sales are added to taxes paid on purchases made in conjunction with both taxable and tax-exempt sales. The sum is then multiplied by the ratio of the taxable transactions, which is the ratio of taxable sales to total sales.
- Taxes paid on taxable purchases are multiplied by the ratio of the taxable transactions.

A business that opts for the second formula must apply that method for two years. A business may, however, change from the first formula to the second without a waiting period.

A business with annual sales of ¥500 million or less can use a simplified formula to calculate tax. The business files a report to the tax office using 80% (90% for wholesalers) of sales as deemed purchase cost. It then pays a 3% tax on 20% (or 10% for wholesalers) of sales or 0.6% (or 0.3% for wholesalers) of the total sales amount. A business which has chosen the simplified formula cannot change this for two years.

Business enterprises with annual sales between ¥30 million and ¥60 million pay tax at less than the standard 3% rate because of a marginal exemption.

Tax returns and payments

The tax period is generally the fiscal year for corporations or the calendar year for individuals. Taxpayers, however, may choose a quarterly tax period.

A corporation must file a tax return and pay the tax due within two months after its fiscal year-end. Also, a corporation must submit an interim return and a payment equal to one-half of the previous year's tax or the actual amount based on the current six-month interim accounts. If the amount of interim tax is less than ¥300,000, however, an interim return and payment are not required.

Tax returns and payments for imported goods must be submitted before the goods may be taken out of the bonded area. A three-month extension is allowed, however, if collateral is provided.

OTHER TAX

Accumulated earnings tax on personal holding companies

Accumulated earnings tax is imposed as an additional tax on current undistributed taxable earnings of personal holding companies. Personal holding companies are corporations, 50% or more of the shares of which are held by three or fewer than three individual shareholders. The tax rate varies from 10% to 20%.

TAX TREATIES

Japan has concluded various international income tax treaties to avoid double taxation. In addition, income tax treaties with some other countries are presently under negotiation.

Most treaties reduce the tax rates on Japanese-sourced income from dividends, interest, royalties, personal services, and ocean and air transportation and also provide relief from double taxation through tax credits. Generally, the treaties reduce the tax rates only when income is not attributable to a non-resident's permanent establishment in Japan.

TAX TREATMENT OF VARIOUS TYPES OF SALES

Installment sales

Where the company sells goods or renders services by installments in accordance with the terms of a contract, the company may choose to record the sales on an installment basis on the condition that the company applies that basis consistently. Profit on installment sales is calculated as follows:

$$\left(\text{Installments sales} - \text{Cost of goods sold} - \text{Sales charge}\right) \times \frac{\text{Installments which become due in a fiscal year}}{\text{Installment sales}} = \text{Profit on installment sales}$$

Consignment sales

A date of a consignment sale is considered to be the date on which the consignee sold the consigned goods, or if a sales statement is prepared and forwarded to a consignor by the consignee for each sale, it may be the date on which the sales statement is received by the consignor. These sales may be transacted on a regular basis such as weekly or monthly.

Approval sales

A date of an approval sale is considered to be the date on which the customer who is holding the delivered goods at its own site notifies its intention of purchase to the seller. In some cases, the approval sales are recognized after a certain time has elapsed since the date the goods were delivered to the customer. Such terms may either be prescribed in the contracts or established by custom in Japan.

Sales by subscription

When a subscription payment has been received, the amount should be recorded in "Deposits Received" account (as a liability). Sales by subscription are recorded when the subscribed goods have been delivered.

Deferred payment sales

When a company sells items such as machinery and plants, vessels and automobiles on a deferred payment basis, on condition that the company records continuously, the profit on sales may be deferred. The following formula is used for the calculation of the profit allocated to a given year:

$$(\text{Total profit}) \times \frac{\text{The amount which has come due during the year}}{\text{Total deferred payment sales}} = \text{The profit for the year}$$

TAX TREATMENT OF VARIOUS OTHER BUSINESS TRANSACTIONS

Selling commission

- bonuses paid to salespersons of specified agents by manufacturers or wholesalers.

These payments are treated as the selling commission and bonuses related to the above are subject to withholding tax as business income. These commission and bonus payments are usually calculated on the sales volume or amount in accordance with a prescribed rate on contracts.

Reserve for warranties on products and guarantees of completed work

A deductible reserve is permitted for resident companies in the construction industry or certain other manufacturing industries. The following are the types of businesses for which this reserve is permitted:

- construction
- manufacturing the following:
  - vessels, pumps and propellers for vessels
  - automobiles
  - air-conditioners

- microwave ovens
- facsimile machines
- television sets
- cameras
- others

Several conditions are prescribed for the reserve to be approved; a tax professional may be consulted for further details.

ACCOUNTING AND AUDITING

The accounting profession

There were certified public accountants, junior certified public accountants and 122 audit corporations registered with the Japanese Institute of Certified Public Accountants (JICPA) as of January 31, 1993.

To qualify as a certified public accountant, a candidate must pass a national examination and must register with the JICPA as stipulated in the Certified Public Accountants Law. The examination is written in three stages. The first examination, from which college graduates are exempt, is intended to judge a candidate's general ability. A candidate who passes the second examination qualifies as a junior CPA; generally, junior CPAs must have three years' training and experience in public accounting to be eligible for the third examination.

The Certified Public Accountants Law, as amended in 1966, gave legal sanction to the incorporation of individual accounting practices into professional audit corporations, which are organizations similar to unlimited partnerships.

These firms provide accounting, auditing, tax and management consulting services. In Japan, as in other countries, the "Big Five" accounting firms provide services through their worldwide networks. The services provided by Japanese accountants, like those provided by accountants in other countries, include:

- consultation and assistance to foreign investors in establishing businesses in Japan, including the choice of business entity, the preparation and filing of the required documents and the handling of registration requirements.

- services provided after the establishment of a branch or the incorporation of a company, such as accounting and bookkeeping, statutory and voluntary audits, and tax services and management consulting services concerning projects such as financial programs, profit plans, management information, EDP systems, reorganizations, mergers and liquidations.

Statutory regulations

The Ministry of Justice regulates financial accounting through the Commercial Code, and the Ministry of Finance specifies financial accounting requirements in the Securities and Exchange Law. The Legislation Deliberation Council, an advisory body to the Ministry of Justice, has embodied its opinions in the "Regulations concerning the Balance Sheet, Income Statement, Business Report and Supporting Schedules of Joint Stock Corporations."

The Business Accounting Deliberation Council, an advisory body to the Minister of Finance, issued the " Financial Accounting Standards for Business Enterprises," which have been reflected in the Ministry of Finance's "Regulations Concerning the Terminology, Form, and Preparation Methods of Financial Statements." The standards required by these regulations are similar to U.S. standards.

Books of account and records The Commercial Code requires all business enterprises to maintain double-entry books of account, including a general ledger and a subsidiary ledger. The books must be retained for a 10-year period.

Financial statements Currently, publicly-owned Japanese companies prepare two similar sets of financial statements. The basic financial report required under the Commercial Code is prepared in accordance with the "Regulations Concerning the Balance Sheet, Income Statement, Business Report and Supporting Schedules of Joint Stock Corporations." These regulations must be observed by all joint stock companies. The form and content of the financial statements required under the Securities and Exchange Law for companies with debt and equity securities traded publicly on securities markets are regulated by the "Regulations Concerning the Terminology, Form and Preparation Methods of Financial Statements."

Reporting under the Commercial Code of Japan Under the Commercial Code, the following financial statements must be prepared by a company for approval at its annual shareholders' meeting:

- a balance sheet
- an income statement
- a proposal for appropriation of retained earnings or disposition of deficit.

In addition, supporting schedules are required for the following:

- changes in capital stock and the statutory reserve
- changes in bonds and other short-term and long-term borrowings
- changes in fixed assets and accumulated depreciation
- collateralized assets
- debt guarantees
- changes in provisions
- amounts due to and from the controlling shareholders
- equity ownership in subsidiaries and the number of shares of the company's stock held by those subsidiaries
- amounts due from subsidiaries
- transactions with directors, statutory auditors, controlling shareholders and third parties with which conflicts of interest exist
- remuneration paid to directors and statutory auditors.

Notes to the financial statements should include the following:

- a summary of significant accounting policies, such as asset valuation methods, depreciation methods and methods of recognizing significant reserves.
- changes in accounting principles and the amounts of the adjustments resulting from the changes.
- the market value of significant current asset items that are substantially lower than their carrying amounts stated at cost.
- the total amount of receivable from and payable to directors.
- material assets or liabilities denominated in foreign currencies.
- assets pledged as collateral.

- debt guarantees, notes receivable discounted or endorsed with recourse, material litigations and other contingent liabilities.
- net income or loss per share.
- in connection with the computation of the amount of earnings available for the distribution of dividends, the excess amount of the sum of certain deferred charges (such as preparation costs, research and development costs, expenditures for the procurement of resources and market development costs) over the amount of the legal reserves.
- amounts of revenues earned and costs and expenses incurred from transactions with subsidiaries and controlling shareholders.

Reporting under the Securities and Exchange Law of Japan In general, the basic financial statements required under the Securities and Exchange Law (SEL) are the same as those required under the Commercial Code; however, the terminology and the form and content of the financial statements and supporting schedules are more precisely defined in the financial regulations of the SEL.

In general, the standards for determining when a separate presentation of items is required (materiality standards) are as follows:

- 1% for balance sheet accounts. For example, a major class of inventory, such as raw materials, must be stated separately if it exceeds 1% of the total assets.
- 10% or 20% for income statement accounts. In this case, the base is the total of the component items that comprise a major section of the income statement. For example, if installment sales or sales to related parties exceed 20% of the total sales, the amount must be stated separately. Similarly, if losses on sales of marketable securities exceed 10% of the total non-operating expenses, the amount must be stated separately.

Commercial and industrial companies are required to present the following schedules in support of the applicable financial statement items:

- Schedule I — marketable securities.
- Schedule II — tangible fixed assets.
- Schedule III — intangible fixed assets.
- Schedule IV — investments in affiliated companies.
- Schedule V — investments in equity other than in the capital stock of affiliated companies.

- Schedule VI — loans to affiliated companies.
- Schedule VII — bonds payable.
- Schedule VIII — long-term borrowings.
- Schedule IX — borrowings from affiliated companies.
- Schedule X — capital stock.
- Schedule XI — capital surplus.
- Schedule XII — legal reserve and voluntary reserves
- Schedule XIII — depreciation, depletion and amortization of fixed assets and deferred charges.
- Schedule XIV — allowances and provisions.

Filing and disclosure Under the Commercial Code, the audit opinions of both the statutory auditor and the independent auditor must be submitted to the annual general shareholders' meeting.

Under the SEL, corporations that have offered securities and filed registration statements in the past and corporations with shares listed on stock exchanges or traded on the over-the-counter market are required to file securities reports annually and semi-annually with the Minister of Finance. The financial statements included in these reports must be audited by an independent accountant or an audit corporation.

Auditors A company may be required to engage two types of auditors: statutory and independent.

Statutory auditors A joint stock company must have at least one statutory auditor, who is not required to have formal professional qualifications. A company with capital of ¥500 million or more or with total liabilities of ¥20 billion or more must have more than one statutory auditor, at least one of whom must be assigned full time. The statutory auditor must not be a director or an employee of the company or its subsidiaries. The statutory auditors are elected by majority vote of the shareholders for a term of two years.

The statutory auditor is responsible for the audit both of the financial statements and of the operations of the company. The statutory auditor's duties and responsibilities vary depending on the size of the company. In a company with capital of ¥100 million or less, the duties and responsibilities are limited to an examination of the financial statements prepared by the directors at the end of each accounting period and to the preparation of a report thereon to be submitted to the shareholders' meeting.

In a company with capital over ¥100 million, the duties and responsibilities are quite broad. Statutory auditors are not only responsible for auditing the financial statements but are also required to supervise the performance of the directors. They can, as necessary, request directors to report on the operations of the company, conduct investigations, and report improper acts to the Board of Directors and to shareholders' meetings. Statutory auditors can attend Board of Directors' meetings and express opinions.

Independent Auditors A company with capital of ¥500 million or more or with total liabilities of ¥20 billion or more must appoint an independent auditor (or auditing firm). The independent auditor must be appointed by resolution at a shareholders' meeting. The independent auditor must be a certified public accountant or an audit corporation whose role is to audit the financial statements of the company.

For answers to specific questions please contact:

Showa Ota & Co.
Hibiya Kokusai Bldg.
2-2-3, Uchisaiwai-cho
Chiyoda-ku, Tokyo 100
Tel: (03) 3503-1191
Fax: (03) 3503-1277

MANAGING YOUR DISTRIBUTION RELATIONSHIPS

LAUNCHING YOUR PRODUCT

A good product can be strangled at birth, even in the hands of a capable distributor, if the exporter is under the illusion that sales somehow take off spontaneously. A good launching program and effective training are absolutely necessary in a well-organized exporting drive.

INTO THE SUNSET...

The starting pistol

One of the most common misconceptions among exporters is that a swarm of salesmen will crisscross Japan showing their products and booking orders as soon as the distribution agreement is signed. They could not be more wrong!

The day after the deal is signed, the distribution company owner has probably had time to think of ten good reasons why your product is no good. The product manager may have chucked your product literature in the filing cabinet because he has more pressing problems to deal with. As for the salesmen, they are probably unwilling to demonstrate your product because they only remember 5% of what you told them and do not want to appear foolish in front of prospective buyers. If thousands of exporters face such situations every year, it is because they mistake a signature for a commitment when all the distributor wished to do is purchase an option for himself.

What is needed at this point is a well-executed launching program. While this program should be mutually agreed to before the distribution agreement is signed, you the supplier must realize that commitment to your product will not flow automatically from a contract and cannot be expected as a right. Commitment is based on human relations and concrete results, both of which can be developed by a conscious effort. This is where the field rep's personality and communication skills really come into play.

Russian roulette

The lack of time is usually cited as the reason so many exporters fall short at this crucial point. Exporters typically swing into Tokyo to exhort their distributors over drinks, then move on to Taipei or Hong Kong for more pep talks over more drinks, followed by Singapore, Bangkok, Sydney, Melbourne, and so on, where the same scene is repeated. Many exporters believe that if ten wet wicks are lighted, one is surely bound to go off! The problem is not time; plenty of it is wasted. Export managers simply must realize that distributors in Asia will not perform well unless field reps have the time and skills required to launch the product properly. Once you have prioritized your target markets, it is far more profitable to develop them one by one in a thorough fashion than to try to cover all of Asia superficially.

JOINT PLANNING

Making goals explicit

Launching programs are usually settled during the final stages of the contract negotiation process. Your goal at that stage is to take the distributor's senior management out of the realm of theory by committing them publicly to subsequent planning meetings, press releases, and sales training sessions.

Sales targets

This program is part of a larger sales promotion plan which must also be made explicit. Amateurs resort to pleading and bullying to push sales; experts rely on negotiated plans to ratchet up distributor performance and develop their in-house market knowledge of Japan. The plan need not be perfect or even good at first: as long as it is reasonable and gives the distributor clear and credible sales targets for the coming year, your product should attract its fair share of distributor resources during the first crucial twelve months when its fate will be decided. The two most effective methods used to define sales targets in the early stages are the **market factor method** and the **promotion plan method**. In both cases, your persuasiveness in the eyes of the distributor will depend on your familiarity with competing products and the customer's buying habits (see Prospecting in Japan – product mapping).

Market factor method

To avoid haggling over numbers until both sides reach the midpoint between two extreme positions, certain suppliers try to identify an independent variable and a target market share to which sales targets can be tied. This independent variable – called market factor – should have a causal relationship with the level of demand for your product.

Example

If a playpen exporter agrees with his distributor that the relevant market factor in Osaka Prefecture is the number of births during the previous year and that 5% is a reasonable market share to aim for during the first year, the sales target could be calculated as follows:

Live births in Osaka (1993)	*86,840*
Target market share	*x .05*
Sales target for 1994	*4,342*

Although market factors are not always as easy to determine as in our example, the advantages of this method are its objectivity and face validity. The distributor can follow its logic without a knowledge of statistics and marketing research. However, this method still leaves plenty of room for quibbling. A distributor could counter that most apartments are too small for playpens. More important, the supplier has not nailed down the distributor as to *how* he intends to sell that number of playpens.

Promotion plan method

Because distributors often think in terms of man-hours spent to achieve certain returns rather than market share, certain exporters think it best to first reach an agreement on a promotional plan before attempting to forecast sales. This is the approach I also recommend. If you have done your research properly, you know something about competing products, who your target customers are and through which intermediaries they are best approached. The next step is to prioritize your target customer groups with your distributor according to sales potential and list the various ways which can be used (along with their cost and expected results within a year) to stimulate sales for each of these groups. What will ensue is a classical bargaining session where a balance is struck between what you would like and are willing to invest in the sales effort, and what the distributor is willing to contribute. Then, and only then, agree to sales targets.

The advantage of this system is that the distributor has a closer stake in achieving his forecasts and a stronger sense of the ways in which the product can be made to grow. If the first year is a success, you can often incorporate the market factor line of reasoning in your argument for augmenting sales targets. By then, the distributor will be far more trusting and receptive.

The product specialist

One final and crucial point to emphasize in a promotion plan is the principle of having a product manager or senior salesman designated for special training related to your product. Ideally, this should be someone with whom you communicate easily, a person with some authority and seniority. This point cannot be overemphasized. Productive franchises often owe their success to the fact that someone within the distributor's organization became personally and enthusiastically involved with the product. As a "product specialist," he will be the one who deals with key and demanding customers, keeps the sales force motivated and maintains inventory levels in your absence. Insist on a product specialist regardless of what the distribution company owner says. If there is no way of getting one, seriously consider giving your business to someone else.

THE LAUNCH

Promotion

Investment in concrete promotional activities such as trade fairs, exhibitions, technical seminars and mailings is generally acceptable to distributors. Advertising, on the other hand, often meets with opposition. The general feeling among distributors is that anything fancy and expensive whose return cannot be quantified should be paid for in part or in whole by the supplier.

Timing

The launching program should follow fast on the heels of the contract. Do not allow the distributor to lose enthusiasm for your product by allowing too much time to elapse between signing the agreement and concrete action.

KISS

This is no time to waste resources on fringe products and territories. Reference has already been made to Japan's limited shelf space and the high cost of storage. Limit your product line during the first year to the few items most likely to succeed. Similarly, concentrate your promotional program in the geographical areas where success is most assured. This is where your early research (see Prospecting in Japan – product mapping) will help you tremendously to steer initial efforts most productively. More difficult territories can be tackled later when you have momentum.

Concessions

Expect your distributor to ask for price concessions, even during the launch. They do this to test you and to make the point that no price list is sacrosanct. It is very important that you resist any such demands or you will never stop being badgered for more discounts. Moreover, new products are, by their very nature, self-promoting and it is unwise to squander special discounts during the launch.

Translation

Another occasional bone of contention is the translation of sales material. This is something you must settle early on with your distributor by examining what successful exporters in your product category are doing in Japan and end-user preferences. It may be that translation or unusual packaging will distinguish your product from the rest and curb parallel imports (see Weak Points and Trouble Spots). Either way, research this question early on and take a joint decision or else translation will come up in every subsequent meeting to explain away poor sales results.

TRAINING

Crucial

Training is probably the most powerful tool in the exporter's hands to win the war for distributor attention. It is a basic, ongoing necessity for success with distributors, and never more important than at the beginning. If done well, it will go a long way towards enhancing the confidence of the sales force in your product and simplify communication when (not if) problems arise. Done in a careless, lackluster way, it will almost certainly lay your product to rest at the bottom of everyone's priority list.

Presentation

Training presentations work best if certain fundamental rules are followed:

- Assume tactfully that your audience knows nothing.

- Speak slowly and avoid slang expressions, especially if your speech is being interpreted.
- Keep technical questions for a separate session.
- Tailor your message to the special interests of your audience: senior management, your product specialist, the sales force, technicians (see section below).
- Pay proper homage to any superiors who may be present by mentioning their names and soliciting comments.
- The Japanese are very visually-oriented. To inject some excitement into the presentation, use visual aids, maintain some physical movement and avoid reading a prepared script.
- Move from the general to the specific. After a brief, self-deprecating and informal introduction, give a general industry background as it relates to Japan. Move on afterwards to your own company's track record and long-term hopes for Japan. Then comes the product. Highlight the unique nature of Japanese customer needs (don't tell them they are not unique; no one will believe you) and the distinctive ways your product can satisfy them. Criticizing the competition does not go down well with the Japanese, so avoid it. Provide a market synopsis outlining the prioritized list of customer groups previously identified with distributor senior management. The salesmen will be most interested to know how many of their present clients fit into our target groups.
- Finally, summarize the key points covered.

zzzzzzzz

The Japanese may be visually-oriented but their capacity to sleep anytime and anywhere is legendary. Lifetime employment, it seems, carries with it a heavy load of stress and anxiety. A typical Japanese salesman can be away from home 270 nights a year. With so few opportunities to relax, sales presentations are an ideal time to catch up on much-needed sleep. Look out for the warning signs: arms folded, eyes closed, the head rolling from side to side until it drops forward signaling complete loss of consciousness. To wake anyone abruptly at this stage, especially company managers, causes damaging loss of face.

The best cure for this is prevention. Keep your presentations short and to the point. Limit yourself only to the few items they will actually be selling during the initial months and make sure there are plenty of opportunities to establish one-on-one relationships with the sales force. Some wily exporters even ask their distributors to take pictures of the audience during a presentation as if it were an important event. That keeps everyone alert! Who wants his photo taken asleep on the job?

Failure

Sadly, many North American field reps do poorly in training presentations for three reasons: they do not know their product sufficiently to answer questions from what can be a sophisticated, internationally-minded audience; their knowledge of the Japanese market is insufficient to capably priorize different customer groups and give meaningful advice as to how best to reach them; and they underestimate the importance of communication skills and personal relationships. Small wholesalers, in particular, respond very well to a form of guidance that is not overbearing yet demonstrates a sincere interest in their well-being – what some would call paternalism.

DIFFERENT AUDIENCES

Owners/senior managers

Assuming the field rep has done his original market prospecting thoroughly (product mapping and channel mapping), much of the training at this level will occur during the process of formal product presentations and negotiations. Subsequent training meetings should emphasize your product in a competitive perspective, its market potential, its compatibility with the distributor's other lines and, of course, its profitability.

Product specialist

This is the person, mentioned earlier in this section, selected for special training because you require someone within the distributor organization who knows your product almost as well as you do. The other (unavowed) goal is to establish a personal relationship with that person so that he becomes committed to your success. The most time-effective way to reach these objectives is usually to invite the product specialist to your home plant. He will not only gain a first-hand impression of your capabilities but you also have his undivided attention and a much greater chance of winning his dedication and loyalty because overseas trips are a special event, long to be remembered. Make sure the distributor has a stake in the product specialist's training. The usual way to share costs is for the distributor to pay for travel expenses while you pick up on-site costs, such as room, board and incidentals.

Salesmen and technical personnel

Because the salesman's greatest challenge is the fear of rejection, arising especially from an ignorance of the product and its application, the most effective training at this level is done through small group sessions followed by hands-on field sales training. One hour of field work is worth a hundred hours of lecturing. Almost as important are the many opportunities field work gives you to strike up a personal relationship with various salespeople. Such relationships go a long way in a Japanese context towards ensuring that your product gets more than its fair share of attention after you are gone.

"Field work training" usually means three basic things:

- Your presence at trade fairs and exhibitions. Foreigners attract attention and that is good for the distributor.
- Opening new accounts. Relationships between Japanese companies are created not by cold calling from below, but rather through go-betweens acting at a high level. Because North Americans and Europeans are accorded a certain respect, your participation in certain sales calls can help the distributor open potentially lucrative accounts.
- Exporters with a direct marketing database for Japan often use it to develop leads and better target the sales force's activities. Japan's labor shortage is making traditional selling techniques – relationship selling, drinking tea with clients, long chats on the phone – very expensive to support.

Training does not mean the imposition of aggressive North American sales techniques on clients. Japanese buyers and sellers do not react well to them.

Sales types and technicians rarely mix well together. It is best, therefore, to organize different sessions for both groups, making sure that the presentation for the technicians is given by a qualified person able to provide all the answers required. Complete familiarity with the product's technical and maintenance requirements is the only way to gain the respect of the engineering and technical staff.

MOTIVATION

Many of the problems faced by foreign exporters dealing with Japan's multi-layered distribution system can be summed up by one word: motivation. What incentives can a supplier use to "push" his product through the system? What criteria should he use when selecting advertising or PR firms to design a promotion campaign that can create demand or "pull" from end-users? I wish to thank Dentsu Burson-Marsteller for contributing the second half of this chapter as well as The Japanese Consumer.

MOTIVATING THE DISTRIBUTOR

Basic principles

Exporters often get so caught up romancing their business that they fall into the trap of treating foreign distributors like religious cults devoted to their products because of their quality or prestige. These things are important, but you must never forget that Japanese middlemen (importers, wholesalers and retailers) are independent businesses whose priorities will often conflict with yours. Here are some basic points to remember:

- The sheer inertia of Japan's overpopulated and multi-layered distribution sector should never be underestimated. "Pushing" products through the system – as opposed to "pulling" them by means of advertising – requires service levels from Japanese manufacturers (rebates, small-batch deliveries, in-channel promotions, personnel sharing, credit) very few importers can match. As a result, many foreign consumer items end up being sold on a spot basis by importers, either as very high-end or low-end niche products.
- Again, to repeat what I said earlier (see Prospecting in Japan – channel mapping), most Japanese middlemen see themselves primarily as purchasing agents for their downstream customers, not as selling agents for their suppliers.
- Most middlemen are in the business of selling product assortments, not individual items, because many customers like to buy multiple products as a group from a single source.
- The rebate systems set up by Japanese manufacturers often distort individual transactions even for imports because terms of trade are tied to volume selling, not profits (see Japanese Distribution Management – the inside view). As a result, many middlemen are focused on annual rather than specific sales even when they result in red ink. The rebates always save the day in the end.

- Finally, the prevalence of rebates and promissory notes in Japanese distribution increases the average middleman's dependency on upstream manufacturers, and makes him a sloppy and conservative manager of his assets. Business relationships must be few and long term; margins in a product category are kept constant whether a given item sells wildly or poorly; and ROI is often extremely low as high service costs are heavily discounted in the scramble to please buyers.

Of course, the situation varies from one product to another and the distribution system is changing, especially at the retail level, but the practices just described remain very much "mainstream." What effect does this have on the traditional tools used by exporters to motivate their foreign distributors: margins, discounts, rebates, credit, training, internal promotion, direct involvement, and overstocking?

Margins

The basic point to remember about gross margins is that they have to be satisfactory. Efficient distributors cut imported lines that take away from their bottom line. Foolish ones accept less and make a mess of everything anyway. The essence of holding a distributor's attention is to become one of his top five to seven profit-makers. Do that and he will bend over backwards to keep you satisfied.

Changing margins to influence distributor behavior, on the other hand, is rarely effective. Exporters used to Hong Kong's freewheeling business style (see my book *Hong Kong/ South China: The Exporter's Distribution Primer*) are often shocked by the relative conservatism of Japanese distributors in this respect. Margins are usually rigidly set across several product lines and apportioned among middlemen according to formulas they think should be stable. No distributor appreciates an exporter who forces him to constantly re-negotiate these profit-sharing arrangements because margins are being fiddled around with.

Discounts and rebates

If Japanese distributors – small ones, especially – ask for small-lot shipments and generous credit terms, volume and trade discounts become meaningless. So don't offer any! Exporters wedded to uniform discount policies often make the mistake of offering too much and end up being bled for extra discounts untied to performance.

The first rule is to stay informed and tie incentives to performance (see the carrot & stick school in Developing a Short List). Trim your discounts to leave an adequate gross margin for the distributor and reserve the rest for specific promotional activities included in the joint sales promotion plan (see Launching Your Product). "But isn't that the distributor's responsibility?" you might ask. "I already give him a very good margin!" True, but with so many suppliers to satisfy, it often happens that a distributor's promises fall through the cracks unless specific incentives are tied to them. Arguing that the distributor's margin is already sufficient may win you the battle but you may ultimately loose the war. Accept these realities of Japanese distribution and plan for it from Day One.

The permutation and combination of incentives can be endless depending on the distributor's circumstances and the joint sales promotion plan. You could offer free samples for trials; share the expense of an advertising program; jointly subsidize a temporary price reduction to customers; offer a special rebate to increase the sales team's commission; participate in certain exhibitions, and so on. Tying incentives to each promotional activity will ensure that the program flies.

Credit

As I explained earlier in Developing a Short List, starting off with small distributors in densely populated niche markets is often a wise move for small and medium exporters. One downside of using smaller, hungrier companies, however, is their need for extended credit.

This is an area where nostrums such as "we're not in the banking business" are widely believed. But if you want to build an export business in Asia, you had better get into the so-called banking business, another name for financing distributor growth. Aggressive distribution strategies almost always go hand in hand with creative management of credit exposure.

The point, first and foremost, is to get paid. The method and time taken to pay should be seen as just another pricing or discounting issue. Depending on the circumstances, you may have to swallow the cost of extended credit, but in most cases, the distributor can be made to pay by adjusting his discounts. Given the Japanese preference for stability, this adjustment is best calculated during the initial negotiating process. Once credit terms are agreed they must be strictly adhered to or each payment will become a test of wills. Then turn to your government for help. Most governments today underwrite excellent export credit programs to assist small and medium firms.

Training

As I pointed out in the previous chapter, training can be a powerful motivating force for a distributor because it simplifies communications and adds to the sale staff's self-confidence. To be effective, however, training has to be treated by the supplier not as a one-shot deal during the launch but as part of an ongoing process with performance evaluations, check points and milestones.

Internal promotion

This is a touchy subject because no distributor wants to loose control of his sales force. Where allowed, cash bonuses are paid to sales teams rather than individuals. Prizes for individual salesmen tend to be of the symbolic kind. Internal promotions work best when they are fair by Japanese standards, easy to understand, and tied to specific targets.

Direct involvement

Over and above the "field training" mentioned in the last chapter, some exporters make very good use of retired Japanese technicians or foreign expats who understand the product and are fluent in Japanese to assist and motivate their distributors. These reps may or may not work full time for the exporter, but what they do is regularly visit the distributor, inquire whether there are any problems or misunderstandings, and report back on new developments and market trends. Given the reticence of the Japanese to report bad news, part-time field reps can sometimes improve communication dramatically. Their visits also act as a powerful reminder pushing the distributor to pay attention to the exporter's products.

Visits from head office have the same effect, provoking an increase in sales activity a month or two before each arrival. Make sure, therefore, to schedule your visits to follow soon after the main selling seasons for your product category.

Use these occasions to also keep in touch with key customers. The Japanese like it when foreign suppliers drop by to see if they are satisfied. It fits their notion of service because the supplier is sending his very best employees to make sure everything is as it should be. You need to get out there directly; you represent the organization.

Overstocking

Inventory is not usually thought of as a motivator; excessive inventory levels force distributors to put pressure on their sales staff to off-load products as a faster rate. Suppliers, therefore, regard overstocking as a legitimate pressure tool as long as their distribution agreements have a no-return-of-merchandise clause. The methods used to incite distributors to overstock include persuasion, bullying, anticipated price increases and real or imaginary threats to supply. Well-organized distributors who adhere to joint sales promotion plans rarely fall for this ploy, but many smaller firms do.

Yes, but...

Never forget that your main challenge in the early days is to attract the distributor's attention away from his existing lines to your own (see Developing a Short List). Important though they are, none of the above "push" techniques will be very effective if some preconditions are not also present:

- **Speed** Suppliers who reply promptly and completely to faxed inquiries attract more attention from distributors. So do those who ship their products on time. Both make their distributors look competent in front of their clients. Both also require adequate sales backup from exporters (see Some Fundamentals).

- **Reliability** Exporters who do well in Japan think twice before making commitments because distributors expect absolute honesty. Reliability that is limited to "big promises" or "most promises" is not good enough.
- **Product development** For many distributors, a key dividing line between exporters deserving special attention and the rest is product development. Are you actively refining your initial product and developing new lines or are you resting on your laurels? Suppliers who stick to a single successful item are usually pushed out as matching products appear on the market (see Weak Points and Trouble Spots). A steady stream of new products, on the other hand, provides continuity to distributors and attracts more promotional efforts.

So much for "push" techniques. "Pull" comes from advertising directed at end-users. What are some of the questions you must ask when selecting an agency specialized in advertising or PR?

CHOOSING AN ADVERTISING OR PR AGENCY

DENTSU BURSON-MARSTELLER

The choice of partners as you enter the Japanese market will be among your most important business decisions. Selecting advertising and public relations support is no exception.

The first step is to understand the difference in the disciplines, as practiced in Japan.

Background

Although Japan has a plethora of consultants, Japanese advertising is dominated by a few large agencies. The largest, in order, are Dentsu, Hakuhodo, Tokyu, Daiko and Asatsu. Foreign-affiliated firms ranking among the top 25 are McCann-Erickson Hakuhodo, Dentsu Young & Rubicam and J.W. Thompson.

Dentsu and Hakuhodo, however, far outweigh the others in size. Billings in 1992, for example, were (in millions of yen):

Dentsu	1,198,255
Hakuhodo	553,618
Tokyo Agency	192,768
Daiko	169,252
Asatsu	147,939

Not surprising, perhaps, in the land of the behemoth corporation; but this has a number of implications that might be new to a foreign firm's experience:

Media might Whereas creative work is valued far more highly than media buying in Western markets, the reverse is the case in Japan because demand for prime time/space by top advertisers exceeds supply and large agencies tightly linked to the media tend to have the advantage. Some of these big spenders therefore use two ad agencies: one for creative and a second for media buying.

Small exporters with modest advertising budgets do not face such dilemmas. Cost trends have nevertheless been favorable to them. In the current "post bubble" economy, demand for media space/time has slackened overall.

Full marketing services The large agencies will be able to provide fully integrated marketing services like research, advertising, public relations, and promotion.

Competitors as clients Two or more clients that might be considered to be conflicts in the U.S. are often housed within one agency in Japan – seemingly with little concern on the part of the Japanese clients.

Japanese advertising strategy

The differences between Western and Japanese advertising worlds go beyond structure. Generally, the approach differs as well. Some have called Japanese advertising emotional; certainly, it could be characterized as more celebrity-oriented and corporate-focused than in many other markets.

Interestingly, consistency in marketing campaigns, and in some cases, long-term celebrity association with a brand or company, is not considered of value. Instead, fresh, new campaigns are demanded. In every season and campaign, Japanese advertisers create new themes and concepts, replacing various *tarento* (celebrity talent) often.

However, consistency of image *is* communicated, by using corporate branding. The corporation, rather than the brand, is usually made the hero. The most common technique is frequent use of corporate logos and trademarks, for example, at the end of a TV commercial. A more sophisticated method is standardizing the "look," tone and/or theme of all campaigns across product lines. In its most effective execution, consumers can immediately spot the corporate identity of any one of many brands or products.

In this respect, foreign firms face a core issue they will encounter in many incarnations: localization vs. standardization. Again and again, marketers will need to decide when to do things the Japanese way, and when, as foreigners, they have the leeway to follow another path. Those whose corporate identities lack the clout of the Japanese marketing giants may choose to build brand franchisees instead, as many foreign firms have been successful doing. Nonetheless, pitfalls exist: they must remain flexible about freshening and recreating their brand identity so as not to be perceived as stale or passé by Japanese consumers. Failure here would surely invite a competitive onslaught.

Trends

With Japanese economic developments – the burst of the economic bubble and ensuing recession; new appreciation for quality of life and a growing sense of individualism – have come trends in advertising's response to changing consumer values. More and more, marketing in

Japan addresses the consumer's desire for services and products that are value-added; competition among marketers will heat up as consumers demand measurable benefits, rather than the amorphous, emotional benefit of image. Marketing experts predict more branding, price competition and perhaps comparative advertising, as a general emphasis on product features and benefits begins to spread.

In response, the way marketers respond will evolve into more spending below the line, supporting product awareness with a sales "pull" – direct mail, point-of-sale, public relations, and so forth.

Choosing agencies

Given this background information, how should a foreign marketer choose partners in Japan? To the criteria you would use in your home market, such as creativity, strategic focus, resources, and capabilities, add the following considerations:

- **Find an advisor you can trust** More than in most markets, you'll need a savvy advisor in Japan, one who has demonstrated he will tell you what he really thinks, rather than what he thinks you want to hear. Consider agencies who are used to servicing foreign multinationals, and who can advise you when to "do it the Japanese way" or when another approach would be more effective.
- **Communicate pro-actively with your advisor** Communication between client and agency often breaks down over distances, both physical and cultural. Ask questions, keep an open mind, put crucial points in writing as often as possible, and consider finding a bicultural "translator" – either within your own organization or by using a foreign-affiliated agency – to ensure you've gotten the messages right.
- **Erase your preconceptions** Avoid the trap of knowing the problem and the solution. As often as not you will be wrong. Let the consultants earn their money. Part of the reason you hire them is to expand the range of options and ideas considered.
- **Be willing to invest** The monetary expense of doing business in Japan is almost legendary, but keep in mind other investments you'll have to make as well. Time and energy spent developing relationships will be crucial to your success. Choose partners who can help by making introductions, adding dimension to relationships, and, if necessary, acting as your surrogate in Japan.
- **Protect your investments** No consultant of any kind can succeed in a vacuum. Do not hold back information – consultants need to fully understand what is going on if they are to contribute. And do not rely on instinct in formulating the marketing plan. Insist on research if none is available. Good research at the beginning can save money later.

- **Ask hard questions** As you have hired expertise, experience and capability to execute, no one should feel defensive when you ask the tough questions. Why does your consultant think the chosen approach will be effective? How does he define effective? How will we measure success?
- **Be realistic and patient** Agree on expectations, and then give your marketing efforts time to work. Don't forget – and don't let the home office forget – that Japan is a huge, complex market, and will not be conquered quickly.

For more specific inquiries, please contact:

Dentsu Burson-Marsteller
Sogo Kojimachi No. 3 Bldg.
6 Kojimachi, 1-chome
Chiyoda-ku, Tokyo 102
Tel: (03) 3264-6701
Fax: (03) 3234-9647

COMMUNICATION, EVALUATION AND GRIEVANCES

The rule of thumb here is that an ounce of prevention is worth a pound of cure. Indeed, the high level of support Japanese distributors sometimes require allows well-organized suppliers to incorporate supervision and evaluation activities in their support programs.

COMMUNICATION

Launching

Contract negotiation is usually the responsibility of senior marketing managers on both sides. Once this is completed, it is best for them to delegate daily communications to certain subordinates and only touch base when they must deal with serious problems or make important decisions. Part of the launching process, therefore, involves the identification of which person talks to whom for the purposes of ordering, shipping, payments, technical advice, and so on. Changes in personnel affecting these lines of communication should promptly be reported.

Reports

This must be defined precisely in writing during the contract negotiation process and not later because distributors hate to write reports. They rightly feel that a greater amount of information in the supplier's hands means more criticism of their performance and more unsolicited advice.

Remember, too, that most middlemen sell product assortments, not individual items (see Prospecting in Japan – channel mapping). Unless given an incentive to do so, they might not maintain separate sales records by product lines sold. Information that could be used by you in promotion planning, product development, packaging, or pricing might be wittingly or unwittingly buried in non-standard records.

Suppliers nevertheless need to know what is happening and those whose training programs are considered most effective are very creative in devising uncomplicated ways to routinize the distributor's information-gathering and reporting system. Critical data are usually reported on a monthly basis; information on the activities of competitors or on market trends can be scheduled quarterly.

Remember that market information is sometimes very difficult to get in Japan. Do not request data unless you have already discussed the availability of this information with the distributor. Distribution companies, are not, after all, market research firms. Small firms, in particular, may not be able to produce sophisticated market studies.

DISTRIBUTOR'S LAMENT

Depending on the product category, the most common complaints about North American suppliers among Japanese distributors revolve around their export readiness, their distrust of middlemen and the behavior of certain irresponsible sales reps.

Not export-minded

Many Japanese distributors feel that North American suppliers are only interested in their own domestic market. Exporting abroad is seen as a stop-gap measure to ensure that plant capacity is fully utilized when domestic demand is insufficient. As a consequence, exporting is not treated with the same professionalism as in Japan: market knowledge is sophomoric, plant capacity is often exaggerated, quality control is spotty, answers to faxed inquiries are slow to come and frequently incomplete, packaging is not downsized or labeled in Japanese, shipping delays are not taken seriously, and products are not altered to fit Japanese tastes.

Uncooperative

Another typical complaint is that North American suppliers are not used to dealing with middlemen, distrust them, and do not consult with them when making decisions which may directly affect the value of the franchise, such as changes in sourcing patterns, pricing, product line composition and in ingredients or components. Worse still, many suppliers assign unrealistic sales quotas without consultation and then switch to other distributors at the drop of a hat if the quota is not reached.

Junketing firemen

All distributors, particularly small ones, are frustrated when field reps or marketing managers make frequent visits with no defined purpose. Protocol often demands that senior people, perhaps even the owner, accompany them around and some reps have come to expect lavish meals, nights out on the town, and other favors. This can become disruptive when pushed beyond a certain point.

Meddling

Some suppliers, forgetting that their item is only one of many carried by the middleman, try to "rationalize" his distribution practices to fit the "best-offer" North American pattern. Negotiate any changes you want to make before the contract is signed. After that, assume that unsolicited advice will not be well received.

THE SUPPLIER'S TURN

No feedback

This is perhaps the most consistently reported difficulty in dealing with the Japanese: problems are often underreported until they grow insurmountable. Trying to get a frank response from a distance or during business hours can be next to impossible. Instead, the focus shifts to face-to-face encounters after business hours.

Make a point, whenever meeting with distributors or training their salesmen, to set aside a few evenings for informal meals and drinks with product managers, trainees and owners. It is practically the only way to get the full picture. This may explain why the Japanese have so little personal time.

Insufficient sales

Suppliers, especially those who select distributors without studying market conditions or who assign sales quotas without a joint promotion plan, are often unhappy with their distributor's performance and are convinced things would improve if only North American marketing techniques were more extensively used.

CANCELLING A DISTRIBUTOR

Scenarios

The two most common scenarios leading to cancellation are that the distributor has failed to meet the exporter's expectations or that the exporter has outgrown his previous arrangements. In the latter case, the original distributor might still play a role in a larger venture: sales branch, subsidiary or joint venture.

Actually, if an imported product is really successful, the opposite may happen and the distributor might actively solicit a licensing deal whereby the exporter exits the Japanese market altogether in exchange for handsome royalties.

Costly

Canceling a distributor is not something a supplier should take lightly. The risks can be real:

- if there is no termination date mentioned in the contract, the courts tend to conclude that the relationship was intended to last forever (see Elements of a Distribution Agreement). Forget the cliché about the Japanese being averse to contracts; they can be as legalistic as any American lawyer when protecting their interests.
- exporters foolish enough to let their agents register or patent their product at the beginning may find that switching is not an option.
- the distributor could disrupt the market by dumping his inventory at bargain prices.
- service levels to existing retail clients could drop precipitously, leading them to cancel your product. For technical products, the same could happen to after-sales service.
- if the distributor owes you money, collecting it or even agreeing on how much is owed could prove difficult.
- your reputation with retailers, end-users and other potential distributors could suffer.
- in certain extreme cases, you ex-distributor could do everything in his power to make life difficult for his successor.

Controlling risks

Prevention is the best way to avoid this. Take the time and make the effort to carefully select your distributor. If problems arise after selection, do you best to ascertain the reason your distributor is not performing and help him find a solution. If cancelling is unavoidable, plan each step carefully.

- Do not cancel anyone unless you have a replacement.
- Find out how much of your product the distributor has on stock and in transit.
- If possible, avoid cancelling your distributor just before a major selling season or just after he has spent money on a major promotion program for your product.

These precautions will probably help you avoid some of the more extreme retaliatory measures I outlined above. During the subsequent negotiations, four issues in particular frequently come up.

- **Transfer of stock** Who will pay for the cost of transferring the stock from the old to the new distributor?
- **Trade receivable** The old distributor will want you or his replacement to pay for any stock he has sold on credit.
- **Promotion expenses** Your old distributor will want to be compensated for promotional and advertising expenses he has incurred which will only profit his successor.
- **Compensation** Some other amount may be asked for to avoid ill will or other "problems." Paying off your ex-distributor is sometimes the least costly alternative.

PLANNING AND REFERENCE

PLANNING AND REFERENCE

ENTRY DETAILS

Visas

Except for Australians and South Africans, tourist and business visitors staying less than 90 days are not required to obtain a visa. Visits involving employment or any kind of locally-paid activity do require an appropriate visa.

In certain cases, because of bilateral visa exemption agreements, visitors from certain countries can stay even longer without a visa as long as no employment is involved.

Up to 6 months Citizens of Austria, Germany, Ireland, Mexico, Switzerland and the U.K.

Up to 3 months Citizens of Argentina, Belgium, Canada, Denmark, Finland, France, Iceland, Israel, Italy, Malaysia, Netherlands, New Zealand, Norway, Singapore, Spain, Sweden, the U.S.A., and a few other countries.

Visa extensions

Obtaining a single 90-day tourist visa extension is usually not a problem. Further extensions, however, require a letter of guarantee, preferably in Japanese. Many long-term residents avoid this extra hassle by making brief visits to South Korea, Taiwan or Hong Kong and coming back.

Any foreigner staying longer than 90 days in Japan must obtain an Alien Registration Card from the closest municipal office. This card must be carried at all times.

Customs

Duty-free articles include:

- Portable professional equipment for your own use during your stay.
- Three 760 ml bottles of alcoholic beverages. (Liquor is very expensive in Japan; bringing some for personal consumption or as gifts might be a good idea.)
- Gifts and souvenirs up to a value of ¥200,000.

Any material, such as men's magazines will be confiscated if photographs show pubic hair. No pubic hair, no problem. The penalties for smuggling drugs are extremely severe.

MONEY

Customs again

There are no controls on the import of foreign or Japanese currency. The export of foreign currency is equally unlimited. However, a ¥5-million limit exists for Japanese currency.

Currency

Japanese yen is available as coins (¥1, ¥5, ¥10, ¥100 and ¥500) and banknotes (¥1000, ¥5000, and ¥10,000). The ¥5 and ¥50 coins have a hole in the middle. As of

September 1, 1994, US$1 was worth ¥100, down from ¥123 two years earlier.

Changing money

If you are carrying currency other than U.S. dollars, you should convert part of it at the airport to make sure you have enough to live on until a bank willing to accept your money is found. Exchanging major Western currencies in hotels and shops is rarely a problem.

Generally, "Authorized Foreign Exchange Banks" offer better exchange rates than the hotels. These banks have English signs and are easy to find in major cities. The best way to carry foreign currency elsewhere is in travelers' cheques, preferably in U.S. dollars. Banks are open Monday to Friday from 9 a.m. to 3 p.m. and closed on Saturdays, Sundays and national holidays.

As long as you follow your common sense, crime will not be a problem. The Japanese themselves prefer cash transactions and often carry great wads of money around without worry.

Credit cards

Although credit cards are becoming more commonplace in Japan, cash still reigns supreme outside of the main cities. The most widely accepted cards are American Express, Visa, MasterCard and Diner's Club. In case of emergency, you can reach them at the following numbers in Tokyo:

- American Express, Tel: 3220-6000, 0120-376-100 (toll free 24 hours)
- Visa, Tel: 3459-4800, 3459-4700
- MasterCard, Tel: 3254-6751
- Diner's Club, Tel: 3499-1311, 3797-7311, 3499-1181

Tipping and taxes

There is no tipping in Japan except for late-night taxis and rental car drivers. All hotels and expensive restaurants add a 10-15% service charge to the bill in lieu of tipping. Japan also has a 3% consumer tax. Finally, a local tax of 3% is added to all restaurant bills exceeding ¥5000 and hotel bills exceeding ¥10,000.

GETTING AROUND

From Narita Airport

Your flight to Tokyo will almost certainly land at Narita Airport, fifty miles northeast of the city. Don't even dream of taking a taxi from the airport to your hotel. It could cost you US$150-200 to get to the city. Take either the Airport Express Bus or Airport Limousine Bus instead; tickets cost about ¥3000 and the trip will take 1 to 2 hours depending on the traffic. Both services run to Tokyo's major hotels, but even if they don't go to your hotel directly, you can get off at the stop nearest to it and take a taxi the rest of the way. Taxis are always easy to find at hotels.

Taxis

Japanese taxis are clean, reliable – and expensive. You will probably have to rely on them at first until you know the city sufficiently well to take the faster and cheaper subway. Remember that most taxi drivers cannot speak English – always carry cards or faxed maps (see Networking and Negotiations) showing your hotel or other destinations in Japanese. And even with a map, your driver may occasionally stop to ask for directions because most streets have no names.

Late at night, some taxis avoid foreigners. You can either go to the nearest hotel or restaurant where taxis tend to congregate or do what the locals do and hold up two or three fingers at passing taxis to signal your willingness to pay double or triple the fare for late night trips. During normal hours, there is no tipping.

Car rental

A very bad idea for most visitors. Highways have few signs in English; road maps are inadequate; parking space is very hard to find; traffic is a nightmare during long rush hours; gas is twice as expensive as in North America; and traffic drives on the left. Stick to public transportation.

Subways and local trains

Apart from Tokyo and Osaka, subway systems operate in Fukuoka, Kobe, Kyoto, Nagoya, Sapporo, Sendai and Yokohama. Subways and local trains are convenient for almost anywhere you want to go. To use them you will probably have to buy your ticket from a machine. First refer to the panels on the wall displaying the various subway lines to find out what you have to pay for each destination. If you can't work the fare out, simply buy a ticket for the lowest fare from the machine and pay the difference at the fare adjustment office once you have arrived at destination. These offices are always near the exit gate.

As a rule, subways are easier to use than local trains. Before boarding a train (called "J.R. Line" in Tokyo) make sure it will stop at your destinations; express lines can whisk you nonstop to the suburbs with no warnings.

Using any form of public transportation during rush hours – 7:30 to 9:30 a.m. and 5 to 7 p.m.. – is not recommended unless you know the lines very well.

Buses

Avoid the buses. Even the locals find them confusing and the bus stop signs are written only in Japanese.

Long-distance trips

For longer train trips between cities, seats can be reserved no more than a month before departure. Ask for the "green car" when reserving first-class seats. Tickets are available at travel agencies and, of course, at train stations. The high-speed bullet train (or *Shinkansen*) links all of Japan's major cities except Sapporo. It is fast, clean, frequent and comfortable.

TOKYO HOTELS

Sprawling over more than 800 square miles, Tokyo is the world's second largest city with a population of about 13 million. Like Paris or London, it serves both as an economic and a cultural center. Its hotels rank with the best in the world. The single occupancy rates listed below are quoted only as guidelines. A 10% service charge and a 3% consumption tax are charged in addition to published rates.

US$170+ (¥18,530+)

Akasaka Tokyu
Tel: 3580-2311
Fax: 3580-6066

Akasaka Prince
Tel: 3234-1111
Fax: 3262-5163

Century Hyatt
Tel: 3349-0111
Fax: 3344-5575

New Otani
Tel: 3265-1111
Fax: 3221-2619

Okura
Tel: 3582-1111
Fax: 3582-3707

Capitol Tokyu
Tel: 3581-4511
Fax: 3581-5822

Imperial
Tel: 3504-1111
Fax:3504-1258

Keio Plaza Inter-Continental
Tel: 3344-0111
Fax: 3345-8269

Tokyo Prince
Tel: 3432-1111
Fax: 3434-5551

Pacific Tokyo
Tel: 3445-6711
Fax: 3445-5733

Takanawa Prince
Tel: 3447-1111
Fax: 3446-0849

Tokyo Hilton
Tel: 3344-5111
Fax: 3342-6094

US$100-200 (¥10,900-21,800)

Fairmont
Tel: 3262-1151
Fax: 3264-2476

Ginza Dai-Ichi
Tel: 3542-5311
Fax: 3264-2476

Ginza Tokyu
Tel: 3541-2411
Fax: 3541-6622

Grand Palace
Tel: 3264-1111
Fax: 3230-4985

Shiba Park
Tel: 3433-4141
Fax: 5470-7519

Hill Top
Tel: 3293-2311
Fax: 3233-4567

Ginza Nikko
Tel: 3571-4911
Fax: 3571-8379

Haneda Tokyu
Tel: 3747-0311
Fax: 3747-0366

Holiday Inn Tokyo
Tel: 3553-6161
Fax: 3553-6040

Sunroute Tokyo
Tel: 3375-3211
Fax: 3379-3040

Takanawa Tobu
Tel: 3447-0111
Fax: 3447-0117

Tokyo
Tel: 3447-5771
Fax: 3447-5250

Takanawa Keikyu
Tel: 3443-1211
Fax: 3443-1221

Takanawa
Tel: 5488-1000
Fax: 5488-1005

OSAKA HOTELS

Home of Japan's pharmaceutical industry, Osaka is the commercial core of the Kansai region. A quarter of the country's industrial output is produced here, including textiles, iron and steel. Its airport and docks handle 40% of total exports.

US$100-200 (¥10,900-21,800)

Plaza
Tel: 543-1111
Fax: 454-0169

Hotel Nikko Osaka
Tel: 244-1111
Fax: 245-2432

Royal
Tel: 448-1121
Fax: 448-4414

Hotel New Otani
Tel: 941-1111
Fax: 941-9769

International Osaka
Tel: 941-2661
Fax: 941-5362

Osaka Dai-Ichi
Tel: 341-4411
Fax: 341-4930

Tennoji Miyako
Tel: 779-1501
Fax: 779-8800

Hanshin
Tel: 344-1661
Fax: 344-3860

New Hankyu
Tel: 372-5101
Fax: 374-6885

Osaka Grand
Tel: 202-1212
Fax: 227-5054

Osaka Tokyu
Tel: 373-2411
Fax: 376-0343

LOCAL INFORMATION

Climate
Japan's length and mountainous topography makes for a varied climate. Hokkaido in the north has long winters and short summers, while the southern Ryukyu Islands enjoy a subtropical climate.

In general, the winter months from December to February are cold and relatively dry in Tokyo; when snow falls, it rarely lasts for long. In contrast, the summer months from June to August can be hot and muggy with a short typhoon season at the end of August. The rest of the year is comparatively mild. Rainfall is relatively low in spring and autumn and the days are often clear.

Clothing
For business meetings, conservative colors and styling are appreciated. Avoid wearing anything that looks too casual or flashy.

Bring along plenty of clothing because finding the right size in Japan, especially in footwear, can be difficult. It may also be necessary to change your shirt twice a day during the hot humid summers. Remember that the Japanese are obsessive about personal cleanliness; showing up for appointments with a wrinkled suit never leaves a favorable impression.

Western businesswomen familiar with Japan try not to overwhelm their hosts with make-up, jewelry, perfume, high heels or way-out hair styles. Dark colors and classic styles project the desired mature image. On occasion, pantsuits are acceptable.

Business hours
Shops are typically open seven days a week from 10am to 8pm. Department stores close slightly earlier, at 6:30 or 7 p.m. They also close one day every week. Office hours in large companies are 9 to 5 or 5:30 p.m.. Factories start at 8 a.m. and work an eight-and-a-half-hour shift. Some office personnel work Saturdays (or every second Saturday), and many salarymen work overtime in the evening. Nevertheless, it is advisable to keep appointments within regular office hours.

Except for business lunches, noon meals are generally short, from noon until 1 p.m. Working breakfasts are uncommon because of late night drinking and long commuting times.

Although factory and shop workers leave on the dot at the end of their shifts, most salarymen spend a good part of the evening drinking in bars with their office colleagues. Visiting businessmen are expected to take part in these outings because they are a perfect occasion to communicate frankly about difficulties and cement relationships. This blending of business and pleasure is made possible by substantial tax-free entertainment allowances. There is a second rush hour at 11:30 p.m. as salarymen stagger to catch the last train or wait in line for taxis. The trip home for most of them takes 90 minutes.

Holidays

There are 13 national holidays in Japan. Business travelers should plan their stays around them, particularly **Obon** season (around August 15) – when many Japanese return to their home towns to visit relatives and remember ancestors – and **Golden Week** between April 29 and May 5.

Jan. 1	New Year's Day
Jan. 15	Coming of Age Day
Feb. 11	National Foundation Day
March 20-21	Spring Equinox
April 29	Greenery Day (i.e., the late emperor's birthday)
May 3	Constitution Day
May 5	Children's Day
Sept. 15	Respect for the Aged Day
Sept. 23-24	Autumn Equinox
Oct. 10	Physical Education Day
Nov. 3	Culture Day
Nov. 23	Labor Day
Dec. 23	Emperor's Birthday

Business Centers

Many of the major hotels in Tokyo and Osaka have "business centers" where you can get documents translated, hire an interpreter, do photocopying, use a computer or fax, and so on. Most hotels restrict usage to guests. You may want to choose your hotel on this basis unless you have access to JETRO's Business Support Center (see Networking and Negotiations).

Hotel business centers are typically open from 8 a.m. to 9 p.m. Their services include:

- Work stations (phone, fax, PCs, photocopiers)
- Typing (¥2000 per page if it is done for you)
- Translation (¥5000 per page)
- Interpretation (¥25,000-30,000 per 2 hours or ¥75,000-80,000 per day)
- Business card printing
- Lounges for informal business get-togethers and meeting rooms with office equipment

Electricity

Electric current in Japan is 100 volts AC. Furthermore, western Japan, including Nagoya, Kyoto and Osaka, is on 60 cycles, while Tokyo and eastern Japan are on 50 cycles. Nevertheless, most North American electrical items still function relatively well on Japanese current even though they are designed to run on 117 volts. The plugs are flat two pins, identical to North American plugs.

Weights and measures

Japan uses the metric system. You can use the following conversion table:

inches x 2.5	=	centimeters
feet x 30.4	=	centimeters
miles x 1.6	=	kilometers
sq. inches x 6.5	=	square centimeters
sq. feet x .09	=	square meters
sq. miles x 2.6	=	square kilometers
gallons x 3.8	=	liters

Tourism

The Japan National Tourist Organization (JNTO) has tourist information centers (TIC) in Narita International Airport and in the Ginza in central Tokyo (Tel: 3502-1451) open every day except Sunday. Their most useful publications include *Your Guide to Japan*, *Tourist Map of Japan*, *Economical Travel in Japan* and *Explore Japanese Culture*. There are also separate brochures on all important tourist destinations. Some of these publications may be available at your hotel front desk.

HEALTH CARE

The following major hospitals have English-speaking doctors:

Tokyo

- Japan Red Cross Medical Center
  4-1-22, Hiroo, Shibuya-ku
  Tokyo 150
  Tel: 3400-1311

- St. Luke's International Hospital
  9-1, Akashicho, Chuo-ku
  Tokyo 104
  Tel: 3541-5151

- International Catholic Hospital
  2-5-1, Nakaochiai, Shinjuku-ku
  Tokyo 161
  Tel: 3951-1111

- International Clinic
  1-5-9, Azabudai, Minato-ku
  Tokyo 106
  Tel: 3582-2646/3583-7831

- Imperial Clinic
  4th Floor, Imperial Hotel
  1-1-1, Uchisaiwaicho
  Chiyoda-ku
  Tokyo 100
  Tel: 3503-8681

Osaka

- Yodogawa Christian Hospital
  2-9 Awaji, Higashi Yodogawa-ku
  Osaka
  Tel: 322-2250

ANNEXES

ANNEX 1

ANNOTATED BIBLIOGRAPHY

No kidding, this is the short version. Thousands of books have been written about Japan. Unfortunately, most of them are produced by academics for academics. The following list is biased towards the practical end. Books marked with an asterix are especially recommended.

* Abegglen, James C., and Stalk, George Jr., **Kaisha, The Japanese Corporation**, Basic Books, 1985.

An excellent introduction to the management policies of Japan's large export champions. Especially strong on market share competition and manufacturing. However, domestic marketing and distribution practices are not covered.

* American Electronics Association (AEA), **Soft Landing in Japan: a market entry handbook for U.S. software companies**, (Version 2.0J), July 1992.

* American Electronics Association (AEA), **Software Partners: the directory of Japanese software distributors**, (Version 1.0J), 1992.

Both of these AEA books are absolute "musts" for software manufacturers interested in the Japanese market. To order or for further information, call the AEA at 1-800-873-1177 (408-987-4200).

Anchordoguy, Mary, **Computers Inc.: Japan's challenge to IBM**, Harvard University Press, 1989.

A very well-researched history of Japan's computer industry.

Asahi Shimbun, **Japan Almanac**, Tokyo, annual.

A very handy pocket-sized compilation of statistics on Japan's society and economy.

* Ashby, Janet, **Gaijin's Guide: practical help for everyday life in Japan**, The Japan Times, 1990.

Although this book is mainly directed towards foreign expats living a year or two in Japan, it contains many helpful hints for business travelers as well. The topics covered are survival Japanese, transportation, eating and drinking, shopping, housing, the bank, the post office, medical care, and leisure activities.

Bartu, Friedemann, **The Ugly Japanese, Nippon's economic empire in Asia,** Yenbooks, Tokyo, 1993.

A more critical overview of Japan's commercial, tourism and investment relations with the rest of Asia.

* Batzer, Eric, and Laumer, Helmut, **Marketing Strategies and Distribution Channels for Foreign Companies in Japan,** Boulder, Westview, 1989.
An extremely detailed overview of Germany's export drive in Japan, especially as it relates to distribution.

Benedict, Ruth, **The Chrysanthemum and the Sword: patterns of Japanese culture**, New American Library, 1946.
A classic study of the Japanese by an anthropologist. The author studied the Japanese during World War II, when travel to Japan was impossible.

Business International, **Finding and Managing Distributors in Asia/Pacific**, Hong Kong, 1989.
A general, rather academic overview. More useful for Hong Kong and Southeast Asia than for Japan. Very expensive (US$500).

* Chapman, William, **Inventing Japan**, Prentice Hall Press, 1991.
A very good post-war history of Japan. Strongly recommended to business readers for the vivid picture it provides of the impact of new-found wealth on Japan's social and political scene.

Choate, Pat, **Agents of Influence**, Touchstone, 1990.
A detailed examination of Japan's lobbying efforts in America. The book is as critical of influence-for-sale in Washington as it is of Japan's activities.

* Christopher, Robert C., **Second to None: American companies in Japan**, Tuttle, Tokyo, 1986.
A study of American multinationals competing successfully in the Japanese market. Designed primarily for a business audience, this book is filled with vivid anecdotes and case studies.

* Cohen, Stephen D., **Cowboys and Samurai: why the United States is losing the battle with the Japanese and why it matters,** Harper Business, 1991.
An excellent overview of the cultural and institutional differences between America and Japan, especially as they affect commercial competitiveness and bilateral trade relations.

* Collins, Robert J., **Japan-Think, Ameri-Think: an irreverent guide to understanding the cultural differences between us**, Penguin Books, 1992.

A very useful and entertaining introduction to Japanese values by an American businessman who has worked in Japan for over 15 years. Highly recommended.

Cusumano, Michael A., **The Japanese Automobile Industry: technology and management at Nissan and Toyota**, Harvard University Press, 1989.
A very thorough analysis of one of Japan's most spectacularly successful industries between 1930 and 1985. For automobile, management, or manufacturing specialists.

* Czinkota, Michael R., and Woronoff, Jon, **Unlocking Japan's Markets: seizing marketing and distribution opportunities in today's Japan**, Probus Publishing 1991.
Extremely well done. The book has a special focus on retailing and wholesaling in Japan.

* De Mente, Boy, **How to do Business with the Japanese**, NTC Business Books, 1987.
An excellent overview of Japan's business scene and protocol from a long-time expat. If you don't have access to the latest edition, be aware that the chapter on consumer spending could be outdated.

Distribution Economics Institute of Japan, **Statistical Abstract of Japanese Distribution**, 1993. (Periodically updated.)
For distribution specialists. Raw numbers with no analysis.

* Dodwell Marketing Consultants (all periodically updated)

***Direct Marketing in Japan**	US$200
***Industrial Goods Distribution in Japan**	US$750
Industrial Groupings in Japan	US$680
R&D Activities of Major Japanese Chemical Companies	US$550
***Retail Distribution in Japan**	US$600
The Structure of the Japanese Electronics Industry	US$700
The Structure of the Japanese Auto Parts Industry	US$830

These publications are by far the most complete – and most expensive – in their fields. The most valuable information they contain are the lists of who supplies whom. Just how an exporter should use this information to succeed in Japan is not really explored. For more information, contact them at G.P.O. Box 297, Tokyo, Japan. Tel: 03-3589-0207, Fax: 03-3589-0516.

Economic Planning Agency, **Economic Survey of Japan**, Tokyo, annual.
The Japanese government's interpretation of recent economic trends.

Eli, Max, **Japan Inc.: global strategies of Japanese trading corporations**, Probus, 1991.

A short general overview of Japan's horizontal keiretsu up to 1987. The focus is on the relationships between core members: top manufacturers, banks and general trading companies.

Encarination, Dennis J., **Rivals Beyond Trade: America versus Japan in global competition**, Cornell University Press, 1992.

Since most world trade is really trade between parent multinationals and their subsidiaries, America's poor export performance in Japan can be explained as a result of the Japanese government's barriers to foreign investment until the mid-'70s. A good book, designed for an academic rather than a business audience.

* Fields, George, **From Bonsai to Levis**, Mentor Book, 1985.

* Fields, George, **Gucci on the Ginza: Japan's new consumer generation**, Kodansha International, 1989.

Although they are a little outdated, Fields' two books (the first, particularly) are still the best introductions to Japanese consumer behavior available. Especially valuable are his many example of good foreign products failing in Japan because exporters ignored local consumer values.

Friedman, **The Misunderstood Miracle: industrial development and political change in Japan**, Cornell University Press, 1988.

For consultants, industrial policy specialists and academics mainly. An in-depth history of Japan's machine tool industry, a sector dominated by small and medium enterprises. According to the author, Japan's success in this field was not due to government guidance or simple market forces, but rather to bottoms-up entrepreneurship, constant product innovation (which is more important than efficiency gains), and the rapid, flexible responses of specialty firms to changing market opportunities.

Gercik, Patricia, **On Track with the Japanese: a case-by-case approach to building successful relationships**, Kodansha International, Tokyo, 1992.

The focus here is on inter-cultural communication, especially for expats working in Japan for long periods of time. The author's numerous case studies are very helpful.

* Graham, John L., and Sano, Yoshihiro, **Smart Bargaining: doing business with the Japanese**, Harper Business, 1989.

A good negotiation book. Because the authors are mostly interested in lengthy and complex deals between multinationals, smaller exporters will probably focus on those sections describing Japanese nonverbal cues and sensitivities.

Hall, Edward, and Hall, M.R., **Hidden Differences: doing business with the Japanese**, Anchor Press, 1987.
Something of a classic in the field of inter-cultural communication, this book will probably mystify readers who have not had an opportunity to stay some time in Japan.

Hamada, Tomoko, **American Enterprise in Japan**, State University of New York, 1991.
The clash of management styles in a Japan-U.S. joint venture as seen from an anthropological perspective. A case study with many concrete examples.

Hampden-Turner, Charles and Tormpenaars, Alfons, **The Seven Cultures of Capitalism**, Doubleday, 1993.
For management consultants mainly. A comparison between American, English, Japanese, French, Dutch, German and Swedish management styles. Unfortunately, these styles tend to be presented as coherent wholes when in fact white and blue collar management in a given country can be very different, at least in Japan. Fascinating nevertheless.

* Hay, Edward J., **The Just-In-Time Breakthrough**, Wiley, 1988.
A good introduction to JIT production systems.

Hendry, Joy, **Understanding Japanese Society**, Routledge, 1989.
An excellent overview of Japanese social interaction beginning with the home and early education. Particular attention is devoted to ritualized behavior and symbols. Very interesting.

* Huddleston, Jackson N. Jr., **Gaijin Kaisha: running a foreign business in Japan**, Tuttle, Tokyo, 1990.
Based on interviews of long-time managers resident in Japan, this book gives an excellent, sometimes brutally candid, overview of the business issues faced by foreign subsidiaries in that market. Fascinating, even though problems encountered by foreign exporters are not the main focus.

Holloway, Nigel (ed.), **Japan in Asia**, Far Eastern Economic Review, 1991.
A country-by-country overview of Japan's economic relations with the rest of Asia and the prospects of a "yen block" being formed in the region.

* Imai, Masaaki, **Kaizen: the key to Japan's competitive success**, Random House, 1986.

"Kaizen" means "continuous improvement." A practical introduction to Japanese-style incremental quality control. A book for manufacturres and would-be suppliers.

Ishikawa, Kaoru, **Introduction to Quality Control**, Chapman and Hall, 1990.

* Ishikawa, Kaoru, **What is Total Quality Control?**, Prentice-Hall, 1985.
Both of these books – the second is an abridged version of the first – are standard books on Japanese-style statistical quality control (SQC). Of interest to manufacturers.

Iwao, Sumiko, **The Japanese Woman: traditional image and changing reality**, Free Press, 1993.
Since Japanese women control family budgets and determine most household consumer spending, exporters of consumer products interested in Japan must understand their values and concerns. This book pulls all the latest data together in a very handy format.

Japan Times, **What's What in Japan's Distribution System**, Tokyo, 1989.
A short comic book introducing Japan's distribution system. Controversial areas are consistently ignored.

* Japan Travel Bureau (JTB) has produced an extremely informative series of 200-page comic-book-style guidebooks on Japanese life and customs. The most relevant from a business perspective are:

Vol. 1	**A look into Japan**
Vol. 2	**Living Japanese Style**
Vol. 3	**Eating in Japan**
Vol. 4	**Festivals in Japan**
Vol. 7	**A Look into Tokyo**
*Vol. 8	**"Salaryman" in Japan**
*Vol. 10	**Today's Japan**

* Japan Travel Bureau (JTB), **Tokyo Today: sightseeing activities, eating and drinking, shopping, accommodations and health**, Tokyo, 1992.
A very effective way to get your bearings in Tokyo.

Johnson, Chalmers, **MITI and the Japanese Miracle**, Stanford University Press, 1982.
A classic history of MITI between 1935 and 1975. Consultants and public policy analysts may find it more to their taste than most business readers.

* Kang, T.W., **Gaishi: the foreign company in Japan**, Basic Books, 1990.

Although this book is mainly directed towards multinationals with subsidiaries in Japan, much of what Kang says about Japanese business practices is equally relevant for exporters. Kang can offer a wealth of concrete examples because he has been doing business in Japan for many years.

* Katzenstein, Gary, **Funny Business: an outsider's year in Japan**, Paladin, 1991.
A revealing account of one American engineer's work experience at Sony. His descriptions of Japanese white collar management are especially interesting.

Kester, W. Carl, **Japanese Takeovers: the global contest for corporate control,** Harvard Business School, 1991.
A very good introduction to the dynamics of Japanese cross-corporate networking. Chapters 2 and 3 on the relationship between companies belonging to the same keiretsu *are especially useful.*

Kobayashi, Koji, **Computers and Communications**, MIT Press, 1986.

Kobayashi, Koji, **The Rise of NEC**, Blackwell Business, 1989.

Kobayashi, Koji, **Rising to the Challenge**, Harcourt Brace Jovanovich, Japan, 1989.
Part autobiography, part management vision, Kobayashi's three books are an insider's account of the evolution of Japan's telecommunications industry. Kobayashi ran Nippon Electric Company (NEC).

* Kodansha, **Japan: a bilingual atlas**, Tokyo, 1991.

* Kodansha, **Kyoto-Osaka, a bilingual atlas**, Tokyo, 1992.

* Kodansha, **Tokyo: a bilingual atlas**, Tokyo, 1991.
Unfortunately, most maps sold in Japan are in Japanese. I recommend these three books for business travelers.

Kotler, P., Fahey, L., and Jatusriptitak, S., **The New Competition**, Prentice-Hall, 1985.
An excellent account of the marketing strategies used by Japan's export champions to penetrate foreign markets. Unfortunately, very little is said about their domestic strategies.

Levy, Sidney M., **Japanese Construction: an American perspective,** Van Nostrand Reinhold, 1990.
A "nuts-and-bolts" overview of the business methods and internal organization of Japan's construction industry, both at home and abroad.

Lynn, Leonard H., and Mckeown, Timothy J., **Organizing Business: trade associations in America and Japan**, American Enterprise Institute, 1988.

The only really substantive English-language book on Japan's trade associations, crucial players in the extraordinarily cooperative relationship between business elites and government in Japan. U.S. associations are also analyzed to point out differences between American and Japanese brands of capitalism.

* March, Robert M., **The Honorable Customer: marketing and selling to the Japanese in the 1990s**, Pitman, 1990.

Like Fields' books, this is an account of Japanese purchasing values. The emphasis, however, is on their service expectations and on Japanese-style selling techniques used within their domestic market. Very useful for exporters.

March, Robert M., **The Japanese Negotiator: subtlety and strategy beyond Western logic**, Kodansha, Tokyo, 1989.

Like most negotiations books, this one focuses on tortuous and complex dealmaking between large multinationals. Exporters will nevertheless find many useful pointers in here.

Matsushita, Konsuke, **Quest for Prosperity: the life of a Japanese industrialist**, PHP Institute, Tokyo, 1988.

The brand names associated with Matsushita – Quasar, Technics and Panasonic – are present in homes around the world. His autobiography is a good introduction to Japan's post-war industrial experience.

* Maurer, P. Reed, **Competing in Japan**, The Japan Times, Tokyo, 1989.

Especially recommended for people in the pharmaceutical business. Licensing, distribution, joint ventures are all discussed by an American executive who knows Japan well.

Miles, Lawrence D., **Techniques of Value Analysis and Engineering**, 2nd Ed., McGraw-Hill, 1972.

For manufacturers interested in value analysis (VA) and value engineering (VE), this is the place to start. Smitka (1991) lists other books on the subject in his bibliography.

* Miyashita, Kenichi, and Russell, David W., ***Keiretsu:* inside the hidden Japanese conglomerates**, McGraw-Hill, 1994.

The best one-volume overview of keiretsu: *the system as a whole, its individual members, and the intricate web of relationships that link banks, manufacturers, suppliers, distributors, and the Japanese government.*

Morgan, James C., and Morgan, J. Jeffrey, **Cracking the Japanese Market: strategies for success in the new global economy**, Free Press, 1991.

Not only an introduction to Japan, but also an analysis of the strategic choices faced by companies interested in that market.

Morita, Akio, with Reingold E.M. and Shimomura M., **Made in Japan: Akio Morita and Sony,** E.P. Dutton, 1986.

This book is both the autobiography of one of Japan's greatest postwar entrepreneurs and an anthology of his thoughts about Japanese and American styles of management. Read it along with Katzenstein's account of his training at Sony (1991); both interpret the same management practices from very different points of view.

Nakane, Chie, **Japanese Society**, Tuttle, Tokyo, 1970.

A classic little book on vertical (i.e., unequal and dependent) relationships as the core organizing principle underlying Japanese society. Frequently praised but extremely academic in style. Most of her conclusions are stated more clearly in Hendry (1989).

* Nevins, Thomas J., **Labor Pains and the Gaijin Boss**, Japan Times, Tokyo, 1983.

* Nevins, Thomas J., **Taking Charge in Japan**, Japan Times, Tokyo, 1990.

Both of Nevin's books are very important for any foreign businessman thinking of setting up an office in Japan. Covers recruitment, compensation, maintaining control, limiting retirement liabilities, etc.

Nikkei Weekly, **Japan Economic Almanac**, Tokyo, annual.

An industry-by-industry review of the previous year. The stress is not on macro-economics (the whole economy) but on meso-economics (the dynamics of particular industries and sectors).

Noh, Toshio, and Kimura, John C., **Japan: a regional geography of an island nation**, (2nd Ed.), Teikoku-Shoin, Tokyo, 1989.

I happen to have found this book but there are any number of equally goods ones on the market. If you are an exporter interested in Japan, make a point of understanding her basic geography and her areas of human and industrial concentration. Many of Japan's unique business practices are really a consequence of geography and demographics.

* NTT Mediascope, **Everything You ever Wanted To Know About Business Otsukiai: a guide to Japanese business protocol**, 1990

"Otsukiai" roughly means "people skills" or "good manners." This handbook was originally written by Japanese managers for inexperienced

colleagues wishing to know how they should behave in certain office situations. As such, it goes much beyond dry rules of etiquette to explain from an insider's perspective what behavior communicates to a Japanese onlooker. There is no other book like this on the market.

* Okimoto, Daniel I., **Between MITI and the Market: Japanese industrial policy for high technology**, Standford University Press, 1989.
Along with Woronoff's 1992 book on Japanese targeting, this book gives the most complete picture of the Japanese government's involvement in the private sector (manufactured exports especially). Exporters of high-tech products should make an effort to read it.

Ono, Keinosuke, and Negoro, Tatsuyuki, **The Strategic Management of Manufacturing Businesses**, 3A Corporation, Tokyo, 1990.
Recommended mainly to manufacturing consultants interested in the latest Japanese thinking concerning the challenges facing transnational manufacturing systems.

Patrick, Hugh T., and Rohlen, Thomas P., "Small-Scale Family Enterprises," in **The Political Economy of Japan: the domestic transformation**, Vol. 1, p. 331-384, Stanford University Press, 1987.
So little has been written in English about small and medium enterprises in Japan that this short article is one of the few pieces around, describing in detail the role they play in the whole economy.

Prestowitz, Clyde V. Jr., **Trading Places: how we are giving our future to Japan and how to reclaim it,** Basic Books, 1989.
Covers almost every gripe American business and congressional leaders have about Japan's business methods. Much of this is covered more succinctly and impartially in Cohen (1991).

Reading, Brian, **Japan: the coming collapse**, Weidenfeld & Nicolson, 1992.
An excellent institutional overview of Japan's postwar economic "system." Especially good in its description of the financial and tax systems.

Rice, Jonathan, **Doing Business in Japan**, BBC Books, 1992.
A good short introduction to the whole subject. Has a special chapter on exporting.

Roberts, John G., **Mitsui: three centuries of Japanese business**, Weatherhill, Tokyo, 1991.
Mitsui is possibly the oldest business entity in the world. For readers interested in studying the growth of a keiretsu *from a historical perspective.*

Rosenbloom, Bert, **Marketing Channels: a management view**, 4th Ed., Dryden Press, 1991.

A good textbook on the management of distribution channels, especially in the U.S.

* Rowland, Diana, **Japanese Business Etiquette**, Warner Books, 1985.

A crash course for foreigners on the "dos and don'ts" of networking, negotiating and socializing in Japan.

Sakiya, Tetsuo, **Honda Motor: the men, the management, the machines**, Kodansha, 1982.

The story of one of Japan's export giants seen from the inside. Honda and Sony are two examples of post-war Japanese companies using foreign expansion to get around the captive distribution networks of older, more entrenched rivals (Toyota and Matsushita, respectively). In that sense, they were not "typical" Japanese companies.

Salacuse, Jeswald W., **Making Global Deals: negotiating in the international marketplace**, Houghton Mifflin, 1991.

A good introduction to the peculiar requirements of successful transnational deal-making.

Schodt, Frederik L., **Inside the Robot Kingdom: Japan, mechatronics, and the coming robotopia**, Kodansha International, 1988.

Visitors to Japan today can see robots starring in feature films and performing sophisticated factory assembly. Why is Japan the world's leader in applied robotics? What is the larger social and cultural significance of Japan's love of robots? This book will answer these questions.

* Schonberger, Richard J., **Japanese Manufacturing Techniques**, Free Press, 1982.

JIT, SQC, plant layout, it's all here.

* Shelley, Rex, **Culture Shock! Japan: a guide to customs and etiquette**, Times Editions, 1993.

Not just etiquette, but also a good introduction to Japanese society in general.

Sheridan, Kyoko, **Governing the Japanese Economy**, Polity Press, 1993.

For economists, consultants and public policy specialists. An account of the Japanese government's economic policies since the Meiji Restoration.

* Smitka, Michael J., **Competitive Ties: subcontracting in the Japanese automotive industry**, Columbia University Press, 1991.

Although it is definitely academic in tone, this book offers a very detailed overview of subcontracting relationships in Japan's auto industry. Separate sections on subcontracting in the electronics, machine tool, printing and shipbuilding industries help complete the picture. Definitely worth consulting for manufacturers looking to become long-term suppliers to Japanese companies at home or abroad.

* Soo, Lennie, **Exporting to Japan**, The ASM Group, Hong Kong, 1992.
A very hands-on export handbook only available by mail-order. Copies cost US$35 plus US$5 for airmail. Contact Asiamag Ltd., Book Dept., GPO Box 12367, Hong Kong, Tel: (852) 555-4777, Fax: (852) 870-0560.

Small and Medium Enterprise Agency, **White Paper on Small and Medium Enterprises in Japan**, Tokyo, annual.
Detailed information on domestic and global trends affecting Japan's small and medium enterprises.

Stern, Louis W., and El-Ansary, **Marketing Channels**, 3rd Ed., Prentice Hall, 1988.
The standard textbook on channel selection and management. Will give you the conceptual framework needed to compare U.S. and foreign distribution systems.

* Tatsuno, Sheridan M., **Created in Japan: from imitators to world-class innovators**, Harper Business, 1990.
For exporters of high-tech products. The best account of Japanese-style R&D and product development in English.

Tedlow, Richard S., **New and Improved: the story of mass marketing in America**, Basic Books, 1990.
Understanding Japan's distinctive distribution arrangements is a lot easier when you see how and why North America came to different solutions. In both cases, geography, government and big business played a crucial role in the final outcome.

Thurow, Lester, **Head to Head: the coming economic battle among Japan, Europe, and America**, William Morrow, 1992.
For readers interested in the "big picture." Reading it back-to-back with Cohen (1991) gives a strong impression of how the collapse of the Soviet Union is bound to increase trade tensions between Japan and America.

Tobin, Joseph J. (ed.), **Re-Made in Japan: everyday life and consumer taste in a changing society**, Yale University Press, 1992.
A series of essays illustrating the ways Western products and consumer values are transformed in a Japanese context. Business readers may be

put off by the book's anthropological verbiage, but it does give valuable insights into Japanese consumer aspirations. Consult it in combination with Fields (1985).

Toyne, Brian, and Walters, Peter G.P., **Global Marketing Management: a strategic perspective**, 2nd Ed., Allyn and Bacon, 1993.
An excellent introductory textbook.

Toyo Keizai, **Japan Company Handbook**, Tokyo, annual.
A good starting point when looking for information on listed companies. Available in a two-volume set.

* U.S. International Trade Commission, **Japan's Distribution System and Options for Improving U.S. Access**, June 1990.
An excellent overview of distribution issues faced by U.S. exporters interested in the Japanese market. Because it is primarily a background study used in bilateral trade negotiations, it does not really try to propose solutions for individual exporters. It is not meant to be a "how-to" book.

Van Wolferen, Karel, **The Enigma of Japanese Power**, Knopf, 1989.
The most detailed "revisionist" critique of Japan's post-war socio-political order. The author's basic point is that Japan's worsening trade conflicts with the rest of the world have no hope of resolution because her blend of factional politics and "production-first" economics leaves no one group in clear control. The system is thus on auto pilot and no one, least of all ordinary Japanese people, has the power to reform it.

Vogel, Ezra, **Comeback**, Simon and Shuster, 1985.

Vogel, Ezra, **Japan as Number One: lessons for America**, Harper Torchbook, 1979.
Vogel's basic thesis in these books is that America has much to learn from Japan, especially with respect to government-business cooperation. Neither book pretends to be a complete portrait of Japanese society. The emphasis is on lessons.

Reischauer, Edwin O., **The Japanese**, Harvard Paperback, 1981.
An excellent one-volume overview of Japan's history, values and society.

* Womack, James P., Jones, Daniel T., and Roos Daniel, **The Machine that Changed the World**, Macmillan, New York, 1990.
From mass production to Japanese-style "lean" production in the car business. A book for people seeking to understand Japan's lead in process technologies.

Woronoff, Jon, **Japan As – Anything But – Number One**, Sharpe, 1990.

A rebuttal of Vogel (1979). Woronoff tries to point out the dark side of Japanese management, education, crime prevention, politics and quality of life.

* Woronoff, Jon, **The Japanese Management Mystique: the reality behind the myth**, Probus, 1992.
Along with Abegglen & Stalk (1985), probably one of the best introductions to the realities of Japanese management for foreign exporters interested in the Japanese market.

* Woronoff, Jon, **Japanese Targeting: successes, failures, lessons**, Macmillan Press, 1992.
An excellent introduction to Japanese industrial policy. Exporters of high-tech products should read it along with Okimoto (1989).

* Woronoff, Jon, **The "No-Nonsense" Guide to Doing Business in Japan**, Yohan, 1991.
A good short business guide.

Woronoff, Jon, **Politics, The Japanese Way**, Yohan, Tokyo, 1986.
By now, a little outdated. Refer to it for insights on the ethos of Japanese political life, not for the latest developments.

Yano Research Center, **Market Share in Japan**, Tokyo, annual.
A useful source book for those doing preliminary market research in Japan. The nearest JETRO office might have a copy.

Young, Alexander K., **The Sogo Shosha, Japan's Multinational Trading Companies**, Tuttle, Tokyo, 1979.
Although the book's statistics are only of historical interest, it does give the reader a clear grasp of the core business activities of Japan's huge general trading companies.

* Yoshino, M.Y., and Lifson, Thomas B., **The Invisible Link: Japan's sogo shosha and the organization of trade**, MIT Press, 1986.
A thorough description of the organization of work within Japan's general trading firms. Reading it will give you a clearer sense of where your product is likely to fit into the scheme of things if you decide to go through a sogo shosha.

Zielinski, Robert, and Holoway, Nigel, **Unequal Equities: power and risk in Japan's stock market**, Kodansha International, 1991.
Although foreign exporters are rarely concerned with foreign stock markets, Japan's own market played a central role in precipitating a domestic "recession" after 1990. This short book explains why.

Ziemba, William T., and Schwartz, **Power Japan: how and why the Japanese economy works**, Probus, 1992.

An institutional overview of Japan's economy with special emphasis on its emergence as the world's greatest creditor nation.

* Zimmerman, Mark, **How to do Business with the Japanese**, Random House, 1985.

Still the best all-around introduction to this subject.

THE FAR SIDE

The foreign executives best able to thrive in Japan often combine an in-depth understanding of their own industry with a warm curiosity about every aspect of life in Japan. The following books are not about business in the narrow sense, but they can definitely broaden the reader's perceptiveness about things Japanese. The topics covered were purposely kept broad to satisfy every taste.

Buruma, Ian, **Behind the Mask: on sexual demons, sacred mothers, transvestites, gangsters and other Japanese cultural heroes**, Meridian, 1984.

Fictional heroes – a John Wayne or a famous samurai – are both atypical characters satisfying their fans' need for escape from stifling routine, and embodiments of social stability perpetually finding some kind of nasty business to clear up. This book tries to illuminate the pressure points of Japanese society through some of its most popular fantasies.

Collins, Robert J., **Max Danger: the adventures of an expat in Tokyo**, Tuttle, Tokyo, 1987.

Collins, Robert J., **More Max Danger: the continuing adventures of an expat in Tokyo**, Tuttle, Tokyo, 1989.

Two very entertaining books from which one can learn quite a lot about the Japanese through the adventures of Max Danger, a fictional character created for the "Tokyo Weekender," a weekly English-language paper.

Edwards, Walter, **Modern Japan Through its Weddings: gender, person, and society in ritual portrayal**, Stanford University Press, 1989.

A fascinating, albeit academic, backstage look at Japan's highly organized wedding industry. At the same time, it reveals a lot about the roles of men and women, the meaning of marriage and the place of the individual in society.

Feiler, Bruce S., **Learning to Bow: inside the heart of Japan**, Ticknor & Fields, 1991.

A well-written account of one American's year-long teaching assignment in a Japanese high school. A story of culture clashes in a microcosm of Japanese society.

Field, Norma, **In the Realm of a Dying Emperor: Japan at century's end**, Vintage, 1991.

An exploration of dissent in Japanese society through the lives of three people: a supermarket owner who burned the national flag; an aging widow who challenged the state's "deification" of fallen soldiers; and the mayor of Nagasaki, who risked his life by suggesting that Hirohito bore some responsibility for World War II.

Freidman, George, and Lebard, Meredith, **The Coming War with Japan**, St. Martin's Press, 1991.

The authors believe that geo-political and economic forces are pushing Japan and the U.S. towards armed conflict. Whether you agree with its conclusions, the book offers a very coherent and well-researched account of Japan's vulnerabilities as both a major importer of raw materials and a global exporter of manufactured goods.

Ishinomori, Shotaro, **Japan Inc.: introduction to Japanese economics**, University of California Press, 1988.

Six themes are explored through the adventures of a small number of comic book characters working for Mitsutomo trading company, a fictitious sogo shosha, *during the 1980s. The themes are trade friction with the United States, the appreciation of the yen, the impact of rising oil prices, the financing of government debt through the issue of government bonds, the internationalization of business and banking, and the adjustment of the domestic market to new consumer tastes.*

Kaplan, David E., and Dubro, Alec, **Yakuza**, Collier Books, 1986.

An exhaustive portrait of Japan's criminal underworld, explaining where and how the gangs mesh with the legitimate world of business and politics.

Prindle, Tamae K. (editor and translator), **Made in Japan and other Japanese "Business Novels,"** Sharpe, 1989.

Seven "business novels" (short stories actually) illustrating Japanese business life from the point of view of its participants.

Reynolds, David K., **The Quiet Therapies: Japanese pathways to personal growth**, University of Hawaii Press, 1980.

People who cannot conform to social expectations often turn to healing techniques which end up reinforcing society's demands. An account of five home-grown Japanese therapies: Morita therapy, naikan, seiza, shadan, *and Zen. The point of view is that of the Japanese patients.*

Rimer, J. Thomas, **A Reader's Guide to Japanese Literature**, Kodansha International, 1991.
Readers wishing to study Japan through the medium of its literature should start with the short summaries contained in this book. Enough details are given to help you decide on your own what to read next.

Rohlen, Thomas P., **Japan's High Schools**, University of California Press, 1983.
Compared to Feiler (1991), this is a much more comprehensive, academic overview of Japan's high schools. It is so well done, however, that it succeeds in explaining education as a cultural mainspring of Japanese social organizations.

Schodt, Frederik L., **Manga! Manga! The World of Japanese Comics**, Kodansha International, 1983.
An entertaining introduction to Japan's comic book industry and creations as a window on the rest of its society.

Ventura, Rey, **Underground in Japan**, St. Edmunsbury Press, 1992.
Japanese society from the point of view of one of its many illegal migrant workers.

Whiting, Robert, **You Gotta Have Wa**, Vintage, 1989.
"Wa" means harmony or team spirit. A close-up view of Japanese-style baseball: its teams, its fans, its rituals and history, as well as the way it has treated visiting American players.

ANNEX 2

JETRO'S INTERNATIONAL NETWORK

JETRO, Tokyo (Headquarters)
2-2-5 Toranomon
Minato-ku, Tokyo 105
Tel: 03-3582-5511
Fax: 03-3587-0219

JETRO, Osaka
Bingo-cho Nomura Bldg.
2-1-8 Bingo-cho, Chuo-ku
Osaka 541
Tel: 06-203-3601
Fax: 06-222-5675

NORTH AMERICA

JETRO, Toronto
Suite 700, Brittanica House
151 Bloor Street West
Toronto, Ontario
M5S 1T7
Tel: 416-962-5055
Fax: 416-962-1124

JETRO, Montreal
1 Place Ville Marie
Suite 1506
Montreal, Qc.
H3B 2B5
Tel: 514-879-5617
Fax: 514-879-5618

JETRO, Vancouver
World Trade Centre
660, 999 Canada Place
Vancouver, British Columbia
V6C 3E1
Tel: 604-684-4174
Fax: 604-684-6877

JETRO, New York
44th Floor, McGraw-Hill Bldg.
Suite 1221
Avenue of the Americas
New York, N.Y.
10020-1060
Tel: 212-819-7762
Fax: 212-997-0464

JETRO, Chicago
401 North Michigan Avenue
Suite 660
Chicago, IL 60611
Tel: 312-527-9000
Fax: 312-670-4223

JETRO, Houston
1221 McKinney
One Houston Center
Suite 2360
Houston, TX 77010
Tel: 713-759-9595
Fax: 713-759-9210

JETRO, Los Angeles
725, S. Figueroa Street
Suite 1890
Los Angeles, CA 90017
Tel: 213-624-8855
Fax: 213-629-8127

JETRO, San Francisco
Suite 1700
235 Pine St.
San Francisco, CA 941014
Tel: 415-392-1333
Fax: 415-788-6927

JETRO, Atlanta
245 Peachtree Center Ave.
Suite 2208, Marquis One Tower
Atlanta, GA 30303
Tel: 404-681-0600
Fax: 404-681-0713

JETRO, Denver
1200 Seventeenth St.
Suite 1110
Denver, CO 80202
Tel: 303-629-0404
Fax: 303-893-9522

JETRO, Puerto Rico
(Frozen Food)
Calle Cruz 03, Bellas Lomas
Miradero Mayaguez
Puerto Rico 00708
Tel: 809-832-0861

EUROPE

JETRO, London
Leconfield House, 6/F
Curzon Street
London, W1Y 7FB England
Tel: 71-493-7226
Fax: 71-491-7570

JETRO, Dublin
BP House
1, Setanta Place, Dublin 2
Ireland
Tel: 1-671-4003
Fax: 1-671-4302

JETRO, Paris
151, rue Saint-Honoré
75001 Paris, France
Tel: 42-61-2727
Fax: 42-61-1946

JETRO, Hamburg
Colonnaden 72, 20354 Hamburg
Bundesrepublik Deutschland
Tel: 49-40-356-0080
Fax: 49-40-346-837

JETRO, Dusseldorf
Konigsallee 58, 4000 Dusseldorf
Bundesrepublik Deutschland
Tel: 0211-136020
Fax: 0211-32-6411

JETRO, Frankfurt
Rossmarkt 17, 6 Frankfurt 1
Bundesrepublik Deutschland
Tel: 69-28-32-15
Fax: 69-28-3359

JETRO, Munich
Prielmayerstrasse 3/IV Elisenhof
8000 Munchen 2, Bundesrepublik
Deutschland
Tel: 49-89-290-8420
Fax: 49-89-290-84289

JETRO, Amsterdam
World Trade Center, Amsterdam
Tower C 4th Fl., Strawinskylaan 447
1077 XX, Amsterdam
The Netherlands
Tel: 31-20-676-5075
Fax: 31-20-664-7597

JETRO, Rotterdam
Groothandelsgebouw B-3 Weena
695 3013AM, Rotterdam
The Netherlands
Tel: 010-4113360

JETRO, Brussels
Rue d'Arlon 69/71 Boite 2, B-1040
Bruxelles, Belgique
Tel: 230-4858
Fax: 230-0703

JETRO, Copenhagen
Vesterbrogade 1c, 1st Flr.
1620 Copenhagen V, Denmark
Tel: 45-33-147312
Fax: 45-33-110136

JETRO, Stockholm
Kungsgatan 48, 4th Floor
11135 Stockholm, Sweden
Tel: 468-411-8173
Fax: 468-411-1888

JETRO, Oslo
Parkveien 55
0256 Oslo 2, Norway
Tel: 47-22-558-611
Fax: 47-22-558-610

JETRO, Zürich
Stampfenbachstrasse 38, 8006,
Zurich, Switzerland
Tel: (01) 362-2323
Fax: (01) 362-7056

JETRO, Geneva
82, rue de Lausanne 1202
Geneve, Switzerland
Tel: 41-22-732-1304
Fax: 41-22-732-0772

JETRO, Vienna
Mariahilferstrasse 41-43/3 Stock
1060 Wien, Austria
Tel: 587-5628/9
Fax: 586-2293

JETRO, Milan
I.N.A. Building Via Agnello 6/1
20121, Milano, Italia
Tel: 392-866-343
Fax: 392-720-23072

JETRO, Rome
Via San Filippo Martire, 1/B 00197
Roma, Italia
Tel: 808-4752
Fax: 907-5230

JETRO, Athens
4 Kubari St. Kolonaki
Athens, Greece
Tel: 363-0820
Fax: 362-1231

JETRO, Madrid
Plaza de Colon
2 Torres de Colon 1
5° B 28046
Madrid, Spain
Tel: 319-5564
Fax: 310-3659

JETRO, Lisbon
Empreendimento das Amoreiras Av.
Eng.° Duarte Pacheco, Torre 2
11° Andar, Sala 1 1000
Lisbon, Portugal
Tel: 659-381
Fax: 691-818

JETRO, Warsaw
UI, Szpitalna 6 M 21, 00-031
Warszawa, Poland
Tel: 48-22-27-84-21
Fax: 48-22-27-95-42

JETRO, Bucharest
Hotel Bucuresti, Strada Luterana
Compound D, Entrance C2
4th Floor, Appartment 14
Bucharest, Romania
Tel: 148-876
Fax: 120-432

JETRO, Sofia
4th Floor, Vela Blagoeva 13
Sofia, Bulgaria
Tel: 52-29-59, 51-81-51
Fax: 59-2-70-5127

ASIA

JETRO, New Delhi
Flat No. 501-505
5th Floor, World Trade Center
Barakhamba Lane
New Delhi-110001, India
Tel: 3312194
Fax: 3313453

JETRO, Karachi
State Life Building #11
Abdullah Haroon Rd.
Karachi, Pakistan
Tel: 510-459
Fax: 568-4392

JETRO, Dhaka
BCIC Bhaban 13th Floor
30-31 Dilkusha, Commercial Area
Dhaka-2, Bangladesh
Tel: 230-575
Fax: 286-3078

JETRO, Colombo
4/F, Carson Cumberbatch Bldg.
#67, Dharmapala
Mawatha Colombo 7
The Republic of Sri Lanka
Tel: 541-221
Fax: 541-221

JETRO, Singapore
Hong Leong Bldg.
16 Rafflesquay #38-05
Singapore 0104
Tel: 221-8174
Fax: 224-1169

JETRO, Jakarta
Summitmas Tower 6th Floor, JL.
Jend Sudirman Kav. 61-62
Jakarta, Indonesia
Tel: 520-0264
Fax: 520-0261

JETRO, Kuala Lumpur
23rd Floor, Menara Tun Razak
(Mail Box 16 & 17)
Jalan Raja Laut
50350 Kuala Lumpur, Malaysia
Tel: 3-293-0244
Fax: 3-293-0132

JETRO, Bangkok
JETRO Building 159 Rajadamri Rd.
Bangkok, Thailand
Tel: 253-6441
Fax: 253-2020

JETRO, Hong Kong
1910-1915 Hutchison House 10

Harcourt Road, Central, Hong Kong
Tel: (5) 264-067/70
Fax: (5) 868-1455

JETRO, Manila
23/F, Pacific Star Bldg.
Sen. Gil J. Pujat Ave.
Makati, Metro Manila
Philippines
Tel: 88-43-73
Fax: 2-818-7490

JETRO, Seoul
7th Floor, The Korea Press Centre
Bldg. 25, 1-Ka Taepyung-Ro
Chung-ku, Seoul
Republic of Korea
Tel: 739-8657
Fax: 739-4658

JETRO, Beijing
303 Chang Fu Gong Office Bldg.
Jia-26, Jian Guo Men Wai St.,
Beijing
The People's Republic of China
Tel: 513-7075
Fax: 513-7079

JETRO, Shanghai
Room 412, West Tower,
Shanghai Center,
1376 West Nanjing Rd., Shanghai
The People's Republic of China
Tel: 21-279-8090
Fax: 21-279-8092

OCEANIA

JETRO, Sydney
Level 19, Gateway 1 Macquarie
Place
Sydney, N.S.W. 2000
Australia
Tel: 241-1181/7
Fax: 251-7631

JETRO, Melbourne
4th Floor, Standard Chartered
House, 30 Collins Street, Melbourne
Victoria 3000 Australia
Tel: 654-4949
Fax: 654-2962

JETRO, Perth
St. George's Court Bldg.
16 St. George's Terrace
Perth, WA 6000 Australia
Tel: 325-2809
Fax: 325-2472

JETRO, Auckland
Room No. 301, Dilworth Bldg.
Customs St. East, Auckland
New Zealand
Tel: 379-7427
Fax: 309-5046

ANNEX 3

SOME JETRO PUBLICATIONS

- *Access to Japan's Import Market Series*
- *Standards Informations Series*
- *Manufacturing Technology Guide Series*
- *Agriculture Product Series*

Books and Directories (partial listing):

Selling in Japan
White Paper on International trade
Investment in Japan

Your Market in Japan Series (partial listing):

Camping and Hiking Goods
Automotive Parts, Accessories and Supplies
Educational Equipment
Jewelry and Personal Accessories
Health-care and Exercise Equipment
Baby Products
Electric Measuring Instruments
Solar Energy Utilization Apparatus
Food Processing Machinery
Computer Hardware
Industrial and Everday-Life Safety Equipment
Pharmaceuticals
Sportswear and Casual Wear
Medical and Dental Instruments
Stationary Goods
Cosmetics
Natural Cheese
Confectionary
Wooden Furniture
Modular Kitchens
Computer Software
Industrial Robots
Environmental Pollution Control Equipment
Wine
Bathroom Equipment
New Materials
Cards and Wrapping Goods
Pet Care Articles
Women's Outer Garments
Winter Sporting Goods
Food Service Industry
Franchise Business
Men's Outer Garments
Optical Frame
Home Lighting Fixtures
Automotive After Market
Resort Market
Men's Fashion Accessories
Formal Wear
Children's Apparel
Swimwear
Party Goods
Interior Art Products – Lithographs
Gift Goods
Games – excluding video games
Kitchen Ware
Central Heating System
Consumer Communication Equipment
Dishwashing Machines

Sports Footwear
High Grade Bicycle and Wear
Golf Goods
Motorcruisers and Yachts
The Door-to-Door Parcel Delivery Market
Mail-Order Market
Bridal Market
Computer Graphics
Office Furniture
Video Software Products
Used Car market
Household Tap Water Purifiers
Health Drinks
Products Related to Pollution Prevention
Toys
Wooden Fittings
Ceramic Tableware
Ornamental Plants
Mineral Water
Meat Products
Construction Materials
Health Care Goods for the Elderly and Disabled Persons
DIY Goods – Electric and Mechanical Hand Tools
Books
Fruit Drinks
Frozen Processed Foods

ANNEX 4

NORTH AMERICAN REGIONAL TRADE CENTERS

CANADA

Newfoundland
215 Water St., Suite 504
PO Box 8950
St. John's, Newfoundland
A1B 3R9
Tel: (709) 772-5511
Fax: (709) 772-2373

Prince Edward Island
Confederation Court Mall
134 Kent Street, Suite 400
PO Box 1115
Charlottetown, PEI
C1A 7M8
Tel: (902) 566-7400
Fax: (902) 566-7450

Nova Scotia
Central Guarantee Trust Building
1801 Hollis Street
PO Box 940, Station M
Halifax, Nova Scotia
B3J 2V9
Tel: (902) 426-7540
Fax: (902) 426-2624

New Brunswick
Assumption Place
770 Main Street
PO Box 1210
Moncton, New Brunswick
E1C 8P9
Tel: (506) 851-6452
Fax: (506) 851-6429

Quebec
Stock Exchange Tower, Suite 3800
800 Victoria Square
PO Box 247
Montreal, Quebec
H4Z 1E8
Tel: (514) 283-8185
Fax: (514) 283-8794

Ontario
Dominion Public Building, 4th Floor
1 Front Street West
Toronto, Ontario
M5J 1A4
Tel: (416) 973-5053
Fax: (416) 973-8161

Manitoba
8th Floor
330 Portage Avenue
PO Box 981
Winnipeg, Manitoba
R3C 2V2
Tel: (204) 983-8036
Fax: (204) 983-2187

Saskatchewan
119-4th Avenue South, Suite 401
Saskatoon, Saskatchewan
S7K 5X2
Tel: (306) 975-5315
Fax: (306) 975-5334

1955 Smith Street, 4th Floor
Regina, Saskatchewan
S4P 2N8
Tel: (306) 780-5020
Fax: (306) 780-6679

Alberta
Canada Place, Suite 540
9700 Jasper Avenue
Edmonton, Alberta
T5J 4C3
Tel: (403) 495-2944
Fax: (403) 495-4507

International Trade Center
510-5th Street, S.W., 11th Floor
Calgary, Alberta
T2P 3S2
Tel: (403) 292-6660
Fax: (403) 292-4578

British Columbia
International Trade Center
Scotia Tower, Suite 900
650 West Georgia Street
PO Box 11610
Vancouver, British Columbia
V6B 5H8
Tel: (604) 666-0434
Fax: (604) 666-8330

Yukon
108 Lambert Street, Suite 301
Whitehorse, Yukon
Y1A 1Z2
Tel: (403) 668-4655
Fax: (403) 668-5003

Northwest Territories
Precambrian Building, 10th Floor
4922-52nd Street, PO Box 6100
Yellowknife, Northwest Territories
X1A 2R3
Tel: (403) 920-8568
Fax: (403) 873-6228

UNITED STATES

Alabama
Rm. 302, Berry Bldg.
2015 2nd Ave. North
Birmingham, Alabama
35203
Tel: (205) 731-1331
Fax: (205) 731-0076

Center for International Trade and Commerce
250 N. Water St., Station 131
Mobile, AL 36602
Tel: (205) 441-7012
Fax: (205) 438-2711

Alaska
Suite 319, World Trade Center
Alaska
4201 Tudor Center Dr.
Anchorage, Alaska 99508
Tel: (907) 271-6237
Fax: (907) 271-6242

Alaska Governor's Office of International Trade
3601 C Street, Suite 798
Anchorage, AK 99503
Tel: (907) 561-5585
Fax: (907) 561-4577

Arizona
Rm. 3412, Federal Bldg.
230 North First Ave.
Phoenix, Arizona 85025
Tel: (602) 379-3285
Fax: (602) 379-4324

Arkansas
Suite 811, USAble Corporate Center
320 W. Capitol Ave.
Little Rock, Arkansas 72201
Tel: (501) 324-5794
Fax: (501) 324-7380

California
Rm. 9200, 11000 Wilshire Blvd.
Los Angeles, California 90024
Tel: (310) 575-7105
Fax: (310) 575-7220

Suite #1, 116-A West 4th St.
Santa Ana, California 92701
Tel: (714) 836-2461
Fax: (714) 836-2332

Suite 230, 6363 Greenwich Dr.
San Diego, California 92122
Tel: (619) 557-5395
Fax: (619) 557-6176

14th Floor, 250 Montgomery Street
San Francisco, California 94104
Tel: (415) 705-2300
Fax: (415) 705-2299

The Center for International Trade Development
1787 Tribute Rd., Suite A
Sacramento, CA 95815
Tel: (916) 263-6578
Fax: (916) 263-6571

Bureau of Export Administration
Western Regional Office
3300 Irvine Ave., Suite 345
Newport Beach, CA 92660-3198
Tel: (714) 660-0144
Fax: (714) 660-9347

Colorado
Suite 680, 1625 Broadway
Denver, Colorado 80202
Tel: (303) 844-3246
Fax: (303) 844-5651

Connecticut
Rm. 610-B, Federal Office Bldg.
450 Main Street
Hartford, Connecticut 06103
Tel: (203) 240-3530
Fax: (203) 240-3473

D.C.
Rm. 1066 HCHB
Department of Commerce
14th St. & Constitution Ave., N.W.
Washington, D.C. 20230
Tel: (202) 482-3181

Japan Export Information Center (JEIC)
Tel: (202) 482-2425
Fax: (202) 482-0469

National Trade Data Bank (NTDB)
Tel: (202) 482-1986

Florida
Suite 224, Federal Bldg.
51 S.W. First Ave.
Miami, Florida 33130
Tel: (305) 536-5267
Fax: (305) 536-4765

128 North Osceola Ave.
Clearwater, Florida 34615
Tel: (813) 461-0011
Fax: (813) 449-2889

c/o University of Central Florida
College of Business Administration,
Rm. 346
CEBA II
Orlando, Florida 32802
Tel: (407) 648-1608

Room 366G, Collins Bldg.
107 West Gaines St.
Tallahassee, Florida 32399-2000
Tel: (904) 488-6469
Fax: (904) 487-1407

Georgia
Plaza Square North, Suite 310
4360 Chamblee Dunwoody Rd.
Atlanta, Georgia 30341
Tel: (404) 452-9101
Fax: (404) 452-9105

Room A-107, 120 Barnard St.
Savannah, Georgia 31401
Tel: (912) 652-4204
Fax: (912) 652-4241

Hawaii
4106 Federal Bldg.
PO Box 50026
300 Ala Moana Blvd.
Honolulu, Hawaii 96850
Tel: (808) 541-1782
Fax: (808) 541-3435

International Business Center of Hawaii
City Financial Tower
201 Merchant Street, Suite 1510
Honolulu, Hawaii 96813
Tel: (808) 587-2792
Fax: (808) 587-2790

Idaho
2nd Floor, Joe R. Williams Bldg.
700 West State Street
Boise, Idaho 83720
Tel: (208) 334-3857
Fax: (208) 334-2787

Illinois
Rm. 1406, 55 East Monroe St.
Chicago, Illinois 60603
Tel: (312) 353-4450
Fax: (312) 886-8025

Illinois Institute of Technology
201 East Loop Road
Wheaton, Illinois 60187
Tel: (312) 353-4332
Fax: (312) 353-4336

PO Box 1747
515 North Court St.
Rockford, Illinois 61110-0247
Tel: (815) 987-8123
Fax: (815) 987-8122

Indiana
Suite 520, One North Capitol Ave.
Indianapolis, Indiana 46204
Tel: (317) 226-6214
Fax: (317) 226-6139

Iowa
Room 817, Federal Bldg.
210 Walnut St.
Des Moines, Iowa 50309
Tel: (515) 284-4222
Fax: (515) 284-4021

Kansas
151 N. Valutsia
Wichita, Kansas 67214-4695
Tel: (316) 269-6160
Fax: (316) 683-7326

Kentucky
Rm. 636B.
Gene Snyder Courthouse and Customhouse Bldg.
601 W. Broadway
Louisville, Kentucky 40202
Tel: (502) 582-5066
Fax: (502) 582-6573

Louisiana
432 World Trade Center
#2 Canal St.
New Orleans, Louisiana 70130
Tel: (504) 589-6546
Fax: (504) 589-2337

Maine
77 Sewall St.
Augusta, Maine 04330
Tel: (207) 622-8249
Fax: (207) 626-9156

Maryland
413 U.S. Customhouse
40 South Gay Street
Baltimore, Maryland 21202
Tel: (301) 962-3560
Fax: (301) 962-7813

Massachusetts
Suite 307, World Trade Center
Commonwealth Pier Area
Boston, Massachusetts 02210
Tel: (617) 565-8563
Fax: (617) 565-8530

Michigan
1140 McNamara Bldg.
477 Michigan Ave.
Detroit, Michigan 48226
Tel: (313) 226-3650
Fax: (313) 226-3657

300 Monroe N.W.
Grand Rapids, Michigan 49503
Tel: (616) 456-2411
Fax: (616) 456-2695

Minnesota
108 Federal Bldg.
110 S. 4th Street
Minneapolis, Minnesota 55401
Tel: (612) 348-1638
Fax: (612) 348-1650

Mississippi
328 Jackson Mall Office Center
300 Woodrow Wilson Blvd.
Jackson, Mississippi 39213
Tel: (601) 965-4388
Fax: (601) 965-5386

Missouri
Suite 610, 7911 Forsyth Blvd.
St. Louis, Missouri 63105
Tel: (314) 425-3302
Fax: (314) 425-3381

Rm. 635, 601 East 12th Street
Kansas City, Missouri 64106
Tel: (816) 426-3141
Fax: (816) 426-3140

International Business Development
301 West High St., Room 720C
Jefferson City, Missouri 65101
Tel: (314) 751-7866
Fax: (314) 751-7384

Nebraska
11133 "O" Street
Omaha, Nebraska 68137
Tel: (402) 221-3664
Fax: (402) 221-3668

Nevada
1755 E. Plumb Lane #152
Reno, Nevada 89502
Tel: (702) 784-5203
Fax: (702) 784-5203

New Jersey
Suite 100, 3131 Princeton Pike
Bldg. #6
Trenton, New Jersey 08648
Tel: (609) 989-2100
Fax: (609) 989-2395

New Mexico
Room 320, 625 Silver SW
Albuquerque, New Mexico 87102
Tel: (505) 766-2070
Fax: (505) 766-1057

New York
1312 Federal Bldg.
111 West Huron St.
Buffalo, New York 14202
Tel: (716) 846-4191
Fax: (716) 846-5290

111 East Ave., Suite 220
Rochester, New York 14604
Tel: (716) 263-6480
Fax: (716) 325-6505

Rm. 3718, 26 Federal Plaza
New York, New York 10278
Tel: (212) 264-0635
Fax: (212) 264-1356

United States Council for
International Business
1212 Avenue of the Americas
New York, N.Y. 10036
Tel: (212) 354-4480
Fax: (212) 575-0327

New York State Department of
Economic Development
1515 Broadway
New York, N.Y.
Tel: (212) 827-6206
Fax: (212) 827-6279

North Carolina
Suite 400, 400 West Market Street
Greensboro, North Carolina 27401
Tel: (919) 333-5345
Fax: (919) 333-5158

Ohio
9504 Federal Office Bldg.
550 Main Street
Cincinnati, Ohio 45202
Tel: (513) 684-2944
Fax: (513) 684-3200

Rm. 600
668 Euclid Ave.
Cleveland, Ohio 44114
Tel: (216) 522-4750
Fax: (216) 522-2235

Oklahoma
6601 Broadway Extension
Oklahoma City, Oklahoma 73116
Tel: (405) 231-5302
Fax: (405) 841-5245

440 S. Houston Streeet
Tulsa, Okalahoma 74127

Tel: (918) 581-7650
Fax: (918) 581-2844

Oregon
Suite 242, One World Trade Center
121 SW Salmon Street
Portland, Oregon 97204
Tel: (503) 326-3001
Fax: (503) 326-6351

Small Business International Trade Program
(same address as above)
Tel: (503) 274-7482
Fax: (503) 228-6350

Pennsylvania
Suite 202, 475 Allendale Road
King of Prussia
Philadelphia, Pennsyvania 19406
Tel: (215) 962-4980
Fax: (215) 951-7959

2002 Federal Bldg.
1000 Liberty Ave.
Pittsburg, Pennsylvania 15222
Tel: (412) 644-2850
Fax: (412) 644-4875

Puerto Rico
Rm. G-55 Federal Bldg.
San Juan (Hato Rey) 00918
Tel: (809) 766-5555
Fax: (809) 766-5692

Rhode Island
7 Jackson Walkway
Providence, Rhode Island 02903
Tel: (401) 528-5104
Fax: (401) 528-5067

South Carolina
Suite 172
Strom Thurmond Federal Bldg.
1835 Assembly St.
Columbia, South Carolina 29201
Tel: (803) 765-5345
Fax: (803) 253-3614

JC Long Bldg., Rm. 128
9 Liberty St.
Charleston, South Carolina 29424
Tel: (803) 724-4361

Tennessee
Suite 1114, Parkway Towers
404 James Robertson Parkway
Nashville, Tennessee 37219-1505
Tel: (615) 736-5161
Fax: (615) 736-2454

301 East Church Ave.
Knoxville, Tennessee 37915
Tel: (615) 549-9268

The Falls Building, Suite 200
22 North Front St.
Memphis, Tennessee 38103
Tel: (901) 544-4137
Fax: (901) 575-3510

Texas
World Trade Center
PO Box 58130
2050 North Stemmons Frwy., S. 170
Dallas, Texas 75242-0787
Tel: (214) 767-0542
Fax: (214) 767-8240

PO Box 12728
816 Congress Ave., Suite 1200
Austin, Texas 78711

Tel: (512) 482-5939
Fax: (512) 320-9674

Room 2625
Federal Courthouse Bldg.
515 Rusk St.
Houston, Texas 77002
Tel: (713) 229-2578
Fax: (713) 229-2203

Texas Department of Commerce
Office of International Marketing
PO Box 12728
Austin, Texas 78711
Tel: (512) 320-9671
Fax: (512) 320-9424

Utah
Suite 105, 324 South State St.
Salt Lake City, Utah 84111
Tel: (801) 524-5116
Fax: (801) 524-5886

State of Utah
International Business Development Office
324 South State St., #500
Salt Lake City, Utah 84111
Tel: (801) 538-8737
Fax: (801) 538-8889

Virginia
8010 Federal Bldg.
400 North 8th Street
Richmond, Virginia 23240
Tel: (804) 771-2246
Fax: (804) 771-2390

Washington
Suite 290
3131 Elliott Ave.
Seattle, Washington 98121
Tel: (206) 553-5615
Fax: (206) 553-7253

West Virginia
Suite 807, 405 Capitol Street
Charleston, West Virginia 25301
Tel: (304) 347-5123
Fax: (304) 347-5408

Wisconsin
Room 596
517 East Wisconsin Avenue
Milwaukee, Wisconsin 53202
Tel: (414) 297-3473
Fax: (414) 297-3470

ANNEX 5

JAPANESE EMBASSIES AND CONSULATES IN NORTH AMERICA

CANADA

Embassy of Japan
255 Sussex
Ottawa, Ontario
Canada K1N 9E6
Tel: (613) 236-8541

Consulate General of Japan
Toronto Dominion Bank Tower
Suite 2702, PO Box 10
Toronto, Ontario
Canada M5K 1A1
Tel: (416) 363-7038

Consulate General of Japan
600 rue de la Gauchetiere W.
Suite 1785
Montreal, Quebec
Canada H3B 4L8
Tel: (514) 866-3429

Consulate General of Japan
Credit Union Central Plaza
730-215 Garry St.
Winnipeg, Manitoba
Canada R3C 3P3
Tel: (204) 943-5546

Consulate General of Japan
2480 Manulife Place
10180-101 Street
Edmonton, Alberta
Canada T5J 3S4
Tel: (403) 422-3752

Consulate General of Japan
Suite 900, 1177 West Hastings St.
Vancouver, British Columbia
Canada V6E 2K9
Tel: (604) 684-6939

UNITED STATES

Embassy of Japan
2520 Massachusetts Ave., N.W.
Washington, DC 20008-2869
Tel: (202) 939-6700

Consulate General of Japan
909 West 9th Ave., Suite 301
Anchorage Alaska 99501
Tel: (907) 279-8428

Consulate General of Japan
250 East First Street, Suite 1507
Los Angeles, California 90012
Tel: (213) 624-8305

Consulate General of Japan
50 Fremont Street, Suite 2300
San Francisco, California 94105
Tel: (415) 777-3533

Consulate General of Japan
Suite 604, Guam International Trade Center Bldg.
590 South Marine Drive
Tamuning, Guam 96911
Tel: 646-1290

Consulate General of Japan
Suite 1501
400 Colongy Square Bldg.
1201 Peachtree St., N.E.
Atlanta, Georgia 30361
Tel: (404) 892-2700

Consulate General of Japan
1742 Nuuanu Ave.
Honolulu, Hawaii, 96817-3294
Tel: (808) 536-2226

Consulate General of Japan
Olympia Center, Suite 1100
737 No. Michigan Ave.
Chicago, Illinois 60611
Tel: (312) 280-0400

Consulate General of Japan
2050 One Poydras Plaza
639 Loyola Ave.
New Orleans, Louisiana 70113
Tel: (504) 529-2101

Consulate General of Japan
Federal Reserve Plaza, 14th Fl.
600 Atlantic Ave.
Boston, Massachusetts 02210
Tel: (617) 973-9772

Consulate General of Japan
2519 Commerce Tower
911 Main Street
Kansas City, Missouri 64105-2076
Tel: (816) 471-0111

Consulate General of Japan
299 Park Ave.
New York, New York 10171
Tel: (212) 371-8222

Consulate General of Japan
2400 First Interstate Tower
1300 S.W. 5th Ave.
Portland, Oregon 97201
Tel: (503) 221-1811

Consulate General of Japan
First Interstate Bank Plaza
Suite 5300
1000 Louisiana St.
Houston, Texas 77002
Tel: (713) 652-2977

Consulate General of Japan
1301 5th Ave., Suite 3110
Seattle, Washington 98101
Tel: (206) 682-9107

ANNEX 6

SOME FOREIGN EMBASSIES AND CONSULATES IN JAPAN

CANADA

7-3-38 Akasaka, Minato-ku
Tokyo 107
Tel: (03) 3408-2101
Fax: (03) 3470-7280/3479-5320

F.T. Building 9F
4-8-28, Watanabe-dori, Chuo-ku
Fukuoka 810
Tel: (92) 752-6055
FAx: (92) 752-6077

Nakato Marunouchi Bldg. 6F
3-17-6 Marunouchi, Naka-ku
Nagoya 460
Tel: (52) 972-0450
Fax: (52) 972-0453

12th Floor, Daisan Shoho Building
2-3 Nishi-Shinsaibashi
2-chome, Chuo-ku
Osaka 542
Tel: (06) 212-4910
Fax: (06) 212-4914

Provincial Offices

Alberta

Place Canada, 3F
7-3-37 Akasaka, Minato-ku
Tokyo 107
Tel: (03) 3475-1171
Fax: (03) 3470-3939

British Columbia

Place Canada, 3F
7-3-37 Akasaka, Minato-ku
Tokyo 107
Tel: (03) 3408-6171
Fax: (03) 3408-6340

The Entente Central Tower
1901, 5-15 Koyo-cho
Higashi, Nada-ku
Kobe, Hyogo-ken 658
Tel: (78) 857-9474
Fax: (78) 858-0547

Quebec

Kojimachi Hiraoka Bldg.
5F, 1-3 Kojimachi, Chiyoda-ku
Tokyo 102
Tel: (03) 3239-5137
Fax: (03) 3239-5140

UNITED STATES

American Embassy
1-10-5, Akasaka, Minato-ku
Tokyo 107
Tel: (03) 3224-5060
Fax: (03) 3589-4235

American Consulate General
2-11-5, Nishitenma, Kita-ku
Osaka 530
Tel: (06) 315-5900
Fax:(06) 361-5978

US & FCS Nagoya
Nagoya Chamber of Commerce
Bldg., 7F.
2-10-19, Sakae, Naka-ku
Nagoya 460
Tel: (052) 203-4011
Fax: (052) 203-4612

American Consulate General
Kita 1-jo, Nishi 28-chome, Chuo-ku
Sapporo 064
Tel: (011) 641-1115
Fax: (011) 641-0211

American Consulate General
2-5-26 Ohori, Chuo-ku
Fukuoka 810
Tel: (092) 751-9331
Fax: (092) 713-9222

U.S. Trade Center
World Import Mart 7F
3-1-3, Higashi Ikebukuro
Toshima-ku
Tokyo 170
Tel: (03) 3987-2441
Fax: (03) 3987-2447

OTHER COUNTRIES

Embassy of Australia
2-1-14 Mita, Minato-ku
Tokyo 108
Tel: (03) 453-0251/9

Embassy of France
4-11-44, Minami Azabu, Minato-ku
Tokyo 106
Tel: (03) 473-0171

Embassy of Germany
4-5-10 Minami Azabu, Minato-ku
Tokyo 106
Tel: (03) 473-0151

Embassy of Italy
2-5-4 Mita, Minato-ku
Tokyo 108
Tel: (03) 453-5291/6

Embassy of Spain
1-3-29 Roppongi, Minato-ku
Tokyo 106
Tel: (03) 583-8531/3

Embassy of the United Kingdom
1 Ichiban-cho, Chiyoda-ku
Tokyo 102
Tel: (03) 265-5511

ANNEX 7

JAPANESE GOVERMENT AND QUASI-GOVERNMENT AGENCIES

Ministry of International Trade and Industry (MITI)
1-3-1 Kasumigaseki
Chiyoda-ku, Tokyo 100
Tel: (03) 3501-1511

- Small and Medium Enterprise Agency: same as MITI
- Agency for Industrial Science and Technology: same as MITI
- Patent Office: 3-4-3, Kasumigaseki
  Chiyoda-ku, Tokyo 100
  Tel: (03) 3581-1101

Prime Minister's Office
1-6-1, Nagata-cho
Chiyoda-ku, Tokyo 100
Tel: (03) 3581-2361

- Fair Trade Commission:
  2-2-1, Kasumigaseki
  Chiyoda-ku, Tokyo 100
  Tel: (03) 3581-5471
- Defense Agency: 9-7-45, Akasaka
  Minato-ku, Tokyo 107
  Tel: (03) 3408-5211
- Economic Planning Agency:
  3-1-1, Kasumigaseki
  Chiyoda-ku, Tokyo 100
  Tel: (03) 3581-0261
- Science and Technology Agency:
  2-1-2, Kasumigaseki
  Chiyoda-ku, Tokyo 100
  Tel: (03) 3581-5271
- Environment Agency:
  1-2-2, Kasumigaseki
  Chiyoda-ku, Tokyo 100
  Tel: (03) 3581-3351

Ministry of Justice
1-1-1, Kasumigaseki
Chiyoda-ku, Tokyo 100
Tel: (03) 3580-4111

Ministry of Foreign Affairs
2-2-1, Kasumigaseki
Chiyoda-ku, Tokyo 100
Tel: (03) 3580-3311

Ministry of Finance (MOF)
3-1-1, Kasumigaseki
Chiyoda-ku, Tokyo 100
Tel: (03) 3581-4161

National Tax Administration
3-1-1, Kasumigaseki
Chiyoda-ku, Tokyo 100
Tel:(03) 3581-4161

Ministry of Education, Science and Culture
3-2-2, Kasumigaseki
Chiyoda-ku, Tokyo 100
Tel: (03) 3581-4211

Ministry of Health and Welfare (MHW)
3-2-2, Kasumigaseki
Chiyoda-ku, Tokyo 100
Tel: (03) 3503-1711

Ministry of Agriculture, Forestry and Fisheries (MAFF)
1-2-1, Kasumigaseki
Chiyoda-ku, Tokyo 100
Tel: (03) 3502-8111

Ministry of Transport (MOT)
2-1-3, Kasumigaseki
Chiyoda-ku, Tokyo 100
Tel: (03) 3580-3111

Ministry of Posts and Telecommunications (MPT)
1-3-2, Kasumigaseki
Chiyoda-ku, Tokyo 100
Tel: (03) 3504-4411

Ministry of Labor
1-2-2, Kasumigaseki
Chiyoda-ku, Tokyo 100
Tel: (03) 3593-1211

Ministry of Construction (MOC)
2-1-3, Kasumigaseki
Chiyoda-ku, Tokyo 100
Tel: (03) 3580-4311

Ministry of Home Affairs
2-1-2, Kasumigaseki
Chiyoda-ku, Tokyo 100
Tel: (03) 3581-5311

National Diet Library
1-10-1, Nagata-cho
Chiyoda-ku, Tokyo 100
Tel: (03) 3581-2331

Japan International Corporation Agency (JICA)
Shinjuku Mitsui Bldg.
2-1-1, Nishi-shinjuku
Shinjuku-ku, Tokyo 163
Tel: (03) 3346-5311

Japan Information Center of Science and Technology (JICST)
2-5-2, Nagata-cho
Chiyoda-ku, Tokyo 100
Tel: (03) 3581-6411

Bank of Japan
2-1-1, Nihonbashi Hongoku-cho
Chuo-ku, Tokyo 103
Tel: (03) 3279-1111

Japan Development Bank
1-9-1, Ohtemachi
Chiyoda-ku, Tokyo 100
Tel: (03) 3287-1221

ANNEX 8

JAPANESE TRADE ASSOCIATIONS

Import Promotion Associations

Japan Federation of Importers Organizations
Hogaku Bldg. 4F
1-19-14 Toranomon
Minato-ku, Tokyo 105
Tel: (03) 3581-9251
Fax: (03) 3581-9217

MIPRO (Manufactured Imports Promotion Organization)
6th Fl., World Import Mart Bldg.
Sunshine City
3-1-3, Higashi Ikebukuro
Toshima-ku, Tokyo 170
Tel: (03) 3542-5023
Fax: (03) 3542-5023

Importers Association for Graphic Arts Machines and Materials
c/o Printing Machines Trading Co. Ltd.
3-21-4, Minami Ohi
Shinagawa-ku, Tokyo 140
Tel: (03) 3763-4141
Fax: (03) 3766-0120

Japan Automobile Importers Association
No. 7 Akiyama Bldg.
5-3, Koji-machi
Chiyoda-ku, Tokyo 102
Tel: (03) 3222-5421
Fax: (03) 3222-1730

Japan Book Importers Association
Chiyoda Kaikan
1-21-4, Nihonbashi
Chuo-ku, Tokyo 103
Tel: (03) 3271-6901
Fax: (03) 3271-6920

Japan Chemical Importers Association
Nihon Shuzo Kaikan
1-1-21, Nishi Shinbashi
Minato-ku, Tokyo 105
Tel: (03) 3501-1304
Fax: (03) 3595-3344

Japan Cosmetics Importers Association, Inc.
Room 107, Azabu Town House
3-2-40, nishi Azabu
Minato-ku, Tokyo 106
Tel: (03) 3408-7541
Fax: (03) 3408-7541

Japan Electronics Products Importers Association
1-1-13, Shinjuku
Shinjuku-ku, Tokyo 160
Tel: (03) 3225-8910
Fax: (03) 3225-9001

Japan General Merchandise Importers Association
World Trade Center Bldg.
2-4-1, Hamamatsu-cho
Minato-ku, Tokyo 105
Tel: (03) 3435-3477
Fax: (03) 3434-6739

Japan Iron & Steel Scrap Importers Association
Fuji Bldg., 8F, 1-5-3, Yaesu
Chuo-ku, Tokyo 103
Tel: (03) 3201-7906
Fax: (03) 3281-3674

Japan Lumber Importers Association
Yushi Kogyo Kaikan
3-13-11, Nihonbashi
Chuo-ku, Tokyo 103
Tel: (03) 3271-0926
Fax: (03) 3271-0928

Japan Machinery Importers Association
Koyo Bldg., 1-2-11, Toranomon
Minato-ku, Tokyo 105
Tel: (03) 3503-9736
Fax: (03) 3503-9779

Japan Marine Products Importers Association
Yurakucho Bldg.
1-10-1, Yuraku-cho
Chiyoda-ku, Tokyo 100
Tel: (03) 3214-3407
Fax: (03) 3214-3408

Japan Paper Importers Association
Kami Pulp Kaikan Bldg.
5-6, Nihonbashi Hisamatsu-cho
Chuo-ku, Tokyo 103
Tel: (03) 3249-4832
Fax: (03) 3249-3834

Japan Textiles Importers Association
Nihonbashi Daiwa Bldg.
1-9-4, Nihonbashi Honcho
Chuo-ku, Tokyo 104
Tel: (03) 3270-0791
Fax: (03) 3243-1088

Japan Watch Importers Association
5th F., Chuo Koron Bldg.
2-8-7, Kyobashi
Chuo-ku, Tokyo 104
Tel: (03) 3563-5901
Fax: (03) 3563-1360

Japan Wool Importers Association
Mengyo Kaikan
2-5-8, Bingo-machi
Chuo-ku, Osaka 541
Tel: (06) 231-6201
Fax: (06) 231-6276

Machine Tool Importers Association of Japan
Toranomon Kogyo Bldg.
1-2-18, Toranomon
Minato-ku, Tokyo 105
Tel: (03) 3501-5030
Fax: (03) 3501-5040

Nippon Wool Importers Federation
Takisada Bldg.
2-3-6, Bingo-machi
Chuo-ku, Osaka 541
Tel: (06) 222-9612
Fax: (06) 232-3625

Major Trade Associations

Japan Foreign Trade Council, Inc.
World Trade Center Bldg.
6F, 2-4-1, Hamamatsu-cho
Minato-ku, Tokyo 105
Tel: (03) 3435-5952
Fax: (03) 3435-5979

Japan Chamber of Commerce and Industry
Tosho Bldg.
3-2-2, Marunouchi
Chiyoda-ku, Tokyo 100
Tel: (03) 3283-7851
Fax: (03) 3216-6497

Osaka Chamber of Commerce and Industry
2-8, Honmachibashi
Chuo-ku, Osaka 540
Tel: (06) 944-6401
Fax: (06) 944-6248

Nagoya Chamber of Commerce and Industry
2-10-19, Sakae
Naka-ku, Nagoya 460
Tel: (052) 221-7211
Fax: (052) 231-5213

All Japan Federation of Lumber Association
Nagatacho Bldg.
2-4-3, Nagata-cho
Chiyoda-ku, Tokyo 100
Tel: (03) 3508-3215
Fax: (03) 3580-3226

Ceramic Association of Japan
2-22-17, Hyakunin-cho
Shinjuku-ku, Tokyo 169
Tel: (03) 3362-5231
Fax: (03) 3362-5714

Database Promotion Center, Japan
7thFl., World Trade Center Bldg.
2-4-1, Hamamatsu-cho
Minato-ku, Tokyo 105
Tel: (03) 3459-8581
Fax: (03) 3432-7558

Electronic Industry Association of Japan (EIAJ)
Tosho Bldg.
3-2-2, Marunouchi
Chiyoda-ku, Tokyo 100
Tel: (03) 3211-2765
Fax: (03) 3287-1712

Federation of Bankers' Association of Japan
1-3-1, Marunouchi
Chiyoda-ku, Tokyo 100
Tel: (03) 3216-3761
Fax: (03) 3201-5608

Federation of Construction Material Industries, Japan
MI Bldg. 5F.
1-4-3, Horidome-cho, Nihonbashi
Chuo-ku, Tokyo 103
Tel: (03) 5640-0901
Fax: (03) 3201-5608

Federation of Japan Towels Manufacturers Association
3-4-5, Ningyo-cho
Chuo-ku, Tokyo 103
Tel: (03) 3663-1087
Fax: (03) 3662-5398

Federation of Pharmaceutical Manufacturers' Association of Japan
Tokyo Yakugyo Kaikan Bldg.
2-1-5, Nihonbashi Hon-cho
Chuo-ku, Tokyo 103
Tel: (03) 3270-0581
Fax: (03) 3241-2090

Glass Manufacturers Association of Japan
3-1-9, Shinbashi
Minato-ku, Tokyo 105
Tel: (03) 3595-2717
Fax: (03) 3595-2719

International Association of Health and Therapy Instruments
7th F., Kokusai Kanko Kaikan
1-8-3, Marunouchi
Chiyoda-ku, Tokyo 100
Tel: (03) 3215-2391
Fax: (03) 3215-2438

International Development Association of the Furniture Industry of Japan
3F, Karukozaka Tanaka Bldg.
2-16-1, kagurazaka
Shinjuku-ku, Tokyo 162
Tel: (03) 3436-2691
Fax: (03) 5261-9404

Japan Advertising Agencies Association
Kochiwa Bldg., 4-8-12, Ginza
Chuo-ku, Tokyo 104
Tel: (03) 3562-0876
Fax: (03) 3562-0889

Japan Amusement Machinery Manufacturers' Association
Room 704, Suwa nagatacho TBR Bldg., 2-10-2, Nagata-cho
Chiyoda-ku, Tokyo 100
Tel: (03) 3593-2563
Fax: (03) 3581-3656

Japan Analytical Instruments Manufacturers' Association
Taimei Bldg.
3-22, Kanda Ogawa-machi
Chiyoda-ku, Tokyo 101
Tel: (03) 3292-0642
Fax: (03) 3292-7157

Japan Asbestos Products Industry Association
Tomono Honsha Bldg.
7-12-4, Ginza
Chuo-ku, Tokyo 104
Tel: (03) 3541-4584
Fax: (03) 3541-4958

Japan Association of Medical Equipment Industries
5F., Ika Kikai Kaikan
3-39-15, Hongo
Bunkyo-ku, Tokyo 113
Tel: (03) 3816-5575
Fax: (03) 3816-5576

Japan Auto Parts Industry Association
1-16-15, Takanawa
Minato-ku, Tokyo 108
Tel: (03) 3445-4211
Fax: (03) 3447-5372

Japan Automobile Manufacturers' Association, Inc.
Ohtemachi Bldg.
1-6-1, Ohtemachi
Chiyoda-ku, Tokyo 100
Tel: (03) 3216-5771
Fax: (03) 3287-2072

Japan Boating Industry Association
Asano Daiichi Bldg.
2-5-1, Ginza
Chuo-ku, Tokyo 104
Tel: (03) 3567-6707
Fax: (03) 3567-0635

Japan Business Machine Makers Association
No. 1 Mori Bldg.
1-12-1, Nishi
Shinbashi, Minato-ku, Tokyo 105
Tel: (03) 3503-9821
Fax: (03) 3591-3646

Japan Chemical Industry Association
Tokyo Club Bldg.
3-2-6, Kasumigaseki
Chiyoda-ku, Tokyo 100
Tel: (03) 3580-0751
Fax: (03) 3580-0764

Japan Cosmetic Industry Association
Hatsumei Kaikan Bldg., 4F.
2-9-14, Toranomon
Minato-ku, Tokyo 105
Tel: (03) 3502-0576
Fax: (03) 3502-0829

Japan Dental Machine Manufacturers' Association
2-16-14, Kojima
Taito-ku, Tokyo 111
Tel: (03) 3851-6124
Fax: (03) 3851-6124

Japan Dental Materials Manufacturers' Association
Kyodo Bldg.
2-18-7, Higashi Ueno
Taito-ku, Tokyo 111
Tel: (03) 3831-3974
Fax: (03) 3831-3983

Japan Department Stores Association
7F., Yanagiya Bldg.
2-1-10, Nihonbashi
Chuo-ku, Tokyo 103
Tel: (03) 3272-1666
Fax: (03) 3281-0381

Japan Direct Marketing Association
6F., No. 32 Mori Bldg.
3-4-30, Shiba-koen
Minato-ku, Tokyo 105
Tel: (03) 3434-4700
Fax: (03) 3434-4518

Japan Electric Measuring Instruments Manufacturers' Association
1-9-10, Toranomon
Minato-ku, Tokyo 105
Tel: (03) 3502-0601
Fax: (03) 3502-0600

Japan Electrical Manufacturers' Association
2-4-15, Nagata-cho
Chiyoda-ku, Tokyo 100
Tel: (03) 3581-4841
Fax: (03) 3593-3198

Japan Farm Machinery Manufacturers' Association
Kikai Shinko Kaikan
3-5-8, Shiba-koen
Minato-ku, Tokyo 105
Tel: (03) 3433-0415
Fax: (03) 3433-1528

Japan Federation of Construction Contracters, Inc.
Tokyo Kensetsu Kaikan
2-5-1, Hatchobori
Chuo-ku, Tokyo 104
Tel: (03) 3553-0701
Fax: (03) 3553-2360

Japan Fisheries Association
Sankaido Bldg.
1-9-13, Akasaka
Minato-ku, Tokyo 107
Tel: (03) 3585-6681
Fax: (03) 3582-2337

Japan Freight Forwarders Federation
Nissei Bldg.
2-13-33, Konan
Minato-ku, Tokyo 108
Tel: (03) 3472-1516
Fax: (03) 3472-6158

Japan Fur Association
3-11-15, Ginza
Chuo-ku, Tokyo 104
Tel: (03) 3541-6987
Fax: (03) 3546-2772

Japan Industrial Robot Association
Kikai Shinko Kaikan
3-5-8, Shiba-koen
Minato-ku, Tokyo 105
Tel: (03) 3434-2910
Fax: (03) 3578-1404

Japan Information Processing Development Center
Kikai Shinko Kaikan
3-5-8, Shiba-koen
Minato-ku, Tokyo 105
Tel: (03) 3432-9371
Fax: (03) 3432-9379

Japan Iron & Steel Federation
Keidanren Kaikan
1-9-4, Ohtemachi
Chiyoda-ku, Tokyo 100
Tel: (03) 3279-3611
Fax: (03) 3245-0144

Japan Leather & Leather Goods Industry Association
2F., Meiyu Bldg.
2-4-9, Kaminarimon
Taito-ku, Tokyo 111
Tel: (03) 3847-1451
Fax: (03) 3847-1510

Japan Light Metal Association
Asahi Seimei Kan
2-1-3, Nihonbashi
Chuo-ku, Tokyo 103
Tel: (03) 3273-3041
Fax: (03) 3213-2918

Japan Machinery Federation
Kikai Shinko Kaikan
3-5-8, Shiba-koen
Minato-ku, Tokyo 105
Tel: (03) 3434-5381
Fax: (03) 3434-6698

Japan Mining Industry Association
Shin Hibiya Bldg.
1-3-6, Uchisaiwai-cho
Chiyoda-ku, Tokyo 100
Tel: (03) 3502-7451
Fax: (03) 3591-9841

Japan Optical Industry Association
Kikai Shinko Kaikan
3-5-8, Shiba-koen
Minato-ku, Tokyo 105
Tel: (03) 3431-7073

Japan Paper Association
Kami Pulp Kaikan
5-6, Nihonbashi
Hisamatsu-cho
Chuo-ku, Tokyo 103
Tel: (03) 3249-4801
Fax: (03) 3249-4826

Japan Perfumery and Flavoring Association
4F., Nitta Bldg.
8-2-1, Ginza
Chuo-ku, Tokyo 104
Tel: (03) 3571-3855
Fax: (03) 3571-3855

Japan Petrochemical Industry Association
Iino Bldg.
2-1-1, Uchisaiwai-cho
Chiyoda-ku, Tokyo 100
Tel: (03) 3501-2151
Fax: (03) 3501-3895

Japan Plastics Industry Federation
Tokyo Club Bldg.
3-2-6, Kasumigaseki
Chiyoda-ku, Tokyo 100
Tel: (03) 3580-0771
Fax: (03) 3580-0775

Japan Plywood Manufacturers' Association
Meisan Bldg.
1-18-17, Nishi-Shinbashi
Minato-ku, Tokyo 105
Tel: (03) 3591-9246
Fax: (03) 3591-9240

Japan Port & Harbor Association
Toranomon Kotohira Kaikan
1-2-8, Toranomon
Minato-ku, Tokyo 105
Tel: (03) 3503-6968
Fax: (03) 3503-6975

Japan Printing Machinery Manufacturers' Association
Rm. 503, Kikai Shinko Kaikan
3-5-8, Shiba-koen
Minato-ku, Tokyo 105
Tel: (03) 3434-4661
Fax: (03) 3434-0301

Japan Refrigeration & Air-Conditioning Industry Association
Kikai Shinko Kaikan
3-5-8, Shiba-koen
Minato-ku, Tokyo 105
Tel: (03) 3432-1671
Fax: (03) 3438-0308

Japan Vending Machine Manufacturers' Association
Shinbashi Tanaka Bldg.
2-37-6, Nishi Shinbashi
Minato-ku, Tokyo 105
Tel: (03) 3431-7443
Fax: (03) 3431-1967

Japan Warehousing Association, Inc.
1-13-3, Eitai
Koto-ku, Tokyo 135
Tel: (03) 3643-1221
Fax: (03) 3643-1252

Petroleum Association of Japan
Keidanren Kaikan
1-9-4, Ohtemachi
Chiyoda-ku, Tokyo 100
Tel: (03) 3279-3811
Fax: (03) 3242-5688

Real Estate Companies Association of Japan
Kasumigaseki Bldg., 23F
3-2-5, Kasumigaseki
Chiyoda-ku, Tokyo 100
Tel: (03) 3581-9421
Fax: (03) 3581-7530

Rubber Trade Association of Japan
2F., Tosen Bldg.
1-10-8, Nihonbashi
Horidome-cho, Chuo-ku, Tokyo 103
Tel: (03) 3666-1469
Fax: (03) 3668-8462

Software Information Center
4F., Toto Bldg., 5-1-4, Toranomon
Minato-ku, Tokyo 105
Tel: (03) 3437-3071
Fax: (03) 3437-3398

Telecommunications Association
11F., Shin Yurakucho Bldg.
1-12-1, Yuraku-cho
Chiyoda-ku, Tokyo 100
Tel: (03) 3201-7816
Fax: (03) 3201-6015

ANNEX 9

NORTH AMERICAN TRADE ASSOCIATIONS IN JAPAN

CANADA

Canadian Chamber of Commerce in Japan (CCCJ)
PO Box 79, Akasaka Post Office
Minato-ku, Tokyo 107
Tel: (03) 3436-8439
Fax: (03) 3436-9295

Canada Beef Export Federation
101 Bran Rouge Akasaka
7-4-8, Akasaka
Minato-ku, Tokyo 107
Tel: (03) 5570-4506
Fax: (03) 5570-4507

Council of Forest Industries (Canada)
Tomoecho Annex-11, 9F.
3-8-27, Toranomon
Minato-ku, Tokyo 105
Tel: (03) 5401-0531
Fax: (03) 5401-0538

UNITED STATES

The American Chamber of Commerce in Japan (ACCJ)
No. 2 Fukide Bldg.
4-1-21 Toranomon
Minato-ku, Tokyo 105
Tel: (03) 3433-5381
Fax: (03) 3436-1446

The American Chamber of Commerce in Japan (ACCJ) Kansai Chapter
Business Center 301
East Court Two
1-14, Koyocho Naka
Higashi Nada-ku, Kobe 658
Tel: (078) 857-9745
Fax: (078) 857-6714

American Electronics Association (AEA) Japan Office
11-4, Yonban-cho
Chiyoda-ku, Tokyo 102
Tel: (03) 3237-7195
Fax: (03) 3237-1237

American Hardwood Export Council, Tokyo Office
Tameike Tokyu Bldg., 7F.
1-1-14, Akasaka
Minato-ku, Tokyo 107
Tel: (03) 3589-0127
Fax: (03) 3265-1419

Pharmaceutical Manufacturers Association, Japan Representative
c/o Nippon Syntex K.K.
Tokyo Tatemono Shibuya Bldg.
3-9-9, Shibuya
Shibuya-ku, Tokyo 150
Tel: (03) 3797-7998
Fax: (03) 3797-7978

U.S. Semiconductor Industry Assn. (SIA) Japan Office
11-4, Yonbancho
Chiyoda-ku, Tokyo 102
Tel: (03) 3237-7683
Fax: (03) 3237-1237

U.S. Automotive Parts Industry, Japan Office
Towa Horidomecho Bldg., 3F.
2-1-1, Nihonbashi Horidomecho
Chuo-ku, Tokyo 103
Tel: (03) 3663-8484
Fax: (03) 3663-8483

Western Wood Products Association, Tokyo Office
Tameike Tokyu Bldg., 7F.
1-1-14, Akasaka
Minato-ku, Tokyo 107
Tel: (03) 3589-1320
Fax: (03) 3505-6710

ANNEX 10

CONVENTION AND EXHIBITION CENTERS

Tokyo International Fair Ground
Tokyo International Trade Center Corp.
5-3-53, Harumi
Chuo-ku, Tokyo 104
Tel: (03) 3533-5311
Fax: (03) 3531-2397

Nippon Convention Center (Makuhari Messe)
2-1, Nakase, Chiba-shi, Chiba 260
Tel: (0472) 96-0001
Fax: (0472) 96-0529

Sunshine City Convention Center
3-1, Higashi Ikebukuro
Toshima-ku, Tokyo 170
Tel: (03) 3989-3486
Fax: (03) 3987-3173

Tokyo Trade Center
1-7-8, Kaigan
Minato-ku, Tokyo 105
Tel: (03) 3434-4241
Fax: (03) 3434-4648

Tokyo Ryutsu Center (TRC)
6-1-1, Heiwajima
Ohta-ku, Tokyo 143
Tel: (03) 3767-2190,
Fax: (03) 3767-2053

Pacifico Yokohama
Pacific Convention Plaza Yokohama
1-1, Minato Mirai, Nishi-ku
Yokohama-shi, Kanagawa 220
Tel: (045) 221-2121
Fax: (045) 221-2136

Nagoya International Exhibition Hall
2-2, Kinjofuto
Minato-ku, Nagoya-shi, Aichi 455
Tel: (052) 398-1771
Fax: (052) 398-1785

International Exhibition Center
Osaka (INTEX Osaka)
1-5-102, Nanko-kita
Suminoe-ku, Osaka-shi, Osaka 559
Tel: (06) 612-8800
Fax: (06) 612-8686

Osaka Merchandise Mart (OMM)
1-7-31, Ohtemae
Chuo-ku, Osaka-shi, Osaka 540
Tel: (06) 943-2020

Kobe International Exhibition Hall
6-11-1, Minatojima Nakamichi
Chuo-ku, Kobe-shi, Hyogo 650
Tel: (078) 302-1020,
Fax: (078) 302-1870

West Japan General Exhibition Center
3-7-1, Asano, Kokurakita-ku
Kitakyushu-shi, Fukuoka 802
Tel: (093) 511-6848
Fax: (093) 521-8845

AXES Sapporo (Sapporo Exposition Center)
4-3-55, Ryutsu Center, Shiraishi-ku
Sapporo-shi, Hokkaido 003
Tel: (011) 865-5811
Fax: (011) 864-1290

U.S. Trade Center
World Import Mart 7F
3-1-3, Higashi-Ikebukuro
Toshima-ku, Tokyo 170
Tel: (03) 3987-2441
Fax: (03) 3987-2447

ANNEX 11

SOME FOREIGN TRANSNATIONAL DISTRIBUTORS IN JAPAN

For more company names, consult the latest American Chamber of Commerce (ACCJ), Canadian Chamber of Commerce in Japan (CCCJ), or European Busniess Community in Japan (EBC) membership directories. The capital letters in brackets refer to the distributor's country of origin: (A) American, (DK) Danish, (U.K.) British, (F) French, (D) German, (I) Italian.

ACI Japan Ltd. (U.K.)
Yurakucho Bldg., 11F.
1-10-1, Yurakucho
Chiyoda-ku, Tokyo 100
Tel: (03) 3213-2571,
Fax: (03) 3213-2574

Biobridge K.K. (D)
7-12, Rokubancho
Chiyoda-ku, Tokyo 102
Tel: (03) 3265-9051,
Fax: (03) 3265-9054

C. Correns and Co. (D, I)
2-1-1, Uchisaiwai-cho
Chiyoda-ku, Tokyo
Tel: (03) 3501-2361
Fax: (03) 3501-5309

C. Holstein Company (D)
1-3-7, Dosho-machi
Chuo-ku, Osaka 541
Tel: (06) 231-0891
Fax: (06) 231-0867

C. Illies & Co., Ltd. (D)
(Irisu Shokai K.K.)
Irisu Bldg.
3-12-18, Kamiosaki
Shinagawa-ku, Tokyo 141
Tel: (03) 3443-4111
Fax: (03) 3443-4118

C. Weinberger & Co. (D)
Shinmachi Grace Bldg., 2/F
2-20-6, Shinmachi
Nishi-ku, Osaka 550
Tel: (06) 541-0191
Fax: (06) 541-0190

Clay & Co., Ltd. (D)
Shikoku Bldg. Annex
1-14-4, Uchikanda
Chiyoda-ku, Tokyo 101
Tel: (03) 3293-8711
Fax: (03) 3293-3872

Cornes & Co. Ltd. (U.K.)
Maruzen Bldg.
2-3-10, Nihonbashi
Chuo-ku, Tokyo 103
Tel: (03) 3272-5771
Fax: (03) 3271-0676

Dodwell & Co. Ltd. (U.K.)
(Inchcape Dodwell K.K.)
Togin Bldg.
1-4-2, Marunouchi
Chiyoda-ku, Tokyo 100
Tel: (03) 3211-2140
Fax: (03) 3211-2179

Douglas Kenrick (Far East) Ltd. (U.K.)
Kowa No. 3 Bldg.
1-11-45, Akasaka
Minato-ku, Tokyo 107
Tel: (03) 3582-0951
Fax: (03) 3585-2591

The East Asiatic Company (Japan) Ltd. (DK)
No. 10 Toyo Kaiji Bldg.
2-31-7, Nishi-Shinbashi
Minato-ku, Tokyo 107
Tel: (03) 3459-8171
Fax: (03) 3459-8238

Francexpa Japan Co. Ltd. (F)
Chatelet Yoyogi Room 1005
4-27-13, Sendagaya
Shibuya-ku, Tokyo 151
Tel: (03) 3746-2822
Fax: (03) 3746-2824

Getz Bros. Co., Ltd. (A)
Sumumoto Seimei Aoyama Bldg.
3-1-30, Minami Aoyama
Minato-ku, Tokyo 107
Tel: (03) 3423-6451
Fax: (03) 3478-5674

GTE Far East (Services) Ltd. (A)
8F, Ohdai Bldg.
1-9-5, Shinjuku
Shinjuku-ku, Tokyo 106
Tel: (03) 3226-9101
Fax: (03) 3226-9107

Hansen & Co. Ltd. (D)
Sannomiya Bldg.
7-1-18, Onoe-dori
Chuo-ku, Kobe 651
Tel: (078) 251-3911
Fax: (078) 232-0165

International Technical Trading, Inc. (INTEC) (A)
209, Asahi Sanbancho Plaza
7-1, Sanbancho
Chiyoda-ku, Tokyo 102
Tel: (03) 3234-6921
Fax: (03) 3234-6915

Isogo Trading Center Inc. (D)
Kashiwano Bldg., 6F
1-5-5, Furo-cho
Naka-ku, Yokohama 231
Tel: (045) 641-6855
Fax: (045) 641-6866

Jardine Matheson K.K. (U.K.)
Nisseki Honkan, 3F
1-3-12, Nishi Shimbashi
Minato-ku, Tokyo 105
Tel: (03) 3502-1421
Fax: (03) 3501-3590

Leybold Co., Ltd. (D)
Tokyo Tatemono Bldg.
1-9-9, Yaesu
Chuo-ku, Tokyo 103
Tel: (03) 3272-1861
Fax: (03) 3281-4490

Minemet Japan (F)
Kokusai Shin Akasaka West Bldg.
13F, 6-1-20, Akasaka
Minato-ku, Tokyo 107
Tel: (03) 3589-1360
Fax: (03) 3589-1370

Nichifutsu Boeki K.K. (F)
(Groupe Denis Freres)
D.F. Bldg.
2-2-8, Minami-Aoyama
Minato-ku, Tokyo 107
Tel: (03) 3403-0330
Fax: (03) 3404-472

Nichio Boeki Co., Ltd. (D)
5-10-15, Higashi Nakano
Nakano-ku, Tokyo 164
Tel: (03) 3364-2781
Fax: (03) 3364-5087

Nihon Olivier, K.K. (F)
Groupe SCOA
2-6, Ichigaya Honmura-cho
Shinjuku-ku, Tokyo 162
Tel: (03) 5261-8701
Fax: (03) 5261-8711

Otto-Sumisho Inc. (D)
Sumumoto Corp. Kanda Bldg.
3-24-4, Kandanishiki-cho
Chiyoda-ku, Tokyo 101
Tel: (03) 3296-4880
Fax: (03) 3219-2988

PMC Co., Ltd. (F, I)
PMC Bldg.
1-23-5, Higashi-Azabu
Minato-ku, Tokyo 106
Tel: (03) 3582-1486
Fax: (03) 3582-1420

Quelle Far East Office (D)
Sanshin Bldg., 503
1-2-1, Sannomiya-cho
Chuo-ku, Kobe 650
Tel: (078) 321-0189
Fax: (078) 332-0179

Rieckermann (Japan) Ltd. (D)
Hibiya Park Bldg., 420
1-8-1, Yurakucho
Chiyoda-ku, Tokyo 100
Tel: (03) 3271-0161
Fax: (03) 3287-1367

SCETI Co. Ltd. (F)
(Groupe Denis Freres)
D.F. Bldg.
2-2-8, Minami-Aoyama
Minato-ku, Tokyo 107
Tel: (03) 3403-0333
Fax: (03) 3404-4472

Siemssen & Co. (D)
Mori Bldg., No. 12
1-17-13, Toranomon
Minato-ku, Tokyo 105
Tel: (03) 3501-2401
Fax: (03) 3501-2405

Thyssen Nippon K.K. (D)
No. 33 Mori Bldg., Suite 702
3-8-21, Toranomon
Minato-ku, Tokyo 105
Tel: (03) 3436-6041
Fax: (03) 3436-6040

Thyssen Tokushuko K.K. (D)
Yokohama Bashamichi Bldg. 6F
4-5, Otamachi,
Naka-ku, Yokohama 231
Tel: (045) 641-6593
Fax: (045) 641-6597

Wolhardt Bros. (Japan) Ltd. (DK)
Fuji Bldg.
1-18-2, Kyobashi
Chuo-ku, Tokyo 104
Tel: (03) 3567-4421
Fax: (03) 3535-4221

ANNEX 12

MARKET RESEARCH & BUSINESS CONSULTING FIRMS

AC Neilsen Company of Japan Ltd.
1-1-71, Nakameguro
Meguro-ku, Tokyo 153
Tel: (03) 3710-6551
Fax: (03) 3791-5880

A.T. Kearney International, Inc.
Akasaka Twin Tower
2-17-22, Akasaka
Minato-ku, Tokyo 107
Tel: (03) 5561-9155
Fax: (03) 5561-9190

ASI-Intech Research, Inc.
(see RBC, Inc.)
Miyakezaka Bldg. 10F.
1-11-1, Nagata-cho
Chiyoda-ku, Tokyo 100
Tel: (03) 3592-6561
Fax: (03) 5467-4722

Access Japan Inc.
Jintan Bldg. 10F.
2-10-10, Shibuya
Shibuya-ku, Tokyo 150
Tel: (03) 5467-4723
Fax: (03) 5467-4722

Access Japan K.K.
4-23-12, Jomyoji
Kamakura, Kanagawa 248
Tel: (0467) 24-5812
Fax: (0467) 24-5814

Advanced Research Corp.
New Korakuen Bldg.
1-22-3, Hongo
Bunkyo-ku, Tokyo 113
Tel: (03) 3818-3551
Fax: (03) 3818-3550

Avant International Services (AVANTIS)
3-4-8, Azuchi-machi
Chuo-ku, Osaka 541
Tel: (06) 262-8228
Fax: (06) 262-8230

Booz, Allen & Hamilton (Japan) Inc.
Imperial Tower bldg. 13F
1-1-1, Uchisaiwai-cho
Chiyoda-ku, Tokyo 100
Tel: (03) 3501-1922
Fax: (03) 3501-2327

Boston Consulting Group K.K.
Time & Life Bldg.
2-3-6, Ohtemachi
Chiyoda-ku, Tokyo 100
Tel: (03) 3279-0761
Fax: (03) 3245-1744

CFI Associates K.K.
4-30-1-202, Nishi-Shinjuku
Shinjuku-ku, Tokyo 160
Tel: (03) 3374-3868
Fax: (03) 33774-3865

CMC Co. Ltd.
1-5-4, Uchikanda
Chiyoda-ku, Tokyo 101
Tel: (03) 3293-7053
Fax: (03) 3293-7985

CRC Research Institute, Inc.
Ozu-Honkan Bldg. 4F
3-6-2, Nihonbashi-honcho
Chuo-ku, Tokyo 103
Tel: (03) 3665-9616
Fax: (03) 5644-7950

De Tok Ltd.
Reinanzaka Annex Bldg.
1-11-3, Akasaka
Minato-ku, Tokyo 107
Tel: (03) 3584-1117
Fax: (03) 3584-1119

Deltapoint International Ltd.
Sanbansho KB-6 Bldg.
6 Sanban-cho
Chiyoda-ku, Tokyo 102
Tel: (03) 3221-1751
Fax: (03) 3221-1753

Diamond Business Consulting Company Ltd. (DBC)
Samon Eleven Bldg.
3-1, Samon-cho
Chiyoda-ku, Tokyo 102
Tel: (03) 3226-6222
Fax: (03) 3226-6226

Dodwell Marketing Consultants
Kowa Bldg. No. 35
1-14-14, Akasaka
Minato-ku, Tokyo 107
Tel: (03) 3589-0207
Fax: (03) 5570-7132

Drake Beam Morin - Japan Inc.
MS Bldg. 9F.
4-11-5, Shiba
Minato-ku, Tokyo 108
Tel: (03) 3452-1461
Fax: (03) 3452-4904

EGIS K.K.
Ichibancho Central Bldg. 8F
22-1 Ichiban-cho
Chiyoda-ku, Tokyo 102
Tel: (03) 3264-1060
Fax: (03) 3265-2260

EPISTAT International
Daikan Plaza #512
1-31-8, Takadanobaba
Shijuku-ku, Tokyo 169
Tel: (03) 3205-9240
Fax: (03) 3205-3234
Portland Office -
Tel: (503) 295-2877
Fax: (503) 226-2519

Farrar Associates
3-7-15, nishi-Azabu
Minato-ku, Tokyo 106
Tel: (03) 3401-2385
Fax: (03) 3401-2385

Finabit Co. Ltd.
1-22-13, Kotesashi-cho
Tokorozawa, Saitama Pref. 359
Tel: (0429) 22-2661
Fax: (0429) 26-7991

Frost International Corporation
1-11-3, Higashi
Shibuya-ku, Tokyo 150
Tel: (03) 3499-5745
Fax: (03) 3499-5074

Fuji Keizai Co., Ltd.
F.K. Bldg., 2-25, Nihonbashi
Kodenma-cho, Chuo-ku, Tokyo 103
Tel: (03) 3664-5816
Fax: (03) 3661-6920

Global Vision Technology, Inc.
875 Mahler Rd., Suite 206
Burlingame, CA 94010
Tel: (415) 697-4594
Fax: (415) 697-0592

High Technology Management (HTM)
Shimizubashi Yabe Bldg., 10F
10-3 Honmachi 3-chome
Shibuya-ku, Tokyo 151
Tel: (03) 5351-2011
Fax: (03) 5351-2018

Howard Roberts Associates
Chisan No. 7 shin-Osaka, Rm 1014
6-2-3 Nishinakajima
Yodogawa-ku, Osaka 532
Tel: (06) 307-1645
Fax: (06) 307-0364

Illies Consult Ltd.
Irisu Bldg.
3-12-18, Kamiosaki
Shinagawa-ku, Tokyo 141
Tel: (03) 3443-4111
Fax: (03) 3443-4118

INBUSCO, Inc.
Kitamura 65 Kan Suite 406
5-16-2, Hiroo
Shibuya-ku, Tokyo 150
Tel: (03) 3447-1851
Fax: (03) 5467-0525

INFOPLAN
Jichiro Kaikan Bldg. 3F.
1, rokuban-cho
Chiyoda-ku, Tokyo 102
Tel: (03) 3265-5411
Fax: (03) 3265-5419

Informatek, Inc.
Grande Maison Akasaka #601
2-17-52 Akasaka
Minato-ku, Tokyo 107
Tel: (03) 3582-0014
Fax: (03) 3582-0040

Institute for Financial Affairs, Inc.
19, Minami-Motomachi
Shinjuku-ku, Tokyo 160
Tel: (03) 3358-1161
Fax: (03) 3359-7947

Institute for Social Behavior Co., Ltd.
Kyoritsu Daiichi Bldg.
14-5, nibancho
Chiyoda-ku, Tokyo 102
Tel: (03) 3239-3011
Fax: (03) 3239-0748

International Business Information, Inc. (IBI)
Izumiya Bldg.
3-1-1, Kojimmachi
Chiyoda-ku, Tokyo 102
Tel: (03) 3230-2151
Fax: (03) 3234-6167

International Consulting of Japan, Inc.
1-1-7, Motoakasaka
Minato-ku, Tokyo 107
Tel: (03) 3497-5661
Fax: (03) 3497-5665

International Investment Consultants Ltd.
Huwa Kioicho TBR Bldg., 1001
5-7 Kojimachi
Chiyoda-ku, Tokyo 102
Tel: (03) 3239-2841
Fax: (03) 3239-2848

International Systems Development, Japan
Kameido Shoko Bldg. 3F
6-27-5, Kameido
Koto-ku, Tokyo 136
Tel: (03) 5626-4541
Fax: (03) 5626-3546

International Transaction Services Co., Ltd.
1-9-4, Kyobashi
Chuo-ku, Tokyo, 104
Tel: (03) 3561-2391
Fax: (03) 3561-3821

JDS Company Ltd.
Rokusan Bldg., 7, Funamachi
Shinjuku-ku, Tokyo 160
Tel: (03) 3358-1601
Fax: (03) 3358-8389

Japan Business Connection Co., Ltd.
Rm 904 Caprice Aoyama
3-12-7, Kita-Aoyama
Minato-ku, Tokyo 107
Tel: (03) 3407-6481
Fax: (03) 5485-2661

Japan Excel-Management Consulting Co., Ltd.
Ginza-Wall Bldg.
6-13-16, Ginza
Chuo-ku, Tokyo 104
Tel: (03) 5565-4104
Fax: (03) 5565-4185

Japan International Commerce Corp., Consulting Division
13-10-604, Sakuragaoka-cho
Shibuya-ku, Tokyo 150
Tel: (03) 3496-4100
Fax: (03) 3496-5005

Japan Management Association Research Institute, Inc. (JMAR)
4-3-13, Toranomon
Minato-ku, Tokyo 105
Tel: (03) 3578-7558
Fax: (03) 3437-1284

Japan Market Research Bureau, Inc.
2-13-2, Kamiosaki
Shinagawa-ku, Tokyo 141
Tel: (03) 3449-8711
Fax: (03) 3473-4029

John Mair & Associates
Homat Grace 101
2-2-9, Shoto
Shibuya-ku, Tokyo 150
Tel: (03) 3460-5233
Fax: (03) 3770-2592

KMG Japan Inc.
1-18-5 Kitagawa
Setagaya-ku, Tokyo 155
Tel: (03) 5478-0163
Fax: (03) 5478-0236

KPMG Peat Marwick Corporate Finance Advisory
Tokyo MI Bldg.
2-2-4, Higashi Shinagawa
Shinagawa-ku, Tokyo 140

Tel: (03) 5462-2812
Fax: (03) 5462-2820

Kaimu Inc.
Kasuga Shima Bldg., 8F.
2-24-11, Kasuga
Bunkyo-ku, Tokyo 112
Tel: (03) 5684-0852
Fax: (03) 5684-0855

Kansai Research Institute (KRI International)
Sumitomo Shiba Daimon Bldg.
No. 2, 1-12-16, Shiba Daimon
Minato-ku, Tokyo 105
Tel: (03) 3578-8661
Fax: (03) 3578-8671

LCC Inc.
Imperial Akasaka Forum #223
7-5-34, Akasaka
Minato-ku, Tokyo 107
Tel: (03) 3589-6398
Fax: (03) 3589-5208

Marcom Inc.
Wako Horidome Bldg.
3-18, Nihonbashi Tomizawa-cho
Chuo-ku, Tokyo 103
Tel: (03) 3663-6891
Fax: (03) 3663-6893

Market Development Research
Miyamasuzaka Bldg., #408
2-19-15, Shibuya-ku, Tokyo 150
Tel: (03) 3498-1561
Fax: (03) 3498-1872

Marketing Intelligence Corporation
2-43-1, Ikebukuro
Toshima-ku, Tokyo 171
Tel: (03) 3590-3421
Fax: (03) 3971-8122

Market Makers Inc.
Senzoku Point #D, 15-14 Senzoku
2-chome, Meguro-ku, Tokyo 152
Tel: (03) 3718-1810
Fax: (03) 3718-4755

Nikkei Research Inc.
1-4-1 Uchikanda
Chiyoda-ku, Tokyo 101
Tel: (03) 3292-5207
Fax: (03) 3292-0330

OA Consultants Co., Ltd.
2-1-1405, Udagawa-cho
Shibuya-ku, Tokyo 150
Tel: (03) 3496-9443
Fax: (03) 3496-9433

ODS Corporation
Daini Kuyo Bldg.
5-10-2 Minami-Aoyama
Minato-ku, Tokyo 107
Tel: (03) 3486-2621
Fax: (03) 3407-8035

Pacific Projects, Ltd.
Kotohira Kaikan Bldg., 9F.
1-2-8, Toranomon
Minato-ku, Tokyo 105
Tel: (03) 3502-0567
Fax: (03) 3508-2047

RBC, Inc.
Miyakezaka Bldg. 10F.
1-11-1, Nagata-cho
Chiyoda-ku, Tokyo 100
Tel: (03) 3592-6561
Fax: (03) 5467-4722

Regency International Trading Company
Cherry Hills
2-247-13, Sakuragaoka
Higashi-yamato City, Tokyo 207
Tel: (0425) 63-6881
Fax: (0425) 63-6798

Roland Berger, Baubel & Partner Ltd.
ARK Mori Bldg., 22F.
1-12-32 Akasaka
Minato-ku, Tokyo 107
Tel: (03) 3587-2271
Fax: (03) 35587-2519

Sanwa Research Institute Corp.
Fukagawa Sanwa Bldg.
2-5-9, Monzennaka-cho
Koto-ku, Tokyo 135
Tel: (03) 3820-8893
Fax: (03) 3820-8894

Shared Systems International Corp. (K.K. SSI)
Flex Doi Bldg., 5F.
1-5, Nanpeidai-cho
Shibuya-ku, Tokyo 150
Tel: (03) 3452-7450
Fax: (03) 3462-7459

Simul Business Communications, Inc.
(Simul International, Inc.)
Kowa Bldg., No. 9
1-8-10, Akasaka
Minato-ku, Tokyo 107
Tel: (03) 3586-7933
Fax: (03) 3505-4794

SMIS Co., Ltd.
Sunshine 60-42F.
3-1-1, Higashi-Ikebukuro
Toshima-ku, Tokyo 170
Tel: (03) 3988-3111
Fax: (03) 3980-2128

Sogo Giken Co., Ltd.
Ito Pia Bldg., 1-6-1, Kaigan
Minato-ku, Tokyo 105
Tel: (03) 3437-1721
Fax: (03) 3437-2823

Soken International Consultants Co., Ltd.
Akihabara Center Bldg., 3F.
3-37, Kanda Sakuma-cho
Chiyoda-ku, Tokyo 101
Tel: (03) 3864-1591
Fax: (03) 3864-1590

Strategic Analysis Japan
3-10-10, Shinjuku
Shinjuku-ku, Tokyo 160
Tel: (03) 3350-8821
Fax: (03) 3350-0272

Sumitomo Business Consulting Co., Ltd.
Shionogi Honcho Kyodo Bldg.
3-7-2, Nihonbashi Honcho
Chuo-ku, Tokyo 103
Tel: (03) 3662-7452
Fax: (03) 3662-7446

Technology Transfer Institute (TTI)
Plaza Mikado Bldg., 6F.
2-14-5, Akasaka
Minato-ku, Tokyo 107
Tel: (03) 3585-6451
Fax: (03) 3584-3786

Technomic Dodwell Consultants K.K.
Kowa Bldg., No. 35, 3F.
1-14-14, Akasaka
Minato-ku, Tokyo 107
Tel: (03) 3589-0418
Fax: (03) 5570-7132

Tohmatsu Touch Ross Consulting Co., Ltd.
Toranomon Kotohira Kaikan
1-2-8, Toranomon
Minato-ku, Tokyo 105
Tel: (03) 3501-8094
Fax: (03) 3580-7675

Trade Balance Incorporated, Japan Office
F Bldg., #403
6-13-12, Minami-Aoyama
Minato-ku, Tokyo 107
Tel: (03) 5467-8258
Fax: (03) 5467-8259

Video Research Ltd.
2-16-7, Ginza
Chuo-ku, Tokyo 104
Tel: (03) 3544-9711
Fax: (03) 3545-2923

Wallace Offutt Consulting
25 Libby Lane Darien
Connecticut 06820, U.S.A.
Tel: (203) 655-6815
Fax: (203) 655-0995

Watt International K.K.
Gosei Bldg., 5-16-7, Minami Azabu
Minato-ku, Tokyo 106
Tel: (03) 3442-7819
Fax: (03) 3442-1958

Yahagi Consultants, Inc.
The New Otani Business Court
2815, Kioi-cho
Chiyoda-ku, Tokyo 102
Tel: (03) 3221-4181
Fax: (03) 3221-4183

Yamato System Development Co., Ltd.
2-22-10, Kamiuma
Setagaya-ku, Tokyo 154
Tel: (03) 3411-6600
Fax: (03) 3487-7961

Yano Research Institute Ltd.
Pola Ebisu Bldg.
3-9-19, Higashi
Shibuya-ku, Tokyo 150
Tel: (03) 5485-4616
Fax: (03) 5485-4681

ANNEX 13

ADVERTISING AND PR FIRMS

Asahi Agency
No. 2 Takachiho Bldg. 2F.
1-6-9 Shiba Daimon
Minato-ku, Tokyo 105
Tel: (03) 3438-3361
Fax: (03) 3438-3672

Chuo Senko Advertising Co., Ltd.
2-6-1 Ginza
Chuo-ku, Tokyo 104
Tel: (03) 3562-0151
Fax: (03) 3535-3576

Cosmo Public Relations Corp.
Isehan Bldg., 8-3-7, Ginza
Chuo-ku, Tokyo 104
Tel: (03) 3572-3666
Fax: (03) 3572-0651

Cove-Ito Advertising Ltd.
Azabu Fuji Bldg.
1-5-6, Nishi-Azabu
Minato-ku, Tokyo 106
Tel: (03) 3403-7251
Fax: (03) 3403-3438

Dai-ichi Kikaku, Co. Ltd.
Hibiya Kokusai Bldg. 9&11 F.
2-2-3, Uchisaiwai-cho
Chiyoda-ku, Tokyo 100
Tel: (03) 3595-1311
Fax: (03) 3595-2160

Dentsu Burson-Marsteller
Sogo Kojimachi No. 3 Bldg.
1-6, Kojimachi
Chiyoda-ku, Tokyo 102
Tel: (03) 3264-6701
Fax: (03) 3237-1244
Author of "The Japanese Consumer" and "Choosing an advertising or PR agency" in this book.

Dentsu Inc.
1-11, Tsukiji
Chuo-ku, Tokyo 104
Tel: (03) 3544-5111
Fax: (03) 3545-5626

Dentsu PR Center Ltd.
2-16-7, Ginza
Chuo-ku, Tokyo 104
Tel: (03) 5565-8429
Fax: (03) 3542-5674

Dynaword Incorporated
Kakihara Asahi Eitai Bldg., 10F
3-7-13, Toyo
Koto-ku, Tokyo
Tel: (03) 5632-5001
Fax: (03) 5632-5011

Fuji Ad Systems Corp.
4-5, Kojimachi
Chiyoda-ku, Tokyo 102
Tel: (03) 3265-2531
Fax: (03) 3264-8257

Gery Daiko Adverstising Inc.
Time & Life Bldg.
2-3-6, Ohtemachi
Chiyoda-ku, Tokyo 100
Tel: (03) 3279-6221
Fax: (03) 3279-4075

Hill and Knowlton Japan
(J. Walter Thompson Co., Ltd.
Hill and Knowlton Division)
Izumikan Sanbancho 5F.
3-8, Sanbancho
Chiyoda-ku, Tokyo 102
Tel: (03) 3288-3671
Fax: (03) 3288-3677

Inoue Public Relations Inc.
Matsuoka Kudan Bldg.
2-2-8, Kudan Minami
Chiyoda-ku, Tokyo 102
Tel: (03) 3230-4351
Fax: (03) 3262-5726

Inter-Image, Inc. Advertising
No. 28 Mori Bldg.
4-16-13, Nishi-Azabu
Minato-ku, Tokyo 106
Tel: (03) 3407-8691
Fax: (03) 3486-0867

International Public Relations Co. Ltd.
Shinbashi Fuji Bldg.
2-1-3, Shinbashi
Minato-ku, Tokyo 105
Tel: (03) 3501-7571
Fax: (03) 3504-0609

J. Walter Thompson Japan Ltd.
1-4-10, Takanawa
Minato-ku, Tokyo 108
Tel: (03) 3449-2511
Fax: (03) 3447-7785

Japan Counselors Inc.
Mita 43 Mori Bldg., 10F.
3-13-16, Mita
Minato-ku, Tokyo 108
Tel: (03) 3457-0311
Fax: (03) 3452-5200

Japan PR Vision Co., Ltd.
Miyuki Bldg., 5-10-6, Ginza
Chuo-ku, Tokyo 104
Tel: (03) 3574-6591
Fax: (03) 3574-0056

KM International Advertising, Inc.
Nakata Bldg.
1-4-6, Akasaka
Minato-ku, Tokyo 107
Tel: (03) 3585-9441
Fax: (03) 3585-3796

Kompass Japan
The Kompass Bldg.
1-32-24, Hatsudai
Shibuya-ku, Tokyo 151
Tel: (03) 5351-1101
Fax: (03) 5351-1125

Kyodo Public Relations Co., Ltd.
Dowa Bldg., 7-2-22, Ginza
Chuo-ku, Tokyo 104
Tel: (03) 3571-5171
Fax: (03) 3574-1005

Mannensha International Inc.
National Bldg. Daini
2-31-9, Hatsudai
Shibuya-ku, Tokyo 151
Tel: (03) 5388-6511
Fax: (03) 5388-6533

McCann-Erickson Hakuhodo Inc.
Shin Aoyama Bldg., E.
1-1-1 Minami Aoyama
Minato-ku, Tokyo 107
Tel: (03) 3746-8111
Fax: (03) 3746-8917

Multilingua Inc.
Kawamura Bldg.
3-21-6, Akasaka
Minato-ku, Tokyo 107
Tel: (03) 3583-0791
Fax: (03) 3587-2077

Nippo, Inc.
Nissan Builnet-2
6-17-2, Ginza
Chuo-ku, Tokyo 104
Tel: (03) 3545-7801
Fax: (03) 3544-0347

OZMA Public Relations Co., Ltd.
Aoyama Tower Bldg.
2-24-15, Minami Aoyama
Minato-ku, Tokyo 107
Tel: (03) 3403-0281
Fax: (03) 3403-0289

Saatchi & Saatchi Advertising
9-2-16, Akasaka
Minato-ku, Tokyo 107
Tel: (03) 5410-8602
Fax: (03) 5410-8612

Simon Marketing International
FAD20 Bldg., 2F.
4-12-5, Akasaka
Minato-ku, Tokyo 107
Tel: (03) 5561-9253
Fax: (03) 5561-9254
(*sales promotion & marketing)

T*COM Corporation
Kuga Bldg., 2F.
2-5-10, Kudan Minami
Chiyoda-ku, Tokyo 102
Tel: (03) 3239-2311
Fax: (03) 3239-2703

Universal Public Relations, Inc.
BR Shinagawa 1 Bldg.
1-20-9, Shinagawa
Shinagawa-ku, Tokyo 140
Tel: (03) 5479-5001
Fax: (03) 5479-5218

Witan Association Ltd.
2-17-13, Nihonbashi Kayaba-cho
Chuo-ku, Tokyo 103
Tel: (03) 3666-5612
Fax: (03) 3639-5498

ANNEX 14

INTERPRETERS AND TRANSLATORS

Access Japan Inc.
Jintan Bldg., 10F.
2-10-10, Shibuya
Shibuya-ku, Tokyo 150
Tel: (03) 5467-4723
Fax: (03) 5467-4722

Berlitz Translation Services
A division of The Berlitz Schools of Languages (Japan) Inc.
Kowa No. 2 Bldg., B1
1-11-39, Akasaka
Minato-ku, Tokyo 107
Tel: (03) 3505-3356
Fax: (03) 3582-7393

Borgnan Corporation
Daisan Taihei Bldg.
1-25-3, Higashi-Ikebukuro
Toshima-ku, Tokyo 170
Tel: (03) 3987-0208
Fax: (03) 3981-9643

Dynaword Inc.
Kakihara Asahi Eitai Bldg.
3-7-13, Toyo
Koto-ku, Tokyo 135
Tel: (03) 5632-5001
Fax: (03) 5632-5011

I.S.S. Service Center Inc.
23-2, Ichiban-cho
Chiyoda-ku, Tokyo 100
Tel: (03) 3265-7891
Fax: (03) 3262-6633

Simul International, Inc.
Kowa Bldg., No. 9
1-8-10, Akasaka
Minato-ku, Tokyo 107
Tel: (03) 3586-7911
Fax: (03) 3583-8336

Sunrise Corporation
Aios Gotanda Annex 202
1-7-11, Higashi-Gotanda
Shinagawa-ku, Tokyo 141
Tel: (03) 3440-8563
Fax: (03) 3440-8564

T.I.S. Corporation (T.I.S. Center)
5-20-27, Tobio, Atsugi-shi
Kanagawa 243-02
Tel: (0462) 41-7679
Fax: (0462) 42-5683

Tandem Access, Inc.
101, Yokosuka Mansion
36-21, Tsutsujigaoka
Midori-ku, Yokohama 227
Tel: (045) 984-7159
Fax: (045) 984-6687

U.S./Japan Information Exchange Inc.
2025 Eye Street, N.W. #520
Washington, D.C. 20006
Tel: (202) 833-1063
Fax: (202) 833-1066

XL Corporation
301 Parkheim, Higashiyama
Meguro-ku, Tokyo 153

Tel: (03) 3760-1224
Fax: (03) 3760-1067

ANNEX 15

CREDIT INVESTIGATION FIRMS

Consumer Credit Clearance Inc.
Kihoh Bldg.
2-2, Kojimachi
Chiyoda-ku, Tokyo 102
Tel: (03) 3222-0490
Fax: (03) 3222-5869

Dun & Bradstreet Business Information Services (Japan) K.K.
4-17-30, Nishi Azabu
Minato-ku, Tokyo 106
Tel: (03) 5485-0451
Fax: (03) 5485-0646
Dun & Bradstreet Corporation
(U.S. head office)
299 Park Avenue
New York, NY 10171

Teikoku Databank, Ltd.
2-5-20, Minami Aoyama
Minato-ku, Tokyo 107
Tel: (03) 3404-4311
Fax: (03) 3404-4339
Teikoku Databank America, Inc.
(New York Office)
750 Lexington Ave., 28th Fl.
New York, NY 10022
Tel: (212) 486-2637
Fax: (212) 486-2638

Tohmatsu & Co. (Deloitte Touche Tohmatsu)
MS Shibaura Bldg.
4-13-23, Shibaura
Minato-ku, Tokyo 108
Tel: (03) 3457-7321
Fax: (03) 3457-1695

Tokyo Shoko Research, Ltd.
Shinichi Bldg.
1-9-6, Shinbashi
Minato-ku, Tokyo 105
Tel: (03) 3574-2258
Fax: (03) 3573-5094

ANNEX 16

PATENT ATTORNEYS

Akasaka International Law, Patent & Accounting Office
Nissanken Kaikan Bldg.
5-3-14, Toranomon
Minato-ku, Tokyo 105
Tel: (03) 5472-4488
Fax: (03) 5472-4491

Finnegan, Henderson, Farabow, Garrett & Dunner
(Roger D. Taylor Gaikokuho Jimu Bengoshi Jimusho)
4F., Hibiya Park Bldg.
1-8-1, Yuraku-cho
Chiyoda-ku, Tokyo 100
Tel: (03) 3215-2773
Fax: (03) 3212-0093

Hanabusa Patent Office
Ochanomizu Square Bldg.
1-6, Kanda Surugadai
Chiyoda-ku, Tokyo 100
Tel: (03) 3291-9721
Fax: (03) 3291-1628

Kohno & Co.
Suite 306, Nagata-cho Hoso Bldg.
2-2-21, Akasaka
Minato-ku, Tokyo 107
Tel: (03) 3583-5043
Fax: (03) 3584-7587

S. Moizumi Patent Office
#809, 3-25-27, Takanawa
Minato-ku, Tokyo 108
Tel: (03) 3280-4088
Fax: (03) 3214-6793

Welty, Shimeall & Kasari International Law and Patent
#405 New Ohtemachi Bldg.
2-2-1, Ohtemachi
Chiyoda-ku, Tokyo 100
Tel: (03) 3241-1526
Fax: (03) 3279-1662

Yuasa and Hara
Section 206, New Ohtemachi Bldg.
2-2-1, Ohtemachi
Chiyoda-ku, Tokyo 100
Tel: (03) 3270-6641
Fax: (03) 3246-0272

ANNEX 17

SHIPPING AND FREIGHT SERVICES

American President Lines, Ltd.
Shin Aoyama Bldg.
1-1-1, Minami Aoyama
Minato-ku, Tokyo 107
Tel: (03) 3423-9000
Fax: (03) 3423-3049

Chikko Corporation
No. 6, Kaigan-dori
Chuo-ku, Kobe 650
Tel: (078) 391-6671
Fax: (078) 391-6673

Dainichi Tsuun Co., Ltd.
1-2-22, Kaigan-Dori
Chuo-ku, Kobe 650
Tel: (078) 391-7170
Fax: (078) 392-1741

Hanshin Electric Railway Co., Ltd.,
Hanshin Aircargo Service Division
2-36-7, Minamisuna
Koto-ku, Tokyo 136
Tel: (03) 3644-2161
Fax: (03) 3644-7346

International Express Co., Ltd.
2-1-17, Kaigan
Minato-ku, Tokyo 105
Tel: (03) 3452-5532
Fax: (03) 3452-4621

Japan Express Co., Ltd.
3-4-1, Marunouchi
Chiyoda-ku, Tokyo 100
Tel: (03) 3216-5024
Fax: (03) 3216-5022

Kintetsu World Express, Inc.
2-3-6, Ohtemachi
Chiyoda-ku, Tokyo 100
Tel: (03) 3270-7252
Fax: (03) 3270-4608

Maersk K.K.
4F., Palace Bldg.
1-1-1, Marunouchi
Chiyoda-ku, Tokyo 100
Tel: (03) 3211-6359
Fax: (03) 3221-6311

Mitsui-Soko Co., Ltd.
1-13-12, Nihonbashi Kayaba-cho
Chuo-ku, Tokyo 103
Tel: (03) 3667-5331
Fax: (03) 3539-5055

Mitsubishi Warehouse & Transportation Co., Ltd.
1-19-1, Nihonbashi
Chuo-ku, Tokyo 103
Tel: (03) 3278-6611
Fax: (03) 3278-6694

Naigai Nitto Co., Ltd.
1-38-8, Higashi-Shinagawa
Shinagawa-ku, Tokyo 140
Tel: (03) 5460-9715
Fax: (03) 5460-9744

Nihon Unyu Kaisha, Ltd.
18, Kanome-cho
Naka-ku, Yokohama 231
Tel: (045) 625-7804
Fax: (045) 621-6210

Omori Kaisoten, Ltd.
123-1, Higashimachi
Chuo-ku, Kobe 650
Tel: (078) 391-3047
Fax: (078) 391-3048

Sea-land Service, Inc.
2F, Shin Kokusai Bldg.
3-4-1, Marunouchi
Chiyoda-ku, Tokyo 100
Tel: (03) 3284-1441
Fax: (03) 3213-3219

Shibusawa Warehouse Co., Ltd.
1-13-16, Nihonbashi Kayaba-cho
Chuo-ku, Tokyo 103
Tel: (03) 3660-4161
Fax: (03) 3660-4050

Sumitomo Warehouse Co., Ltd.
2-1-5, Kawaguchi
Nishi-ku, Osaka 550
Tel: (06) 581-1181
Fax: (06) 581-3879

Utoku Express Co., Ltd.
5-85, Benten-Dori
Naka-ku, Yokohama 231
Tel: (045) 201-6360
Fax: (045) 201-1941

Yusen Air & Sea Service Co., Ltd.
30-1, Nihonbashi Hakozaki-cho
Chuo-ku, Tokyo 103
Tel: (03) 3669-6915
Fax: (03) 3669-8540

ANNEX 18

CUSTOMS BROKERS

Chikko Corporation
No. 6, Kaigan-dori
Chuo-ku, Kobe 650
Tel: (078) 391-6671
Fax: (078) 391-6673

Dainichi Tsuun Co., Ltd.
1-2-22, Kaigan-Dori
Chuo-ku, Kobe 650
Tel: (078) 391-7170
Fax: (078) 392-1741

Hanshin Electric Railway Co., Ltd.,
Hanshin Aircargo Service Division
2-36-7, Minamisuna
Koto-ku, Tokyo 136
Tel: (03) 3644-2161
Fax: (03) 3644-7346

International Express Co., Ltd.
2-1-17, Kaigan
Minato-ku, Tokyo 105
Tel: (03) 3452-5532
Fax: (03) 3452-4621

Japan Express Co., Ltd.
3-4-1, Marunouchi
Chiyoda-ku, Tokyo 100
Tel: (03) 3216-5024
Fax: (03) 3216-5022

Kintetsu World Express, Inc.
2-3-6, Ohtemachi
Chiyoda-ku, Tokyo 100
Tel: (03) 3270-7252
Fax: (03) 3270-4608

Mitsui-Soko Co., Ltd.
1-13-12, Nihonbashi Kayaba-cho
Chuo-ku, Tokyo 103
Tel: (03) 3667-5331
Fax: (03) 3539-5055

Naigai Nitto Co., Ltd.
1-38-8, Higashi-Shinagawa
Shinagawa-ku, Tokyo 140
Tel: (03) 5460-9715
Fax: (03) 5460-9744

Nihon Unyu Kaisha, Ltd.
18, Kanome-cho
Naka-ku, Yokohama 231
Tel: (045) 625-7804
Fax: (045) 621-6210

Omori Kaisoten, Ltd.
123-1, Higashimachi
Chuo-ku, Kobe 650
Tel: (078) 391-3047
Fax: (078) 391-3048

Shibusawa Warehouse Co., Ltd.
1-13-16, Nihonbashi Kayaba-cho
Chuo-ku, Tokyo 103
Tel: (03) 3660-4161
Fax: (03) 3660-4050

Sumitomo Warehouse Co., Ltd.
2-1-5, Kawaguchi
Nishi-ku, Osaka 550
Tel: (06) 581-1181
Fax: (06) 581-3879

Utoku Express Co., Ltd.
5-85, Benten-Dori
Naka-ku, Yokohama 231
Tel: (045) 201-6360
Fax: (045) 201-1941

Yusen Air & Sea Service Co., Ltd.
30-1, Nihonbashi Hakozaki-cho
Chuo-ku, Tokyo 103
Tel: (03) 3669-6915
Fax: (03) 3669-8540

ANNEX 19

KANSAI REGION BUSINESS SUPPORT ORGANIZATIONS

Business consultants & research firms

A.C. Neilson Company of Japan, Ltd., Osaka Branch
Higashi Umeda Bldg.
9-6, Nozaki-cho
Kita-ku, Osaka 530
Tel: (06) 313-0781
Fax: (06) 313-2929

ASI Market Research (Japan) Inc., Osaka Branch
West Bldg., 7F.
6-4-10, Fukushima
Fukushima-ku, Osaka 553
Tel: (06) 452-4791
Fax: (06) 452-4793
For English inquiries contact Tokyo:
Tel: (03) 3432-1701
Fax: (03) 3433-3395

Avant International Services
Toko Bldg., 6F.
3-4-8, Azuchi-machi
Chuo-ku, Osaka 541
Tel: (06) 262-8228
Fax: (06) 262-8230

Dentsu Research Inc., Osaka Office
Dojima Axis Bldg.
2-2-28, Dojimahama
Kita-ku, Osaka 530
Tel: (06) 342-3325
Fax: (06) 342-3334

EES Corporation International Ltd.
Osaka Ekimae No. 3 Bldg., 25 F.
1-1-3, Umeda
Kita-ku, Osaka 530
Tel: (06) 344-8576
Fax: (06) 347-0660

Howard Roberts Associates
7-18-402, Hashinouchi 2-chome
Ibaraki-shi, Osaka 567
Tel: (06) 307-1645
Fax: (06) 307-0364

ITEK
Matsumoto Mansion 103
18-13 Kamihigashi 4-chome
Hirano-ku, Osaka 547
Tel & Fax: (06) 792-6156

International Consulting Service Association
Osaka Woodbell Bldg., 3F.
2-1-34 Nishi-Honmachi
Nishi-ku, Osaka 550
Tel: (06) 541-3821
Fax: (06) 541-3949

ISMAC (International Sports Management & Consultants)
Fix 213 Bldg., 2F
2-13-14, Yamamoto Dori

Chuo-ku, Kobe 650
Tel: (078) 222-6116
Fax: (078) 241-7325

Kogito Co., Ltd.
Eiwa Oike Bldg., 8F.
435 Sasaya-cho
Higashinotoin-higashiiru, Oike
Nakagyo-ku, Kyoto 604
Tel: (075) 231-8767
Fax: (075) 231-4776

Management and Communications Consultancy Inc. (Macc Inc.)
Suite 704 Cofio Bldg.
5-2-19, Kitanagasa-dori
Chuo-ku, Kobe 650
Tel: (078) 341-0546
Fax: (078) 341-0580

McKinsey & Company, Inc.
Umeda Center Bldg., 9F
4-12 Nakazaki Nishi 2-chome
Kita-ku, Osaka 530
Tel: (06) 359-0350
Fax: (06) 359-2840

Mitsubishi Research Institute, Inc., Kansai Branch Office
Kintetsu Dojima Bldg.
2-2-2, Dojima
Kita-ku, Osaka 530
Tel: (06) 341-5981
Fax: (06) 341-5984

Nomura Research Institute Ltd., Kansai Regional Head
1-8-15, Azuchi-machi
Chuo-ku, Osaka 541
Tel: (06) 266-1478
Fax: (06) 266-3615

OrBS Urban Architectural Design Inc.
Shukugawa Bldg., 501
3-11, Oide-cho
Nishinomiya-shi, Hyogo 662
Tel: (0798) 71-6031
Fax: (0798) 71-6971

Plan-Do, Inc.
Minami-semba Daiji Bldg.
1-8, Minami-semba, 3-chome
Chuo-ku, Osaka 542
Tel: (06) 243-1358
Fax: (06) 243-9480

Sakura Institute of Research, Inc., Osaka Research Center
1-8-13, Koraibashi
Chuo-ku, Osaka 541
Tel: (06) 201-1346
Fax: (06) 223-0440

Sanwa Research Institute Corp., Osaka Main Office
Shinanobashi Sanwa Bldg.
6-1, Awaza, 1-chome
Nishi-ku, Osaka 550
Tel: (06) 534-7306
Fax: (06) 534-7315

Sumitomo Business Consulting
Ginsen Yokobori Bldg., 2F.
4-6-2, Koraibashi
Chuo-ku, Osaka 541
Tel: (06) 228-1755
Fax: (06) 228-0409

Yano Research Institute Ltd., Osaka Branch Office
1-8-6, Azuchi-machi
Chuo-ku, Osaka 541

Tel: (06) 266-1381
Fax: 906) 266-1389

Zen International Business Promotions, Inc.
Sunlight Heights 305
21-10 Minami-kaneden 2-chome
Suita-shi, Osaka 564
Tel: (06) 387-5483
Fax: (06) 337-6809

Production, Advertising Companies

Asia-Pacific Productions
3-17 Higashi Maruyama-cho
Nagata-ku, Kobe 653
Tel: (078) 691-2450
Fax: (078) 641-3394

McCann-Erickson Hakuhodo Inc., Osaka Office
Watanabe-bashi Bldg., 8F
1-4-16, Dojima Hama
Kita-ku, Osaka 530
Tel: (06) 342-6800
Fax: (06) 342-6890/2

Nova Incoporated
No. 5-18, Utsubo-honmachi
2-chome, Nishi-ku, Osaka 550
Tel: (06) 445-7531
Fax: (06) 445-7860

Interpretation & Translation Services

Excell Communication Co., Ltd.
7-6 Tonoshima-cho
Kadomo, Osaka 571
Tel: (06) 900-4189
Fax: (06) 900-4190

GK Associates Inc.
Tohwa City Corpo, Otemae II
1-2-10-805 Ote-dori
Chuo-ku, Osaka 540
Tel: (06) 946-6016
Fax: (06) 946-6087

Inter Group Co., Ltd.
3F., Shiroguchi Bldg.
2-15 Kakuta-cho
Kita-ku, Osaka 530
Tel: (06) 372-8048
Fax: (06) 372-6120

International Communication Co., Ltd.
1B-505 Center Bldg.
4-1-13 Isogami-dori
Chuo-ku, Kobe 651
Tel: (078) 251-8821
Fax: (078) 251-8694

Ivy International Co., Ltd.
Rokkaku-Kaikan Bldg., 4F
245 Donomae-cho
Karasuma Higashi-iru, Rokkaku-dori
Nakagyo-ku, Kyoto 604
Tel: (075) 255-1500
Fax: (075) 255-3232

Japan Convention Service Co., Ltd., Kansai Branch
Sumitomo-seimei Midosuji Bldg., 13F.
4-14-3 Nishitenma
Kita-ku, Osaka 530
Tel: (06) 311-2131
Fax: (06) 311-2130

Seikosha Co., Ltd.
Nukata Bldg., 3F
1-5-7 Koraibashi
Chuo-ku, Osaka 541
Tel: (06) 201-5771
Fax: (06) 223-1020

Showa Human Resources Co., Ltd.
11 Kaneichi Bldg.
15-22 Funabashi-cho
Tennoji-ku, Osaka 543
Tel: (06) 763-4934
Fax: (06) 764-5900

Simul International, Inc.
New Bingomachi Bldg., 5F
3-3-15 Bingomachi
Chuo-ku, Osaka 541
Tel: (06) 263-5091
Fax: (06) 263-5097

Patent Attorneys' Association

Kinki Branch
Kinki-Toyama Kaikan 2F
1-9-15, Utsubo-honmachi
Nishi-ku, Osaka 550
Tel: (06) 443-2566

Commercial Arbitration Association

Osaka Branch
Osaka Chamber of Commerce & Industry Bldg., 5F
2-8 Honmachi-bashi
Chuo-ku, Osaka 650
Tel: (06) 944-6164

Kobe Office
Kobe Chamber of Commerce & Industry Bldg.,
6-1 Minatojima Nakamachi
Chuo-ku, Kobe 650
Tel: (078) 303-5806

Chambers of Commerce

Osaka Chamber of Commerce & Industry, International Division
2-8 Honmachi-bashi
Chuo-ku, Osaka 650
Tel: (06) 944-6400

Kobe Chamber of Commerce and Industry, International Division
6-1 Minatojima Nakamachi
Chuo-ku, Kobe 650
Tel: (078) 303-5806

Kyoto Chamber of Commerce and Industry, International Division
Ebisugawa-agaru, Karasuma-dori
Nakagyo-ku, Kyoto 604
Tel: (075) 231-0181

Economic Organizations

Kansai Economic Federation (Kankeiren)
Nakanishima Center Bldg., 30F
6-2-27, Nakanoshima
Kita-ku, Osaka 530
Tel: (06) 441-0101

The Kansai Committee for Economic Development (Kansai Keizai Doyukai)
Nakanoshima Center Bldg., 28F.
6-2-27, Nakanoshima
Kita-ku, Osaka 530
Tel: (06) 441-1031

Convention Bureaus

Osaka Convention Bureau
c/o Osaka Chamber of Commerce and Industry
2-8 Honmachi-bashi
Chuo-ku, Osaka 540
Tel: (06) 944-6484

Kobe International Association
6-9-1 Minatojima-nakamachi
Chuo-ku, Kobe 650
Tel: (078) 302-5200

Kyoto Convention Bureau
Kyoto City International Exchange Association Bldg.
2-1 Torii-cho Awataguchi
Sakyo-ku, Kyoto 606
Tel: (075) 212-4110

Nara Convention Bureau
c/o Nara Chamber of Commerce & Industry
36-2 Noborioji-machi, Nara 630
Tel: (0742) 26-7700

Fukui Convention Bureau
Phoenix Plaza, 1-13-1, Tahara
Fukui 910
Tel: (0776) 20-5151

International Fair Association
2-33 Honmachibashi
Chuo-ku, Osaka 540
Tel: (06) 941-2661

Osaka International Trade Fair Commission
INTEX Osaka, 1-1-12 Nanko-kita
Suminoe-ku, Osaka 559
Tel: (06) 612-1212

Exhibition Facilities

INTEX Osaka
1-1-12 Nanko-kita
Suminoe-ku, Osaka 559
Tel: (06) 612-8800

Mydome Osaka
2-5 Honmachibashi
Chuo-ku, Osaka 540
Tel: (06) 947-4321

Osaka Merchandise Mart
1-7-31, Otemae
Chuo-ku, Osaka 540
Tel: (06) 943-2020

International Conference Center, Kobe
6-9-1, Minatojima-nakamachi
Chuo-ku, Kobe 650
Tel: (078) 302-5200

Kyoto International Conference Hall
Takaragaike, Sakyo-ku, Kyoto 606
Tel: (075) 791-3111

Nara Prefecture New Public Hall
101 Kasugano-cho, Nara 630
Tel: (0742) 27-2630/5

Industrial Standard Association

Japan Industrial Standard Association, Kansai Branch
Honmachi Nomura Bldg.
7F, 3-4-10 Honmachi
Chuo-ku, Osaka 541
Tel: (06) 261-8086

ANNEX 20

ASIA PACIFIC FOUNDATION OF CANADA OFFICES

Head Office
666-999 Canada Place
Vancouver, British Columbia
Canada V6E 3E1
Tel: (604) 684-5986
Fax: (604) 681-1370

Ontario
65 Queen St., W., Suite 1100
Toronto, Ontario
Canada M5H 1P6
Tel: (416) 869-0541
Fax: (416) 869-1696

Quebec
525 Cherrier Street East
Montreal, Quebec
H2L 1H2
Tel: (514) 982-9300
Fax: (514) 982-9060

Saskatchewan
Hong Kong Bank Building
1874 Scarth St.
Regina, Saskatchewan
Canada S4P 4B3
Tel: (306) 791-8778
Fax: (306) 359-7066

Alberta
40 McDougall Centre
455 6th Street S.W.
Calgary, Alberta
T2P 4E8
Tel: (403) 297-4393
Fax: (403) 297-4276

Japan
3F Place Canada
3-37 Akasaka 7-chome
Minato-ku, Tokyo 107 Japan
Tel: (03) 5410-3838
Fax: (03) 5410-3020

INDEX

INDEX

Title soon to be released in the EXPORTER'S DISTRIBUTION PRIMER series.

SOUTHEAST ASIA

Each book covers:

- the political, social and economic trends which directly affect distribution in the booming and increasingly integrated markets,
- the purchasing behaviour of importers of capital goods and consumer products,
- the marketing strategies used by distributors,
- a step-by-step approach to effectively selecting a distributor,
- crucial contacts : trade associations, credit investigation firms, government trade offices, law and accounting firms, market research organizations.

Fax this form to (819) 956-5539 or mail it to:
Publications Management,
Canada Communication Group-Publishing,
45 Sacré-Coeur Blvd, Room A2404, Hull, Quebec,
CANADA K1A 0S9

YES, I would like to be informed when the new title in ***The Exporter's Distribution Primer*** series becomes available.

Name: ______________________________

Organization: ______________________________

Address: ______________________________

____

City: ______________________________

Province: ________________ Postal Code: __________

Country: ______________________________

This is not an order form.

ALSO AVAILABLE...

THE TAIWAN BUSINESS PRIMER

The primer covers:

- guidance on local customs and how to develop successful business relationships,
- clear summaries of Taiwan's political, social and economic trends,
- profiles of major industries and professions,
- valuable information on Taiwanese business practices: business values, the legal framework, employment, distribution, exporting, sourcing and investment,
- useful addresses: trade associations, credit investigation firms, audit corporations, law and patent firms,
- advice on getting around.

This primer is the result of a project sponsored by the *Asia Pacific Foundation of Canada.*

$20 (**US$26** - Other countries) 12.5 x 18 cm
Catalogue No. K49-1-1991E Paperbound 314 pages

Également disponible en français sous le titre ***TAIWAN LE GUIDE DES GENS D'AFFAIRES*** (N° de catalogue K49-1-1991F).

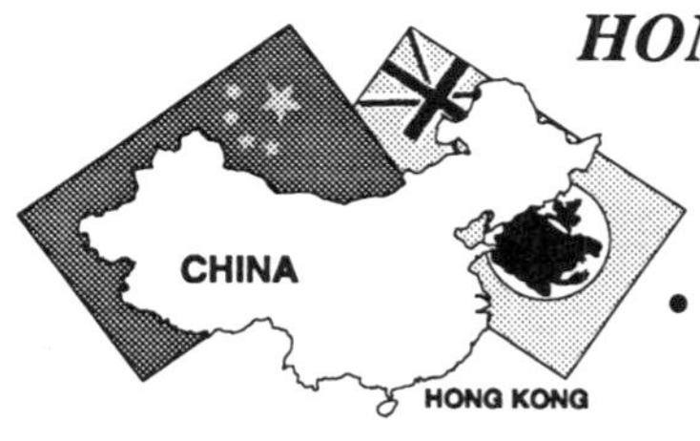

HONG KONG / SOUTH CHINA

THE EXPORTER'S DISTRIBUTION PRIMER

The primer examines:

- the political, social and economic trends directly affecting distribution in Hong Kong/South China markets;
- the purchasing behaviour of Hong Kong and mainland importers of capital goods and consumer products;
- the marketing strategies used by Hong Kong distributors active in the mainland Chinese market;
- crucial contacts: trade associations, credit investigation firms, and market research organizations.

This primer is the result of a project sponsored by the *Asia Pacific Foundation of Canada.*

$35 (**US$29.95** - Other countries) 12.5 x 18 cm
Catalogue No. K49-2-1993E Paperbound 253 pages

Également disponible en français sous le titre ***HONG KONG / LA CHINE DU SUD: INTRODUCTION À LA DISTRIBUTION POUR LES EXPORTATEURS*** (N° de catalogue K49-2-1993F).

ORDER FORM

YES, send me

___ copies of **UNLOCKING JAPAN'S DISTRIBUTION SYSTEM IN THE 90's: The complete exporter's guide** (Cat. No. K49-3-1994E) at the unit cost of $39.95 (US$51.95 for other countries).

___ copies of **HONG KONG/SOUTH CHINA: The Exporter's Distribution Primer** (Cat. No. K49-2-1993E) at the unit cost of $35 (US$29.95 for other countries).

___ copies of **THE TAIWAN BUSINESS PRIMER** (Cat. No. K49-1-1991E) at the unit cost of $20 (US$26 for other countries).

Add to this amount the shipping and handling fees (in Canada, add 7% GST).

Please print

Name : ______________________________

Firm: ______________________________

Address: ______________________________

____

City: ______________________________

Province : ______________ Postal Code: __________

Country: ______________ Telephone : (____) ________

Refer to the following pages for ***Method of Payment***, ***Shipping and Handling Fees*** and ***Distributors' Addresses***.

FOR ORDERS FROM CANADA

Send your orders to:
Canada Communication Group - Publishing
Ottawa **CANADA**
K1A 0S9

Tel.: 819) 956-4802
Fax: (819) 994-1498

These publications are also available at or may be ordered through Canadian booksellers.

METHOD OF PAYMENT

Purchase Orders are accepted from governments, registered companies and educational institutions. Federal government must provide official purchase orders. All others must prepay.

Purchase Order No.: ____________

◯ Cheque/Money Order (payable to the Receiver General for Canada) enclosed

◯ **Visa/MasterCard**

Account No. ____________

Expiry Date: ____________

Signature : ____________

Shipping and Handling Fees

Order Value	Fees
$5.01 to $25	$3.50
$25.01 to $75	$5.40
$75.01to $200	$10.50
Over $200	6% of the total order value

FOR ORDERS FROM THE UNITED STATES

Send your orders to:

International Specialized Book Services
5804 Hassalo Street NE
Portland OR 97213

Tel.: 1-800-547-7734 (toll free)
Tel.: (503) 287-3093 (in Oregon)
Fax : (503) 280-8832

Accents Publications Service Inc.
911 Silver Spring Avenue,
Suite 202
Silver Spring, MD 20910

Tel.: (301) 588-5496
Fax : (301) 588-5249

FOR ORDERS FROM OTHER COUNTRIES

Send your orders to:

Canadian Books Express
The Abbey Bookshop
29, rue de la Parcheminerie
75005 Paris
FRANCE

Tel.: 33.1.46.33.16.24
Fax : 33.1.46.33.03.33

Asia Book House
16/17 Bangla Bazaar
Dhaka 1100
BANGLADESH

Tel.: 91.800.2.245650
Fax : 91.800.2.833983

Books Express
P.O. Box 10
Saffron Walden
Essex CB 114 EW
UNITED KINGDOM

Tel.: 44.799.513726
Fax : 44.799.513248

MicroInfo Ltd.
Box 3 Omega Park
Hampshire, England
GU34 2PG
UNITED KINGDOM

Tel.: 44.0420.86848
Fax : 44.0420.89889

Academic Book Store
P.O. Box 128
00100 Helsinki
FINLAND

Tel.: 358.0.121.4325
Fax : 358.0.121.4441